The Legal Status of the Financial Action Task Force in the International Legal System

International and Comparative Business Law and Public Policy

VOLUME 7

The titles published in this series are listed at *brill.com/blpp*

The Legal Status of the Financial Action Task Force in the International Legal System

By

Ilda Cristina Ferreira

BRILL | NIJHOFF

LEIDEN | BOSTON

Library of Congress Cataloging-in-Publication Data

Names: Ferreira, Ilda Cristina, author.
Title: The legal status of the Financial Action Task Force in the international legal system / by Ilda Cristina Ferreira.
Description: Leiden ; Boston : Brill/Nijhoff, 2025. | Series: International and comparative business law and public policy | Includes bibliographical references and index. |
Identifiers: LCCN 2024045461 | ISBN 9789004715127 (hardback) | ISBN 9789004715134 (ebook)
Subjects: LCSH: Financial Action Task Force. | Money laundering–Law and legislation. | Money laundering–Prevention–International cooperation. | Banking law–Criminal provisions. | Terrorism–Finance–Law and legislation–Criminal provisions. | Banks and banking, International–Corrupt practices.
Classification: LCC K5223 .F47 2025 | DDC 345/.0268–dc23/eng/20240926
LC record available at https://lccn.loc.gov/2024045461

Typeface for the Latin, Greek, and Cyrillic scripts: "Brill". See and download: brill.com/brill-typeface.

ISSN 2667-3495
ISBN 978-90-04-71512-7 (hardback)
ISBN 978-90-04-71513-4 (e-book)
DOI: 10.1163/9789004715134

This book is printed on acid-free paper and produced in a sustainable manner.

To my parents
In memory of my grandparents

Contents

Preface

> *If we have a prince* said Pliny to Trajan, *it is so that he may preserve us from having a master*
>
> In JEAN-JACQUES ROUSSEAU, *Second Discourse*, 1753

This book is based on my doctoral (DPhil) dissertation submitted to the Faculty of Law of the University of Hong Kong in 2023 which has been updated, revised and improved.

In this process, I would like to express my gratitude to the Dissertation Committee, especially Professor Michelle Gallant for her valuable contribution and words of encouragement and to my outstanding supervisor Professor Simon Young.

This book addresses an important and recognised organisation – the Financial Action Task Force (FATF), the world's leading organisation responsible for the integrity, security, transparency of the international financial system, via international standards to counter money laundering, the financing of terrorism and the proliferation financing of weapons of mass destruction, and its legal position in the international legal system.

I first became aware of the FATF in 1999, during the Portugal's presidency of the organisation. For the past two decades, I have been following its activities and those of the Asia-Pacific Group on Money Laundering. As a legal counsel in international law, I have witnessed the gradual metamorphosis from a specialised technical body into a complex and multi-layered organisation, whose legitimacy is undermined by the lack of clarity regarding its legal standing.

I became intrigued with the organisation's scope and far-reaching impact of its policies and measures to respond to global trends and threats that pose a risk to the international financial system, as well as how members, non-members, IOs and other international actors have accepted and implemented them, without close scrutiny (checks and balances) and questioning its legal status.

In this regard, a word of deep appreciation to Mr. Gil Galvão, President of the FATF in 1999–2000 and, for many years, head of delegation of Portugal to the FATF, to Mr. Duarte Chagas, senior legal counsel of the Gaming Inspection and Coordination Bureau of the Macao Special Administrative Region and to Professor Simon Young for their expertise, wisdom and insightful comments.

The topic may be of interest in the fields of Public International Law, Law of International Organisations or International Institutional Law, International Economic Law, International Relations, and to a potential audience of policy-decision makers, scholars, legal practitioners, lawyers, regulators, and students.

Acknowledgements

I would like to express my deepest gratitude to my supervisor, Professor Simon Young for the understanding and generosity shown during this long process as well for the unwavering support for the thesis' direction and insightful comments that enriched this project over the years.

A word of appreciation to the Faculty of Law and its staff at the University of Hong Kong and a special thanks to the Education and Youth Development Bureau of the Macao Special Administrative Region for its scholarship for my doctoral programme.

It is very difficult to name all the colleagues and friends that throughout the last 10 years have helped me and given me the strength to overcome the various challenges and complete this almost lifetime project; to all my gratitude. Nevertheless, acknowledgements have to be made to Ana Bento, Ana Paula Barros, António Costa, Carlos Morais José, Diane Aguiar, Diogo Baptista, João Palla, Mário Duque, Miguel Rosa Duque, Paula Mendonça, Paulo Cardinal, Rui Simões and Vera Varela.

I am profoundly grateful and in debt particularly to Isira Makuloluwe, Joaquim Menano, Selina Lei and Silvia de Sousa for their support and guidance with the English language, research referencing and editorial process.

I also need to express my special thanks to my Brill publishers, especially Beth Derr and the editors' team who kindly support me in revising my dissertation, a project that landed in the printed pages of Brill.

Finally, and most important to my family who never gave up believing in me and my stubbornness. I would like to thank my daughter and son, who bring light into my life, for their encouragement, patience and kindness, particularly for the time I did not spend with them. I am also indebted to my sister and parents for their unconditional support and love.

Abbreviations

ADB	Asian Development Bank
AEOI	Automatic Exchange of Information
AfDB	African Development Bank
AML	Anti-Money Laundering
APG	Asia-Pacific Group on Money Laundering
APUNCAC	Additional Protocol to the Merida Convention
ASEAN	Association of Southeast Asian Nations
AU	African Union
BCBS	Basel Committee on Banking Supervision
BENELUX	*Union Économique Benelux*
BIS	Bank for International Settlements
BO	Beneficial Ownership
BSEC	Black Sea Economic Co-operation
BSTDB	Black Sea Foreign Trade and Investment Bank
CAN	Andean Community
CARIN	Camden Asset Recovery Inter-Agency Network
CBRS	Correspondent Banking Relationships
CDD	Customer Due Diligence
CEMAC	Customs and Economic Union of Central Africa
CFATF	Caribbean Financial Action Task Force
CFT	Countering Financing of Terrorism
CICAD	Inter-American Drug Abuse Control Commission
CICTE	Inter-American Committee against Terrorism
CLAB	Anti-Money Laundering Liaison Committee of the Franc Zone
CoE	Council of Europe
COPS	Conference of the Parties
COSUNS	Co-operating and Supporting Nations
CPF	Countering Proliferation Financing
CPLP	Community of Portuguese Language Countries
CSCE	Conference on Security and Co-operation in Europe
CTED	Counter-Terrorism Committee Executive Directorate (see UNCTED)
CTITF	United Nations Counter-Terrorism Implementation Task Force
DARIO	Draft Articles on the Responsibility of International Organisations
DNFBPS	Designated Non-Financial Businesses and Professions
EAG	Eurasian Group on Combating Money Laundering and Terrorist Financing
EBA	European Banking Authority
EBRD	European Bank for Reconstruction and Development

ECB	European Central Bank
ECG	Evaluations and Compliance Group
ECHR	European Convention on Human Rights
ECJ	European Court of Justice
ECOWAS	Economic Community of West African States
ECtHR	European Court of Human Rights
EFTA	European Free Trade Association
EOIR	Exchange of Information on Request
ESAAMLG	Eastern and Southern Africa Anti-Money Laundering Group
EU	European Union
EUROJUST	European Union Agency for Criminal Justice Co-operation
EUROPOL	European Union Law Enforcement Agency
FAO	Food and Agriculture Organisation
FATF	Financial Action Task Force
FIFA	Fédération Internationale de Football Association
FIS	Financial Institutions
FIUS	Financial Intelligence Units
FSB	Financial Stability Board
FSRBS	Financial Action Task Force-Style Regional Bodies
FT	Financing of Terrorism
FUR	Follow-up Report
GABAC	Task Force on Money Laundering in Central Africa
GAFILAT	Financial Action Task Force of Latin America
GATT	General Agreement on Tariffs and Trade
GDP	Gross Domestic Product
GIABA	Inter-Governmental Action Group against Money Laundering in West Africa
GIFCS	Group of International Finance Centre Supervisors
GNCG	Global Network Co-ordination
HKSAR	Hong Kong Special Administrative Region
HLPOS	High-Level Principles and Objectives
HR	Human Rights
HRC	Human Rights Council
IAEA	International Atomic Energy Agency
IAIS	International Association of Insurance Supervisors
IBRD	International Bank for Reconstruction and Development
ICAO	International Civil Aviation Organisation
ICC	International Criminal Court
ICITO	Interim Commission for the International Trade Organization
ICJ	International Court of Justice

ICRG	International Co-operation Review Group
IDB	Inter-American Development Bank
IFCS	International Financial Centres
IFIS	International Financial Institutions
IGP	Internal Governance Principles
ILC	International Law Commission
ILO	International Labour Organisation
IMF	International Monetary Fund
IMO	International Maritime Organisation
INote	Interpretive Note
INTERPOL	International Criminal Police Organisation
IO	International Organisation
IOC	International Olympic Committee Board
IOM	International Organisation for Migration
IOSCO	International Organisation of Securities Commissions
IPU	Inter-Parliamentary Union
ITLOS	International Tribunal for the Law of the Sea
ITO	International Trade Organisation
ITTO	International Tropical Timber Organisation
JCPOA	Joint Comprehensive Plan of Action
JEM	Joint Experts' Meeting
KRA	Key Recommended Actions
KYC	Know Your Customer
LCCS	Low-Capacity Countries
ME	Mutual Evaluation
MENAFATF	Money Laundering and Terrorist Financing to Countries in the Middle East and North Africa Region
MER	Mutual Evaluation Report
MERCOSUR	Southern Common Market
ML	Money Laundering
MONEYVAL	Committee of Experts on the Evaluation of Anti-Money Laundering Measures and the Financing of Terrorism
MoU	Memorandum of Understanding
MSAR	Macao Special Administrative Region
MSBS	Money Service Businesses
MTOS	Money Transfer Operators
MVTS	Money Value Transfer Services
NAFTA	North American Free Trade Agreement
NATO	North Atlantic Treaty Organisation
NCCT	Non-Cooperative Countries and Territories

NGOS	Non-Governmental Organisations
NPOS	Non-Profit Organisations
NRA	National Risk Assessment
OAS	Organisation of American States
OECD	Organisation for Economic Co-operation and Development
OGBS	Offshore Group of Banking Supervisors
OMCT	World Organisation against Torture
OPEC	Organisation of the Petroleum Exporting Countries
OSCE	Organisation for Security and Co-operation in Europe
OTIF	Intergovernmental Organisation for International Carriage by Rail
PDG	Policy Development Group
PEPS	Politically Exposed Persons
PF	Proliferation Financing
RBA	Risk-Based Approach
ROSC	Risk-Based Reports on the Observance of Standards and Codes
RTMG	Risk, Trends and Methods Group
RUSI	Royal United Services Institute
SCO	Shanghai Co-operation Organisation
SDD	Simplified Customer Due Diligence
SEATO	Southeast Asia Treaty Organisation
SR	Special Recommendation
STRS	Suspicious Transaction Reports
TC	Technical Compliance
TCRR	Technical Compliance Re-Ratings
TF	Terrorist Financing
TFS	Targeted Financial Sanctions
UIC	International Union of Railways
UIT	International Telegraph Union
UN	United Nations
UNCTAD	United Nations Conference on Trade and Development
UNCTE	United Nations Conference on Trade and Employment
UNCTED	United Nations Counter-Terrorism Committee Executive Directorate
UNEP	United Nations Environmental Program
UNESCO	United Nations Educational, Scientific and Cultural Organisation
UNGAS	United Nations General Assembly
UNIDO	United Nations Industrial Development Organisation
UNODC	United Nations Office on Drugs and Crime
UNSC	United Nations Security Council
UPO	United Planning Organisation
UPU	Universal Postal Union

VA	Virtual Assets
VASPs	Virtual Assets Service Providers
VCLT	Vienna Convention on the Law of the Treaties
WB	World Bank
WCO	World Customs Organisation
WG	Working Group
WHO	World Health Organisation
WMD	Weapons of Mass Destruction
WMO	World Meteorological Organisation
WTO	World Trade Organisation

CHAPTER 1

Introduction

> At the turn of the twenty-first century, a new generation of international organisations started to emerge in response to the changing character of the international system and demands for a more representative, effective and responsive governance system. These new and innovative 'hybrid' international organisations vary widely in size, composition and functional capacity and go by a variety of names – global public policy networks, inter-organisational networks, public-private partnerships and (*ad hoc*) global alliances and coalitions. They represent a new approach to solving or managing complex issues and problems currently on the global agenda, a significant departure from the traditional form of international organisations and conventional understanding of their role(s) in the governance of the international system.[1]

There is a general consensus on the emergence of new forms and designs of organisations operating in the international system in response to the challenges faced by the international community. The Financial Action Task Force (FATF), which is the organisation responsible for setting the international standards to counter money laundering, financing of terrorism, and the financing of the proliferation of weapons of mass destruction (the 'Forty Recommendations') with the aim of guaranteeing the integrity and security of the international financial market, is one of them. It was established in 1989, by a G-7 Declaration in a collective effort to fight money laundering resulting from drug trafficking. It currently consists of 40 members, representing the world's wealthiest and emerging economies.[2]

1 James Muldoon, 'New Types of Organizations and the Global Governance in the Twenty-First Century: The Case of ICANN' in J.E. Oestreich (ed), *International Organizations as Self-Directed Actors – a Framework Analysis* (Routledge 2012), 241–242.

2 Russian Federation membership has been suspended since February 2023. At: https://www.fatf-gafi.org/en/publications/Fatfgeneral/outcomes-fatf-plenary-october-2023.html. Also, 2024 Ministerial Declaration, para. 2 and 4.

 | DOI:10.1163/9789004715134_002

The mandate and powers of the FATF are complex, broad, and multi-layered, comprising policy and lawmaking powers, monitoring and sanctioning powers, such as blacklisting, that extend to non-members.

The FATF has built a network of nine regional bodies, the FATF Style Regional Bodies (FSRBS) interconnecting 206 jurisdictions that I call the *octopus-effect network*. An ingeniously designed system in which all jurisdictions around the world implement the same standards, adopt similar regimes in their national systems, share identical compliance mechanisms, and are supervised at both regional and FATF levels using uniform methods and core common values. In practical terms, the FATF has devised an optimal solution to maintain its limited membership policy and *status quo*, wherein the decision-making capacity and processes lie in the "hands" of an elite (the 'octopus head'), while the FSRBS (the 'octopus arms') ensure compliance in the respective regions.

As a result of its mission, the FATF performs relevant public functions in global governance matters, as it is self-evident that protecting the integrity and security of the international financial system is in the best interest of the global public good, with obvious implications for the integrity of States and, ultimately, for the benefit of the population.

Its legitimacy to act in the international landscape stems not only from a worldwide convergent political will, but also from the highest-level endorsement of its mandate by international organisations (IOS), such as the United Nations (UN), particularly its Security Council (UNSC), the Council of Europe (CoE), the European Union (EU), the International Monetary Fund (IMF) and the World Bank (WB), as well as the G-20, the leading international economic forum.

The FATF has been the subject of extensive literature, particularly in relation to the scope of the Forty Recommendations and its role in global governance, as well as the impact of its regulatory, monitoring, and sanctioning frameworks, or on topics, such as legitimacy, transparency, and accountability. Although certain writings must be contextualised in light of the evolving nature of the organisation, others remain valid.

However, no in-depth study of the legal status of the FATF under international law has been found. In States or IOS statements, expert reports, and academic literature, the FATF is described in different ways, namely as an IO, a soft organisation, an inter-governmental body or a transgovernamental network. There is no clear understanding of its legal nature. This ambivalence is also noticeable in the organisation when it makes vague and ambiguous statements about its own legal standing.

This circumstance is even more problematic when international law, in particular international institutional law, struggles to provide a comprehensive definition and identify universally accepted requirements for the legal personhood of IOs. As Jan Klabbers wisely noted:

> [P]erhaps the most difficult question to answer is the one which is, in some ways, a preliminary question: what exactly is an international organisation? (...) The short answer is, quite simply, that we do not know. We may, in most of the cases, be able to recognise an international organisation when we see one, but it has so far appeared impossible to actually define such organisation in a comprehensive way.[3]

I consider that the FATF is a unique organisation. Despite the lack of a treaty foundation and the fact that members have not resolved its international legal personality, the FATF has attained a singular and significant status in international affairs that should not be unnoticed, especially considering its public functions.

My own view is that the FATF has evolved and is now an IO, where the dynamics of the international system is itself a driving force of FATF's evolutionary character. It is contended that due to the evolution of the mandate, institutional setting, and *modus operandi* of the FATF, its nature has gradually evolved into an IO, changing its *modus constituendi.* The interaction between the different international actors at the international plane plays a crucial role, signalling a general practice and acquiescence with the FATF as an international legal person.

An empirical study and a conceptual approach based on existing sources of international law and legal theory with a critical review are used to determine the legal nature of the FATF. For this purpose, a coherent, structured, and comprehensive reasoning of five elements is drawn to ascertain the legal personhood of the FATF. This reasoning provides a rational basis whenever an organisation does not meet the traditional and consensual criteria of being treaty-based, created by States, and 'having an organ of its own with a separate will', and the organisation's distinct will (*volunté disctincte*) needs to be proven.

These five elements are:

i) Membership, to be constituted by States or other entities with recognised legal status under international law;

3 *An Introduction to International Institutional Law* (2nd edn, Cambridge University Press 2009), 6.

ii) Created under international law, treaties or other acts of international law, such as Resolutions, Declarations and Final Acts of a constitutive nature;
iii) To have an organ with a distinct will, ie. to have a separate and independent body with self-governing capacities, acting in the interest of the organisation and assuring a distinct and autonomous will between the organisation and its members;
iv) To operate on the international plane according to international law;
v) External recognition by other subjects of international law.

This reasoning is of the utmost importance since it will inevitably have implications for the field of public international law. Being recognised as a subject of international law means bearing rights and obligations under international law and being bound by international law.

Furthermore, this reasoning gains higher significance when the organisation is entrusted with public functions, where its actions have a transversal and cross-sector impact, affecting a diversity of stakeholders (States, institutions, legal persons and individuals), and covering both public and private sectors and a wide range of subject matters (eg. legal, financial, law enforcement, international co-operation).

The FATF, like any other IO that has a part in global governance matters, should be governed by the rule of law and other principles of good governance, together with internal and external oversight mechanisms, as its decisions and actions have ramifications at global and national scales and affect natural and legal persons.

The FATF case-study is relevant from the viewpoint of international institutional law as it sheds light on the legal status of organisations *in* and *under* international law, with the prospect of enjoying rights, such as the right to conclude treaties (*ius tractum*) and the right to enjoy privileges and immunities (*ius legationis*). At the same time, it entails respecting general principles and rules of international law and being responsible for breaching international law.

A precise understanding of FATF's legal standing on the international plane may enable us to identify other organisations that share analogous features, especially if performing public authority functions and to provide some clarity and legal certainty to the architecture of the international legal system of the twenty-first century.

This hypothesis is even more pertinent given that the FATF is most likely inspiring and shaping other organisations. Indeed, the FATF may be understood as a contemporary or *avant-garde* type of IO, and if it is being used as a framework model for the new generation of IOs, it is critical to assess any shortcomings and suggest ways for improvement.

In our increasingly complex knowledge-based society, the emergence of novel institutional designs of IOs that are created outside the traditional paradigm of a domestic ratification procedure requires new insights and a holistic vision, as they capture theoretical and practical consequences in international law. Does the legal status of IOs still matter? It is believed that it does, and that these forms of multilateral co-operation created by the international legal system according to its own dynamics and challenges need to be studied on a case-by-case basis to their core.

The lack of a clear-cut definition of what an IO is echoes their heterogeneity. Given the diversity of patterns, it is not prudent to 'compartmentalise IOs into boxes', such approach may run the risk of stereotyping or misrepresenting the objective reality of the legal system, while avoiding adequate scrutiny.

We may be witnessing a global trend in international institutional law, where IOs' founding and constitutional instruments are less formal and more dynamic in nature, where organisations have a higher degree of flexibility and adopt pragmatic decisions or actions to the concerns of the international community, while being part of the international legal system, bound by the principles of international law and no less accountable, especially when affecting the rights of individuals.

No institution is therefore free from scrutiny, particularly when it performs heavy leadership functions with global outreach, such as ensuring the stability and integrity of the international financial system. The exercise of public powers presupposes upholding a *corpus* of fundamental principles and norms either of a constitutional or administrative nature; an international law *ethos* that results from the cross-fertilisation of ethical and legal values and principles of the international legal system, which transcend the constituent instruments of an organisation and should guide and frame the *modus operandi* of an IO.

The FATF is an unconventional organisation. The nature, complexity, and impact of FATF's mission on the international plane go far beyond that of a mere soft organisation or a transgovernamental network. As the FATF professes to be the global standard-setter, guardian and arbiter for combating money laundering, financing of terrorism and financing of the proliferation of weapons of mass destruction, its legal personality deserves our full attention and scrutiny.

This book consists of six chapters. Chapter 2 provides historical background and a brief analytical overview of the FATF's institutional, regulatory, and operational frameworks, highlighting its evolving and complex nature. Chapter 3 examines the ongoing debate surrounding the definition of an IO and the identification of its essential elements. This analysis considers the diverse sources of international law and the various theoretical approaches to international legal personality. It also crafts a comprehensive conceptual approach to the key elements for determining the legal personhood of the FATF when traditional and consensual criteria are lacking and its *volunté distincte* needs to be established. Chapter 4 brings a new insight into the legal status of the FATF based on the conceptual approach outlined in the preceding Chapter, presenting sustainable *indicia* that the FATF, an organisation with global governance powers, has morphed into an IO. This transformation is evident through the organisation's current characteristics and capacities, which are often ascribed to those of formal IOs. Chapter 5 discusses the relevance of this case-study in the context of public international law and international institutional law. It also addresses the challenges associated with being entrusted with public functions and suggests a new IO paradigm. Chapter 6 concludes with a concise overview of the main findings.

To ascertain the legal nature of the FATF, its constitutive elements (*modus constituendi*) and institutional, regulatory, and operational frameworks (*modus operandi*) are analysed, including its relationship with its FSRBs and other international actors in the international system, in an evolutionary perspective based on the doctrinal method, empirical analysis, comparative method and model-testing.

A behaviour analysis of FATF and FSRBs members and non-members, as well as a behaviour analysis of relevant IOs, such as the UN/UNSC, CoE and EU and other international bodies, such as the G-20, is carried out to comprehend how the FATF is perceived in the international system, based on fact-finding, internal rules, practice and acquiescence.

Some concrete cases of State behaviour (from common law and civil law jurisdictions) were selected to illustrate the impact of FATF actions at national level and in different domains, which are analysed based on comparative methods. Additionally, quantitative and qualitative data from expert reports (eg. IMF, WB or UN) are provided to substantiate impact findings.

Relevant international legal instruments, both 'hard' and 'soft' law, as well as general and customary international law, judicial decisions, legal doctrine, fact-finding and experts' reports are therefore considered. These sources can provide insight into the perception of the FATF in the international realm. There is a general, expressive, and representative acceptance of the mission and powers of the organisation, and an exceptional compliance behaviour by its members and non-members to meet its Recommendations, action plans, and calls for countermeasures.

Following the aforementioned, I have endeavoured to produce satisfactory evidence that the FATF is an *institutional legal fact*, an independent international organisation with a distinct will (*volonté distincte* – the *quintessential* element) from its members in the international legal landscape, and that the source of its legal personhood results from international law, ie. from the operation and recognition of such an organisation in the international legal system.

It is also hoped that this research may enhance the understanding of the FATF and its effective place in the international legal system, while identifying possible trends or even the emergence of novel models of IOs that deviate from the traditional institutional-building paradigm as subjects of international law.

CHAPTER 2

Description of the Financial Action Task Force

1 Historical Background and Raison d' Être

The FATF was set up at the G-7 Paris Economic Summit in 1989,[1] by the Heads of State and Governments of the seven major industrialised countries (France, Germany, Italy, Japan, United Kingdom (UK), United States of America (USA) and Canada) and the President of the Commission of the European Communities (now European Commission of the EU), as the first comprehensive global response to counter money laundering from drug cartels in the finance sector.[2]

It is no coincidence that the timing of this collective action concurred with the recent adopted United Nations Convention against Illicit Traffic in Narcotic Drugs and Psychotropic Substances of 1988 (1988 Vienna Convention[3]) aiming at fighting drug trafficking and related crimes, including money laundering.

1 The G-7 or Group of Seven is an international finance group created in 1975 by France, Germany, Italy, Japan, United Kingdom, United States of America (former Group of Six) with the addition of Canada in 1976.

2 G-7 Economic Declaration (16/07/1989), para. 52. The influence of the EU, CoE and European Commission drafting the AML global regime (FATF) as well as the hegemonic influence of the USA are outlined by Jason Sharman, 'The Global Anti-Money Laundering Regime and Developing Countries: Damned If They Do, Damned If They Don't?' (International Studies Association Annual Conference, San Diego, 22–25 March 2006). Amongst others, Liliya Gelemerova notes that the USA was one of the main founders of the FATF aiming at imposing the American AML standards on a global scale. *The Anti-Money Laundering System in the Context of Globalization: A Panopticon Built on Quicksand*? (Wolf Legal Publishers 2011), 258. Nicholas Turner also refers that many of the core Recommendations resembled the USA Federal Law, 'The Financial Action Task Force: International Regulatory Convergence through Soft Law' (2014) 59 *New York Law School Law Review*, 557. Along these lines, Sofia de Oliveira mentions the influence of the USA in the setting of the FATF, including the partnership with the IMF and WB, and the correlation of powers within the FATF. The author comments that the FATF is "managed by a group of great powers USA and core allies twist in global governance", 'The Governance of the Financial Action Task Force: An Analysis of Power and Influence throughout the Years' (2018) 69 *Crime, Law and Social Change*, 156–160.

3 Adopted in Vienna on 20/12/1988, entered into force on 11/11/1990. It has 192 State Parties. At: https://treaties.un.org/Pages/ViewDetails.aspx?src=TREATY&mtdsg_no=VI-19&chapter=6&clang=_en (last visited 15/05/2025).

 | DOI:10.1163/9789004715134_003

The 1988 Vienna Convention is pioneering as it is the first multilateral legal instrument addressing the problem of money laundering.[4] Organised crime, drug trafficking and the flow of illicit money from narcotics into the financial and banking systems were clearly marked. States are called to ensure stronger and closer co-operation, particularly in legal co-operation matters, where the fight against drug trafficking and related crimes must be a shared responsibility.

In response to this plea for deeper co-operation, the G-7 Economic Declaration of 16 July 1989 established a *task force* with the following mandate:

> [T]o assess the results of co-operation already undertaken in order to prevent the utilisation of the banking system and financial institutions for the purpose of money laundering, and to consider additional preventive efforts in this field, including the adaptation of the legal and regulatory systems so as to enhance multilateral judicial assistance.[5]

The G-7 Economic Declaration is the FATF's founding instrument, establishing its mandate and purpose.[6] Besides the G-7 members and the Commission of the European Communities, the Summit was open to other participants, namely Australia, Austria, Belgium, Luxemburg, The Netherlands, Spain, Sweden and Switzerland that were invited to join the task force, while France took the presidency.

The first meeting was led by France, and three working groups (WG) were formed with a mission of producing a report by April 1990: the WG on Money Laundering and Statistics Methods, the WG on Legal Questions and the WG on Administrative and Financial Co-operation. The report was divided into three segments: (1) extent and nature of money laundering process; (2) programmes

4 The 'Guidelines on the Prevention of Criminal Use of the Banking System for the Purpose of Money-Laundering' by the Basel Institute aimed at the banking sector were adopted on 28/12/1988. The CoE Convention on Laundering, Search, Seizure and Confiscation of the Proceeds from Crime was adopted on 08/11/1990.

5 Para. 53, point 8.

6 For a comprehensive understanding of the international global efforts to counter money laundering and, particularly, of the FATF, amongst others, John Broome, *Anti-Money Laundering – International Practice and Policies* (Sweet and Maxwell Asia 2005); Alain Damais, 'The Financial Action Task Force' in W.H. Muller, C.H. Kalin and J.G. Goldsworth (eds), *Anti-Money Laundering: International Law and Practice* (John Wiley & Sons 2007); James Jackson, 'The Financial Action Task Force: An Overview' (2017) Congressional Research Service Report, at: https://sgp.fas.org/crs/misc/RS21904.pdf. Nicholas Ryder provides a brief overview of the evolution of the concept of money laundering and how it became part of the international agenda. 'The Financial Services Authority and Money Laundering, a Game of Cat and Mouse' (2008) 67(3) *Cambridge Law Journal*.

already in place to combat money laundering (national and international); and (3) Forty Recommendations.

The 'Forty Recommendations' were drawn to assist States to combat the misuse of financial systems by persons laundering money from illicit production and trafficking of drugs and to promote information sharing and co-operation among States.[7] Their scope comprised a general part of a political nature urging States to commit to implementing the 1988 Vienna Convention and to adopt an effective Anti-Money Laundering (AML) programme; a part covering national legal frameworks to combat money laundering; a part focusing on the role of the financial system and its reinforcement; and, lastly, a part addressing the strengthening of international co-operation.

The report with the Forty Recommendations was endorsed by the Finance Ministers and later adopted at the G-7 Houston Summit in 1990.[8] Meanwhile, participants at the Summit became mindful that the FATF could play a decisive role as a *technical specialised body* (as a standard-setter) in the fight against money laundering and, equally, serve as a forum for global co-ordination and co-operation, including with non-members and other IOs. To this end, widespread implementation and dissemination of the Recommendations would be instrumental to maximising international co-operation and strengthening the role of the FATF.[9]

Accordingly, "all countries of the Organisation for Economic Co-operation Development (OECD) and financial centre countries" were invited to participate in FATF's mission, and politically pressured to endorse FATF's Recommendations.[10] The FATF was well aware that the universal and effective implementation of the Recommendations could only be attainable with the formal endorsement and commitment of all States (jurisdictions).[11]

New jurisdictions were, therefore, invited to join the task force, particularly those with major financial centres,[12] increasing the level of expertise and

7 1990 FATF Report, 3.

8 1990–1991 FATF Report, 4.

9 Ibid, 5.

10 Ibid, 4.

11 As there are jurisdictions that are not sovereign States but have international legal status or have been granted external relations powers, the term 'jurisdictions' is preferred, and more commonly used in the present text.

12 Denmark, Finland, Ireland, New-Zealand, Norway, Portugal and Turkey. The FATF also invited the three most important offshore banking centres: Hong Kong, Singapore and the Gulf Co-operation Council (Bahrain, Kuwait, Oman, Qatar, United Arab Emirates and Saudi Arabia). Singapore, although endorsing the Recommendations, took one year to become a full member (1990–1991 FATF Report, 4 and 13).

know-how of different systems with distinct backgrounds ranging from legal to law enforcement, from finance to supervision.

Further, in order to ensure the "worldwide mobilisation against money laundering",[13] the FATF created a unique mechanism to determine and monitor the degree of implementation of the measures against money laundering,[14] while assisting non-members who wish to endorse and apply the Forty Recommendations.

The strategic plan was to evaluate the progress of all members after endorsing the Forty Recommendations by 1996.[15] Accordingly, a self-evaluation mechanism was introduced,[16] a mutual evaluation peer review mechanism was designed,[17] a technical assistance programme was established (between members and non-members upon request),[18] and a minimum institutional framework was set up.[19]

It was agreed that the FATF should function as an *ad hoc* group for the next five years, with a mid-term review every three years. The FATF Presidency would rotate among members on an annual basis and be supported by a Steering Group.[20] In the meantime, the OECD would provide administrative backup while negotiations to establish a specialised Secretariat within the OECD took place.[21] Membership policy, participation in FATF's meetings and other policy issues were to be addressed in the following years.[22]

2 Legal Nature and Mandate

2.1 *Character and Mandate*

The FATF characterises itself in the 2019 Mandate as an "inter-governmental body"[23] whose purposes are to: "protect financial systems and the broader economy from threats of money laundering and the financing of terrorism and

13 1991–1992 FATF Report, 20.
14 1990–1991 FATF Report, 3.
15 Ibid, 17–18.
16 Ibid, 3, 17–18.
17 Ibid.
18 Ibid, 3–4, and 18.
19 Ibid, 3 and 19.
20 Ibid and 1991–1992 FATF Report, para. 7.
21 Ibid and 1991–1992 FATF Report, para. 7 and 12.
22 1991–1992 FATF Report, para. 100.
23 Para. 1.

proliferation, thereby strengthening financial sector integrity and contributing to safety and security".[24]

The mandate, membership, lifespan and nature of the FATF have changed, coherently or not, throughout the years in a flexible manner in order to provide prompt, robust and efficient responses to the global challenges and illicit activities and trends that threaten the integrity of financial systems. In its 2008–2012 Mandate, FATF's flexible nature is emphasised:

> Over the long-term, it will be vital for the FATF to evolve if it is to maintain an effective response to the constantly changing threats facing the international financial system. It will therefore be essential that the structure, organisation and operational planning of the FATF remain flexible and able to adapt to meet new challenges as they arise.[25]

Consequently, the FATF's mandate has been regularly revised and gradually broadened whether to incorporate new functions, to review its Recommendations and enforcement mechanisms, or to engage in structural reforms.

Following the G-7 Houston Summit in 1990, a mid-term review conducted in 1993–1994 decided to extend the mandate of the FATF for five more years.[26] This period was then expanded to periods of eight years starting from 2004.[27]

From 1991 to 1996, the FATF's main tasks were: i) setting standards and reviewing money laundering methods; ii) monitoring the implementation of AML measures by member governments; and iii) promoting the adoption of countermeasures.[28]

In 1996, the FATF's mandate and its Recommendations were revised to "reflect evolving money laundering trends and techniques", in particular to broaden their scope far beyond drug related-money laundering (Section 6.1. below). At the same time, its membership expanded to 26 jurisdictions and two IOs,[29] and its former mandate to "assess and evaluate" established in the

24 Para. 2–3. Slightly different, the 2022–2023 FATF Report states that the FATF is an "independent inter-governmental body that develops and promotes policies to protect the global financial system against money laundering, terrorist financing and the financing of proliferation of weapons of mass destruction", 2.

25 Para. 19.

26 1993–1994 FATF Report, para. 2, 10 and 15.

27 Ministries renewed the FATF's eight-year mandate on 28/04/1998 (1997–1998 FATF Report, para. 22), 14/05/2004 (2003–2004 FATF Report, para. 15 and 20) and 20/04/2012 (2011–2012 FATF Report, 8 and 10).

28 1997–1998 FATF Report, para. 13.

29 1996–1997 FATF Report, para. 8.

G-7 Economic Declaration of 1989 has evolved into a multi-disciplinary body whose purpose is the *development and promotion of policies to combat money laundering* (policy-making body). The 1996 Forty Recommendations were endorsed by more than 130 jurisdictions and were recognised as the international standard to counter money laundering.[30]

From 1996 to 1999, the FATF determined as priorities to: i) establish a worldwide AML network and disseminate the FATF's message across all continents and regions; ii) improve members' implementation of the Forty Recommendations; and iii) actively assess money laundering (ML) trends and countermeasures.[31]

The 1999–2004 initial mandate covered the same priorities.[32] However, following the 9/11 terrorist attacks in the USA, it was expanded in October 2001 to counter the financing of terrorist acts and terrorist organisations. The 'Eight Special Recommendations (SR) on Terrorist Financing' were added and complemented the Forty Recommendations.[33] FATF members then included 29 jurisdictions and two IOs.[34]

The key priorities of the FATF were:

i) Reviewing the Forty Recommendations;
ii) Countering the financing of terrorism (CFT);
iii) Spreading the AML message throughout the world;
iv) Trends and techniques in ML and Terrorist Financing (TF); and
v) Improving the implementation of the Forty Recommendations.[35]

For the second time, in 2003, the FATF Recommendations were fully revised to incorporate updated techniques to counter ML as well as financing of terrorism (FT). The Forty Recommendations together with the Eight SR on Terrorist Financing (later, in 2004, Nine SR) provided "an enhanced, comprehensive and consistent framework of measures for combating money laundering and terrorist financing".[36]

30 2003–2004 FATF Report, para. 15.

31 1997–1998 FATF Report, para. 16–19.

32 2001–2002 FATF Report, para. 4.

33 Ibid, para. 15. Amongst others, on the role of FATF in the context of the global fight against terrorism, Andrew Ayers, 'The Financial Action Task Force: The War on Terrorism Will Not Be Fought on the Battlefield' (2002) 18(3) *New York Law School Journal of Human Rights*; Joel Sollier, 'The United Nations Security Council – and the Efforts to Combat Money Laundering and the Financing of Terrorism' in W.H. Muller, C.H. Kalin and J.G. Goldsworth (eds), *Anti-Money Laundering: International Law and Practice* (John Wiley & Sons 2007); Kern Alexander, *Economic Sanctions – Law and Public Policy* (Palgrave Macmillan 2009).

34 2002–2003 FATF Report, para. 11.

35 2002–2003 FATF Report, para. 14.

36 2003 FATF Recommendations, 2.

In the 2004–2012 Mandate priorities were updated to:

i) Continue to set standards to combat ML and FT;
ii) Carry out typologies and compliance work to ensure global action against ML and FT;
iii) Develop closer co-operation with the IMF and the WB; and
iv) Enhance FATF's relationships with the FSRBs.[37]

With a new eight-year mandate, the FATF requested all jurisdictions to take "the necessary steps to bring their national systems for combating money laundering and terrorist financing into compliance with the new FATF Recommendations, and to effectively implement these measures".[38]

In 2004, the FATF consisted of 31 jurisdictions and two IOs, with approximately 140 jurisdictions universally recognising the FATF's Recommendations as the international AML/CFT standard.[39]

Acknowledging the new challenges of the international financial system, FATF's mandate was renewed again in 2012 for an additional eight years period (2012–2020).[40] The rising threat of proliferation financing (PF) of weapons of mass destruction (WMD) from countries, such as Iran and North Korea, along with cyber-attacks and the use of virtual assets (VA) in criminal schemes triggered a review of the mandate.[41]

The 2012–2020 Mandate established as main priorities to "set standards and to promote effective implementation of legal, regulatory and operational measures for combating money laundering, terrorist financing and other related threats to the integrity of the international financial system" and "to identify national-level vulnerabilities with the aim of protecting the international financial system from misuse".[42]

In 2012, the FATF included 34 jurisdictions and two IOs, and more than 180 jurisdictions universally accept FATF's Recommendations as the international standard for AML, CFT and Countering Proliferation Financing (CPF).[43]

A new mandate was adopted in 2019, marking the beginning of a new era by introducing a major structural novelty – an unlimited mandate. The 2009

37 2003–2004 FATF Report, para. 14.

38 2003 FATF Recommendations, 3.

39 2003–2004 FATF Report, para. 2; 2004–2005 FATF Report, para. 5; 2005–2006 FATF Report, para. 6 and 17.

40 2011–2012 FATF Report, 10.

41 20 Years FATF Report, 12, 15–16; 25 Years FATF Report, 3 and 12 *et seq.*

42 2012–2020 Mandate, para. 2.

43 2012–2013 FATF Report, 33–34.

Mandate identifies four key areas of action for the FATF, that remain in place to this day. These areas are to:

i) Identify threats to the financial system;
ii) Develop robust standards to fight these threats;
iii) Assess countries compliance with the FATF Standards; and
iv) Identify countries that fail compliance.[44]

To protect financial systems and the global economy from ML/FT/PF, as specified in the 2019 Mandate,[45] a significant number of functions and tasks have been assigned, including continuous updating of the standards and close mentoring with relevant partners and stakeholders.[46]

In practice, the FATF has been adapting, without objection, its priorities and tasks in its mandates and mid-term reviews to respond to the collective needs and threats in the fields of ML/FT/PF. As commented by Heba Shams:

> Following its creation at the Summit, the FATF assumed a life of its own, without any limitation of mandate or timeframe. It is left to the FATF to decide its own destiny and to define its own mission.[47]

At the present, the FATF consists of 40 members – 38 jurisdictions and two IOs, with 206 jurisdictions universally endorsing the FATF Recommendations as the international standard for AML, CFT and CPF.[48]

2.2 *Lifespan*

In terms of its lifespan, the FATF was a non-permanent body for three decades, with a successively renewed lifespan of eight years, with the last renewal of

44 Para. 3; 30 Years FATF Report, 13. The mandate also includes *inter alia* to assist vulnerable or low-capacity jurisdictions, to co-operate with other IOs and bodies, and to engage with private sector and civil society.

45 Para. 2.

46 Ibid, para. 3. About the expansion of FATF's mandate, and FATF as a model of 'experimentalism governance', amongst others, Mark Nance. The author acknowledges that FATF's "evolution into a major financial actor" was "unexpected", 'Re-Thinking FATF: An Experimentalist Interpretation of the Financial Action Task Force' (2018) 69 *Crime, Law and Socials Change*, 117–120.

47 'Club Multilateralism and Global Supranationalism: The Case of FATF' in J.B. Attanasio and J.J. Norton (eds), *Multilateralism v Unilateralism: Policy Choices in a Global Society* (British Institute of International and Comparative Law and SMU Dedman School of Law 2005), 461.

48 2022–2023 FATF Report, 4; 2024 Ministerial Declaration, para. 2.

eight-years on 20 April 2012.[49] In the 2012 Ministerial Declaration it is clearly affirmed that:

> The FATF is a task force of its Members, and its activities have continued to evolve whilst remaining focussed on achieving concrete results. We believe that the task force structure of the FATF has served it well. The FATF should therefore retain this flexibility as it continues to consolidate and build on what it has already achieved.[50]

However, on 12 April 2019, in an unprecedented landmark decision, the Ministers changed the traditional position and established an open-ended mandate in the 2019 Mandate.[51] This evolution of FATF's lifespan is explained in the 30 Years FATF Report:

> Three decades ago, the G-7 created the FATF as a temporary forum to find a solution to the money laundering problem that was a global priority at the time (...) This year, Ministers (...) agreed to make the FATF's mandate open-ended. This reflects the fact that money laundering, terrorist financing and the financing of proliferation are enduring challenges for the integrity of the financial system, and that a sustained political commitment to fight money laundering, terrorist financing, and proliferation financing is required.[52]

In the 2022 Ministerial Declaration, in an abbreviated form, Ministers announced: "We made the FATF's mandate open-ended starting in 2020, recognising that the FATF has evolved from a time-bound forum to a permanent body".[53]

This change of status to a permanent body should be viewed as a natural and logical step, considering the role of the FATF as a global standard-setter and its political engagement amidst the international community, including the UN/UNSC, IMF, WB and G-20, without disregarding its pivotal mission in the 'FATF Global Network' (Chapter 4, Sections 5 and 6 below).

---

49 2012–2020 Mandate, para. 49 (until 31 December 2020).

50 Para. 11.

51 2019 Ministerial Declaration, para. 16; 2019 Mandate, para. 49. Also, 30 Years FATF Report, 13.

52 At: 83–84.

53 Para. 2.

In fact, what is peculiar about such a decision is its significant postponement. From another angle, the political reason behind its 30-year delay can be questioned, given that it was and continues to be evident that FATF's mission and objectives are long-lasting.[54] As once voiced, as long as "there is crime, there will be money laundering".[55]

The arguments in favour of a fixed lifespan and midterm reviews were that Ministers should constantly ensure that the FATF remains consistent with its functions and aims, and the other, the ongoing need to review its mission and standards to keep pace with global threats.[56] This understanding is undeniably superseded in 2019 by a contrasting approach in which the FATF's (long-term) aims and functions require a permanent basis organisation.[57]

This modification should not be ignored. As a matter of fact, it should be analysed in the context of international institutional law, ie. how the FATF maps itself (its legal status) in the international legal system? How is the FATF perceived by other subjects of international law in the international arena? In other words, is the FATF an international legal person – an IO?

2.3 *Legal Nature*

The FATF has been classified as an informal organisation (or 'soft' organisation),[58] a standard-setter,[59] a transnational policy network,[60] or an

54 Over the past three decades, the FATF's mandate has been firmly reaffirmed and strengthened. If one considers the fact that its main objective is to combat transnational financial crimes, it is not difficult to conclude that its mission will be permanent.

55 30 Years FATF Report, 42.

56 2007–2008 FATF Report, para. 45.

57 2018–2019 FATF Report, 29–31.

58 Amongst others, Shawn Donnelly, 'Informal International Lawmaking: Global Financial Market Regulation' in A. Berman *et al* (eds), *Informal International Lawmaking: Case Studies* (Torkel Opsahl Academic EPublisher 2012), 201–202; Joost Pauwelyn, Ramses Wessel and Jan Wouters, 'When Structures Become Shackles: Stagnation and Dynamics in International Lawmaking' (2014) 25(3) *European Journal of International Law*, 746 and 752–754; Leonardo Borlini, 'Soft Law, Soft International Organizations e Regolamentazione 'Tecnica' di Problemi di Sicurezza Pubblica e Integrità Finanziaria' (2017) 2 *Rivista di Diritto Internazionale*, 378; Nathanael Tilahun, 'The Re-organization of the FATF as an International Legal Person and the Promises and Limits to Accountability' in A. Arcuri and F.C. Kund (eds), *Technocracy and Multi-level Governance: What Role for Accountability?* (Routledge 2021). On-line version, 2, at: https://papers.ssrn.com/sol3/papers.cfm?abstract_id=4127120.

59 On FATF's role as a worldwide standard-setter, amongst others, Alexander, 'The International Anti-Money Laundering Regime: The Role of the Financial Action Task Force' (2001) 4(3) *Journal of Money Laundering Control*; Broome (n 6); Ross Delston and Stephen Walls, 'Reaching Beyond Banks: How to Target-Based Money Laundering

IO.[61] The FATF is identified as an IO in the 2023 Yearbook of International Organisations.[62]

In the 2009 Report of the European Union Committee of the UK House of Lords (2009 House of Lords Report), the uniqueness of FATF's standing is discussed at length:

> Most international bodies in which a number of States participate have a formal structure and constitution contained in a treaty, convention or other agreement. The FATF is not one of them (...) but Sir James Sassoon told us that the organisation as described by Professor Alldridge did not bear much resemblance to anything that he recognised. When he first came to the FATF it struck him as 'a rather extraordinary entity in its way', but he thought its interesting constitutional set-up had served it reasonably well over the last 20 years. We agree that the constitutional set-up of

and Terrorist Financing Outside the Financial Sector' (2009) 41(1) *Case Western Reserve Journal of International Law.*

60 Nance classifies FATF as a "transnational public policy network", (n 46), 137. Amongst others, Kenneth Blazejewski, 'The FATF and Its Institutional Partners: Improving the Effectiveness and Accountability of Transgovernamental Networks' (2008) 22(1) *Temple International* and *Comparative Law Journal*, 11–13; Anja Jakobi, 'Governing Illicit Finance in Transnational Security Spaces: The FATF and Anti-Money Laundering' (2018) 69 *Crime, Law and Social Change*; Nance, 'The Regime that FATF Built: An Introduction to the Financial Action Task Force' (2018) 69 *Crime Law and Social Change*, 115.

61 Navin Beekarry affirms that "[it] is now recognised as one, if not the most, influential international organisation in the international campaign against both ML and FT", 'The International Anti-Money Laundering and Combating the Financing of Terrorism Regulatory Strategy: A Critical Analysis of Compliance Determinants in International Law' (2011) 31(1) *Northwestern Journal of International Law & Business*, 169. Amongst others, Klabbers, 'Formal Intergovernmental Organizations' in J.K. Cogan, I. Hurd and I. Johnstone (eds), *Oxford Handbook of International Organisations* (Oxford University Press 2016) 137; Borlini and Francesco Montanaro, 'The Evolution of the EU Law against Criminal Finance: The 'Hardening' of FATF Standards within the EU' (2017) 48(4) *Georgetown Journal of International Law*, 17–18. Habibollah Habibi and Shahram Zanershan, mention the controversial nature of FATF as an IO and attempt to demonstrate that that the FATF is an IO. 'The Role & Position of FATF in International Law System' (2021) 20 (45) *Journal of Legal Research*, (Abstract) – Arabic/Persian.

62 2022–2023 Yearbook of International Organisations – Guide to Global Civil Society Networks, vol. 5 – Statistics, Visualisations and Patterns (5th edn, UIA and BRILL), at: https://uia.org/sites/uia.org/files/misc_pdfs/pubs/yb_2022_vol5_lookinside.pdf (last visited 15.02.2023). The FATF is classified as 'Type I F': organisations of special form and 'Type II gy': intergovernmental and international organisation membership, at: https://uia.org/ybio?name=Financial+Action+Task+Force (last visited 18/04/2024).

> the FATF is unusual – extraordinary is perhaps not too strong a word – but we feel it is none the worse for that.[63]

The FATF has also issued different statements with differentiated terminology over the years regarding its legal nature, including an unexpected statement in the 30 Years FATF Report. Chronologically, in 1990, the FATF self-identified as an "*ad hoc* group"[64] and, in 1991, affirmed that it "is not an international organisation, but a group of governments that has agreed to adopt and to implement a comprehensive set of recommendations with the aim of combating money laundering".[65]

In subsequent reports, the FATF characterises itself as an "independent *ad hoc* group"[66] or as a "free-standing *ad hoc* group reporting to Finance Ministers or other competent ministers and authorities of its member governments".[67] From 1998 until 2003, this matter, intentionally or not, was left out of the reports. In the mid-term review of 2003,[68] the topic of the legal nature of the FATF was brought up again. At this meeting, Ministers recalled their late statement of April 1998 where it was agreed that the FATF "is not a permanent international organisation".[69]

In 2006, the FATF brands itself as an "inter-governmental body" and its status as a "policy-making body" is commonly referred.[70] In 2007, the FATF identifies itself as an "inter-governmental policy-making body" whose purpose is to "establish international standards, and develop and promote policies, both at national and international levels, to combat money laundering and terrorist financing".[71] In the 2022–2023 FATF Report, the FATF assumes that it "is an independent inter-governmental body".[72]

The term "independent inter-governmental body" has been consistently used in FATF reports since 2008,[73] as well as in the 30 Years FATF

63 UK House of Lords – European Union Committee, Nineteenth Report-Money Laundering and the Financing of Terrorism (2008–09) (2009 House of Lords Report), para. 17, 25–26.

64 1990–1991 FATF Report, 19.

65 1991–1992 FATF Report, para. 83.

66 1993–1994 FATF Report, para. 15.

67 Ibid, para. 24.

68 2003–2004 FATF Report, para. 15.

69 1997–1998 FATF Report, para. 12.

70 2004–2005 FATF Report, para. 1; 2005–2006 FATF Report, para. 2; 20 Years FATF Report, p. 6; 25 Years FATF Report, 7.

71 2007–2008 FATF Report, para. 1.

72 At: 2.

73 2008–2009 till 2022–2023 FATF Reports, colophon page or 2, except 2013–2014 and 2014–2015 FATF Reports.

Report,[74] and is reiterated in the Forty Recommendations (as last updated in November 2023).[75] The term "inter-governmental body" is affirmed in the 2019 Mandate[76] and in the Forty Recommendations.[77]

As regards international obligations, both the 2019 Mandate and the (previous) 2012–2020 Mandate are categorical in stating that the "FATF mandate does not intend to create any legal rights or obligations".[78]

The flexible and informal nature of the FATF has been a cornerstone characteristic of the organisation;[79] often lauded and defended as an almost *sine qua non* condition for its efficiency and success. In several FATF Reports, it is stated:

> As the main money laundering policy maker, the FATF has once again proved that its flexible structure did not impede effective results.[80]
>
> One of FATF's crucial advantages, as the key money laundering policy making body, lies in its highly flexible structure. This puts the Task Force in an excellent position to take the lead in tackling the increasingly global character of the money laundering phenomenon.[81]
>
> The success of the FATF's work so far demonstrates that there is no alternative international organisation, body or group, which has the necessary expertise, ie. of a multidisciplinary nature with the experience and ability to assume responsibility of the FATF in a flexible and efficient way.[82]
>
> The FATF's task force structure has enabled it to respond decisively and promptly to emerging threats and to accommodate efficiently several expansions in its membership. This structure remains broadly the right one for the organisation and should be maintained.[83]

74 Colophon page.

75 At: 1 (last visited 15/05/2024).

76 Para. 1.

77 At: 7.

78 Para. 48 in both mandates.

79 1990–1991 FATF Report, 13; 2007–2008 FATF Report, para. 45; Declaration of the FATF President, 2012–2013 FATF Report, 8. This feature was also commended, amongst others, 2009 House of Lords Report (n 63) para. 25–26; Blazejewski (n 60) 10–13.

80 1991–1992 FATF Report, para. 100.

81 1993–1994 FATF Report, para. 122.

82 1997–1998 FATF Report, para. 20.

83 2008–2012 Mandate, para. 18.

The preceding statements reflect a general belief that the adopted informal model was the best option.[84] Nevertheless, in the 30 Years FATF Report, under the title: "FATF's new mandate as an international organisation", FATF's status as an IO is unequivocally affirmed:

> This year, Ministers recognised that the FATF had evolved from a time-bound task force to an international organisation whose work was crucial to the integrity of the global financial system.[85]

This public declaration directly contradicts earlier FATF's statements, placing FATF's acclaimed informal legal nature into perspective with obvious consequences in the sphere of international law if recognised as a subject of international law (Chapter 5 below).

Moreover, prior to the 30 Years FATF Report, the legal nature of the FATF was discussed internally, particularly during the Spanish (2016–2017)[86] and Argentina (2017–2018) Presidencies,[87] and subsequently reported by the FATF to the G-20 Hamburg Summit in 2017[88] and to the G-20 Buenos Aires Finance Ministers and Central Bank Governors Meeting in 2018:[89]

---

84 This understanding was reproduced in the FATF's website in 'General Questions' by asserting that the FATF "was not formed as a formal international organisation" rather a "task force composed of member governments who agree to fund the FATF on temporary basis with specific goals and projects (a 'mandate')". Its time-bound was addressed and not updated in FATF's website until 15/09/2022. This topic was in the meantime left out from general questions. At: https://www.fatf-gafi.org/en/pages/frequently-asked-questions.html#tabs-36503a8663-item-bb71634027-tab (last visited 15/05/2024).

85 At: 83–84.

86 Some members raised the need for a debate on the FATF's legal and institutional status, international position and governance matters. See 'Proposals to Strengthen FAFT's Institutional Basis, Governance and Capacity' in the Outcomes of the FATF Plenary meeting in June 2017.

87 'Objectives for FATF-XXIX (2017–2018) Paper by the Incoming President Priorities for the Argentina Presidency of FATF (2017–2018)' – Executive Summary, para 17.

88 Para. 3–5 on how to enhance 'FATF's Institutional Basis' (French proposal). At: https://www.fatf-gafi.org/content/dam/fatf-gafi/reports/FATF-Report-to-G20-July-2017.pdf. The G-20 Leaders in response welcomed the: "intention to further explore its transformation into a legal person, which recognises that the FATF has evolved from a temporary forum to a sustained public and political commitment to tackle AML/CFT threats", G-20 Hamburg Action Plan (08/07/2017), 13. Also, The Hamburg G-20 Leaders' Statement on Countering Terrorism (08/07/2017), para. 12.

89 Para. 1 and 6. At: https://www.fatf-gafi.org/media/fatf/documents/FATF-G20-FM-CBG-March-2018.pdf.

> FATF members reaffirm their intention to strengthen FATF international status as the inter-governmental body in charge of setting standards globally for anti-money laundering, counter terrorist financing and counter proliferation financing. In that regard, FATF members continue to explore ways to improve FATF's institutional basis, including through further consideration of legal personality in the host country of the Secretariat or under international public law.[90]

The affirmation in the 30 Years FATF Report is indeed an unprecedented stand that can be understood as reflecting the objective reality of the organisation. However, the absence of publicly accessible information on further developments is manifest, resulting in an unresolved ambiguity that overshadows FATF's legal position in the international legal system.

Another possible interpretation is that the use of this terminology simply accommodates the idea of an organisation with a permanent standing deprived of international personality. Did the Ministers exclusively approach the mandate of the FATF from the viewpoint of its lifespan and long-term "enduring concerns", failing to determine the legal status of the organisation in international affairs? Or should the affirmation be considered an explicit assumption of the true legal nature of the FATF?

The lack of explanation of what "a permanent body" means in the Ministerial Declarations raises doubts regarding the nature of this institutional change.[91] While it may be agreed that there is a material need for a permanent body to fulfil the mandate of protecting the integrity, transparency, and security of the

90 Ibid, para. 6. There are no more references to this topic in subsequent presidencies.

91 Tilahun addresses the informal nature of the FATF and proposes three modes of legitimation: 1) international legal personality with a constitutive treaty; 2) domestic legal personality through a legal agreement with the host State; 3) international legal personality without a constitutive treaty circumscribed to a set of privileges, immunities and powers through an agreement by the members. The author also explores the advantages and disadvantages of each model, (n 58) 6–9. The legal nature of the FATF was also discussed at the 2023 RUSI Roundtable (November) about the FATF entitled 'The Future of the Financial Action Task Force – Improving the Least Bad Option?' with no conclusive suggestion, (2024 RUSI Conference Report) 1, at: https://www.rusi.org/explore-our-research/publications/conference-reports/future-financial-action-task-force-improving-least-bad-option. In this Report, reference is made to the UN Panel on Global Financial Integrity that recommended the FATF to establish a formal "legal foundation for an inclusive intergovernmental body on money laundering (Recommendation 14C)", FACTI, 'Financial Integrity for Sustainable Development' (February 2021) Executive Summary, Report of the High-level Panel on International Financial Accountability, Transparency and Integrity for Achieving the 2030 Agenda, x.

international financial system, rather than a body with a limited-term, subject to constant renewal, how to explain FATF's current functions and far-reaching powers? How should these elements be understood in terms of international institutional law?

The term may refer to an ordinary permanent forum for communication, dialogue and concertation of wills,[92] or it may refer to an institutional feature consistent with a formal IO. Actually, it may be interpreted that: (a) Ministers justifying that the *evolution* of the FATF requires a "sustained public and political commitment"; (b) Ministers endorsing FATF's decision-making role; (c) Ministers formalising bi-annual meetings; and (d) the unprecedent affirmation in the 30 Years FATF are signs of an implicit recognition of the FATF as a permanent organisation with legal standing.

2.4 *Political Accountability*

As regards accountability, the FATF has always been accountable to the Ministers of its member jurisdictions, reporting on a regular basis on main aspects of its work.[93]

Ministerial meetings, equivalent to a Conference of the Parties to a multilateral treaty, are the high-level political forum that endorse and provide the political authority for the FATF to operate, including FATF's strategic guidelines and policy-making priorities, as well as its institutional setting and mandate.[94]

Normally, Ministers would meet for the mid-term reviews, mandate renewal or on an *ad-hoc* basis in exceptional circumstances.[95] This situation changed on 12 April 2019 when Ministers decided that a Ministerial meeting shall be held every two years.[96]

The first biannual meeting took place in Washington D.C. on 21 April 2022. In this meeting, Ministers reiterated:

> At our last meeting in April 2019 in Washington D.C., we agreed to enhance the FATF's capacity to respond to these threats all countries face (…) We decided to deepen our engagement as Ministers by meeting every

92 Ibid, Tilahun mentions that the FATF "operates essentially as a permanent conference", 2.

93 2019 Mandate, para. 49–50. Also, 2008–2012 FATF Revised Mandate, para. 26 (Annex of 2007–2008 FATF Report); 2012–2020 Mandate, para. 50.

94 Ibid.

95 Two extraordinary meetings were held, the first, in October 2001, following the 9/11 terrorist attacks (2001–2002 FATF Report, para. 16) and the second, in December 2015, following the Paris and Brussels terrorist attacks (2015–2016 FATF Report, 13).

96 2019 Ministerial Declaration, para. 16; 2019 Mandate, para. 49.

two years, starting in 2022, to set out the FATF's strategic direction for the next biennium.[97]

The reporting procedure includes annual reports, mid-term reviews and communiqués of the FATF President, and his/her participation in Ministerial meetings, including the biannual Ministerial meeting or any extraordinary meeting. This reporting procedure seems to be the FATF's only direct accountability mechanism.[98]

The current position of the G-7 in FATF's framework is somehow imperceptible, most likely due to its diminishing role in international financial affairs, where referencing to FATF after 2008 is poor.[99] On the other hand, it appears that FATF's Ministerial meetings have become self-determining and the *sole high-level political body*, especially after the 2019 revision of FATF's mandate as a permanent organisation and the holding of biannual meetings.

In a differing direction, the political role of the G-20 has become increasingly prominent in FATF's work, particularly after the 2008 world financial crisis, when the G-20 assumed a leadership position for international economic co-operation in international affairs.[100]

The G-20 and the FATF have built a strong institutional relationship, in which the G-20 provides political backup by endorsing FATF's mission, encouraging new studies and actions, and measuring results. In other words, the G-20 implicitly oversees FATF's actions.[101] The same holds true for the UN/UNSC (Section 9 below).

97 2012 Ministerial Declaration, para. 2.

98 2019 Mandate, para. 50.

99 Few references to FATF can be found in G-7 Statements. However, at the G-7 London Summit in 2021, G-7 Finance Ministers and the Central Bank Governors recalled the implementation of FATF's standards and FRSBs' work, and committed to provide "expertise and funding" to support ME, G-7 London Finance Ministers Communiqué (05/06/2021), para. 9.

100 De Oliveira underlines the decrease in influence of the G-7 on financial matters after 2005, and a sort of "transfer of politics concerns" to the G-20, which assumed world leadership in financial inclusion, tax transparency and corruption with a broader political scope, (n 2), 158.

101 2020–2021 FATF Report, 26. As stated by the FATF President: "They [standards] are backed-up in many areas by the legal authority of the UN Conventions and Security Council Resolutions and by strong political support from the G-20", 2020 OSCE Wide Counter-Terrorism Conference (15/09/2020). At: https://www.fatf-gafi.org/publications/fatfgeneral/documents/2020-osce-counter-terrorism-conference.html. With Indonesia's recent acceptance as a member, all G-20 members are now fully represented in the FATF.

During the 2024 Ministerial biannual meeting, Ministers reiterated their unconditional support to FAFT's mission, pledging "to fully, swiftly and effectively implementing the FATF Standards". Additionally, and for the first time, an explicit mention is made to the need to promote a "robust and inclusive governance" and to uphold principles of "integrity, accountability, and transparency".[102]

3 Internal Legal Order

The FATF encompasses a Plenary (general assembly), which is the decision-making body, the President and Vice-President, the Steering Committee, which is an advisory body, and the Secretariat, which supports the work of the FATF.[103] The FATF is based in Paris, in the OECD headquarters, as an independent organisation.[104]

3.1 *The FATF Bodies*

3.1.1 The Plenary

The Plenary, which meets at least three times a year (usually February, June and October), comprises all members' jurisdictions and organisations.[105] Extraordinary meetings may be held whenever deemed appropriate, as well as extraordinary ministerial and deputy-minister level meetings.[106] The FATF Plenary meetings are chaired by a President.

The functions of the Plenary are to: a) determine the manner in which the FATF conducts its affairs; b) appoint the President, the Vice-President and the Steering Group members; c) approve the work programme and budget; d) adopt standards, guidance and reports developed by the FATF; e) decide on membership, FSRB status and observer status; and f) decide on any other matter governing the business and affairs of the FATF.[107]

The Plenary has the responsibility to determine what actions should be taken against a member who does not comply or fails to comply with the standards as well as to determine "which countries pose a significant risk to

102 2024 Ministerial Declaration, para. 2 and 21.

103 2019 Mandate, para. 17–19.

104 Are the FATF and OECD related? At: https://www.fatf-gafi.org/en/pages/frequently-asked-questions.html (last visited 15/05/2024).

105 2019 Mandate, para. 24.

106 Only two extraordinary meetings were held in 2001 and 2015, (n 95).

107 2019 Mandate, para. 20.

the financial system due to strategic deficiencies in their legal, regulatory or operational frameworks".[108]

According to the 30 Years FATF Report, a Plenary meeting involves seven days of WGs and Plenary sessions, with 700 officials and an "average of 180 papers, from country assessments to policy work".[109]

Working groups and *ad hoc* WG may be created to study relevant subject matters and to make recommendations according to the Plenary's needs. The chairs of the WG and subgroups are selected from and appointed by the Plenary at the President's recommendation. They report their work programmes to the Plenary.[110]

The current five WGs are the: Evaluations and Compliance Group (ECG), Global Network Co-ordination (GNCG),[111] International Co-operation Review Group (ICRG), Policy Development Group (PDG) and the Risk, Trends and Methods Group (RTMG).[112]

There is no description, even general, of the functions of the majority of the said WGs in FATF's core papers and reports. However, it can be surmised that the ECG has the task of ensuring the quality of the Mutual Evaluation Reports (MERs) and Follow-Up Reports (FURs) before publication; the GNCG strengthens the co-operation partnership spirit among the FATF and the FRSBs; the PDG is responsible for developing FATF Standards and guidance towards an effective implementation of the Recommendations; and the RTMG promotes studies and analysis aiming at identifying threats, risks and providing red flags and solutions.[113]

In contrast, there is clear reference to ICRG's functions, as FATF's WG responsible for analysing potential and high-risk jurisdictions (including proposals for blacklisting), recommending action plans to address significant AML/CFT/CPF deficiencies, establishing timelines and monitoring progress.[114]

108 30 Years FATF Report, 25.

109 Ibid.

110 1991–1992 FATF Report, para. 25; 2019 Mandate, para. 26–30.

111 In FATF's Reports there are few references to the GNCG. See 2012–2013 FATF Report, 32; 2014–2015 FATF Report, 25.

112 2019 Mandate, 15.

113 More at: https://home.treasury.gov/about/offices/terrorism-and-financial-intelligence/terrorist-financing-and-financial-crimes/financial-action-task-force-fatf.

114 30 Years FATF Report, 64–65; 2020–2021 FATF Report, 55; 2022–2023 FATF Report, 39–41. The new procedures for next round of ME provides more information as regards the operation of the ICRG (see Section 7 below).

3.1.2 The President

The FATF President is appointed on a consensual basis by the Plenary from among its members for a term of two years non-renewable (since 2019),[115] and is assisted by a Vice-President. The nomination is governed by a chair rotation and geographical distribution policy.

The Presidencies have been occupied in the following order: France, Switzerland, Australia, UK, The Netherlands, USA, Italy, Belgium, Japan, Portugal, Spain, Hong Kong (China), Germany, Sweden, France, South Africa, Canada, UK, Brazil, The Netherlands, Mexico, Italy, Norway, Russian Federation, Australia, South Korea, Spain, Argentina, USA, China, Germany, and Singapore.[116] From this spectrum, it is possible to sustain that geographical representation (chair rotation) has been balanced (fair and consistent) considering its members.

The President of the FATF must act in his/her personal capacity, being fully committed to the organisation's goals, where the exercise of the office must be performed in strict independence, autonomy and impartiality from his/her own jurisdiction and from "other authorities or institutions".[117]

Each Presidency chooses and presents its priorities and timelines to FATF's Ministers in the beginning of the term.[118] Germany took the first FATF Presidency with a two-year mandate, which started on 1 July 2020 and ended on 30 June 2022, setting its priorities on digital transformation, and studies on ethnically or racially motivated terrorism, migrant smuggling, environmental crimes and illicit arms trafficking.[119]

Singapore assumed FATF's leadership on 1 July 2022 for two years (2022–2024).[120] Its priorities are: strengthening asset recovery, countering cross-border cyber enabled crimes (eg. on-line scams and phishing activities), increasing global AML measures and FSRBs' partnership including by charting

115 Formerly, the chair rotation occurred annually. The first chair rotation happened in June 1991 when Switzerland replaced France (1990–1991 FATF Report, 19).

116 The only one woman to hold the Presidency was Mrs. Claire Lo from Hong Kong (China) in 1989. On 01/07/2024, Ms. Elisa de Anda Madrazo, from Mexico, will be the second woman to occupy this position.

117 2019 Mandate, para. 34.

118 The appointment for the President and Vice-President takes place at the February Plenary, their respective terms start 1 July (2019 Mandate, para. 31 and 33).

119 At: https://www.fatf-gafi.org/media/fatf/documents/German-Presidency-Priorities.pdf.

120 According to the 2022 March Plenary outcomes, there were several candidates to the chair and a comprehensive consultation procedure was carried out. At: https://www.fatf-gafi.org/en/publications/Fatfgeneral/Outcomes-fatf-plenary-march-2022.html.

out a roadmap to improve capability and capacity development.[121] Mexico will be the next Presidency from 1 of July 2024 to 30 June 2026.[122]

As noted, the President convenes and chairs Plenary and Steering Group meetings, as well as supervises the Secretariat. The President addresses all Plenary decisions and actions required to achieve FATF's objectives and reports on the fundamentals of FATF's activity. He/she is the FATF's prime spokesperson, representing the FATF at external level, issuing statements, and addressing other stakeholders, while promoting FATF's public outreach.[123]

During the last decade, Presidencies have undertaken an active role in the international arena, addressing the UNSC, EU, Organisation for Security and Co-operation in Europe (OSCE), G-20 and other international actors, including non-State actors.[124]

The role of the Vice-President was created in 2008 due to the increasing amount of work of the FATF and the "need to ensure consistency in the leadership".[125] The Vice-President assists the President in carrying out his/her functions, strengthening FATF's position and visibility in the international *fora*. The Vice-President is also chosen in FATF's Plenary from among its members, with a two-year term (since 2019).[126] In previous Mandates, the vice-presidency was one year and the next presidency-to-be.[127]

Canada occupies the Vice-Presidency since 1 July 2023 for the current term.[128] Mexico previously held this position on 1 July 2020, and was reappointed for a mandate of two years from 1 July 2021 to 30 June 2023. Differently from the Presidency, there is no express time-limitation for the Vice-Presidency in the 2019 Mandate.

3.1.3 The Steering Group

The Steering Group, created in 1991,[129] is an advisory body to assist the President as well as the Plenary in carrying out their functions and decision-making.[130]

121 At: https://www.fatf-gafi.org/media/fatf/documents/Singapore-Presidency-Priorities.pdf.

122 At:https://www.fatf-gafi.org/en/publications/Fatfgeneral/outcomes-fatf-plenary-february-2024.html.

123 At: https://www.fatf-gafi.org/about/fatfpresidency/ and https://www.fatf-gafi.org/about/fatfpresidency/.

124 30 Years FATF Report, 15–16.

125 Ibid, 16.

126 2019 Mandate, para. 35.

127 2012–2020 Mandate, para. 35.

128 At:https://www.fatf-gafi.org/en/publications/Fatfgeneral/outcomes-fatf-plenary-june-2023.html.

129 Ibid, 3. Also 1991–1992 FATF Report, para. 7.

130 1990–1991 FATF Report, 19.

The configuration of the Steering Group is decided by the Plenary at the proposal of the President.

Before it was composed of seven elements: four members (jurisdictions) plus the current President, the immediate past Presidency and the Presidency-to-be to ensure a smooth operational transition.[131] There is, presently, no public information available about the number of elements, the term of office or the elected members. The following criteria are listed in the 2019 Mandate: balanced geographical representation, size of the economy, participation level and international engagement.[132]

The responsibilities of the Steering Group include to: a) monitor and guide the progress of the FATF's ongoing work; b) promote co-ordination across the WG; c) ensure effective information flow to all members; and d) take forward, in consultation with the Plenary, any other work necessary for the FATF to fulfil its mandate.

3.1.4 The Secretariat

The FATF Secretariat initially supported by the OECD Secretariat in 1990, became an autonomous body in the following year.[133] The Secretariat currently comprises two divisions, the Human Resources, Finance and Communication Division and the Support Staff Division, and five teams to assist the five designated FATF WGs.[134]

It is led by a Permanent Executive Secretary who is nominated by the Plenary on the President's recommendation, reporting directly to him/her, and it is seconded by a Deputy Executive Secretariat, position instituted in 2015–2016.[135]

The main responsibilities of the Secretariat include to:

i) Support the activities of the FATF, including its WGs;
ii) Facilitate co-operation between members, associate members and observers;
iii) Ensure efficient communication to members and others;

131 2004–2012 FATF Mandate, para. 13.

132 Para. 38.

133 1991–1992 FATF Report, para. 7–12.

134 Evaluation and Compliance Team, Policy Development Team, Risk, Trends and Methods Team, International Co-operation and Review Team, and Global Network Co-ordinating Team (2019 Mandate, 15).

135 2015–2016 FATF Report, 55. Violaine Clerc, a French national, is the first woman to occupy the position of the FATF Executive Secretary (since 01/06/2022). At: https://www.fatf-gafi.org/about/fatfsecretariat/.

iv) Ensure the quality and consistency of MERs in applying the FATF Recommendations within the Global Network, including through the participation of the relevant FSRBs;[136]
v) Assist the Secretariats of the FSRBs;[137]
vi) Manage the financial, material and human resources allocated to the FATF;
vii) Maintain the records, running internal and external websites and FATF's;
viii) Carry any other functions assigned by the President or the Plenary;[138] and
ix) Assure an effective communication system with diverse stakeholders, including the *media*.[139]

The Secretariat is composed of highly qualified staff who are not exclusively responsible for the administrative and bureaucratic work but also for technical matters. It should be underscored that from a small administrative unit it has developed over time into a well-structured and professionalised operational body of 68 professionals.[140]

This "multicultural team" includes professionals from 15 countries with distinct background and expertise "from law enforcement and intelligence agencies, financial intelligence units, policy advisors and the legal profession", covering 10 languages.[141] It may also incorporate, on a temporary basis, experts from members' jurisdictions (financially supported by them). These experts provide technical assistance, expertise, strengthening the Secretariat's human resources whilst reducing FATF's financial burden.[142]

136 2006–2007 FATF Report, para. 39.

137 Ibid, para. 38.

138 2019 Mandate, para. 43–46.

139 2020–2021 FATF Report, 72. A new and updated description is provided in the 2022–2023 FATF Report, 50.

140 2022–2023 FATF Report, 50. In 2012, the Executive Secretary explained that the 2012–2013 revision of the Recommendations, mandate and the internal procedures contributed significantly to the increased workload of the Secretariat (2012–2013 FATF Report, 9).

141 At: http://www.fatf-gafi.org/about/fatfsecretariat (last visited 15/05/2024). The 2022–2023 FATF Report mentions "27 nationalities", 50.

142 See 2017–2018 FATF Report, Annex I, 66 or 2022–2023 FATF Report, 50.

4 Membership, Affiliation and Observers

4.1 *Membership*

The FATF comprises 40 members, including jurisdictions with sovereign and non-sovereign status and two IOs: Australia (1990), Austria (1990), Belgium (1990), Canada (1990), France (1990), Germany (1990), Italy (1990), Luxembourg (1990), Japan (1990), The Netherlands (1990), Spain (1990), Sweden (1990), Switzerland (1990), UK (1990), USA (1990), European Commission (EU) (1990), Denmark (1991), Finland (1991), Greece (1991), Hong Kong (China) (1991), Ireland (1991), New Zealand (1991), Norway (1991), Portugal (1991), Turkey (1991), Gulf Co-operation Council (1991), Iceland (1992), Singapore (1992), Argentina (2000), Brazil (2000), Mexico (2000), Russian Federation (2003),[143] South Africa (2003), China (2007), South Korea (2009), India (2010), Malaysia (2016), Israel (2018), Saudi Arabia (2019), and Indonesia (2023).[144]

The membership expansion policy of the FATF has been adjusted during these three decades according to the perceived needs of the Plenary. In the early years, a conservative approach was adopted, one might even say restrictive, when it was understood that the organisation was "clearly approaching the maximum membership possible".[145] This policy was later modified.

Indeed, in 1998–1999, the FATF decided to expand its membership policy by adopting a pro-active approach, inviting countries that strategically could play a major role in FATF's mission in their regions, particularly in areas of the world where the FATF was under-represented.[146] Geographical representation and bringing together the major financial centres into the organisation became a prime objective of the FATF.[147]

143 Membership has been suspended since February 2023. See FATF Statement on the Russian Federation of 24/02/2023, at: https://www.fatf-gafi.org/en/publications/Fatfgeneral/fatf-statement-russian-federation.html.

144 Year of membership is in parenthesis.

145 1991–1992 FATF Report, para. 96. This conservative approach was re-affirmed in 2004–2012 Mandate, para. 6: "However, the FATF has perhaps approached the limit of members if it is to continue to retain its current structure and character. Any future identification of possible strategically important countries should address the issue of geographical balance and the impact on the efficiency of FATF".

146 1997–1998 FATF Report, para. 17, 21, 23 and 139; 1998–1999 FATF Report, para. 1, 6, 148–152; 1999–2000 FATF Report, para. 16.

147 2008–2012 Mandate, para. 20; 2012–2013 FATF Report, 33.

The invitation of Argentina, Brazil, and Mexico in 1999[148] or South Korea and India in 2008[149] or Malaysia in 2014 are evident examples of such plan.[150] In 2017–2018, in line with the "limited membership expansion" policy, the FATF invited Indonesia, Israel and Saudi Arabia to join the organisation.[151] Indonesia is the most recent member.

Predictably, considering the flexible and dynamic nature of the organisation, the membership criteria have also evolved over the years, with an increasing number of conditions that needed to be satisfied for a jurisdiction to become a member.

The year 1998–1999 also marks a shift in governance transparency. For the first time the membership policy was tangible, with the qualifications laid down in 'black and white' (ie. made publicly available) along with members' rights and obligations.[152]

At the present, the fundamental criteria under consideration are as follows:

i) Quantitative indicators – the size of gross domestic product (GDP), the size of the banking, insurance and securities sectors and population;
ii) Qualitative indicators – impact on the global financial system, including the degree of openness of the financial sector and its interaction with international markets, active participation in FRSBs and regional prominence in AML/CFT efforts, level of commitment to AML/CFT efforts, level of AML/CFT risks faced and efforts to combat those risks; and

148 1999–2000 FATF Report, para. 17: "Latin America, for its relevance in the global economy, represents a region in which fighting money laundering is crucial. With the addition of these three countries to the worldwide network of anti-money laundering systems, the overall effort in the Americas is thus reinforced. The FATF will now consider the possible membership of other strategically important countries from regions in which the FATF wants to strengthen representation".

149 2007–2008 FATF Report, para. 45.

150 2014–2015 FATF Report, 23: "Malaysia, a country with a dynamic and open economy was one of the candidate countries and would enhance the representation of the Asian region in the FATF membership".

151 2017–2018 FATF Report, 59.

152 1998–1999 FATF Report, para. 150–151: "The minimum and *sine qua non* criteria for admission are as follows: a) to be fully committed at the political level: (i) to implement the 1996 Recommendations within a reasonable timeframe (three years), and (ii) to undergo annual self-assessment exercises and two rounds of mutual evaluations; b) to be a full and active member of the relevant FATF-style regional body (where one exists), or be prepared to work with the FATF or even to take the lead, to establish such a body (where none exists); c) to be a strategically important country; d) to have already made the laundering of the proceeds of drug trafficking and other serious crimes a criminal offence; and e) to have already made it mandatory for financial institutions to identify their customers and to report unusual or suspicious transactions".

iii) Additional factors: level of adherence to financial sector standards and participation in other relevant international organisations.[153]

Aside from the fundamental criteria, a lengthy procedure must be undertaken from the application date to acceptance. Primarily, it is requested from the candidate jurisdiction to provide a written political undertaking that it is committed to FATF's aims, and wishes to endorse the FATF Recommendations.

The candidate jurisdiction will undergo a peer review mutual evaluation process with the AML/CFT Methodology applicable at the time, and subsequent FURs. The jurisdiction will actively participate in FATF activities in all relevant *fora*.

A high-level visit will be organised to all the relevant ministries, members of the legislature and competent authorities of the candidate jurisdiction, to determine whether the level of technical compliance reflects a sound AML/CFT/CPF regime, in particular in what concerns the core Recommendations and the ability and resources to assess and address ML/FT/PF risks (Recommendation 1).[154]

Following the high-level visit, a report will be submitted to the Plenary to decide whether to grant (or not) the observer status to the jurisdiction. The Mutual Evaluation (ME) assessment should start and be concluded within a maximum of three years.

Membership will be granted if the ME is satisfactory followed by FATF Plenary approval.[155] If the identified deficiencies are not substantial, as long as the jurisdiction is politically engaged to meet FATF standards, a detailed action plan with a maximum timeframe of four years will be designed to assist the jurisdiction.[156]

If the deficiencies reveal a weak AML/CFT/CPF regime, the observer status will not be granted and an *ad hoc* group to assist the jurisdiction to undergo a

153 Technical and other criteria are also considered. The jurisdiction must be a "full and active member" of an FSRB. The criteria and procedure for application are available at: https://www.fatf-gafi.org/en/the-fatf/fatf-membership-policy.html (last visited 15/05/2024). For a comparative analysis with previous requirements, see 2008–2009 FATF Report, Annex 5 (membership criteria).

154 At: https://www.fatf-gafi.org/en/the-fatf/membership-process-criteria.html (last visited 15/05/2024).

155 A ME shows serious deficiencies, if the jurisdiction: i) has 8 or more NC/PC ratings for TC; ii) is rated NC/PC on any one or more of Recommendations 3, 5, 10, 11 and 20; iii) has a low or moderate level of effectiveness for 7 or more of the 11 Immediate Outcomes; or iv) has a low level of effectiveness for 4 or more of the 11 Immediate Outcomes. Ibid.

156 Ibid.

successful ME may be constituted. This Group will meet on a regular basis and report on the jurisdiction's progress at each Plenary meeting.[157]

Member jurisdictions must: a) commit and endorse the development of the FATF standards, guidance, AML/CFT/CPF policies as well as related to other threats to the integrity of the international financial system; b) co-operate in carrying out the objectives and tasks of FATF's mandate, including peer-reviews; c) actively participate in the work of the FATF, including in its outreach initiatives with the private sector.[158]

All members have the right to attend any Plenary or WG meetings and are encouraged to firmly contribute and join FATF's activities, such as heading WG meetings, leading and giving studies/typologies, or offering technical assistance while financially contributing to the organisation. All members enjoy equal status, including voting rights, and decisions are carried out by consensus.[159]

Delegations are usually headed by high-level representatives of a jurisdiction's finance ministry or central bank and composed of government representatives from the ministries of justice, interior and external affairs, as well as financial regulatory authorities and law enforcement agencies.[160]

Membership rules do not clearly state what sort of measures will be applied if a member fails to perform its obligations either in full or partially. This information is non-existent in the 2019 Mandate as in previous mandates.

By contrast, there are prescribed actions for members in case of non-compliance with the standards. In paragraph 91 of the 4th Round of ME Procedures for the FATF (as last amended),[161] several measures are established

157 The FATF Secretariat assists the Group, which includes at least one Steering Group member and is open to all FATF and associate members.

158 2019 Mandate, para. 6–8.

159 2019 Mandate, para. 19. There is no written rule how consensus is achieved as consensus does not mean unanimity. This aspect is also mentioned at 2023 RUSI Roundtable about the FATF. The lack of a "threshold to determine what consensus means" and how negotiations are carried out at the FATF (persuasion and lobby not necessarily "constructive debate") signal transparency and legitimacy concerns. A "formal framework or rules for establishing a level of agreement needed to approve decisions" was discussed at the roundtable, (n 91) 2–3. Koos Couvée mentions that "FATF makes decisions by consensus, which in practice means that only three or four of the group's 39 members can scuttle a plan by objecting". 'Exclusive: FATF Spared Large Economies from Pressure Over AML Gaps' (06/01/2023) *ACAMS*, at: https://www.moneylaundering.com/news/exclusive-fatf-spared-large-economies-from-pressure-over-aml-gaps/.

160 1996–1997 FATF Report, para. 10.

161 Last amended February 2023 (last visited 15/05/2024).

in case of lack of compliance or failure, including, as ultimate measures, suspension and termination of membership (Section 7.2. below).

The FATF was aware that defining a policy for non-compliant members was critical to safeguard its mission;[162] however, there is limited information (at least publicly available) on sanctions if a member fails to comply with its financial obligations or if is not fully committed to FATF's goals, or does not participate in FATF's activities.

The recent military invasion of Ukraine by the Russian Federation in February 2022 'opens the door' to this issue, especially at the level of FATF's principles and values: how to handle a member who violates FATF's core principles?

On 4 March 2022, in a ground-breaking Public Statement, the FATF declared:

> At the heart of the work of the FATF are the principles of international co-operation, dialogue and mutual respect among countries. In light of the Russian Federation's military intervention of Ukraine, the FATF, as the global standard setting body for combating money laundering, terrorist financing and proliferation financing, expresses its grave concern about the invasion's impact on the money laundering, terrorist financing and proliferation financing risk environment as well as the integrity of the financial system, the broader economy and safety and security. The actions of the Government of the Russian Federation run counter FATF core principles and represent a gross violation of the commitment upon which FATF Ministers agree to implement and support the FATF Standards. The FATF is reviewing Russia's role at the FATF and will consider what future steps are necessary to uphold these core values.[163]

On 16 March 2022, Ukraine as a member of the Evaluation of Anti-Money Laundering Measures and the Financing of Terrorism (MONEYVAL (FSRB)) and a jurisdiction of the FATF Global Network submitted a public petition asking the FATF to:

---

162 1995–1996 FATF Report, para. 60: "Although there were few members in this situation, this was clearly damaging to the FATF and its mission. The FATF considered it had a responsibility to make every effort to ensure that the necessary actions were taken. Consequently, FATF defined a policy for dealing with these few members which were not in compliance with the existing forty FATF Recommendations. The measures contained in this policy represent a graduated approach aimed at enhancing peer pressure".

163 At: http://www.fatf-gafi.org/publications/fatfgeneral/documents/ukraine-2022.html; https://www.fatf-gafi.org/en/countries/detail/Russian-Federation.html; https://www.fatf-gafi.org/en/publications/Fatfgeneral/Outcomes-fatf-plenary-march-2022.html.

i) Suspend immediately Russian Federation's membership;
ii) Proceed with membership expulsion under para. 20(e) of the FATF Mandate;[164]
iii) Request the MONEYVAL and Eurasian Group on Combating Money Laundering and Financing of Terrorism (EAG) to terminate Russian Federation's membership, and request the Asia-Pacific Group on Money Laundering (APG) and the Middle East and North Africa Financial Action Task Force (MENAFATF) to terminate Russian Federation's observership; and lastly
iv) Insert Russian Federation in FATF's 'Black List'.[165]

Pursuant to Recommendation 19 (High-Risk Countries), one of the grounds for blacklisting is the nomination of a jurisdiction by a FATF or FSRB member due to specific ML/TF/PF concerns or the threat posed by that jurisdiction. Under these grounds, Ukraine alleged that Russian Federation not only is breaking FATF's values, principles, and mandate but equally undermining the global efforts against financial crime, thus posing a threat to the international financial system.[166]

On 21 April 2022, at the first Ministerial biannual meeting, Ministers seconded FATF's statement, recalling and reaffirming that the "ongoing Russian invasion runs counter to the FATF core principles and represents a gross violation of the commitment upon which FATF Ministers agree to implement and support the FATF Standards".[167]

In its third stand, at the FATF Plenary meeting in June 2022, the FATF reiterated the previous statements and, while recognising Russian Federation's engagement in the "Global Network in the Eurasian region" since it joined the FATF in 2003, decided not to suspend Russian Federation's membership, but rather to limit its membership rights:

> However, as a result of the invasion, the FATF has decided to severely limit the Russian Federation's role and influence within the FATF. In particular, the Russian Federation can no longer hold any leadership or advisory roles or take part in decision-making on standard-setting,

164 This provision stipulates that decisions on membership status lies in the Plenary.

165 'Support the Petition: Expel Russia from the FATF and add it to the Blacklist', The State Financial Monitoring Service of Ukraine (19/03/2022), at: https://fiu.gov.ua/en/pages/funkcional/news/pidtrimajte-peticziyu-viklyuchiti-rosiyu-z-FATF-i-vnesti-jiji-v-chornij-spisok-FATF.html.

166 Ibid.

167 2022 Ministerial Declaration, para. 4.

> FATF peer review processes, governance and membership matters. The Russian Federation can also no longer provide assessors, reviewers or other experts for FATF peer-review processes.[168]

Additionally, the FATF urged jurisdictions to be vigilant as to the possible threats and risks that the armed conflict could cause to the international financial system, declaring that the Russian Federation continues under monitoring, and that further consideration will be given at each FATF Plenary meeting whether there are grounds to impose the aforementioned restrictions.[169]

At the FATF Plenary meeting in October 2022, prior decisions and political stance were upheld with additional membership restrictions. Russian Federation was barred from participating in FATF's project teams and to participate as a FATF member in FSRBS meetings.[170]

At the time, Russian Federation was a member of two regional bodies: the MONEYVAL of the CoE and the EAG. At present, the Russian Federation is no longer a member of MONEYVAL after its formal exclusion from the CoE in mid-March 2022.[171] The jurisdiction has also lost its observer status in the APG, following a decision at the APG Annual meeting in July 2022 to terminate the status of the Russian Federation,[172] however it retains its observer status in the MENAFATF.[173]

---

168 At: http://www.fatf-gafi.org//publications/fatfgeneral/documents/ukraine-june-2022.html.

169 The Ukraine Government congratulated FATF's decision and requested tougher measures: "Ukraine will request further steps from the FATF during the October Plenary in relation to violations of the FATF standards committed by Russia, including breaches of specific technical requirements and failure to meet the effectiveness criteria, which were raised by Ukraine (…) The Ministry of Finance calls on other States to provide assistance in this process and support the ultimate exclusion of Russia from the FATF and its inclusion on the Black List", 'Ministry of Finance of Ukraine Welcomes FATF Decision to Suspend Russia's Member Rights, Calls on Further Action to Exclude and Blacklist Russia' (27/06/2022) Ukraine Government portal, at: *kmu.gov.ua*.

170 At:https://www.fatf-gafi.org/en/publications/Fatfgeneral/Outcomes-fatf-plenary-october-2022.html.

171 On 17 March 2022 the Russian Federation was excluded from the CoE at the extraordinary meeting of the Committee of Ministers, under Article 8 of the Statute of the CoE. As a result, its membership also ceased to exist in MONEYVAL. At: https://www.coe.int/en/web/moneyval/-/the-russian-federation-is-excluded-from-the-council-of-europe-and-moneyval.

172 The Russian Federation acquired APG's observer status in 2010. At: http://www.apgml.org/news/details.aspx?n=3188 or http://www.apgml.org/about-us/page.aspx?p=fe4fce1a-2579-49f3-be93-598430e1b08a.

173 At: https://www.menafatf.org/about/Members-Observers/observers (last visited 15/05/2024).

On 24 February 2023, the FATF suspended Russian Federation's membership. Nevertheless, it was decided that the Russian Federation continues to be an "active member" of EAG with membership rights. Moreover, regardless of membership suspension, the jurisdiction continues to be obliged to implement the FATF Standards and to fulfil its financial obligations. In FATF's Public Statement it is affirmed that:

> The Russian Federation's continuing and intensifying war of aggression against Ukraine runs counter to FATF's principles of promoting security, safety and the integrity of the global financial system and the commitment to international cooperation and mutual respect upon which FATF Members have agreed to implement and support the FATF Standards. As a result, the FATF Plenary has today suspended the membership of the Russian Federation.[174]

After one year, the FATF reiterated the suspension of the Russian Federation's membership in its Statement dated 23 February 2024, maintaining the same conditions. This decision was endorsed by the Ministers at the 2024 biannual meeting.[175]

This particular case should trigger an in-depth discussion inside the organisation as regards its core principles and values and conceivable implications in case of infringement. The FATF stresses that the principles of international cooperation, dialogue, and mutual respect among jurisdictions are "at the heart of the work" of the organisation, and both FATF public statements and FATF Ministers vowed to adhere to these principles, which are general principles of international law.

However, they are not explicitly referred to or even enshrined in any foundation or constitutional document, such as the G-7 Declaration, Mandate(s), the High-Level Principles and Objectives for the FATF and the FSRBS (HLPOS),[176] or the Consolidated Processes and Procedures por Mutual Evaluations and Follow-Up (Universal Procedures).[177]

174 FATF Public Statement on the Russian Federation of 24/02/2023, at: https://www.fatf-gafi.org/en/publications/Fatfgeneral/fatf-statement-russian-federation.html.

175 At: https://www.fatf-gafi.org/en/publications/Fatfgeneral/fatf-statement-russian-federation-feb-2024.html; 2024 Ministerial Declaration, para. 4.

176 Last amended February 2019 (last visited 15/03/2023).

177 Last amended September 2022 (last visited 15/03/2023). New Universal Procedures were adopted to be in line with the new methodology and procedures for the next round of ME (see Section 7).

Even so, these principles can be inferred from the FATF mission, especially within the context of the Global Network, co-operation programmes, ICRG mechanism, and technical assistance. Considering their relevance and the principle of legal certainty, an express reference to these principles at the minimum in the Mandate of the FATF is highly recommended.

The Russian Federation's membership is also an interesting case to be charted in the context of the policy and decision-making capacities of the FATF (Chapter 4, Section 4 below).

4.2 *Associate Membership*

Associate members are regional or sub-regional bodies (FSRBs) formed by jurisdictions of such regions or sub-regions, which endorse FATF's Standards and policies and assure their implementation at regional level. According to FATF's Mandate, the associate membership status is awarded to FSRBs who:

> a) endorse the FATF Recommendations, guidance and other AML/CFT/CPF policy as determined by the FATF; b) promote effective implementation of the FATF Recommendations among their member jurisdictions and support systematic peer reviews (ME) and follow-up processes using the assessment methodology and procedures in place at the time; and c) participate in the development of the FATF Standards, guidance and other AML/CFT/CPF policies and other threats to the integrity of the international financial system.[178]

The position of 'associate member' was established in 2005–2006[179] and the concept of 'FSRBs' was referred to for the first time in the 1997–1998 FATF Report.[180]

Based on the experience of the pre-existing two regional organisations – the Caribbean Financial Action Task Force (CFATF) and the APG, created in 1992 and 1997 respectively, the FATF pictured the potential role of regional bodies in its project of building a secure financial global environment: a *network* that would ensure the worldwide implementation of the FATF Recommendations.[181] In the 1999–2000 FATF Report, it is stated:

178 At: 6.

179 2005–2006 FATF Report, para. 19–21.

180 1997–1998 FATF Report, para. 2, 17, 19, 21.

181 Ibid. Also, 30 Years FATF Report, 68.

> As the primary objective of its current mandate, the FATF is committed to promoting anti-money laundering initiatives in all continents and regions of the globe and to building a worldwide anti-money laundering network. This strategy consists of three main components: enlarging the FATF membership, developing credible and effective FATF-style regional bodies, and increasing co-operation with the relevant international organisations.[182]

In the following years, the setting-up of regional bodies became a priority and a cornerstone of FATF's strategic policy, recognising their role "as a way to leverage global efforts and ensure effective implementation of the FATF Recommendations in all regions of the world".[183]

However, the formation of regional bodies increased the risk of discrepancies or dual criteria regarding the implementation of the FATF's Recommendations and/or of the ME process, as well as their potential misapplication or misinterpretation.

The need to control the implementation of the Recommendations and the quality of the ME process proved to be of the utmost importance. In order to guarantee countries' effective engagement with the AML/CFT standards and policies of the FATF, and to ensure coherence and consistency in the implementation of the Recommendations,[184] the organisation created a new status within its institutional framework – the associate member. This position aims to build a closer *politico-institutional bond* and partnership between the FATF and the FSRBS and respective jurisdictions.

The 2005–2006 formula intended to encourage the development of regional groups that share the same aims as the FATF, while ensuring that these bodies endorse the FATF Recommendations and its assessment methodology. As an added 'privilege', FRSBS are entitled to attend closed FATF and WGS meetings and participate in policy-making and standard-setting processes.[185]

182 Para. 13.

183 2000–2001 FATF Report, para. 19: "Active efforts have continued to support or foster the development of FATF-style regional bodies in all parts of the world. These groups, which have similar objectives and tasks to those of the FATF, provide the same peer pressure". Also, 2005–2006 Report para. 16; 2007–2008 FATF Report, para. 5; 2008–2009 FATF Report, para. 5.

184 2005–2006 FATF Report, para. 17–19; 2006–2007 FATF Report, para. 7; 2007–2008 FATF Report, para. 8; 2012–2013 FATF Report, 20.

185 2005–2006 FATF Report, para. 17–19; 2012–2020 Mandate, 4. The degree of influence of these bodies and their jurisdictions that are non-FATF members in FATF decision-making is questionable. As mentioned in the 2023 RUSI Roundtable about the FATF: "There was a widespread view that the FATF's structure gives Global North Countries (typically full

Although partnership and co-operation have been a long practice amidst the FATF and its FSRBs either through common projects or studies, joint meetings, common ME processes, the associate membership status awards *direct access* and an *active role* in FATF's affairs.[186]

Presently, all nine FSRBS enjoy the status of associate member. The MONEYVAL, Financial Action Task Force of Latin America (GAFILAT), APG, MENAFATF, CFATF, EAG, Eastern and Southern Africa Anti-Money Laundering Group (ESAAMLG), Inter-Governmental Action Group against Money Laundering in West Africa (GIABA) and Task Force on Money Laundering in Central Africa (GABAC) became associate members of the FATF, respectively in 2006, 2006, 2007, 2007, 2008, 2010, 2010, 2010 and 2015.

The decision as to whether a body qualifies as an FSRB, and thus eligible to participate in the FATF as an associate member, rests in FATF's Plenary.[187]

4.3 *Observers*

As regards observers, there are three types of observers: i) the observer that is a potential candidate to be a member of the FATF;[188] ii) observers that enjoy a special status in the FATF, namely the IMF and the WB;[189] and iii) observers which are IOs and international institutions that share the same concerns and goals as the FATF.

The IMF and the WB have built a special partnership with the FATF since its inception by attending FATF's meetings and collaborating in its work through conferences and studies.[190] In 2001, both IOs recognised the FATF as the AML global standard-setter and agreed in 2004 to incorporate FATF's Recommendations and assessment methodology into their own framework. The IMF and the WB may assess FATF jurisdictions and conduct joint assessments under the umbrella of the FATF (Section 9 below).

Other IOs and international institutions that at the moment enjoy observer status include the following: African Development Bank (AfDB), Anti-Money Laundering Liaison Committee of the Franc Zone (CLAB), Asian Development Bank (ADB), Basel Committee on Banking

---

FATF members rather than members of an FSRB) the power to dominate the deliberations that ultimately determine the 'consensus' view of the membership", (n 91) 4.

186 Ibid, para. 20. An 18 months transition period was given to each group for adjustment to FATF requirements (ibid, para. 17–19).

187 2019 Mandate, para. 12.

188 See the recent case of Indonesia (2021–2022 FATF Report, 56; 2022–2023 FATF Report, 54).

189 2019 and 2012–2020 Mandates, both para. 13.

190 1990–1991 FATF Report, 19; 1993–1994 FATF Report, para. 99–100.

Supervision (BCBS or Basel Committee), Camden Asset Recovery Inter-agency Network (CARIN), CoE, Egmont Group of Financial Intelligence Units, European Bank for Reconstruction and Development (EBRD), European Central Bank (ECB), Eurojust, Europol, Group of International Finance Centre Supervisors (GIFCS – formerly the Offshore Group of Banking Supervisors (OGBS)), Inter-American Development Bank (IDB), International Association of Insurance Supervisors (IAIS), International Organisation of Securities Commissions (IOSCO), INTERPOL, Organisation of American States (OAS)/ Inter-American Committee Against Terrorism (CICTE), OAS/Inter-American Drug Abuse Control Commission (CICAD), OECD, OSCE, UN[191] and World Customs Organisation (WCO).[192]

The granting of the observer status follows a formal request and specific proceedings. The candidate must be geographically and/or sectorally relevant to FATF's mission, ie. must play a role in the field of combating ML/FT/PF and support FATF Recommendations, guidance, and other policies.[193] The decision belongs to the FATF Plenary, where reciprocity is a key prerequisite to attend FATF's non-closed meetings, sharing of information on AML/CFT/CPF issues, or participating in FATF's activities.[194]

Non-governmental organisations (NGOs) have no observer status in the FATF.

5 Budgetary Matters

Members must financially contribute to FATF's budget to fund its activities, including its Secretariat. The contribution scale is based on a formula related to the size of the country's economy (ie. a fixed equal base and a proportional one in concordance with the OECD contribution scales).[195] FATF's financial

191 United Nations Office on Drugs and Crime (UNODC), United Nations Counter-Terrorism Committee Executive Directorate (UNCTED), The Analytical Support and Sanctions Monitoring Team pursuant to resolutions 1526 (2004) and 2253 (2015) concerning ISIL (Da'esh), Al-Qaida and the Taliban and associated individuals and entities, The Expert Group to the Security Council Committee established pursuant to UNSCR 1540 (2004), Panel of Experts to the Security Council Committee established pursuant to UNSCR 1718 (2006) and the Security Council Subsidiary Organs. At: https://www.fatf-gafi.org/about/membersandobservers/ (last visited 15/05/2024).

192 Ibid.

193 2019 Mandate, para. 14–16.

194 At: https://www.fatf-gafi.org/en/the-fatf/membership-process-criteria.html (last visited 15/05/2024).

195 2019 Mandate, para. 47. Also, 2022–20023 FATF Report, 51.

resources also rely on members' voluntary contributions either into the general budget or to a particular project. For instance, the establishment of the FATF Training Institute in Busan, in the Republic of Korea, was possible because of the voluntary contribution of Korea and the Metropolitan City of Busan.[196]

The budget and the Finance Activity Report are approved by the FATF Plenary on an annual basis. FATF's Reports started to be publicly available since 1991, yet the Finance Activity Report only started to be published in 2004–2005 with the purpose of guaranteeing *higher standards of transparency* and *accountability* of FATF's work.[197]

From a brief overview of all FATF reports, it is possible to establish that the format and contents, including of the Finance Activity Reports, have evolved over time.[198] FATF's reports from the previous decade or two were more informative, objective, comprehensive, and less repetitive than those issued today. In contrast, the Finance Activity Reports are concise, providing a general prospect of FATF's budget and expenditures.[199]

The HLPOs also provide guidance on financial transparency and good governance practices in Annex I, entitled: "Principles of Financial Governance for the FATF/FRSBs", including:

i) The organisation should prepare annual or multi-year budgets;
ii) The sources of funding should not interfere with the impartiality and/or effectiveness of the organisation' activities;
iii) To establish rules on budget preparation, work plan approval and management;
iv) To develop financial management regulations, with detailed guidelines, procedures and processes on all stages of the budget cycle;
v) To regularly reporting to members and to introduce regular independent auditing functions (at least once a year) and external audit (at least every three years);
vi) To ensure circulation of information and a mechanism to grant access to these documents.[200]

196 2004–2012 FATF Mandate, para. 15; 2016–2017 FATF Report, 19; 2020–2021 FATF Report, 65.

197 2004–2012 FATF Mandate, para.15: "A mechanism for providing the annual financial statements to members should be established". Also, 2004–2005 FATF Report, Executive Secretariat Introductory Remarks, 5.

198 For instance, as a Section of FATF's report (eg. 2004–2005 FATF Report) or as an Annex of FATF's Report (eg. 2017–2018 FATF Report).

199 The FATF's budget includes: i) staff cots (salaries and indemnities); ii) travel; iii) operating costs (including office rental); iv) OECD overhead charges; v) Meeting costs, translation, interpretation; vi) IT investment and maintenance costs (2022–2023 FATF Report, 51).

200 HLPOs, para. 28–29 and Annex I.

These principles are primarily intended to provide budgetary transparency, efficient cost management of an organisations' assets and resources, and management responsibility.

Table 1 below shows the budget expenditure after the adoption of the 2012 Recommendations with the launching of the new FATF reporting cycle – the 4th Round of ME.

TABLE 1 FATF budget expenditure from 2012 to 2023

Fiscal year	Euros	Fiscal year	Euros
2012	3,273,639	2018	6,227,159
2013	3,474,404	2019	9,207,423
2014	3,511,280	2020	11,824,844
2015	4,044,092	2021	11,824,444
2016	4,093,700	2022	12,882,792
2017	4,839,992	2023	14,076,599

SOURCE: FATF REPORTS FROM 2011–2012 TO 2022–2023

From the figures, it may be concluded that in over 10 years the FATF's expenditure rose from 3,273,639 euros to 14,0764,599 euros (330% increase). In the years 2012 to 2017, there was a steady increase, and afterwards there were significant increases.[201]

The rise in question can be ascribed to several factors, including the FATF's expanded responsibilities, the growth of the Global Network, concerns related to branding and consistency, the publication of a considerable number of guidance and research papers, as well as outreach activities and the growth of the Secretariat's workforce.

The budget expenditure for 2020 and 2021 can be explained by the global pandemic situation (Covid-19) that resulted in the drastic reduction of travel costs and related expenses, but with the notable increase in the Secretariat staff from 51 members to 65 (27% increase).

From a financial standpoint, the FATF, as an organisation, seems to be in a favourable position. Members are deeply committed politically and financially. At the 2022 Ministerial meeting, FATF's Ministers reiterated and strengthened their undertaking to financially support FATF's activities:

201 Financial Statement page from 2012–2013 to 2022–2023 FATF Reports.

> We will ensure that the FATF has the necessary resources and support to fulfil its mandate, and that all members have adequate capacity to play a meaningful and effective role in its working group and assessment work, and contribute fully, fairly and proportionally to its funding (…) We recognise that the implementation of the FATF's strategic priorities must be funded in a sustainable way, and we commit to ensuring that regular Membership contributions can achieve this objective.[202]

At the 2024 Ministerial meeting, FATF's Ministers expressed their unwavering commitment to funding FATF's mission to "promote global security and integrity of the international financial system and sustainable and economic and social development", declaring:

> [W]e the FATF Ministers commit to increase our core funding to ensure sustainability of the FATF's budget. We recognise the important role voluntary contributions play and continue welcoming such contributions from FATF members. We will continue to use our resources efficiently and focus their use to deliver on the FATF's strategic priorities to enhance the effective implementation of the FATF Standards.[203]

6 Policy and Lawmaking Powers

As mentioned in Section 2 above, the FATF is a policy and lawmaking body[204] that has been actively engaged in the development of a coherent and strategic global AML/CFT/CPF policy wherein the strengthening of its regulatory (lawmaking) power is pivotal.[205] FATF's ongoing influence and gradual recognition as a standard-setter gained *momentum* with the open and formal acknowledgment of the UNSC in its Resolution 1617 (2005) in the context of countering terrorism and FT:

---

202 2002 Ministerial Declaration, para. 23.

203 2024 Ministerial Declaration, para. 3.

204 25 Years FATF Report, 6: "The FATF is a policy-making body that develops international standards that will help countries detect, prevent, and punish the abuse of the international financial system".

205 The FATF's role as the ML/FT global regulator has been commended, amongst others, Jackson (n 6); Neupane Samridha, 'Money Laundering: Current Issues and Challenges' (15/11/2010) Legal Services India (blog), at: https://www.legalservicesindia.com/article/436/Money-Laundering.html#google_vignette.

> Strongly urges all member States to implement the comprehensive, international standards embodied in the Financial Action Task Force's (FATF) Forty Recommendations on Money Laundering and the FATF Nine Special Recommendations on Terrorist Financing.[206]

This was the first time that the FATF and its Forty Recommendations were referred to in a Resolution of the UNSC acting under Chapter VII of the UN Charter.[207] Subsequent Resolutions of the UNSC have reinforced FATF's status,[208] particularly Resolution 2462 (2019) by explicitly "*stressing* the essential role of the FATF in setting global standards for preventing and combatting money laundering, terrorist financing and proliferation financing".[209] This chief paragraph has been replicated in recent Resolutions 2610 (2021) and 2617 (2021).[210]

The UN General Assembly also mentions the FATF, for the first time, in September 2006 with a Resolution that sets the 'UN Global Counter-Terrorism Strategy', encouraging States to implement the Forty Recommendations and the Nine SR, referring to them as 'international standards'.[211]

The policy and lawmaking powers of the FATF encompass internal and external acts. The first acts are the acts within the organisation, which include acts related to the internal legal order of the organisation (that govern its functioning and operational aspects)[212] and to the relationship of the FATF *vis-à-vis* its members, FRSBs and respective jurisdictions (but not limited to) within the *octopus-effect network*.[213] The external acts are those adopted or conducted by the FATF at external relations level with its counterparts.

206 Para. 7. Also, 2007–2008 FATF Report, para. 5; 25 Years FATF Report, 12–13.

207 Resolutions adopted by the UNSC under Chapter VII of the UN Charter have binding nature pursuant to its Articles 24, 25, 39 *et seq.*

208 Eg. UNSCR 1989 (2011), UNSCR 2083 (2012), UNSCR 2160 (2014), USNCR 2161 (2014), UNSCR 2166 (2014), UNSCR 2195 (2014), UNSCR 2253 (2015), UNSCR 2255 (2015), UNSCR 2331 (2016), UNSCR 2322 (2016), UNSCR 2347 (2017), UNSCR 2368 (2017), UNSCR 2501 (2019), UNSCR 2610 (2021), UNSCR 2617 (2021).

209 Preamble, para. 12.

210 Respectively, Preamble, para. 33 and Preamble, para. 27. These are one of the latest UNSC Resolutions on threats to international peace and security related to terrorism. At: https://www.un.org/securitycouncil/content/resolutions (last visited 15/05/2024).

211 A/RES/60/288, 08/09/2006, Part II – 'Measures to Prevent and Combat Terrorism', op.para. 10.

212 In general, these acts are not accessible to the public with the exception of the Mandate. Reference is made to Internal Governance Principles (IGP) in the 4th ME Procedures, para. 97 or in the 5th ME Procedures (draft) para. 177.

213 For example, calling the FRSB's jurisdictions to adopt a certain conduct towards non-members. More at Chapter 4, Sections 4 and 5.

In the first category, a paraphernalia of acts may be pointed out from Recommendations, Interpretive Notes (INotes), Best Practices and Guidance Papers to Typologies Reports, from ME Reports, Procedures and Methodologies for the ME to HLPOs, from Public Statements to joint reports and studies.

The gradual and wide range of acts (of different nature, purposes, and addressees) enacted by the FATF during the last 30 years, as it will be evidenced, reveals in a vivid manner the evolutionary character of this organisation as a policy and lawmaker.[214] At the same time, it consolidates FATF's position as an organisation embodied with public authority (Chapter 5, Section 2 below). Navin Beekarry gives a good description of this evolution:

> The constantly evolving normative structure of the FATF system, which leads to greater institutionalisation, has enhanced and provided more sustainability to its identity formation. Confronted with changing demands resulting from testing situations, it has regularly reconfigured its institutional setting (through regular reviews of its norms) and adapted itself into a more dynamic institutional framework enabling it to perform its functions and confirm its relevance as a permanent forum. This expansion of its role and functions to address TF issues on a global scale, providing a platform and process to identify jurisdictions that facilitate TF and strengthening co-operation networks, significantly reinforced the FATF setup and its compliance role.[215]

6.1 *FATF Recommendations*

The Forty Recommendations aim to set up high-level standards with universal application and to provide a multidisciplinary and integrated framework to tackle ML, FT and PF. They cover finance and banking, law enforcement, legal, judicial and regulatory areas, international co-operation, including legal co-operation in criminal matters, and target public and private sectors, individual and legal persons, member and non-member jurisdictions.[216] The Forty Recommendations affect and shape domestic legal orders at all levels, while crossing a diversity of sectors and actors.[217]

214 Shams names it an organisation of "fluid nature", (n 47) 463.

215 (n 61) 169. Nance conceives the FATF as good example of "global governance through experimentalism" (n 46) 131–132, 149–150.

216 1997–1998 FATF Report, para. 20; 2019–2020 FATF Report, 25; 2012 FATF Recommendations (as amended), 7–9.

217 The current 40 Recommendations are divided in seven segments: 1) AML/CFT Policies and Co-ordination; 2) ML and Confiscation; 3) FT and PF; 4) Preventive Measures; 5) Transparency and BO of Legal Persons and Arrangements; 6) Powers and

The FATF Recommendations together with its INotes and the attached Glossary with the applicable definitions form the so-called 'FATF Standards'. The INotes intend to clarify the scope of Recommendations, their correct interpretation and implementation.[218]

As referred in Section 2 above, the FATF Recommendations (and INotes) were subject to substantial and in-depth revision in 1996, 2003 and 2012. Specific or tailored amendments were adopted in 2001, 2004, 2013, 2015, 2016, 2017, 2018, 2019, 2020, 2021, 2022 and 2023.[219]

The 1996 revision of the Forty Recommendations extended the scope of the ML offence to comprise the UN Convention against Transnational Organised Crime (Palermo Convention) and introduced some key developments, *inter alia*:

i) AML measures to financial activities performed by non-financial businesses or professions;
ii) Legal obligation to report suspicions transactions;
iii) Prevention of the unlawful use of shell corporations;
iv) Reinforcement of customer due diligence (CDD) measures;
v) AML measures to minimise the threat of the use of new technologies;
vi) AML regulations to bureaux de change;
vii) Cross-border currency monitoring; and
viii) Controlled delivery techniques.[220]

The following revision, which started in 2000,[221] culminated with a structural review in 2003.[222] In the mid-period, in 2001, the Eight Special Recommendations were adopted expanding FATF's mandate to combat FT.[223]

The Forty Recommendations plus the Eight SR strengthened the existing AML measures, acknowledging new techniques and trends in ML crimes, and the weaknesses and gaps identified throughout the 1st Round of ME and the

Responsibilities of Competent Authorities and Other Institutional Measures; and 7) International Co-operation.

218 Ibid (2012 FATF Recommendations, as amended), 8. Within FATF's regulatory framework, FATF's Recommendations, together with their INotes, are conceived to be binding, unlike other documents adopted by the FATF. See, 1991–1992 FATF Report, para. 5 and para. 68–70; 1995–1996 FATF Report, para. 17; 2017–2018 FATF Report, 37.

219 For a chronological understanding of the changes, see https://www.fatf-gafi.org/publications/fatfrecommendations/documents/fatf-recommendations.html (last visited 15/05/2024).

220 1995–1996 FATF Report, para. 2 and 18–27.

221 2000–2001 FATF Report, para. 84–87.

222 2002–2003 FATF Report para. 19.

223 2001–2002 FATF Report, para. 1, 3 and 16–18.

Non-Cooperative Countries and Territories (NCCT) process. As referred in the 2002–2003 FATF Report:

> [M]oney laundering methods and techniques change in response to the countermeasures that are developed to combat this crime (...) These factors, combined with the experience gained through the FATF's Non-Cooperative Countries and Territories (NCCT) process, and a number of national and international initiatives, led to the FATF deciding to review and revise the Forty Recommendations.[224]

The measures included: i) stronger standards for ML predicate offences; ii) reinforcement of the CDD process for financial institutions in particular enhanced CDD measures for high-risk customers and transactions; iii) wide coverage of designated non-financial businesses and professions (DFNBPS) subject to AML measures (casinos, real estate agents, dealers of precious metals/stones, accountants, lawyers, notaries and independent legal professionals, trust and company service providers);[225] and iv) stronger control measures to increase transparency of legal persons and arrangements.

A novel international standard to counter FT was established and jurisdictions were asked to:

i) Ratify and implement the relevant UN instruments;
ii) Criminalise the FT, terrorist acts and terrorist organisations;
iii) Freeze, seize and confiscate terrorist assets;
iv) Report suspicious transactions linked to terrorism;
v) Provide and facilitate assistance to other countries' law enforcement and regulatory authorities for FT investigations;
vi) Impose AML measures on money remittance systems;
vii) Strengthen CDD measures in international and domestic wire transfers; and
viii) Ensure that entities, in particular non-profit organisations (NPOS), cannot be misused for FT purposes.[226]

The review process was quite inclusive. Comments were collected from different stakeholders and a Public Consultation Paper was released in May 2002. A Forum with the private sector representatives and non-members

224 Para. 16.

225 In this revision, the FATF enumerates which entities should be classified as DNFBPS instead of leaving such classification to jurisdictions.

226 2001–2002 FATF Report, para. 18.

was organised in October 2002 to facilitate dialogue with the industry.[227] According to the 2002–2003 FATF Report, "more than 150 written comments were received (…) Many of these proposals have been incorporated into the text of the Recommendations that was finally agreed".[228]

In 2004, the Eight SR on FT were expanded to nine to include "the threat posed by cash couriers by introducing measures to detect physical cross border transportation of cash and bearer monetary instruments", which culminated, for instance, with the (gradual) elimination of bearer negotiable instruments and the implementation of a cross-border declaration system of currency and bearer negotiable instruments.[229]

In 2010, the FATF engaged in another major reform returning to its classic 'Forty Recommendations' format.[230] The review merged the Nine SR, expanded the FATF's mandate to include PF,[231] and set forth a new strategic model focused on risk assessment. Logically, the review took into consideration the "changing threats to the international financial system", as well as the "shortcomings and loopholes in the existing Recommendations, reflecting the lessons learnt from implementing and evaluating them".[232]

Besides the adoption of a *risk-based approach* (RBA) at national and sectorial levels, and the inclusion of PF of WMD pursuant to Resolutions 1718 (2006) and 2231 (2015) of the UNSC and subsequent Resolutions, the revision reinforces:

i) CDD measures to foreign and domestic politically exposed person (PEPS), international organisations, PEPS family and close associates;
ii) Co-operation mechanisms between investigative, supervisory and prosecutorial agencies and the financial institutions and, in particular with the Financial Intelligence Unit (FIU);
iii) Investigative techniques and powers of investigative, supervisory and prosecutorial agencies (eg. to obtain and analyse financial information about suspect or parallel financial investigations of major proceeds-generated from predicate offences);

227 2000–2001 FATF Report, para. 85; 2001–2002 FATF Report, para. 8; 2002–2003 FATF Report, para. 2, 17–18.

228 2002–2003 FATF Report, para. 17 and 19.

229 2004–2005 FATF Report, para. 3, 12–14.

230 2009–2010 FATF Report, 17–18; 2010–2011 FATF Report, 8–9; 2011–2012 FATF Report, 15.

231 The concerns with PF of WMD has been in FATF's agenda since 2008, see 25 Years FATF Report, 12–13.

232 2011–2012 FATF Report, 15; 2015–2016 FATF Report, 19. The recent revision related to asset recovery also illustrates a recognised gap (2022–2023 FATF Report, 10–11).

iv) Stronger transparency requirements on ownership and control of legal persons and legal arrangements and parties, and in particular in what concerns electronic funds transfers;
v) Predicate offences underlying ML to include tax crimes; and
vi) National co-operation and co-ordination.[233]

The revised FATF Recommendations were adopted in February 2012 and its process was open and inclusive like the previous one, with the participation of a sizeable number of stakeholders from public to private sectors, and civil society.[234]

The 2012 reform endeavoured to find a balance between technical standards compliance and effectiveness, placing emphasis on the outcomes of the adopted regimes and measures, whether members successfully and fully implemented the recommendations in practice or, conversely, shown inadequacies or had demonstrated shortcomings in this regard.

Accordingly, Governments and different sectors of society are required to evaluate the efficiency of the implemented measures and to understand the ML/FT/PF risks,[235] by finding or predicting vulnerabilities, as well devising preventive measures or addressing the identified vulnerabilities. Each jurisdiction must determine its low and high-risk sectors, along with priorities and areas of improvement. The chosen method to identify these risks is the mentioned 'RBA'. In 2012–2013 FATF Report, it is explained that:

> [C]ountries should clearly understand the money laundering and terrorist financing risks which affect them, and adapt their AML/CFT system to the nature of these risks. This approach will allow them to apply enhanced measures where the risks are higher and it will give them the option to apply simplified measures where the risks are lower. A well-implemented risk-based approach will result in a more effective, flexible, and less costly AML/CFT system.[236]

233 2011–2012 FATF Report 15–18.

234 As stated in the Report: "The review of the FATF standards was a complex process (...) The private sector and civil society are vital partners in ensuring the integrity of the financial system, the FATF therefore took an inclusive approach to the review, involving not only governments but also the private sector and civil society", ibid, 7.

235 The 2020 October amendment added PF to Recommendation 1 (Assessing Risks and Applying an RBA) and Recommendation 2 (National Co-operation and Co-ordination).

236 At: 16.

The RBA has the advantage of tailoring AML/CFT/CPF strategies to the specific needs and circumstances of individual jurisdictions. This enables a better evaluation and management of the available (and desirable) resources, and simultaneously assists public and private sectors on how to use them in an effective and prudent manner.[237] As emphasised in the 30 Years FATF Report:

> Given each country's unique risk situation, the FATF Recommendations provide countries a level of flexibility to determine which actions they need to take to address the particular money laundering and terrorist financing risks they face.[238]

As noted, a number of events and circumstances compelled a comprehensive review of the standards and/or successive amendments to Recommendations or INotes.[239] Just to name a few:

i) The 9/11 terrorist attacks in 2001;
ii) The world financial crisis in 2008;[240]
iii) The UNSCRs on non-proliferation to counter the PF of WMD in 2008;[241]
iv) The G-20 calls to enhance transparency to counter proceeds of corruption in 2009;[242]
v) The UNSCRs targeting the Islamic State in Iraq and the Levant (ISIL) and other affiliates of Al-Qaida in 2014;[243]
vi) The terrorist attacks in Tunisia, Paris, Brussels, Istanbul and other places in the world in 2015–2016;[244]
vii) The Panama Papers in 2016;[245]

237 Ibid.

238 At: 42.

239 1995–1996 FATF Report, para. 17: "Money laundering is a fluid, evolving phenomenon. Efforts to combat laundering, therefore, must be similarly dynamic. It has always been understood that the FATF's Recommendations should not be set in stone, but rather subject to periodic review". Also, 2015–2016 FATF Report, 23–24.

240 2012–2013 FATF Report, 6; 25 Years FATF Report, 4.

241 2007–2008 FATF Report, 5, 10–11, 19 and 21; 2008–2009 FATF Report, 24–25.

242 G-20 Leaders Statement: The Pittsburgh Summit 2009, para. 15 and 42; 20 Years FATF Report, 15.

243 2014–2015 FATF Report, 5.

244 Ibid.

245 At: https://www.icij.org/investigations/panama-papers/. As stated in the 2015–2016 FATF Report: In April 2016, the 'Panama papers' (the Mossaka-Ferreira case) "highlighted the need for many countries to fully implement the FATF Standards. Over 11 million leaked documents identified 214,000 offshore entities in 21 jurisdictions, all over the world. The documents highlighted the intricate structures that are used for legal and illegal activity, including tax avoidance, tax evasion, corruption, sanctions evasion, terrorist financing

viii) The use of technology to circumvent the financial system such as artificial intelligence digital solutions and VA (2018 onwards);[246] and

ix) The Pandora Papers in 2021.[247]

The *rationale* behind each review is explained with clarity in the 2017–2018 FATF Report:

> The FATF keeps the international standards and their implementation under ongoing review, in order to identify where there is a need for further guidance and best practices at international level, or where the Standards themselves may need to be updated, clarified, or expanded. This can include responding to new and emerging risks (such as the financing of foreign terrorist fighters); correcting widespread misunderstandings of the Standards with unintended consequences (such as de-risking in the correspondent banking sphere). The FATF also updates its standards and guidance to assist countries with implementing the most difficult aspects of the AML/CFT requirements and to reflect evolving practices and technologies in the public and private sectors.[248]

The preceding events had both a theoretical and practical impact, namely at the level of criteria and requirements (eg. review of the Recommendations, methodology and benchmarks), at methodological level (shifting from a technical compliance (TC) approach to an RBA) and at institutional level (eg. powers and tasks of FATF's bodies re-designed, expansion of *ad-hoc* WGs, typologies, guidance papers, work volume, human resources and expenditures, together with the demand for stronger political commitment).

From the adoption of the current Forty Recommendations and/or INotes in February 2012 until November 2023 (last amendment),[249] 13 amendments to the Recommendations,[250] 18 amendments to the INotes,[251] and eight revisions

and other predicate offences for money laundering", 25–26. The improvement of BO information and transparency requirements were reinforced following a call from the G-20, see G-20 Chengdu Finance Ministers and Central Bank 2016 Communiqué, para. 10 and 12. Also, 30 Years FATF Report, 57.

246 2017–2018 FATF Report, 9; 30 Years FATF Report, 86–87.

247 At: *icij/investigations/pandora-papers/*.

248 At: 37.

249 At: https://www.fatf-gafi.org/publications/fatfrecommendations/documents/fatf-recommendations.html (last visited 15/05/2024).

250 Recommendations 8, 21, 2, 15, 1, 2, 24, 25, 4, 30, 31, 38, and 8 (by order of modification).

251 INotes 5, 8, 5, 7, 18, 15, 1, 2, 15, 22, 23, 24, 25, 4, 30, 38, 40 and 8 (by order of modification).

or adding of definitions to the Glossary[252] can be accounted for.

For instance, INote to Recommendation 5 (Criminalisation of Terrorist Financing) was subject to amendments in 2015 and 2016 to be in conformity with Resolution 2178 (2014) of the UNSC,[253] and subsequent Resolutions.[254] Recommendations 1 and 2 and respective INotes were revised to include PF in the National Risk Assessment (NRA) and within the national co-operation and co-ordination contexts, in October 2020.[255]

The latest amendments relate to strengthening the control and transparency of BO information related to trusts and similar arrangements (Recommendation 24) in February 2023.[256] The October 2023 changes cover the definition of legal and operational frameworks that "prioritise asset recovery" and a "non-conviction-based confiscation" procedure, while enhancing means of international co-operation in these areas (Recommendations 4 and 38).[257] The scope of Recommendation 8 regarding NPOs was also clarified following a study on unintended consequences and a public consultation in June 2023 (Chapter 5, Section 2 below).[258]

In short, the FATF Recommendations provide a holistic and systematic regime to counter ML, FT and PF aiming universal observance. As described, their evolution and degree of normative and regulatory activity in the past three decades are deeply associated with the dynamics of society and constant trends and threats related to international financial crime.[259]

---

252 'Funds or other assets', 'designed persons or entity', 'designation' and 'without delay', 'virtual assets' and 'virtual assets service provider', 'designated categories of offences', 'financial group', 'nominator' and 'nominee shareholder or director', 'beneficial owner', 'beneficiary', 'legal arrangements' and 'asset recovery' (by order of modification).

253 It incorporates the financing of travelling of foreign terrorists' fighters and related activities into the FT offence, 2014–2015 FATF Report, 6 and 16; 2015–2016 FATF Report, 13–15.

254 It clarifies that the term 'economic support' covers trade in oil and other natural resources, and other assets which could be used to obtain funds to finance terrorism (UNSCR 2199 (2015) and UNSCR 2253 (2015)), 2016–2017 FATF Report, 22.

255 At:https://www.fatf-gafi.org/en/publications/Fatfgeneral/Outcomes-fatf-plenary-october-2020.html.

256 At:https://www.fatf-gafi.org/en/publications/Fatfgeneral/outcomes-fatf-plenary-february-2023.html.

257 Previously, Recommendation 4 asked jurisdictions to consider adopting measures that allow non-conviction-based confiscation or reverse the burden of proof, if "consistent with the principles of their domestic law". The new version compels jurisdictions to have in place measures to "confiscate criminal property through non-conviction-based confiscation". The reference to being "consistent with fundamental principles of domestic law" was moved to INotes. At: https://www.fatf-gafi.org/en/publications/Fatfgeneral/outcomes-fatf-plenary-october-2023.html.

258 Ibid.

259 1995–1996 FATF Report, para. 17; 25 Years FATF Report, 12–13.

The translation of the Forty Recommendations into 13 languages should also be emphasised, as it reveals the significance of FATF's policy-making and lawmaking authority at the national and regional levels. They are officially translated into English and French and unofficially translated into Arabic, Armenian, Chinese, Czech, Dari, Estonian, Mongolian, Pashto, Portuguese, Russian and Spanish.[260] This circumstance is remarkable and extremely relevant as to their worldwide impact and observance.

6.2 *Typologies, Best Practices and Guidance Papers*

The other acts that are regularly produced by the FATF aim at providing know-how, guidance or assistance at practical level on how to better implement the FATF Recommendations. These auxiliary documents together with the Recommendations set out a comprehensive and sound operational framework to counter ML/FT/PF.[261]

The typologies-exercise began at the onset of the formation of the FATF as an expert forum where law enforcement agents shared their experience, know-how, concerns and solutions.[262] As stated in the 1996–1997 FATF Report, it was designed as "a forum for law enforcement experts – those primarily tasked with combating money laundering – to discuss recent trends in the laundering of criminal proceeds, emerging threats, and effective countermeasures".[263] Over the years, this technical think-thank has been expanded to other areas and to a widerrange of experts.

Today, the Joint Experts' Meeting (JEM) brings together more than 100 operational experts from the Global Network, including from other IOs (eg. IMF, WB, UN), often organised in partnership with the FSRBs. It gathers experts from law enforcement, financial intelligence, security agency experts, prosecutors, and judges to debate cross-cutting matters related to current and emerging ML/FT/PF threats.[264]

Within this context, a reference should be made to the Global Threat Assessment (GTA) exercise adopted in 2010 that has its origins in the typologies

260 At: https://www.fatf-gafi.org/publications/fatfrecommendations/documents/fatf-recommendations.html (last visited 15.05.2024).

261 2000–2001 FATF Report, para. 86; FATF Recommendations (as amended), 8.

262 1991–1992 FATF Report, para. 68–70.

263 Para. 2–4. The designation 'typologies report' was first used in the 1996–1997 FATF Report.

264 Eg. 2019 FATF/MONEYVAL JEM, Tel Aviv, 25–26 March (2018–2019 FATF Report, 35–36); 2020 Virtual JEM, 23–26 November (2020–2021 FATF Report, 38); 2023 FATF JEM, New Delhi, 3–6 April (2022–2023 FATF Report, 23).

work and in the Strategic Surveillance Initiative. It aims at anticipating long-term ML, TF and PF threats and providing strategic means of response.[265]

The annual typologies meetings (JEM) and related reports offer an exhaustive analysis of the vulnerabilities of a specific sector based on real case-studies as well as guidance for future action, such as red flag indicators and best practices to counter the misuse of the sector under study.[266] These documents are particularly important to low-capacity jurisdictions by providing direction on policy development and decision-making along with choices for the rational and sound allocation of resources.

On the other hand, as Mark Nance accurately observes, "although [typologies] are not generally acknowledged as such", they also "play a monitoring role" in terms of "diagnostic and generative".[267] Indeed, typologies may afford useful information about the status of a given field, as well as the level of implementation of standards, making them a valuable monitoring tool from this viewpoint .

During the past three decades, the FATF has issued over 100 publications, including on methods and trends,[268] guidance[269] and best practices,[270] guidance related to RBA,[271] as well on joint studies[272] and workshop

265 2010–2011 FATF Report, 26–27.

266 25 Years FATF Report, 10; 30 Years FATF Report, 36.

267 (n) 46, 139.

268 Eg. Football Sector (2009); Free Trade Zones (2010); Trade-based ML (2012); Legal Professionals (2013); Emerging TF (2015); Financial Flows from Human Trafficking (2018); Crowdfunding for TF (2023).

269 Eg. Capacity-building for ME and Implementations of FATF Standards within LCC (2008); National ML/TF Risk Assessment (2013); Transparency and BO (2014); TF Risk Assessment (2019); Digital ID (2020); Guidance on PF Risk Assessment and Mitigation (2021); BO and Transparency of Legal Arrangements (2024).

270 Eg. Cash Couriers – Illicit Cross-border Transportation (2005); Trade Based ML (2008); Managing the AML and CFT Policy Implications of Voluntary Tax compliance Programmes (2012); FATF Recommendations to Combat Corruption (2013); BO for Legal Persons (2019); Combating the Abuse of NPOs (2023).

271 Eg. RBA for Dealers in Precious Metals and Stones, Trust and Company Service Providers, Accountants, Real Estate Agents (2008); Prepaid Cards, Mobile Payments and Internet-based Payment Services (2013); Virtual Currencies (2015); MVTs (2016); Risk Based Supervision (2021); Real Estate Sector (2022); ML and TF Risks arising from Migrant Snuggling (2022).

272 Eg. Joint FATF-GIABA-GABAC Report on TF in West and Central Africa (2016); Joint FATF-Egmont Group Study on Concealment of BO (2018); ML and the Illegal Wildlife Trade Study (2020); FATF/Egmont Trade-based ML: Trends and Developments Report (2020); FATF/Egmont Digital Transformation of AML/CFT for Operational Agencies (2021);

findings,[273] which are publicly available.

Some of these studies and data collected concern the identification of new threats and methods, while others concern the identification of gaps either in the Recommendations or INotes or address new topics that are directly or indirectly related to the Recommendations, resulting in the development and creation of new Recommendations and INotes as well as the improvement of the ME process.[274]

Such is the case of the typologies report on PF in 2008 and Recommendation 7,[275] or on 'Trusts and Company Service Providers' in 2010 and Recommendations 24 and 25,[276] or on the 'Risk of Terrorist Abuse in Non-Profit Organisations' in 2014 and Recommendation 8,[277] or on 'Virtual Currencies-Key Definitions and Potential AML/CFT Risks' (2014) or 'Guidance for a Risk-Based Approach to Virtual Currencies' (2015) and Recommendation 15 and VA Red Flag Indicators on ML/FT/PF (2020, 2021 and 2022).[278]

Drive by the ambition of being at the "forefront to identify and understand new threats that challenge the safety and security of the financial system",[279] the FATF is constantly surveying new vulnerabilities,[280] or new threats, such as "proceeds-generating crimes stemming from the Covid-19 crisis" (ML, fraud or cybercrime).[281]

Joint Project with the OECD on the Misuse of Citizenship and Residency by Investment Programmes (2023).

273 Eg. FATF Workshop on the Role of Judges and Prosecutors in Tackling ML/TF in Africa and Middle East (2018), Joint FATF/MONEYVAL Experts' meeting and TF Prosecution Workshop (2019).

274 2008–2009 FAFF Report, 10; 25 Years FATF Report, 11.

275 2008–2009 FATF Report, 24–25; 2009–2010 FATF Report, 18.

276 2010–2011 FATF Report, 17.

277 2015–2016 FATF Report, 19, 23–24.

278 2014–2015 FATF Report, 9; 25 Years FATF Report, 10.

279 30 Years FATF Report, 19.

280 UNSCR 2462 (2019), op.para. 14: the sectors of construction, commodities and pharmaceutical industries.

281 2019–2020 FATF Report, 9–10; 2020–2021 FATF Report, 6–7. The outbreak was declared a public health emergency of international concern (PHEIC) by the WHO on 30/01/2020 and a pandemic on 11/03/2020. On 05/03/2023, the WHO declared that Covid-19 "no longer constitutes a PHEIC". See WHO Statements, at: https://www.who.int/groups/covid-19-ihr-emergency-committee. Gabrielle Marceau emphasises the role of IOs in providing quick and efficient solutions in times of worldwide crisis and how their pragmatic and innovative responses benefit the international community (eg. WHO with SARS or IMF/WB with the 2008 financial crisis). Times of crisis may create a stimulus for new creative methods, including informal lawmaking and practices, as well as "appropriate institutional changes". However, these new normative frameworks also need to be supported in transparency and accountability mechanisms, peer pressure, and global administrative

The Covid-19 pandemic is therefore a paradigmatic example of FATF's capacity to react to adverse effects in a prompt, positive and efficient manner, by diligently identifying the loopholes in the international realm that could be exploited in this unprecedented global crisis.[282]

Additionally, a number of studies were conducted from 2021 to 2023 on different subjects, such as the use of new technologies,[283] environmental crime,[284] ethnically or racially motivated FT,[285] illicit proceeds generated from the supply chains for fentanyl and related synthetic opioids,[286] ML through art, antiquities and other cultural objects,[287] together with projects on countering the proceeds from ransomware attacks[288] and asset recovery,[289] which may foster new guidance, benchmarks or even standards.

7 Monitoring and Sanctioning Powers

The success of the FATF model is also attributable to its monitoring power that comprises: i) a complex and thorough peer review mechanism of evaluation

law principles. 'IGOs in Crisis? Or New Opportunities to Demonstrate Responsibility?' (2011) 8 *International Organizations Law Review*, 2.

282 2020–2021 FATF Report, 10. In April 2020, the FATF President made a statement warning on the probability of financial crimes being committed (eg. corruption, fraud, counterfeiting of essential goods, such as medical supplies and medicine, fundraising for fake charities). Statement by the FATF President: Covid-19 and Measures to Combat Illicit Financing of 01/04/2020, at: https://www.fatf-gafi.org/publications/fatfgeneral/documents/statement-covid-19.html. In May, a study was conducted to assess the 'Challenges, Good Practices and Policy Responses to New Money Laundering and Terrorist Financing Threats and Vulnerabilities Stemming from the Covid-19 Crisis', which was subsequently updated in December 2020. Webinars were held with the public and private sectors (July 2021) and red flag indicators on ML/TF risks were published (September 2021). At: https://www.fatf-gafi.org/en/publications/Fatfgeneral/Updated-covid-19-ml-tf.html.

283 Digital solutions to counter ML/FT/PF, data pooling & analysis and data protection (2021–2022 FATF Report, 18–21). Eg. Report on Illicit Financial Flows from Cyber-enabled Fraud (2023).

284 Ilegal trade in wildlife, forestry crime, illegal mining and waste trafficking (2019–2020 FATF Report, 21–23). Eg. Report on Money Laundering from Environment Crime (2021).

285 Eg. Report on Ethnically or Racially Motivated Financing of Terrorism (2021).

286 Eg. Report on Money Laundering from Fentanyl and Synthetic Opioids (2022).

287 Eg. Report on Money Laundering and Terrorist Financing in the Art and Antiquities Market (2023).

288 Eg. Report on Countering Ransomware Financing (2023); Countering Ransomware Financing-Potential Risk Indicators (2023).

289 Eg. Report on Recovering International Proceeds of Crime through Inter-Agency Networks (2023).

that is consistently reviewed (ME); ii) a specific monitoring process for jurisdictions that present serious deficiencies in the AML/CFT/CPF domestic systems (the ICRG); and iii) a sanction mechanism (blacklisting) for jurisdictions that show systemic deficiencies or lack of compliance. A considerable part of this monitoring power, in particular the ME process, is delegated to the FSRBS to oversee their member jurisdictions.

The ME process is reproduced with some procedural adjustments according to the regional context and risks of each regional or sub-regional group. However, the sanctioning power lies in the 'hands' of the FATF, mirroring our concept of the *octopus-effect network*. The FSRBS are just 'agents' of this multi-layered compliance architecture, designed by the 'octopus head'. As Nance properly affirms: "FATF's monitoring powers are among the farthest reaching of any international organisation".[290]

7.1 *Mutual Evaluation Process*

The ME process is a mechanism to evaluate and monitor how jurisdictions are implementing the FATF Recommendations; in other words, it assesses if the AML, CFT and CPF domestic systems are properly in place, both at legal/regulatory and at operational levels.[291]

The FATF describes the ME process as "an in-depth and intrusive assessment of the measures a country is taking".[292] Indeed, it is a complex, laborious and thorough analysis (an X-ray) of a jurisdiction's AML/CFT/CPF national policies and practices covering public and private sectors, and civil society.[293]

Briefly, the ME process consists of a report that is drafted by a team of experts (assessors) in co-operation with the assessed jurisdiction, which culminates with a debate and subsequent report approval at the FATF Plenary, where key findings and shortcomings are shared and recommendations are made.[294]

---

290 The author stresses the two mechanisms: the ME/typologies and the ICRG/backlisting, (n 60) 116.

291 2006–2007 FATF Report, para. 16; 2010–2011 FATF Report, 11; 2016–2017 FATF Report, 29–30.

292 2015–2016 FATF Report, 35.

293 Ben Hayes refers that the "mutual evaluation process is crucial because it *de facto* extends the FATF Recommendations by imposing extraordinarily detailed guidance", establishing over 250 criteria or benchmarks to assess jurisdictions' compliance with the Recommendations. 'Counter-Terrorism, 'Policy Laundering' and the FATF: Legalizing Surveillance, Regulating Civil Society', (2012) Transnational Institute and Statewatch Report (2012 Hayes Report) 19.

294 2006–2007 FATF Report, para. 25. More in 'Procedures for the FATF Fourth Round of AML/CFT Mutual Evaluations' (4th Round of ME Procedures, as last amended February 2023) (last visited 15/05/2024).

The MER and its corresponding Executive Summary Report are published on the FATF website, which is a fundamental criterion for both members and members of associate members.[295] The non-publication "with the common FATF/FSRBS mutual evaluation cover page"[296] indicates that the jurisdiction in question did not undergo an assessment. Initially, MERS were only made publicly available upon consent of the concerned jurisdiction, as mentioned in the 2004–2005 FATF Report:

> [A] summary of each Report will be published on the FATF website and FATF members have agreed in principle to make public the full mutual evaluation reports (with the ultimate decision being left to each FATF member for its own report).[297]

The drafting of the report is a long process, during which the assessed jurisdiction provides information and evidence on technical compliance and effectiveness in relation to the implementation of the Forty Recommendations.[298] All pertinent information that offers a clear picture of the existing AML, CFT and CPF systems and how they work in practice must (should) be given to the assessment team, which is bound by a confidentiality clause.[299]

A minimum on-site visit of 10 days is conducted by assessors to all main institutions (both public and private),[300] after which a preliminary draft report is submitted to the assessed jurisdiction for comments. In its last stage, the draft report is distributed to a team of reviewers and to the assessed jurisdiction. The former must ensure that the assessment and its findings are addressed accurately, and that the MER meets an "acceptable standard of quality and consistency", and the later must provide its final comments.[301]

Before the Plenary meeting, face-to-face meetings are carried out between the assessment team and the assessed jurisdiction for final clarification and/or any final adjustments.[302]

The ME process may take approximately 14 months.[303] During this process, the FATF Secretariat has the responsibility, *inter alia*, to support the assessment

295 2019 Mandate, para. 6(b) and 12(b); HLPOS, para. 35–36.
296 HLPOS, para. 35.
297 2004–2005 FATF Report, para. 19.
298 2015–2016 FATF Report, 35; Universal Procedures, para. 14–18, 20, 24.
299 4th Round of ME procedures, para. 32; Universal Procedures, para. 19.
300 Annex II, 4th Round of ME Procedures.
301 Ibid, para. 42–44.
302 Ibid, para. 47–49; Universal Procedures, para.27.
303 Universal Procedures, para. 6. The 5th ME Round establishes 18 months.

team, to co-ordinate the relationship between the assessors and assessed jurisdiction, to co-ordinate the relationship between the assessors and reviewers, and to ensure the quality and consistency of the report.[304]

Before being submitted to the FATF's Plenary, both the MER and the Executive Summary Report are distributed among the FATF and FRSBS members for comment, ie. the documents are made available to all jurisdictions of the Global Network.[305]

This process facilitates a common comprehension and systematic application of the standards, increasing the transparency of the assessment through proper implementation of the methodology. It also enables jurisdictions to partake in the exercise, establishing a fair and equitable playing field, where jurisdictions from all over the world can express their views. Furthermore, by sharing and disseminating the findings of the draft MERS and FURS and contributing to them, it nurtures a 'sense of belonging', allowing jurisdictions to feel that they are effectively part of the network.[306]

In the FATF Plenary, a list of "high-level and key substantive issues" is discussed by all stakeholders, including ratings (downgrade/upgrade) and recommendations, with the MER being approved by consensus.[307] The MER is reviewed with changes agreed in the FATF Plenary, assessed jurisdiction and FATF Secretariat.[308]

If no agreement is reached the adoption of the MER is deferred. Assessors, the jurisdiction, and the Secretariat need to address the outstanding issues either for written approval when the changes are minor, or for the next FATF Plenary meeting when amendments are substantial.[309]

The final version of the FATF or regional bodies MERS will be reviewed for quality and consistency (Q&C) by the FATF Secretariat, as a mandatory requisite "regardless of the assessing body" to ensure "a consistently high standard for all assessments" within the FATF Global Network, as explained in the 2016–2017 FATF Report.[310]

---

304 Ibid, para. 12; 4th Round of ME Procedures, para. 18, 60, 63–64, 71.

305 Ibid, para. 28; 4th Round of ME Procedures, para. 61–64, 71–72.

306 2012–2013 FATF Report, 33.

307 A preliminary debate may be held at the ECG. Key issues resolved by consensus are submitted to the Plenary for endorsement, whilst unsolved key issues are debated at the Plenary. 4th Round of ME Procedures, para. 56; 2012–2013 FATF Report, 9; 2016–2017 FATF Report, 30 and Universal Procedures, para. 28–31.

308 4th Round of ME Procedures, para. 57; Universal Procedures, para. 32.

309 Ibid, para. 58; Universal Procedures para.34.

310 At: 30. Also, 4th Round of ME Procedures, para. 57–72; 2012–2013 FATF Report, 12.

Whenever the assessed jurisdiction or other parties (ie. other jurisdictions from the Global Network, Secretariats, International Financial Institutions (IFIs)) identify considerable Q&C problems with the final version for publication that is being circulated, a post-Plenary Q&C process will be conducted.

The ECG with the assistance of the FATF Secretariat reviews the claim and either decides that it does not meet the substantive threshold of "serious or major issues of Q&C with the potential to affect the credibility of the FATF brand as a whole",[311] and is therefore in conditions for publication or, in case it meets the threshold, the ECG reports the matter to the FATF Plenary for final decision considering the seriousness of the matter.[312]

The control of the Q&C of the reports is associated with FATF's brand concerns (Chapter 4, Section 5 below). The publication of a MER from a regional body in FATF's website suggests that these reports bear the FATF 'seal of guarantee'. As highlighted in the 2013–2014 FATF Report:

> The credibility of the FATF as the global standard-setter for AML/CFT matters relies on the fact that the approach to assessing compliance with the FATF standards, and the quality of the mutual evaluation reports, are the same, regardless of the assessing body.[313]

The MERs of the FATF and quality-control of the MERs of the FSRBs reflect FATF's work as a reliable and robust monitoring organisation and emphasise the role of the FATF not exclusively as a global standard-setter, but also as an international supervisory authority - as a global keeper (Section 7 below).[314]

311 Meeting a substantive threshold means that: "a) the ratings are clearly inappropriate and not consistent with the analysis; b) there has been a serious misinterpretation of the standards, methodology and/or procedures; c) an important part of the methodology has been systematically misapplied; or d) laws that are not in force and effect have been taken into account in the analysis and ratings of a report", 4th Round of ME Procedures, para. 59.

312 Ibid, para. 60–72; Universal Procedures, para. 38–46.

313 2013–2014 FATF Report, 29–30. "The final MER is a report of the FATF and not of the assessors", as noted in para. 59 of the 4th Round of Procedures. Also, HLPOs, para. 35–36.

314 The 2015–2016 FATF Report states: "The aim is to ensure a standard of operating and reciprocity across the FATF Global Network, which is in the interest of both FATF and FSRB. If one of the organisations is functioning poorly and not delivering rigorous assessments for example, then this can have an impact on all organisations in the FATF Global Network and the credibility of their work and the FATF brand. In February 2016, the FATF updated the high-level principles and objectives to ensure they remain relevant and allow each organisation sufficient flexibility to develop within its own governance structure", 51.

The FATF reports are usually lengthy and extensively detailed (around 250–300 pages), comprising an additional Executive Summary (around 10–15 pages).[315] The FATF has published more than 600 MERs and FURs to date.[316]

7.1.1 Common Methodology

A common methodology – the 'Methodology for Assessing Compliance with the Forty Recommendations and the Nine Special Recommendations Report' (2004 Methodology) – was adopted in 2004 and endorsed by the FSRBs, IMF and WB for the 3rd Round of ME, envisioning a global, consistent and high-quality assessment mechanism.[317] In the 2003–2004 FATF Report, the FATF highlights the significance of sharing a common methodology:

> The 2004 Methodology will be a very useful tool to carry out mutual evaluations. It will help identify the key elements of the systems and mechanisms developed by countries with diverse legal, regulatory and financial frameworks and determine whether those countries are in compliance with the current FATF standards.[318]

Logically, the FATF methodology, procedures and related documents, in line with the FATF Standards and strategies, have been subject to development, and improvement through time.[319] The 2004 Methodology, the 'AML/CFT Handbook for Countries and Assessors' (2004),[320] and the 'Key Principles for ME and Assessments' (2010)[321] were revised, refined, and finally replaced by the '2013 Methodology for Assessing Compliance with the FATF Recommendations and the Effectiveness of AML/CFT Systems' (2013 Methodology)[322] together

315 Eg. The MER of Japan (August) 2021, MER of South Africa (October) 2021, MER of Germany (August) 2022, MER of Brazil (December 2023) accounted, respectively, 292, 240, 330 and 359 pages.

316 At: https://www.fatf-gafi.org/publications/mutualevaluations/?hf=10&b=0&s=desc(fatf_releasedate) (last visited 15/05/2024). In this respect, 2018–2019 FATF Report, 45–51; 2019–2020 FATF Report, 29–33.

317 2003–2004 FATF Report, para. 37–39. The co-operation with the FSRBs, IMF and WB in this process as main partners is highlighted in 2004–2005 FATF Report, para. 17–21. Also, 2012–2013 FATF Report, 12.

318 Para. 40.

319 2006–2007 FATF Report, para. 24; 2012–2013 FATF Report, 16; 2016–2017 FATF Report, 9 and 12.

320 2006–2007 FATF Report, para. 25. In 2009, it is entitled '3rd Round of AML/CFT Mutual Evaluations and Procedures'.

321 2009–2010 FATF Report, 21.

322 Last amended June 2023 (last visited 15/05/2024).

with the '2013 Procedures for the 4th Round of AML/CFT Mutual Evaluations' (4th Round of ME Procedures)[323] and the '2014 Consolidated Processes and Procedures for Mutual Evaluations and Follow-Up' (Universal Procedures).[324] These documents have also been regularly updated, and constitute the cornerstone documents to assess jurisdictions.[325]

The 2013 Methodology was subject to a 'Strategic Review' and new procedures for the 5th Round of ME were approved at FATF's Plenary meeting, on 4 March 2022.[326] The main objective is to assess all jurisdictions based on identical criteria and benchmarks for each of the Forty Recommendations.

In the 1st Round of ME, the assessment was rather focused on countries' national legal framework to implement the Recommendations (technical compliance),[327] whereas in the last round – the 4th Round – the focus shifted to effectiveness and to an RBA,[328] as stated (Section 2 above). As the 2013–2014 FATF Report elucidates:

> The methodology for the fourth round of mutual evaluations is different from the one used during the previous round. While measuring technical compliance has remained more or less the same, the assessment of effectiveness has been significantly strengthened. In order for an assessment team to judge the level of effectiveness a country has achieved in its AML/CFT system, it will now need to have a sound understanding of the country's AML/CFT regime in practice as well as a clear picture of its risks and context.[329]

Currently, evaluation is undertaken in two spheres: i) technical compliance, which determines whether the elements of an AML/CFT/CPF system are in place, and ii) effectiveness, which determines how well these elements work

323 Last amended February 2023 (last visited 15/05/2024).

324 2013–2014 FATF Report, 10, 29–30. The Universal Procedures have been amended, last amendment in September 2022 (last visited 15/05/2024). The new Universal Procedures have entered recently in effect (May 2024) for the new round of ME.

325 These procedures ensure consistency, quality and timely reports of all ME and FURS within the Global Network. See 2011–2012 FATF Report, 18–20; 2012–2013 FATF Report, 33; 2016–2017 FATF Report 32.

326 At: https://www.fatf-gafi.org/en/publications/Fatfgeneral/Outcomes-fatf-plenary-march-2022.html.

327 1997–1998 FATF Report, para. 14.

328 2012–2013 FATF Report, 16–19.

329 At: 9.

together in practice to meet the objectives of an effective AML/CFT/CPF system.[330]

Technical compliance ratings are: 'Non-Compliant (NC)', 'Partially Compliant (PC)', 'Largely Compliant (LC)' and 'Compliant (C)', whilst effectiveness is assessed based on 11 Immediate Outcomes that represent key goals for achieving a sound AML/CFT/CPF system with ratings of: 'High', 'Substantial', 'Moderate' or 'Low' levels of effectiveness.[331]

A jurisdiction under assessment should provide evidence that "adequately understands its risks" and that adopted "proportionate and effective measures" to reduce the ML/FT/PF risks.[332] Technical requirements and effectiveness outcomes are measured in a detailed and exhaustive manner without disregarding risk factors (RBA).[333] As pointed out in the 2012–2013 FATF Report:

> [Assessors] will determine whether the key objectives of an effective AML/CFT system are being met. This is not a statistical exercise, with a checklist of specific requirements. The assessment of the effectiveness of a country's AML/CFT system will rely on the judgement by the assessors, based on their understanding of how the country's AML/CFT regime works in practice, taking into account the country's risk and context.[334]

The ME process is a peer-assessment conducted by a team of five to six members from the legal, financial, supervisory and law enforcement fields, selected from a pool of experts after attending with success an assessors' training,[335] and staff from the FATF Secretariat.[336] Experts from the IMF and WB may

330 Technical Compliance is cross checked with a series of criteria and benchmarks established in the methodology related to the correct implementation of the Forty Recommendations.

331 Immediate Outcomes cover the following fields: i) policy, co-ordination and international co-operation to mitigate AML/CFT/CPF risks; ii) FIs and DFNBPs' prevention, detection and reporting proceeds of crime and funds related to ML/FT/PF; and iii) prevention, detection and disruption of ML/FT/PF resources and implementation of effective, dissuasive and proportionate sanctions for criminals (2013 Methodology, 16). Also, 2012–2013 FATF Report, 16–19.

332 Each jurisdiction must conduct its own NRA to identify, assess and tackle their ML/FT risks. See 2012–2013 FATF Report, 19; 2015–2016 FATF Report, 35.

333 2012–2013 FATF Report, 19; 2016–2017 FATF Report 29–30.

334 2012–2013 FATF Report, 17.

335 2006–2007 FATF Report, para. 23; 2009–2010 FATF Report, 22–23; 2015–2016 FATF Report, 35; 4th Round of ME Procedures, para. 15–16; Universal Procedures para. 10–11.

336 2004–2005 FATF Report, para. 18; 2016–2017 FATF Report, 33; 4th Round of ME Procedures, para. 15.

integrate the FATF and FSRBs' teams on a reciprocal basis; in the case of joint assessments, experts for the assessment team are selected among the concerned bodies.[337]

In the selection of assessors, several factors, including language and legal background of the jurisdiction to be assessed (civil or common law system) or specific characteristics (eg. size and composition of the economy and financial sector, geographical factors or cultural background) are considered to ensure a balanced, impartial and fair assessment.[338] The appointment of the team experts is carried out in co-ordination with the jurisdiction to be assessed under the guidance of the FATF President or FATF Secretariat. The agreed team of assessors is subsequently appointed by the FATF President.[339]

The FATF runs assessors training courses frequently, sometimes together with other assessor's bodies, including the IMF and WB.[340] The assessors' role is to critically examine whether the legal, regulatory and operational frameworks are producing the expected outcomes of a sound financial and economic system, protected against ML, FT and PF threats.[341]

The methodology indicates the elements, requirements and benchmarks that must be considered during the assessment, and provides guidance through examples and suggestions, recalling that each jurisdiction is unique, with specific characteristics and contexts.[342] Assessors/reviewers being trained based on a common methodology is crucial to ensure that all "have achieved the same level of knowledge".[343]

Jurisdictions are regularly called to provide experts to participate in assessors training programmes in order to actively contribute to a paramount function of the FATF which is the peer review mechanism. Jurisdictions that fail to provide a minimum number of assessors are obliged to contribute financially "in an amount equivalent to the cost of providing such assessors".[344]

337 4th Round of ME Procedures, para. 16. The FATF has the discretion to decide the number of FATF assessments that can be conducted by the IMF or WB (para. 74–82).

338 Ibid, para. 14–18; Universal Procedures para. 10–11.

339 Ibid, para. 14.

340 2009–2010 FATF Report, 22–23, 32; 2016–2017 FATF Report, 33; 2020–2021 FATF Report, 64–67. According to the 2022–2023 FATF Report, there are 1,320 professionals that have been qualified as assessors since 2013, 18.

341 2010–2011 FATF Report, 11; 2015–2016 FATF Report, 35; 2016–2017 FATF Report, 29–30.

342 2010–2011 FATF Report, 11; 2016–2017 FATF Report, 29–30.

343 2006–2007 FATF Report, para. 23.

344 An update list of assessors is maintained by the ECG. The amount is decided by the FATF Plenary, 4th Round of ME Procedures, para. 17. There is no public information available about the practical application of this measure.

7.1.2 Follow-up Process

After the adoption of the MER, the FATF will monitor the progress of the jurisdiction in relation to the shortcomings and deficiencies identified in the report, or if standards' implementation is being adequately sustained.[345]

Depending on the ratings, a jurisdiction may be subject to a simple 'regular follow-up' in case of showing a substantial degree of compliance or subject to an 'enhanced follow-up' in case of showing insufficient progress or deficiencies in its AML/CFT/CPF system. The first follow-up process requires reporting after three years of the adoption of the MER, addressing the identified shortcomings, while the second requires consecutive reporting over the next three years, starting the year following the adoption of the MER.[346]

The decision of placing a jurisdiction under enhanced follow-up is at the discretion of the FATF Plenary based on technical compliance and effectiveness factors. Jurisdictions will be immediately placed into enhanced follow-up if:

i) It has 8 or more NC/PC ratings for technical compliance;
ii) It has NC/PC on any one or more of Recommendations 3, 5, 10, 11 and 20;
iii) It has a low or moderate level of effectiveness for 7 or more of the 11 Immediate Outcomes; or
iv) It has a low level of effectiveness for 4 or more of the 11 Immediate Outcomes.[347]

Jurisdictions may also be placed into enhanced follow-up, if the Plenary concludes after assessing the regular follow-up report:

a) That major priority actions have not been addressed in an adequately and timely manner;
b) That levels of compliance with the FATF Standards have fallen to a level as equivalent to NC/PC on any one or more of Recommendations 3, 5, 10, 11 and 20.[348]

Jurisdictions subject to the ICRG are not expected to report in relation to the Recommendations under the ICRG's action plan rather to focused on the parts of Recommendations which are not covered, demonstrating progress.[349]

345 "The follow-up process is intended to: (i) encourage members' implementation of the FATF Standards; (ii) provide regular monitoring and up-to-date information on countries' compliance with the FATF Standards (including the effectiveness of their AML/CFT systems); (iii) apply sufficient peer pressure and accountability; and (iv) better align the FATF and FSAP assessment cycle". Ibid, para. 83.

346 Ibid, para. 84–85, 87 *et seq.*

347 Ibid, para. 88; Universal Procedures, para. 47–48.

348 Ibid.

349 Ibid, para. 93–94.

Apart from thorough monitoring, which comprises an action plan with timelines, other actions may be taken in case of lack of progress within the expected timeframe, such as letters to relevant minister(s) by the FATF President, high-level missions, formal FATF statements in conformity with Recommendation 19 (High-Risk Countries),[350] membership suspension[351] or termination of membership.[352]

In the past, action was taken against Turkey with a high-level mission visit in 1996,[353] and Austria with a warning of membership suspension in 2000.[354] On 21 June 2019, the FATF issued a Statement expressing membership concerns over Brazil.[355] The Brazilian Government's incapacity to remedy the deficiencies highlighted in its MER (June) 2010, especially those pertaining to terrorism

350 Recommendation 19: FIs should be required to apply enhanced due diligence measures to business relationships and transactions with natural and legal persons, and FIs, from countries for which this is called for by the FATF. The type of enhanced due diligence measures applied should be effective and proportionate to the risks. Countries should be able to apply appropriate countermeasures when called upon to do so by the FATF. Countries should also be able to apply countermeasures independently of any call by the FATF to do so. Such countermeasures should be effective and proportionate to the risks.

351 During suspension, the jurisdiction cannot attend meetings or provide input into FATF processes except for the process to determine whether deficiencies have been adequately addressed (4th Round of ME Procedures, para. 90).

352 Ibid.

353 1995–1996 FATF Report, para. 61: "Turkey is the only FATF member which has not passed anti-money laundering legislation and whose compliance with the Forty Recommendations is seriously deficient. Therefore, the former President of the FATF wrote a letter to the relevant ministers about Turkey's lack of progress on the anti-money laundering front. Subsequently, a FATF high-level mission met with several members of the Turkish Government in Ankara at the end of April 1996, in order to encourage Turkey to expedite the enactment of its anti-money laundering Bill. If this legislation is adopted, it will avoid the FATF Plenary having to take more serious steps after September 1996 regarding Turkey's non-compliance with the Forty Recommendations".

354 1999–2000 FATF Report, para. 4: "On 3 February 2000, in accordance with its policy for members who do not comply with the Forty Recommendations, the FATF decided to suspend Austria as one of its members in June 2000 unless action was taken on the issue of anonymous passbooks. Following this unprecedented move, the Government of Austria took the appropriate steps to meet the conditions required by the FATF and thus avert suspension of membership".

355 At: https://www.fatf-gafi.org/en/publications/Mutualevaluations/Brazil-statement-june-2019.html. The FATF Statement of 19 February 2019 in relation to Brazil does not mention membership issues, however this topic is addressed at FATF Plenary meeting in June 2018. See 2017–2018 FATF Report 49; 2018–2019 FATF Report, 50.

and FT,[356] and the successive unanswered appeals for action were at the root of such concern.[357]

At the FATF Plenary meeting in October 2019, the FATF decided that "no longer considers [Brazil] a membership concern" considering the new legislation and measures adopted to identify and freeze terrorist assets.[358]

Turkey and South Africa are the two FATF members currently under heightened monitoring; both have committed to implement an action plan to resolve their AML/CFT deficiencies.[359] Turkey was designated a jurisdiction of concern in October 2021, based on its MER (December) 2019.[360] Similarly, South Africa was listed in February 2023 following its MER (October) 2021.[361]

The aim of the enhanced follow-up process is to address all the identified shortfalls by the third year. Meanwhile, any jurisdiction may request updates to technical compliance ratings rated 'NC' and/or 'PC', whereas effectiveness will not be evaluated until the end of the fifth year.[362] If significant progress is achieved, jurisdictions under enhanced follow-up may be upgraded to regular follow-up.[363] Exceptionally, as referred, jurisdictions may be downgraded if the Plenary becomes aware that they have lowered their compliance requirements.[364]

Re-rating(s) procedure is a written process that encompasses a peer review, report analysis and consultation mechanism among members, associate

356 MER of Brazil (June) 2010, 259–269. There was no standalone criminalization of FT and no freezing regime in place (non-compliant with the 2012 Recommendations on FT and PF).

357 June and October 2016, February, June, November 2017, June 2018, February and June 2019.

358 At:https://www.fatf-gafi.org/en/publications/Fatfgeneral/Outcomes-plenary-october-2019.html. In 2020, Brazil was still being monitored because of loopholes on information sharing and restrictions on the use of financial intelligence (2019–2020 FATF Report, 35). Brazil was recently assessed, shortcomings were identified in relation to Recommendations 5 and 6 (both rated 'PC'), MER of Brazil (December) 2023, 8–9, 15.

359 At:https://www.fatf-gafi.org/en/publications/High-risk-and-other-monitored-jurisdictions/Increased-monitoring-february-2024.html.

360 At: 10–11. At: https://www.fatf-gafi.org/en/countries/detail/Turkey.html and https://www.fatf-gafi.org/content/fatf-gafi/en/publications/High-risk-and-other-monitored-jurisdictions/Increased-monitoring-october-2021.html.

361 At: 12–14. At: https://www.fatf-gafi.org/en/countries/detail/South-Africa.html and https://www.fatf-gafi.org/en/publications/Fatfgeneral/outcomes-fatf-plenary-february-2023.html.

362 4th Round of ME Procedures, para. 85 and 94–96.

363 Ibid, para. 91–92.

364 Ibid, para. 89. Eg. Re-ratings in the 2022–2023 FATF Report: upgrades of China, Finland, Hong Kong (China), Japan, Mexico and Norway and downgrades of Hong Kong (China) and Norway, 35.

members, and observers.[365] It needs written approval by the FATF Plenary[366] and subsequent publication.[367]

Irrespective of being under regular or enhanced follow-up, jurisdictions will be subject to an assessment after five years with a focus on effectiveness where particular attention is given to high-risks sectors, as well as to priority areas identified in the most recent MER.[368]

7.1.3 The 5th Round of Mutual Evaluations

After a decade of applying the 2013 Methodology and common procedures, the FATF conducted for the first time a stocktake of the existing status of the AML/CFT/CPF framework collecting data from 120 MERs of the Global Network.[369] At the Royal United Services Institute (RUSI) meeting in November 2019, the FATF Executive Secretary underscored the goals of this exercise:

> It will consist of a stocktake, then work to review and modernise the mutual evaluation and follow-up processes, including the work of FATF's international co-operation and review group that leads to the so-called Grey and Black Lists.[370]

The Strategic Review began in 2019 and culminated with the 'Report on the State of Effectiveness and Compliance with the FATF Standards' (2022 FATF Status Report), wherein the strengths and weaknesses of the AML/CFT/CPF regimes were identified. The Report acknowledges that although most of the jurisdictions had a "satisfactory" legal framework in place, revealing a "significant improvement in technical compliance" when compared to 2012 data, jurisdictions still face considerable challenges in terms of effectiveness and application of an RBA.[371]

---

365 It may include experts from the previous MER, and/or experts nominated by the delegation of the ECG, ibid.

366 Ibid. If there are concerns raised by the delegation, members, associate members or observers, an analysis is conducted in the ECG, and in case of no consensus, a discussion is undertaken in the Plenary on the matter for final decision (para. 96).

367 Only reports with re-ratings are published. Final FURs are also offered for comments to all assessment bodies in the Post-Plenary Q&C review. Ibid para. 100–101.

368 Ibid, para. 101–103; Universal Procedures, para. 85 and 95.

369 2019–2020 FATF Report, 10–11, 32–33; 2020–2021 FATF Report, 28.

370 At:http://www.fatf-gafi.org/publications/fatfgeneral/documents/rusi-fatf-strategic-review.html.

371 The 2022 FATF Status Report concludes that in general over half of the FIs and MVTS have a "very good risk understanding", while DNFBP "mostly have below-average to poor understanding of money laundering and terrorist financing risks, with the exception of

The Report also provides valuable inputs for improvement, henceforth being at the basis of the revision/drafting of the new methodology and procedures for the 5th Round of ME.[372] These inputs are divided into three main segments: the ME, the ICRG and the methodology, endeavouring to streamline time, resources, and the efficiency of the ME process. The following suggestions from the Report should be highlighted:

i) To give more weight to the quality of international co-operation;
ii) To assess the FIs and the DNFBPs in separate Immediate Outcomes;
iii) The methodology and ME framework should provide more information and references to risk, major risks, and context, so that assessors may focus in areas of predominant risk;
iv) To extend the ME process to one month;
v) To issue strategic 'Key Recommended Actions' (KRA) and a KRA Roadmap as an outcome of the ME process; and
vi) To insert the ICRG process in FATF's procedures and ME process, and improve ICRG procedures.[373]

These suggestions are mirrored in the new Methodology for the 5th Round of ME, which was available on-line, although "not in effect" for two years. According to the document, the new methodology will: a) give more focus to effectiveness and the jurisdiction's risk and context but only as regards major identified risks; b) require assessments to be more results-orientated and

casinos. Just over half (51%) of countries reviewed demonstrated an average to very good understanding of the risks they faced". Difficulties were also encountered in relation to investigation and prosecution of high-profile cross-border cases and in the prevention of anonymous shell companies and trusts used for illicit purposes, 5, 28 and 48. Also, 2021–2022 FATF Report, 8–9. Simon Young makes a brief comparative analysis in policing and prosecution of ML as regards effectiveness under the 2013 Methodology in which 48 jurisdictions were assessed, choosing three jurisdictions with high ratings and other three with low ratings. In this study, the author recognises the benefits of the exercise (by revealing a "gap between law and practice") but also the 'variation' of the assessors that conduct ME, the lack of information available on how they are selected and the lack of a comprehensive guidance by FATF on how risk should be assessed. 'Policing and Prosecution of Money Laundering' in V. Mitsilegas, S. Hufnagel and A. Moiseienko (eds), *Research Handbook on Transnational Crime* (Edward Elgar Publishing 2019).

372 At: https://www.fatf-gafi.org/publications/fatfgeneral/documents/outcomes-fatf-Plenary-march-2022.html. Also, 2022–2023 FATF Report, 36.

373 2022 FATF Status Report, 49–51. Also, FATF Handout of the 5th Round of ME (April 2022), at: https://www.fatf-gafi.org/media/fatf/documents/methodology/Handout-5th-Round-Methodology.pdf.

focused on specific actions, and c) have shorter ME cycles (from ten to six or seven years).[374]

The on-line document related to the procedures for the next round of ME – 5th Round of ME Procedures, also "not in effect" for two years, displayed some substantial changes.[375] First of all, FATF members for the 5th Round of ME will be scheduled based on risk-related considerations, including the last MER, the general AML/CFT/CPF risks as determined by the FUR (and ICRG, if under review), and the relative size of the economy and financial sector.[376]

Second, 'technical compliance' will be assessed uniquely in relation to "Recommendations under review", ie. legal, regulatory, or operational frameworks in need of improvement based on past assessments (MER, FUR or Technical Compliance Re-Ratings (TCRR)).[377] 'Effectiveness' will be assessed in relation to all eleven Immediate Outcomes.[378]

Third, after the adoption of the MER, a KRA and a KRA Roadmap will be designed setting the core priorities for action and for reducing the AML/CFT/CPF risks based on each jurisdiction's contextual factor. A copy of the KRA Roadmap will be submitted to the "appropriate Minister of the assessed country" and advise will be given as regards "FATF's expectations" in the FURs.[379] The KRA's of jurisdictions will be assessed according to the following scale: 'Fully Addressed', 'Largely Addressed', 'Partly Addressed', and 'Not Addressed'.[380]

Fourth, there are stricter requirements for placing a jurisdiction under enhanced follow-up, namely jurisdictions rated with 5 or more 'PC' for technical compliance (before eight); jurisdictions with 6 or more moderate levels of

---

374 The on-line first version was completed in February 2022, later revised in February 2024 to take into consideration the recent amendments to the Forty Recommendations and INotes, although stating that the "document is not yet in effect". At: https://www.fatf-gafi.org/media/fatf/documents/methodology/5th-Round-Revised-Methodology.pdf (last visited at 15/03/2024). Also, 2022–2023 FATF Report, 36. The document has been in force since May 2024 and publicly available, at: https://www.fatf-gafi.org/en/publications/Mutualevaluations/Assessment-Methodology-2022.html.

375 The on-line version dates from April 2022, stating that the "procedures in this document are not yet in effect". At: https://www.fatf-gafi.org/media/fatf/documents/methodology/5th-Round-Procedures.pdf. The document has been in force since May 2024 and publicly available, at: https://www.fatf-gafi.org/en/publications/Mutualevaluations/5th-Round-Procedures.html.

376 5th Round of ME Procedures, para. 9. Plenary may consider requests on a voluntary basis as well (para. 10).

377 Ibid, para. 72–74.

378 Ibid, para. 82.

379 Ibid, para. 116.

380 Ibid, para. 137. Countries will report 3 years after the adoption of their MER and address all KRA, especially Recommendations rated NC or PC (para. 126).

effectiveness out of 11 Immediate Outcomes (before 7 or more); and jurisdictions with 1 or more low levels of effectiveness out of 11 Immediate Outcomes (before 4 or more) will be signalled.[381]

There is also a proposal to refer a jurisdiction to the ICRG, namely jurisdictions rated with 15 or more 'NC'/'PC' for technical compliance (before 20). Furthermore, the criteria for a FATF or FSRB jurisdiction to nominate a jurisdiction to the ICRG are more detailed and streamlined, comprehending when a jurisdiction's legal and regulatory framework does "not comply with important portions of the FATF Standards"[382] or when does not provide "adequate international co-operation related to AML/CFT/CPF".[383]

Fifth, FATF's public statements are addressed for the *first time* in the ME procedures,[384] which will be of three kinds:

i) A statement announcing that the jurisdiction is under the ICRG review (agreed revised KRA Roadmap), and that it is highly committed to address the identified AML/CFT deficiencies;[385] or

ii) A separate statement calling on members of the Global Network to consider the risks arising from the shortages in the absence of a high-level political undertaking or insufficient progress on the jurisdiction's revised KRA Roadmap ('Grey List'). In this scenario, the FATF will declare the following:

> The FATF calls on its members to advise their financial institutions to apply enhanced due diligence measures proportionate to the risks arising from the deficiencies associated with each jurisdiction as described below.[386]

---

381 Ibid, para. 124.

382 The term "portions" is vague and unclear, it requires clarification.

383 Ibid, para. 150. Although not a new concept, the term "diminished compliance" is introduced. Any delegation or Secretariat cognisant of a situation justifying a decrease in a jurisdiction's compliance ratings equivalent to NC/PC in relation to Recommendations 3, 5, 6, 10, 11 and 20 may address the Plenary for proper action (para. 134–136). See 4th Round of ME Procedures, para. 93.

384 Indeed, there is no reference in the HLPOs, and just briefly mentioned in the Universal Procedures, para. 57.

385 5th Round of ME Procedures, para. 173.

386 Ibid, para 174. As regards enhanced measures, para. 188: "[t]hey will automatically activated if a country fails to fully or largely address all KRA outlined in its KRA Roadmap. These enhanced measures include: a high-level mission to determine political commitment, on-going reporting, and issuance of a FATF public statement, depending on the concrete case, Recommendation 19 may be applied based on risk and proportionality context. Furthermore, the Plenary may also whether the country's FATF membership status should be suspended or withdrawn as outlined in the Internal Governance Principles".

The statement must make clear that it does not intend to call for the countermeasures described in the second part of Recommendation 19;[387] or

iii) A statement calling all jurisdictions of the Global Network to apply the countermeasures under Recommendation 19, if the jurisdiction "continues to fail to provide a high-level political commitment to a revised KRA roadmap or to complete the roadmap".[388]

One novelty worth stressing compared with the previous ME procedure is that the ICRG procedures are "formalised for the first time" and made publicly available.[389] The operation of this WG, with the authority to submit proposals to FATF's Plenary for blacklisting, has been kept secretive and obscure. The process for the 5th Round of ME Procedures acknowledges that this formalisation envisages "greater transparency".[390]

There are now perceptible rules governing: the ICRG decision-making process,[391] the selection, appointment, and term of ICRG Joint Group Co-chairs, the selection and appointment of ICRG lead reviewers,[392] and the appointment of independent ICRG experts, the latter to reinforce the technical nature of the ICRG.[393]

The new methodology – 'Methodology for Assessing Technical Compliance with the FATF Recommendations and Effectiveness of AML/CFT/CPF Systems' and the revised procedures – 'Procedures for the FATF AML/CFT/CPF Mutual Evaluations, Follow-Up and ICRG' for the 5th Round of ME, approved at the

387 The Plenary may provide examples of countermeasures as enumerated in the INote to Recommendation 19.

388 5th Round of ME Procedures, para. 175–176.

389 Annex I of the 2022 FATF Status Report: 'Overview of Changes from the FATF Strategic Review Process', 50.

390 Ibid, the Annex of the Report refers to the "existing ICRG Procedures and Guidelines" which were not public.

391 Ibid, para. 149–172.

392 Ibid, para. 55–56. Eg. clear mandate lengths and composition of joint group rules. As mentioned by Couvée, "But the process has at times struggled for legitimacy, not least because FATF until April of last year disclosed very little about the inner workings of the ICRG, which has power to recommend the addition or removal of countries from the group's blacklist of jurisdictions with significant AML deficiencies and gray list of those subject to 'increased monitoring'", (n 159).

393 Ibid, para. 53–54. Other substantives changes that deserve to be highlighted are the: replacement of the term 'action plan', introduction of new type of experts ('follow-up experts') (para. 48–52), introduction of specific procedures for jurisdictions with supra national context (para. 15–20), and the possibility of two-Plenary reporting cycles for countries under the ICRG's review (para. 170).

FATF Plenary meeting in March 2022, have come into effect, respectively in April and May 2024.[394]

As a consequence, the Universal Procedures were also reviewed to be in accordance with the new requirements and policies for the next round of assessments. FSRBs are required to revise their own internal procedures to align them with the FATF 2023 Universal Procedures and to apply the FATF ME Procedures or similar procedures.[395] As explained in the new Universal Procedures:

> When the Universal Procedures are updated, eg., after the FATF Procedures are changed, all FSRBs' evaluation procedures should be updated within a reasonable amount of time and will be checked against the updated Universal Procedures.[396]

The document 'Universal Procedures 2023' states that it was adopted in October 2023, however it was only made public available in May 2024 and also updated on that date. At the FATF Plenary meeting in October 2023, it was announced that the "FATF agreed to a comprehensive set of procedures that all relevant assessment bodies (…) will use to assess countries' compliance with the FATF Standards in the next round of mutual evaluations",[397] namely FSRBs and FIs.

Mutual Evaluations that are still under the 4th Round of ME will continue to use the 2013 Methodology and respective procedures. The 5th Round will begin in April 2025, with Belgium and Malaysia being the first members to be assessed under the new methodology.[398]

This new 2025 reporting cycle focusing on high-risks and effectiveness will be extremely difficult to implement, particularly to FSRBs' jurisdictions that are already handling with low effectiveness rates, which is visible in the 2022 FATF Status Report. Risk factors and risk contexts should be clearly defined to facilitate the interpretation and application of the criteria by all stakeholders, especially assessors when conducting ME assessments. Flexibility should also be accorded to the specific context of low or medium capacity-building jurisdictions.

394 At: https://www.fatf-gafi.org/en/publications/Fatfgeneral/Outcomes-fatf-plenary-march-2022.html.

395 Para. 1–2 of the 2023 Universal Procedures (May 2024).

396 Ibid, para. 2.

397 At: https://www.fatf-gafi.org/en/publications/Fatfgeneral/outcomes-fatf-plenary-october-2023.html.

398 At: https://www.fatf-gafi.org/en/calendars/assessments.html (last visited 15/04/2024).

7.2 *Sanctioning Power: 'Name and Shame' Policy and Countermeasures*

The FATF monitoring process is complemented by another ongoing enhanced monitoring mechanism for jurisdictions that demonstrate serious deficiencies in their national AML/CFT/CPF regimes, thus posing a threat to the international financial system. This enhanced mechanism includes a 'name and shame' policy (blacklisting) and calls on jurisdictions for the application of countermeasures.[399]

The logic of this process is straightforward, as described by Nance:

> The internal logic is reasonable. FATF names States or jurisdictions that are non-compliant, signalling to market actors that transactions with institutions in those jurisdictions may be subject to additional scrutiny by the blacklisting States. This potential added difficulty compels market actors to either divest currently held assets or avoid new transactions in targeted countries, which harms the targeted jurisdiction's economy. Targets, or would-be targets, comply with FATF's standards to avoid that fate.[400]

The fear of losing reputation *vis-à-vis* compliance is also underpin by Saby Ghoshray:

> [D]espite the traditional lack of institutional imprimatur of soft law, the FATF publication process of blacklisting countries introduced a unique dimension of coerced compulsion. Via the associative dynamics of

---

399 Amongst others, Brigitte Unger and Joras Ferwerda, 'Regulating Money Laundering and Tax Havens: The Role of Blacklisting (2008) Utrecht School of Economics, Tjalling C. Koopmans Research Institute, Discussion Paper Series 08–12 at: https://www.uu.nl/sites/default/files/rebo_use_dp_2008_08-12.pdf; Rainer Hülsse, 'Even Clubs Can't Do Without Legitimacy: Why the Anti-Money Laundering Blacklist Was suspended' (2008) 2(4) *Regulation & Governance*. Louis de Koker, John Howell and Nicholas Morr make a comprehensive description of FATF's backlisting process, acknowledging that this process "has changed over time and distinguish four broad periods reflecting different messaging." The authors divide the process into four periods: Period I from 2000 to 2006 (NCCT); Period II from 2007 to 2009 (transition period); Period III from 2010 to 2015 (initial stage of the ICRG); Period IV from 2011 onwards (consolidation period and greatest impact on backlisted jurisdictions). 'Economic Consequences of Greylisting by the Financial Action Task Force' (2023) 11 *Risks*.

400 (n 46), 133. The 2021 IMF Paper on the 'Impact of Gray-Listing on Capital Flows: An Analysis Using Machine Learning' reveals that there is a real impact in capital inflows of jurisdictions that are grey-listed (Working Paper Mizuho Kida and Simon Paetzold).

> conformance and reputational injury, the social nature of the FATF has transformed into a legal paradigm.[401]

In 1999, the FATF realised that its mission would be ineffective unless all jurisdictions around the world implemented identical high-level AML standards into their national systems; otherwise, the organisation's efforts to promote a sound and transparent international financial system would be in vain. In its 1999–2000 Report, the FATF remarked:

> Recent years have seen a considerable increase in the number of jurisdictions which offer financial services without appropriate regulation or control, coupled with very strict banking secrecy. Over the last ten years, many countries have developed measures to combat money laundering. However, any weak link in international arrangements jeopardises the entire international financial system.[402]

An ambitious strategy had to be devised with a particular emphasis on non-FATF members and an all-encompassing application of the Recommendations in mind. In the first phase, jurisdictions were 'encouraged' to endorse and adopt FATF's Standards, and to be part of an FSRB.[403] In the second phase, irrespectively of being a FATF or a non-FATF member, an FSRB member or a non-FSRB member, jurisdictions would be assessed, monitored and subject to countermeasures in case their AML/CFT rules and practices impaired the setting up and maintenance of a transparent international financial system.[404]

As explained in the 1999–2000 FATF Report:

> [I]t is increasingly desirable that all financial centres across the world have comprehensive controls, regulations and supervisory arrangements in place and that all financial agents assume anti-money laundering obligations (…) [I]n the shorter term, it would be appropriate for all countries or territories forming part of the international financial system to amend

401 'Compliance Convergence in FATF Rulemaking: The Conflict Between Agency Capture and Soft Law' (2014/2015) 59(3) *New York Law School Law Review*, 542.

402 Para. 76.

403 Ibid, para. 77.

404 1997–1998 FATF Report, para. 14. See 1999–2000 FATF Report, para. 75: "Since the end of 1998, the FATF has embarked on substantive work on the problems raised by countries and territories which do not co-operate in the combat of money laundering". Also, 2000–2001 FATF Report, para. 48; 2005–2006 FATF Report, para. 47.

their rules and practices which hamper anti-money laundering measures conducted in other countries.[405]

7.2.1 Non-Cooperative Countries and Territories

This initiative started in 1998 by setting an *Ad-Hoc* Group on NCCT to assist FATF's Plenary in terms of criteria and methodology to identify jurisdictions "whose detrimental rules and practices seriously and unjustifiably hamper the fight against money laundering"[406] and what sort of actions should be taken against them.[407] The supervision scope included "all major financial centres, offshore or onshore" centres, whether they were FATF members or not.[408]

The Initial NCCT Report (14 of February 2000) established 25 requirements to meet the agreed criteria, defined the methodology, and distinguished three

405 Para. 77.

406 Initial NCCT Report (14/02/2000), para. 38; 2001–2002 FATF Report, para. 69–70; 2004–2005 FATF Report, para. 37. The *Ad-Hoc* Group was backed by four regional groups (Americas, Asia/Pacific, Europe, Africa and Middle East), 1999–2000 FATF Report, para. 70. Also, 2002–2003 FATF Report, para. 116. This exercise was well received at the G-7 Leaders Statement: The Okinawa Summit 2000, para. 26. According to Nance, who provides an historical background of FATF's blacklisting process: "States initially rejected blacklists, but as described in the Annual Report (1996), developed them in response to the perception that continued non-compliance by Turkey and Austria was 'clearly damaging' their efforts. Members developed the NCCT process in reaction to the move by Seychelles to profit from money laundering", (n 46) 142–143. Also, Nance, 'Naming and Shaming in Financial Regulation: Explaining Variation in the Financial Action Task Force on Money Laundering' in H.R. Friman (ed), *The Politics of Leverage in International Relations – Name, Shame and Sanction* (Palgrave Macmillan 2015), 128–133.

407 1999–2000 FATF Report, para. 10, 78–82; 2001–2002 FATF Report, para. 69; 2004–2005 FATF Report, para. 37; 30 Years FATF Report, 63. Guy Stessens contends that the FATF's reviewing mechanism is far stricter than the one conducted by the OECD in the context of harmful tax practices, classifying the NCCT exercise as the "most drastic measure so far taken to as part of the FATF strategy to spread the recommendations geographically". The author critically comments that the FATF is focused on jurisdictions external to its 'group', neglecting an unbiased analysis towards its members, a circumstance that shakes significantly FATF's credibility, like the British or French offshores. 'The FATF 'Black List' of Non-Cooperative Countries or Territories' (2001) 14 *Leiden Journal of International Law*. For an overview of the NCCT process, amongst others, Jesse Morgan, 'Dirty Names, Dangerous Money: Alleged Unilateralism in US Policy on Money Laundering' (2003) 21(3) *Berkeley Journal of International Law*; Nance, ibid. Broome provides a clear picture of the NCCT process and its background, as well as its inconsistencies and the causes for its suspension, (n 6) 65–66, 556–558, 565–568. Karen Bravo also addresses in detail the NCCT list, 'Follow the Money? Does the International Fight Against Money Laundering Provide a Model for International Anti-Trafficking Efforts?' (2008) 6(1) *University of St. Thomas Law Journal*.

408 1999–2000 FATF Report, para. 78; 2000–2001 FATF Report, para. 49.

categories for which a jurisdiction could be classified as NCCT.[409] Each category according to the levels of non-compliance would "trigger different degrees of action":

i) Clearly non-cooperative (severe deficiencies in many areas);
ii) Partly non-cooperative (impediments in various areas); and
iii) *De facto* non-cooperative (no significant impediments in laws and regulations but ineffective regime in practice).[410]

The selection method was based on members experience and data (law enforcement intelligence, sharing of financial information, international cooperation) and financial factors related to AML investigations (eg. jurisdiction bank secrecy laws or vulnerability of the financial sector to criminal activities), and the difficulties encountered to collect information following a proposal from a member. Any of these factors could lead to a fact-finding survey by the *Ad-Hoc* Group, and FATF Secretariat's input for further review.[411]

The chosen jurisdiction would be notified and invited to provide information and feedback ("right to reply") in relation to the findings in the draft report.[412] Face-to-face meetings to discuss the final draft would be undertaken until the adoption of the report by the FATF Plenary. These reports remained confidential, and the jurisdiction's name would only become public through the NCCT list.[413]

Any jurisdiction inserted in the NCCT list would be "encouraged to adopt constructive anti-money laundering action" to overcome the identified deficiencies.[414] In this respect, Emmanuel Ebikake comments:

> Non-cooperative governments have found themselves under heavy moral, political and economic pressure to be up to standard through the reviews. For example, Austria eventually agreed to prohibit anonymous

409 1999–2000 FATF Report, para. 79; 2002–2003 FATF Report, para. 115. Also reproduced in the Appendix of the 2000 NCCT Review Report (First Review).

410 Initial NCCT Report, para. 38.

411 Ibid, para. 39–40. Jurisdictions' inability to provide information or having legislation that precluded mutual legal assistance resulted in being placed in the NCCT list (2004–2005 FATF Report, para. 38).

412 2005 NCCT Review Report (Sixth Review), para. 80: To ensure a fair process, "in addition to electronic exchanges and letters, the reviewed jurisdictions were invited to comment on the draft NCCT reports, and their views were considered by the review group. The countries were also invited to present their cases in person during face-to-face meetings. All these steps took place before the presentation of the draft reports to the Plenary.".

413 Ibid, para. 81.

414 1999–2000 FATF Report, para. 81; Initial NCCT Report, para. 44–47.

> savings accounts as a result of pressure from the FATF, and the States of Eastern Europe and the former Soviet Union (including Russia) have embarked upon urgent national legislative programmes in a very short space of time as a result of their inclusion on the Non-Cooperative Countries and Territories (NCCT) List.[415]

De-listing would require a jurisdiction to address all shortfalls and to demonstrate that sound reforms are in place and/or being put into practice.[416] As stated in the 1999–2000 FATF Report: "the ideal course would obviously be for non-co-operative jurisdictions to adopt laws and regulations to bring them into compliance with the Forty FATF Recommendations and to ensure they are effectively implemented".[417]

Notwithstanding only conducting two rounds of nominations under the NCCT exercise, respectively 2000 and 2001,[418] the FATF assessed 47 jurisdictions and listed 23 jurisdictions during seven years. By the end of 2007, these jurisdictions were no longer blacklisted due to the recognition of "substantial legal reforms", which increased "their capacity to co-operate at the international level in the fight against money laundering and terrorist financing".[419]

Collective action for the application of countermeasures under Recommendation 21 (2003 FATF Recommendations)[420] would be conducted in a "gradual, proportionate and flexible manner" depending on the case,[421]

415 'Money Laundering: An Assessment of Soft Law as a Technique for Repressive and Preventive Anti-Money Laundering Control' (DPhil Thesis, Liverpool John Moores University, 17/05/2021), 188, at: https://researchonline.ljmu.ac.uk/id/eprint/16216/1/THE%20THESIS.pdf.

416 2000–2001 FATF Report, para. 52; Initial NCCT Report, para. 44–47.

417 1999–2000 FATF Report, para. 82; Initial NCCT Report, para. 49.

418 Fifteen in 2000 and 8 in 2001. At: https://www.fatf-gafi.org/en/publications/Fatfgeneral/Aboutthenon-cooperativecountriesandterritoriesncctinitiative.html.

419 2004–2005 FATF Report, para. 38 and 52; 2005–2006 FATF Report, para. 47; 2007–2008 FATF Report, para. 51–54. But still considered as a 'priority item' in following plenaries, see 2002–2003 FATF Report, para. 118; 2004–2005 FATF Report, para. 35–36.

420 Recommendation 21: FIs should give special attention to business relationships and transactions with persons, including companies and financial institutions, from countries which do not or insufficiently apply the FATF Recommendations. Whenever these transactions have no apparent economic or visible lawful purpose, their background and purpose should, as far as possible, be examined, the findings established in writing, and be available to help competent authorities. Where such a country continues not to apply or insufficiently applies the FATF's Recommendations, countries should be able to apply appropriate countermeasures.

421 Eg. failure to apply or poor application of the FATF Recommendations or failure to address deficiencies or to demonstrate progress in their AML/CFT system. See, 2000–2001 FATF Report, para. 54; 2002–2003 FATF Report, para. 121; 2004–2005 FATF Report, para. 40.

regardless of members' ability to implement countermeasures individually.[422] The countermeasures could range from enhanced CDD measures to financial institutions to conditioning, restricting, targeting or even prohibiting financial transactions with a NCCT.[423]

According to the FATF, the NCCT exercise was successful[424] and proved to be a "very useful and efficient tool",[425] which contributed to the improvement of the "AML/CFT regimes of more than 20 countries",[426] as well as to the safety and integrity of the international financial market. This exercise also influenced the development of some Recommendations because of the loopholes, inadequacies or ambiguities that were discovered during its course.[427] The first NCCT Review Report was published in June 2000 and the last one in October 2007.[428]

However, this 'name and shame' policy and ability to call for countermeasures were not exempt from strong and wide criticism from IOs, such as the IMF and WB,[429] academics and professionals,[430] in which inconsistencies, double standards and selection bias were highlighted. Todd Doyle describes this process as "extraterritorial bullying", a highly intrusive and direct interference in jurisdictions' national strategies.[431]

---

422 Initial NCCT Report, para. 20.

423 Ibid, para. 50–54.

424 2006–2007 FATF Report, para. 45; 2007–2008 FATF Report, para. 52.

425 2005–2006 FATF Report, para. 47; 2005 NCCT Report, para. 79.

426 2007 NCCT Review Report (Eight Review), para. 4–7.

427 Eg. BO in relation to legal persons, bearer shares or CDD measures for intermediaries (2005 NCCT Report, para. 82).

428 At: https://www.fatf-gafi.org/en/publications/Fatfgeneral/Aboutthenon-cooperative-countriesandterritoriesncctinitiative.html.

429 2002 IMF Press Release (08/08/2002): 'IMF Advance Efforts to Combat ML and TF Directors' Views on the NCCT Exercise, its Suspension and Compatibility with Risk-Based Reports on the Observance of Standards and Codes (ROSC) Principles'. At https://www.imf.org/en/News/Articles/2015/09/28/04/53/pn0287.

430 Amongst others, Todd Doyle, 'Cleaning Up Anti-Money Laundering Strategies: Current FATF Tactics Needlessly Violate International Law (Financial Action Task Force)' (2002) 24(2) *Houston Journal of International Law*. Broome mentions IMF's and WB's pressure and refusal to cooperate with the FATF while the NCCT list was in place, (n 6) 66 and 568–569. Also, Nance (n 46) 142 and (n 406), 138. Hülsse explains in detail why the list was suspended and considered illegitimate, (n 399) 462–466. Koker, Howell and Morris also mention that the "NCCT listing process did not follow a comprehensive compliance assessment of each country", (n 399) 4.

431 Ibid, 281. The author claims that "in an effort to encourage constructive [anti-money laundering] action (...) the FATF has threatened an economic embargo of any recalcitrant State refusing to mend its wayward ways. This development is disturbing and suggests a policy redolent of extraterritorial bullying. From a policy perspective, economic sanctions have a history of negatively impacting the general populace without accomplishing

In line with these concerns, Karen Bravo writes in relation to Caribbean countries:

> The standards were formulated by a non-representative body – that is, no input from the countries that would be subject to those standards. The project was intended to force non-member States and jurisdictions with deficient anti-money laundering systems to create new legislation by adopting a 'name-and-shame' device – in the form of the published list of non-compliant jurisdictions – and by encouraging FATF members to take actions to convince NCCTs of the importance of adopting such legislation.[432]

Jared Wessel also outlines the Caribbean case (eg. Cayman Islands' placed in the NCCT list in June 2002), claiming lack of due process and duality of standards:

> Caribbean nations argued that European jurisdictions, specifically Austria and Monaco, were allowed to negotiate compliance agreements that kept them off the NCCT. In contrast, Caribbean jurisdictions were forced to work under the name-and-shame rubric of the NCCT while similarly situated European jurisdictions were allowed to stay off the list by implementing domestic legislation that the Caribbean areas would have enacted if given the chance.[433]

Despite conceding that the NCCT list "had the unintentional effect of straining the relationship between the FATF and the FATF-Style Regional

---

the desired effects upon the behaviour of those for whom the sanctions were intended". Moreover, Doyle contends that FATF's blacklist violates international law to the extent that it contravenes "the letter and the spirit of the Forty Recommendations", concluding in high critical note that the "NCCT [process] went too far", 279 and 298.

432 At: 19. The author argues that "most part, Caribbean countries have complied with the regulations established regarding money laundering, but they have had to do so because if they did not, economic disaster would result -their economies simply are not strong enough to survive for long while under siege from the world powers". Bravo also criticises the FATF's intrusive method of compelling sovereign States to change their domestic law in accordance with the Standards, without voting rights. 'Challenges to the Caribbean Economic Sovereignty in a Globalising World' (2011) *Michigan State University College of Law Journal of International Law*, 40–41.

433 'Financial Action Task Force: A Study in Balancing the Sovereignty with Equality in Global Administrative Law' (2006/2007) 13(1) *Widener Law Review*, 181.

Bodies",[434] the FATF only suspended the NCCT exercise in 2007. It is believed that the pressure from the IMF and WB for its suspension was decisive in the elimination of the NCCT list, most likely as one of the IFIs conditions for continuing to collaborate with the FATF and strengthen co-operation.[435]

7.2.2 The FATF's Grey and Black Lists

The NCCT exercise was replaced for a new mechanism in 2007, which consists in identifying high-risk jurisdictions that pose a threat to the international financial system and, whenever adequate, to take "firm action when a country chooses not to engage with the appropriate FSRB or the FATF or to reform its systems".[436] However, it also envisages assistance and permanent dialogue with jurisdictions. This mechanism can be seen as a response to a quest for more transparency, impartiality, mutual collaboration and shared responsibility.

The ICRG was thus set up to continue the FATF's ongoing monitoring function by introducing novel rules and procedures to identify, monitor and assist jurisdictions that are vulnerable to financial criminal activities, including proposing concrete actions to jurisdictions with systemic AML/CFT deficiencies or that are not in compliance.[437] It also recommends jurisdictions for listing

434 2000–2001 FATF Report, para. 55. Notwithstanding the elimination of the NCCT list, the FATF re-assured its "vigilance" and ability to act without hesitations, if necessary (2007–2008 FATF Report, para. 540). Also, 25 Years Report, 18.

435 2004 IMF Press Release (02/04/2004): 'IMF Executive Board Reviews and Enhances Efforts for AML and CFT'. It is clearly stated: "some Directors expressed concern that the FATF had left open the possibility of further rounds of the NCCT exercise, and noted that if the FATF were to resume the NCCT exercise, the Fund would need to reconsider collaboration with the FATF, as the exercise is at odds with the uniform, voluntary, and cooperative nature of the Risk-Based Reports on the Observance of Standards and Codes (ROSC) exercise. They indicated that the suspension of the exercise should continue to be a condition for the Fund's joint work". At: https://www.imf.org/en/News/Articles/2015/09/28/04/53/pn0433. Also, in this respect, 2011 IMF Paper on 'Anti-Money Laundering and Combating the Financing of Terrorism (AML/CFT) Review on the Effectiveness of the Program', para. 14–17, (2011 IMF Paper AML/CFT Review). Amongst others, Hülsse and Dieter Kerwer explained that IFIs request was "based on the argument that it violates the principles of how international regulators should function" and that although using benchmarking and peer review to improve participation, the FATF also needed "to take into consideration the rules of the game of global governance" since there is a certain "institutionalised environment", 'How International Organizations Rule the World: the Case of the Financial Action Task Force' (2011) 2(1) *Journal of International Organisations Studies*, 59.

436 2007–2008 FATF Report, para. 8. Also, 2018–2019 FATF Report, 54.

437 25 Years FATF Report, 18; 30 Years FATF Report, 65.

or de-listing and advises the FATF Plenary on steps to be taken, which are reflected in FATF's public statements after each FATF Plenary meeting.[438]

This blacklisting mechanism was strengthened following the G-20's endorsement of the FATF at the G-20 Pittsburgh Summit in 2009 "to reinvigorate its process for assessing countries' compliance with international AML/CFT standards and to publicly identify high-risk jurisdictions by February 2010".[439] This request served as an additional stimulus for the 2012 revision of the Recommendations and the related 2013 Methodology.[440]

In 2015, the ICRG procedures were also revised to align with the new standards and methodology, though there is no information on the terms of the update and little information on its internal proceedings as previous noted.[441]

Built on the principle of co-operation and interaction between the FATF, FSRBs and nominated jurisdiction, the ICRG process is more inclusive, partnership-oriented, and transparent than the NCCT, offering the nominated jurisdiction higher scrutiny and means of defense. Co-operation and dialogue are pursued constructively.[442]

The blacklisting process is also a reflection of the dynamics of the international scenario and its agents, as outlined by Nance:

> They developed the ICRG process in 2007 as a synthesis model, merging the member and the NCCT processes in light of protests from FATF members, targets of the NCCT process, and, most importantly, the World Bank and IMF, who refused to co-operate with FATF while the NCCT process was still in place (…) There is a clear pattern within the blacklisting process, a process that many see as vital to FATF's operation, whereby members alter it in light of perceptions about the challenges of implementation.[443]

438 There are three statements every year – February, June and October.

439 G-20 Leaders Statement: The Pittsburgh Summit 2009, para. 15. Also, 2009–2010 FATF Report, 28–29; 2010–2011 FATF Report, 20.

440 2017–2018 FATF Report, 53.

441 There is no information on this matter in the 2014–2015 FATF Report or 2015–2016 FATF Report. Brief background, at: https://www.fatf-gafi.org/publications/high-risk-and-other-monitored-jurisdictions/more/more-on-high-risk-and-non-cooperative-jurisdictions.html?hf=10&b=0&s=desc(fatf_releasedate).

442 Regional Groups from Africa/Middle East, the Americas, Asia/Pacific, and Europe/Eurasia work together with the ICRG in carrying out the reviews and supporting the target jurisdiction within their region. 2018–2019 FATF Report, 57; 30 Years FATF Report, 66.

443 (n 46) 142.

Normally, a jurisdiction will be under the ICRG review following a weak MER result, namely if it has 20 or more 'NC' or 'PC' ratings for technical compliance, or it is rated 'NC/PC' on 3 or more of Recommendations 3, 5, 6, 10,11, and 20, or if it has a low or moderate level of effectiveness for 9 or more of the 11 Immediate Outcomes, with a minimum of 2 lows or it has a low level of effectiveness for 6 or more of the 11 Immediate Outcomes (Section 7.1. above).[444]

A jurisdiction will be automatically under the review of the ICRG if it does not participate in an FSRB, or if it does not allow the ME results to be published in a timely manner, or if is nominated by a FATF or an FSRB member due to a specific ML, TF or PF risk or threat, as mentioned.

Being under the ICRG review means that designated-jurisdictions will be constantly monitored, in which the FATF will develop action plans to overcome the identified AML/CFT deficiencies with strict timelines, ongoing reporting and face-to-face meetings.[445] Additionally, a *high-level political commitment* is requested by the FATF as a *sine qua non* condition that the jurisdiction is willing and fully committed to implement the required legal, regulatory and operational reforms.[446]

Jurisdictions under the ICRG process may be identified as "Jurisdictions under Increased Monitoring" list (previously called 'Improving Global AML/CFT Compliance: Ongoing process'), also known as the 'Grey List',[447] being subject to the above measures.[448] If the results are not satisfactory or meaningful progress is not achieved based on the agreed "milestones and timelines",[449] jurisdictions will be classified as 'high-risk'.

Jurisdictions nominated as 'High-Risk Jurisdictions subject to a Call for Action' (previously called 'Public Statement'),[450] also known as the 'Black List',[451] indicates that the jurisdiction reveals a level of risk, vulnerability or detected deficiencies that requires members to adopt *enhanced due diligence measures* against the nominated jurisdiction.

444 2017–2018 FATF Report, 53; 2018–2019 FATF Report, 57; 30 Years FATF Report, 64.

445 2017–2018 FATF Report, 54.

446 30 Years FATF Report, 66.

447 This change occurred in 2019. Also, 2018–2019 FATF Report, 58–59; 2019–2020 FATF Report, 37.

448 Jurisdictions under the ICRG Review are subject to a one-year observation period to work together with the FATF and/or its FSRB to overcome deficiencies before a public identification and formal review by the FATF, 2018–2019 FATF Report, 57.

449 2016–2017 FATF Report, 39–40; 30 Years FATF Report, 65.

450 This change occurred in 2019. See 2018–2019 FATF Report, 58–59; 2019–2020 FATF Report, 37.

451 2019–2020 FATF Report, 37.

These measures should be proportional to the identified risk or deficiency, and may include obtaining additional information on the customer, on the source of funds and on the source of wealth of the customer, as well as enhanced monitoring of the business relationship.[452]

If jurisdictions show "serious, longstanding strategic deficiencies" and fail to make progress, *specific countermeasures* may be applied pursuant to Recommendation 19, ranging from enhanced due diligence and systematic reporting of transactions involving the jurisdiction, to a limitation or prohibition of financial transactions with the nominated jurisdiction.[453]

In all circumstances, jurisdictions within the Global Network should be able to implement the specific measures against the nominated jurisdiction when urged to do so by the FATF.[454]

To be removed from ICRG's mechanism and be placed in normal follow-up process, the jurisdiction has to demonstrate it has addressed substantially "all the components of its action plan" and that it is deeply committed to undergo the necessary reforms to build a sound AML/CFT/CPF framework.[455]

Jason Sharman mentions that this blacklisting process is a powerful tool in global governance, generating not only *post compliance*, after being blacklisted with the logical reputational damages and material economic losses but also *pre-emptive compliance*, where jurisdictions endeavour efforts anticipating blacklisting.[456]

Throughout almost two decades, Iran[457] and the Democratic People's Republic of Korea (DPRK)[458] have been blacklisted and subject to a series of public statements and calls for countermeasures.

In 2016, Iran provided a high-level undertaking to address its AML/CFT deficiencies, which resulted in the suspension of the countermeasures in the succeeding years.[459] However, due to Iran's lack of progress in certain outstanding

452 2017–2018 FATF Report, 54–55; 2018–2019 FATF Report, 58–59.

453 Ibid.

454 2017–2018 FATF Report, 55. Under INotes to Recommendations 10 and 19, it is the responsibility of each country to implement the measures deemed to be necessary. Also, FATF's website: At: https://www.fatf-gafi.org/en/publications/High-risk-and-other-monitored-jurisdictions/Call-for-action-february-2024.html.

455 2016–2017 Report, 40–41; 2018–2019 FATF Report, 57.

456 'The Bark is the Bite: International Organizations and Blacklisting' (2009) 16(4) *Review of International Political Economy*.

457 2008–2009 FATF Report, 17; 2009–2010 FATF Report, 28–29; 2011–2012 FATF Report, 30; 2016–2017 FATF Report, 39–40.

458 2011–2012 FATF Report, 21; 2016–2017 FATF Report, 39–40.

459 2015–2016 FATF Report, 40; 2016–2017 FATF Report, 40; 2017–2018 FATF Report, 56.

requirements, the countermeasures were called back in 2019 and remained since.[460]

The DPRK was identified as a high-risk jurisdiction with strategic AML/CFT deficiencies in 2011, and has been on the 'Black List' since then. A specific public statement was issued in 2017 in relation to the risks of proliferation of WMD and PF following relevant UNSCRs.[461]

In October 2022, at FATF's Plenary meeting, Myanmar became the third country to be added to the 'Black List'.[462] After a series of unsuccessful appeals for Myanmar to comply with the FATF (ICRG) action plan, which ended in September 2021, the FATF decided to "call on its members and other jurisdictions" to apply *enhanced due diligence measures* to business relations and transactions with Myanmar.[463]

Enhanced measures applied to Myanmar must be proportional to the risk, without undermining NPO funding for humanitarian assistance, or any NPO legitimate activity and money remittances.[464] Unlike Iran and DPRK, the FATF does not requests the application of *specific countermeasures* against Myanmar.

According to the 2022–2023 FATF Report, from June 2007 to June 2023, the organisation conducted 125 reviews and publicly identified 101 jurisdictions; of these, 72 have made significant reforms to address their AML/CFT weaknesses and have been removed from the review process.[465]

As of February 2024, there are 21 jurisdictions on the 'Grey List', with Barbados, Gibraltar, Uganda, UAE removed (October 2023) and Kenya and Namibia added,[466] and three jurisdictions in the 'Black List' (Iran, DPRK and Myanmar).[467]

---

460 2018–2019 FATF Report, 56; 2019–2020 FATF Report, 39; 2022–2023 FATF Report, 41. More on Chapter 4, Section 5.

461 2018–2019 FATF Report, 55–56; 2019–2020 FATF Report, 38; 2022–2023 FATF Report, 41 More on Chapter 4, Section 5.

462 At: https://www.fatf-gafi.org/publications/high-risk-and-other-monitored-jurisdictions/documents/call-for-action-october-2022.html.

463 Ibid.

464 Ibid.

465 At: 39. The FATF considers this process to be a "very successful tool to safeguard the integrity of the global financial system", 25 Years Report, 18.

466 Bulgaria, Burkina Faso, Cameroon, Croatia, Democratic Republic of Congo, Haiti, Jamaica, Kenya, Mali, Mozambique, Namibia, Nigeria, Philippines, Senegal, South Africa, South Sudan, Syria, Tanzania, Turkey, Vietnam and Yemen. At: https://www.fatf-gafi.org/en/publications/High-risk-and-other-monitored-jurisdictions/Increased-monitoring-february-2024.html. See October 'Grey List', at: https://www.fatf-gafi.org/en/publications/High-risk-and-other-monitored-jurisdictions/Increased-monitoring-october-2023.html.

467 Although inserted on the 'Black List', Myanmar is only subject to enhanced due diligence. At:https://www.fatf-gafi.org/en/publications/High-risk-and-other-monitored-jurisdictions/Call-for-action-february-2024.html.

Amidst the Covid-19 pandemic crisis, jurisdictions under review were afforded flexibility in reporting and timelines, which consequently resulted in a lengthier assessment. An additional fact pertains to the lack of information concerning certain jurisdictions. The FATF Statement of February 2024 calling for countermeasures against Iran and DPRK expressly indicates that it is based on its Statement of February 2020 (including data), which originates an unusual circumstance of not reflecting changes or progress achieved, if any, in their AML/CFT/CPF regimes.[468] This circumstance bears obvious socio-economic costs (Chapter 5, Section 2 below).

7.3 *Technical Assistance*

Another key component of the FATF activity and deeply associated with the ME is the provision of technical assistance to jurisdictions that have low AML/CFT capacity and a "less mature AML/CFT/CPF framework".[469] Indeed, the ME process also helps to better identify and assess jurisdictions' needs, being a valuable background tool (information) for jurisdictions and donors to determine priorities and strategic areas of intervention and burden-sharing.[470]

Technical assistance may be provided by the FATF and/or its members,[471] and/or in partnership with other IOs, such as the IMF, WB or UN. As declared by the Ministers in April 2022:

> We continue to foster the effective implementation of the FATF Standards in the wider Global Network through individual FATF members offering

468 Reference is made to the fact that although it submitted a report in January 2024, no substantial progress has been achieved by Iran, such as the application of the International Convention for the Suppression of the Financing of Terrorism or Palermo Convention. Ibid.

469 The 2009–2010 FATF Report states: "The provision of technical assistance, in particular in drafting laws and regulations, and adapting bank supervisory and law enforcement authorities' structures. This could be provided by individual task force members, or by the secretariat, within the limits of its resources", 1990–1991 FATF Report, 3–4 and 18. A special module related to Low Capacity Countries (LCCs) was designed by the FATF together with the IMF and the WB for assessors training to address jurisdictions "with severe capacity constraints", 21–22. Also, 2015–2016 FATF Report, 21.

470 2011 IMF Paper AML/CFT Review (n 435) para. 11. The UNSC also refers to the MERs as an assessment tool to understand technical assistance needs (eg. op.para. 102 of UNSCR 2610 (2021)).

471 2000–2001 FATF Report, para. 53; 2004–2005 FATF Report, para. 39.

> technical assistance and engaging in other international *fora*, including by the G-20 and G-7, to shore up political will. We call on the IMF, the World Bank, the United Nations and multilateral technical assistance providers to increase their capacity building to support these efforts.[472]

In 2016, a Training and Research Institute (TREIN) was set up in Busan, Korea with the aim of offering "training and research programmes, workshops, seminars and other events" to assist AML/CFT/CPF capacity building of FATF's and FSRBs jurisdictions.[473] This Training Institute has a broad reach targeting government officials, assessors and reviewers, and the private sector from all over the Global Network.[474] Webinars have been conducted on a regular basis by the FATF on a wide range of topics providing an opportunity to enhance capacity-building, information sharing and expertise.[475]

An e-learning platform for specialised training (intermediate and advanced levels) and basic knowledge about the FATF and its ME process and the 'FATF @cademy' targeting officials across the FATF Global Network were launched, respectively in 2019 and mid-2020.[476] Both initiatives are particularly relevant at a time when on-site training options were extremely limited due to COVID-19.[477]

The TREIN in Busan contributes to the expansion of the FATF's outreach activities to the Asia-Pacific Region and it is a hub for learning and training. According to the 2022–2023 FATF Report, 316 professionals attended Standard Training Courses and 1,847 professionals benefit from e-learning courses during that year. Furthermore, new courses have been launched such as the 'Train the Trainer' or 'ICRG Reviewer Training'.[478]

472 2022 Ministerial Declaration, para. 11.

473 2015–2016 FATF Report, 21; 30 Years FATF Report, 22; 2020–2021 FATF Report, 64–65.

474 Ibid. Also, 2020–2021 FATF Report, 65; 2022–2023 FATF Report, 46–48.

475 More at: https://www.fatf-gafi.org/publications/?hf=10&b=0&q=webinar&s=desc(fatf_releasedate).

476 The 2020–2021 FATF Report refers: "The FATF's e-learning platform for the Global Network membership has been a great success. The FATF Training Institute in Busan, Korea has completed a number of virtual courses, including with experts from FATF-style regional bodies (FSRBS) GIABA, ESAAMLG, the Eurasian Group and others", 65. The FATF @cademy is also available to FSRBs Secretariats and FATF Observers. At: FATF.e-learning@fatf-gafi.org.

477 2019–2020 FATF Report, 47; 2020–2021 FATF Report, 64–65.

478 At: 46–49.

8 The FATF Regional Bodies

As mentioned, the FATF's *octopus-effect* network comprises to this date nine regional bodies that were gradually established from 1992 (CFATF) until 2004 (EAG and MENAFATF). Despite their differences, all regional bodies are jointly committed to FATF's standards and policies, as well as to ensuring and monitoring their implementation within their respective regions.

As it is described below, the large majority of the FSRBs are formal IOs, regardless of the format of their founding legal instrument. The EAG is treaty-based, whereas MONEYVAL, GIABA and GABAC are organs created under the auspices of formal IOs (the CoE, the Economic Community of West African States (ECOWAS) and the Economic and Monetary Community of Central Africa (CEMAC), respectively).

The CFATF and the GAFILAT, though established via less formal legal instruments (Memorandum of Understanding (MoU)),[479] are endowed with international legal personality, as expressly stated in the respective Headquarters Agreements or Privileges and Immunities Agreements.

The ESAAMLG was also created through a MoU, but nothing is mentioned about its legal nature. It is set up for an indefinite period and its foundational norms, including the requirements to enter into effect (only after member States "have signed and advised the President that their constitutional requirements have been satisfied")[480] and to withdrawal (only "take effect three months after receipt by the Secretariat of written notice of intention to withdraw")[481] are formally consistent with the Vienna Convention on the Law of Treaties (VCLT).

Both APG and MENAFATF assert that their legal status is informal. The MENAFATF was created through a MoU, with fewer formal requirements than the ESAAMLG and has no limited term.[482] The APG was established by a Declaration and is subject to a time-limit. Of the two FSRBs, the APG has closely followed the FATF institutional model (Chapter 5, Section 1 below).

479 About nature and legal effects of MoUs, amongst others, Anthony Aust, *Modern Treaty Law and Practice* (3rd edn, Cambridge University Press 2013), 28–53.

480 Section XX of the MoU.

481 Ibid. Section XXI.

482 Section 2 of the MoU: "[ESAAMLG] is voluntary and co-operative in nature and independent from any other international body or organisation; it was established by agreement between the governments of its members and is not based on an international treaty. It sets its own work, regulations, rules and procedures and co-operates with other international bodies, notably the FATF, to achieve its objectives."

Eight of the nine regional bodies, excluding the APG, have constituent instruments that are more formal than those of the FATF, with the majority being regarded as formal IOs. Nonetheless, irrespective of the diversity of their constituent instruments, the institutional structure, decision-making procedures, and operational models are largely similar among them, and similar to those of the FATF.

At institutional level, all FSRBs have a minimum of a Plenary and Secretariat, and comparable to the FATF, all FSRBs have WGs that may vary in number from two (GABAC or MENAFAFT) to six (ESAAMLG), covering *inter alia* policy matters, evaluations and compliance, risk, trends and methods, technical assistance and training.

Decision-making also differs from FSRB to FSRB, with no discernible pattern between formal and less formal FSRBs; it ranges from a consensus requirement (eg. APG and EAG, like the FATF) to qualified majorities (eg. GIABA and MENAFATF).

In general, failure to perform membership duties, similar to FATF, implies limited or suspended participation in the organisation, suspension of voting rights, membership suspension and expulsion. There are particulars, for instance: issuance of a warning (GABAC), non-recruitment of its citizens to international posts in the Secretariat (GIABA), suspension of all forms of assistance (GIABA), or referral to the ICRG (APG and CFATF).

Of all regional bodies, only the CFATF has established additional Recommendations to FATF's – the Nineteen Aruba Recommendations (1990) and an internal ICRG WG to consider AML/CFT international co-operation matters and adopt recommendations. The CFATF also issues its own public statements in accordance to its own rules and procedures.[483]

8.1 *The Caribbean Financial Action Task Force*

The CFATF[484] is the oldest FSRB with a membership of 24 jurisdictions: Anguilla, Antigua and Barbuda, Aruba, Barbados, Belize, Bermuda, Cayman Islands, Curacao, Dominica, Grenada, Guyana, Haiti, Jamaica, Montserrat, Saint Kitts and Nevis, Saint Lucia, Saint Vincent and the Grenadines, Sint

483 At: https://www.cfatf-gafic.org/how-are-we-organized; https://www.cfatf-gafic.org/home/public-statements and https://www.cfatf-gafic.org/cfatf-public-statement-process (last visited 15/05/2024). Pursuant to Section 17 of the MoU among Member Governments of the CFATF, apart from being automatically suspended, a member may be referral to the CFATF ICRG in case of failure of its membership fees. The non-compliant member will also be referral to FATF's ICRG.

484 At: https://www.cfatf-gafic.org/.

Maarten, Suriname, The Bahamas, Trinidad and Tobago, Turks and Caicos Islands, Venezuela and Virgin Islands.[485]

It was created in Jamaica with the Kingstown Declaration on Money Laundering, 5–6 November 1992,[486] aiming at implementing and monitoring compliance with the Aruba Recommendations and the FATF Forty Recommendations in the Caribbean Region.[487]

The core documents that form the basis of the CFAFT are the: Kingstown Declaration and the MoU among Member Governments of the Caribbean Financial Action Task Force signed at San Jose, Costa Rica, on 10 October 1996, which has been regularly updated,[488] together with the Agreement between the Caribbean Financial Action Task Force and the Republic of the Trinidad and Tobago on the Headquarters of the Caribbean Financial Action Task and its Privileges and Immunities, signed in Port of Spain, on 23 March 1999.

This Agreement recognises the Task Force and its Secretariat as a regional agency and grants to it and its officials and representatives' certain privileges and immunities, setting the headquarters of the CFATF at Port of Spain, in Trinidad and Tobago.[489]

The bodies of the CFATF are the: Council of Ministers, which is the main policy-decision body, Plenary of Seniors Officials, Steering Group and Secretariat.[490] The Council meets at least once annually and decisions are carried out by a two thirds majority whilst the Plenary is the decision-making body at technical level that meets twice annually and decisions are consensus-based or two thirds majority.[491]

Apart from members and observers, the CFATF established the category of Co-operating and Supporting Nations (COSUNs) which relates to some members of the FATF that support the work and/or provide resources to CFATF jurisdictions in accordance with their national laws and policies.[492] The list of COSUNs includes Canada, France, Mexico, The Netherlands, Spain, UK and USA.[493]

485 At: https://www.cfatf-gafic.org/who-are-our-24-members (last visited 15/05/2024).
486 Meetings convened in Aruba in May 1990 and Jamaica in November 1992. Kingstown Declaration, para. 2.
487 Ibid, para. 2.
488 Last amended February 2013 (last visited 25/02/2023).
489 Articles 11 and 2, respectively.
490 Sections III, VIII, XI, XIII and XIV of the MoU.
491 Ibid, Sections VIII and XII.
492 Ibid, Section IV.
493 At: https://www.cfatf-gafic.org/home/cfatf-overview (last visited 15/05/2024).

Differently from the FATF, the CFATF is embodied with legal personality with an indefinite term.[494]

8.2 *The Asia-Pacific Group on Money Laundering*

The APG was established through the Bangkok Declaration on 27 February 1997 to combat ML in the Asia-Pacific region.[495] It comprises 42 members: Afghanistan, Australia, Bangladesh, Bhutan, Brunei Darussalam, Cambodia, Canada, China, Chinese Taipei, Cook Islands, Fiji, Hong Kong (China), India, Indonesia, Japan, South Korea, Lao PDR, Macao (China), Malaysia, Maldives, Marshall Islands, Mongolia, Myanmar, Nauru, Nepal, New Zealand, Niue, Pakistan, Palau, Papua New Guinea, Philippines, Samoa, Singapore, Solomon Islands, Sri Lanka, Thailand, Timor-Leste, Tonga, Tuvalu, USA, Vanuatu and Vietnam.[496]

The core constitutional instrument is the APG 2019 Terms of Reference (as amended), which incorporates the previous Terms of Reference, APG Explanatory Note on Membership and APG Governance Committee Terms of Reference.[497]

The APG framework includes the: Plenary (Membership), Governance Committee, Operations Committee and Secretariat.[498] The Plenary is led by two Co-chairs, a permanent chair (Australia) and a rotating one (another member with a two-year tenure); this distinction is the result of an arrangement with Australia under which the APG's headquarters location is in Sydney.[499]

The APG Plenary is the decision-making body which meets regularly once a year and where decisions are consensus-based and a minimum quorum of two-thirds of its members is required.[500]

The APG describes itself as a 'technical nature' organisation, stating in its Terms of Reference that it is a "non-political inter-governmental

494 Section XXIII of the MoU and Article 3 of the Headquarters and Privileges and Immunities Agreement.

495 At: http://www.apgml.org/about-us/page.aspx?p=91ce25ec-db8a-424c-9018-8bd1f6869162.

496 At: http://www.apgml.org/members-and-observers/members/default.aspx. Eight countries enjoy observers' status: Democratic People's Republic of Korea, Federated States of Micronesia, France, Germany, Kazakhstan, Kiribati, UEA and UK (last visited 15/05/2024).

497 Last amended in July 2023 (last visited 15/05/2024). See Sections 2.7, 2.9 and 2.10 of the Preamble. The APG also adopted specific policy and strategic documents and business plans. At: http://www.apgml.org/about-us/page.aspx?p=73c287fe-ed93-41d2-8e26-22f028eed804.

498 Section 5 of the Terms of Reference.

499 It is hosted at the Australian Federal Police. At: http://www.apgml.org/about-us/page.aspx?p=6e984e5c-5293-4d25-ba71-0099edb28954.

500 Sections 5 and 6 of the Terms of Reference.

organisation"[501] with an eight-year mandate (regularly renewed). The APG's current mandate expires in December 2028.[502]

8.3 *The Council of Europe Committee of Experts on the Evaluation of Anti-Money Laundering Measures and the Financing of Terrorism*

The MONEYVAL[503] is a permanent body created in September 1997 within the framework of the CoE.[504] It is an independent monitoring mechanism that reports directly to the Committee of Ministers since the adoption of Resolution CM/Res (2010)12 on the Statute of MONEYVAL on 13 October 2010. The Statute of MONEYVAL has been amended by Resolution CM/Res (2013)13 and subsequent Resolutions.[505]

The MONEYVAL has 35 members, which are: Albania, Andorra, Armenia, Azerbaijan, Bosnia and Herzegovina, Bulgaria, Croatia, Cyprus, Czech Republic, Estonia, Germany, Georgia, Gibraltar, Guernsey, Holy See, Hungary, Isle of Man, Israel, Latvia, Liechtenstein, Lithuania, Jersey, Malta, Moldova, Monaco, Montenegro, North Macedonia, Poland, Romania, San Marino, Serbia, Slovak Republic, Slovenia, Ukraine and UK.[506] It includes non-CoE members and two FATF jurisdictions selected to participate as full members for a two-year term.[507]

The main bodies of MONEYVAL are: The Plenary of the delegates, the Bureau (Chairperson, two Vice-Chairs and two other persons with two years term) and the Secretariat. The MONEYVAL holds at least two Plenary meetings a year, and decisions on issues arising in MERs, progress and follow-up reports and compliance reports shall be reached by consensus.[508]

MONEYVAL headquarters are located in Strasbourg, France.

501 Ibid, Section 3.

502 Ibid, Section 2.11 (b) of the Preamble.

503 At: https://www.coe.int/en/web/moneyval/. It was the former Select Committee of Experts on the Evaluation of Anti-Money Laundering Measures (PC-R-EV), a subcommittee of the European Committee on Crime Problems (CDPC). In 2002, the name was modified to the existing one. See Resolution Res (2005)47. It became an independent monitoring mechanism directly accountable to the Committee of Ministers on 01/01/2011.

504 The CoE is a regional IO created by the Treaty of London on 05/05/1949.

505 Articles 1, 5, 6, 9 and 10. Last amended by Resolution CM/Res (2022)13 (last visited 15/05/2024).

506 At: http://www.coe.int/en/web/moneyval/jurisdictions (last visited 15/05/2024). Since March 2022, the Russian Federation is no longer a member.

507 Due to its membership in both bodies, Israel is the only member that is evaluated simultaneously by the FATF and MONEYVAL. Currently, the two FATF jurisdictions are Germany and the UK (last visited 15/05/2024).

508 Articles 5, 6, 9 and 10.

8.4 *The Eastern and Southern Africa Anti-Money Laundering Group*

The ESAAMLG[509] was established through a MoU in Arusha, Tanzania, on 27 August 1999, which has been regularly amended,[510] and accounts 21 members, namely Angola, Botswana, Burundi, Eritrea, Eswatini, Ethiopia, Kenya, Lesotho, Madagascar, Malawi, Mauritius, Mozambique, Namibia, Rwanda, Seychelles, South Africa, South Sudan, Tanzania, Uganda, Zambia and Zimbabwe.[511]

Like the CFATF, in addition to the status of members and observer, the COSUNS status was also created to countries that provide technical or financial support to ESAAMLG.[512]

The main bodies of the ESAAMLG are the: Council of Ministers, Task Force of Senior Officials, Steering Committee and the Secretariat. The Council is the decision-making body and meets at least once a year while the Task Force is the executive body accountable to the Council, meeting twice annually.[513] Council Resolutions are adopted by three quarters majority.[514]

The ESAAMLG headquarters are in Dares Salaam, Tanzania.

8.5 *The Inter-Governmental Action Group against Money Laundering in West Africa*

The GIABA[515] was set up within the framework of ECOWAS[516] in Lomé, Togo, on 10 December 1999, and its statutes were adopted in Mali on 3 November 2000 and revised in 2006.[517]

The GIABA comprises 16 members that include Benin, Burkina Faso, Cape Verde, Côte d'Ivoire, Gambia, Ghana, Republic of Guinea, Guinea Bissau, Liberia, Mali, Niger, Nigeria, São Tomé and Príncipe, Senegal, Sierra Leone and Togolese Republic.[518]

---

509 At: https://www.esaamlg.org/index.php/about.

510 MoU Eastern and Southern Africa Anti-Money Laundering Group, last amended in September 2021 (last visited 15/05/2024). Also, ESAAMLG Procedures for Holding Task Force of Senior Officials and Council of Ministers Meetings (05/09/2020).

511 At: https://www.esaamlg.org/index.php/about (last visited 15/05/2024). The Democrat Republic of Congo is a regional observer. Portugal, UK, USA are also observers. At: https://www.esaamlg.org/index.php/about_countries_cooperative_partiner (last visited 15/05/2024).

512 Section III of the MoU.

513 Ibid, Section VI, VII, IX, IX-A and XI.

514 Ibid, Section X.

515 At: https://www.giaba.org/.

516 ECOWAS is a regional IO founded by the Treaty of Lagos on 28/05/1975.

517 At: https://www.giaba.org/about-giaba/index.html (last visited 15/05/2024).

518 At: http://www.giaba.org/member-States/index_-1.html (last visited 15/05/2024).

The institutional structure of GIABA integrates: an *Ad Hoc* Ministerial Committee (decision-making body), a Secretariat, a Technical Commission (experts from States) and a Network of national correspondents. Decisions of the Committee are taken by a two thirds majority.[519]

Like the MONEYVAL, the GIABA is a specialised body of the ECOWAS focused on AML/CFT embodied with legal personality.[520] It has indefinite term and its headquarters are in Dakar, Senegal.

8.6 *The Financial Action Task Force of Latin America*

The GAFILAT, initially named Financial Action Task Force of South America (GAFISUD),[521] was launched through a MoU in Cartagena de Indias, Colombia, on 8 December 2000. The constitutive document, originally signed by nine countries of the current 18, has been subject to amendments whenever necessary.[522]

The members of GAFILAT are: Argentina, Bolivia, Brazil, Chile, Colombia, Costa Rica, Cuba, Dominican Republic, Ecuador, El Salvador, Guatemala, Honduras, Mexico, Nicaragua, Panama, Paraguay, Peru and Uruguay.[523]

The main bodies are: the Council of Authorities, the Plenary of Representatives, and the Executive Secretariat. The Council is the decision-making body and meets when it is necessary. The Plenary meets twice a year and decisions are made by consensus.[524]

The GAFILAT is a permanent organisation with headquarters in Buenos Aires, Argentina, as stipulated in the Agreement of the GAFISUD Headquarters between the Republic of Argentina and GAFISUD, signed on 3 December 2001.[525] This Agreement expressly recognises the international legal personality and capacity of the organisation, establishing its immunities and privileges, including for its staff.[526]

The GAFILAT regards itself as "a regional intergovernmental organisation";[527] the structure of the MoU and its contents, in addition to its diplomatic

519 Articles 8, 9, 10 and 11 of the MoU.
520 At: https://www.giaba.org/about-giaba/index_656.html.
521 At: https://www.gafilat.org/index.php/en/. The name was changed to include all Latin American countries. At: http://www.gafilat.org/content/quienes/&lang=en.
522 The latest on 12 December 2014, in Ciudad de Antigua, Guatemala (last visited 25/02/2023).
523 At: https://gafilat.org/index.php/es/inicio (last visited 15/05/2024).
524 Section VI of the MoU.
525 Article 2.
526 Articles 1, 4, 10.
527 At: https://www.gafilat.org/index.php/es/gafilat/que-es-gafilat. Also, GAFILAT Strategic Plan 2020–2025, 6.

status in the Argentine Republic support the understanding that this is a formal organisation.

8.7 *The Task Force on Money Laundering in Central Africa*

The GABAC[528] like the MONEYVAL and the GIABA was created within the CEMAC[529] as a specialised institution to counter money laundering and the financing of terrorism in the region.

It was founded in N'Jamena, Chad, on 12 December 2000, Additional Act 9/00/CEMAC-086/CCE-02, which jointly with Regulation 00001/17/GABAC/PLEN, on establishing the Rules of Procedure of the GABAC (as amended)[530] and the Regulation 01/CEMAC/UMAC/CM, on the Prevention and Punishment of Money Laundering and the Financing of Terrorism and Proliferation in Central Africa (as amended)[531] and Directive 01/16/CEMAC/UMAC/CM, on the Model Text for the Creation, Organisation and Operation of the AML, CFT and CPF Coordinating Committees (as amended)[532] constitute the core documents of the organisation.

The GABAC encompasses seven members: Cameroon, Central African Republic, Chad, Republic of the Congo, Democratic Republic of the Congo, Equatorial Guinea and Gabon.[533] The Governor of the Banks of the States of CEMAC, the President of the CEMAC Commission, the President of the Committee of Police Chiefs of CEMAC and the Secretary General of the Banking CEMAC are also members of the GABAC.[534]

The main bodies of the GABAC are: the Plenary, which is the decision-making body and meets on an annual basis, the Permanent Secretariat and the WGs. Decisions are taken by a two thirds majority.[535]

The GABAC is a permanent organisation "endowed with legal personality"[536] and its headquarters are located in Libreville, Gabon.

528 At: http://spgabac.org/.

529 It is a regional IO, formerly known as the Customs and Economic Union of Central Africa (UDEAC), established by the Brazzaville Treaty in 1964. The CEMAC was established in N'Jamena, Chad, 10/03/1994. It officially supersedes UDEAC in June 1999.

530 Brazzaville, 16/01/2017 (last visited 15/05/2024).

531 Bangui, 11/04/2013 (last visited 15/05/2024).

532 Bangui, 12/12/2016 (last visited 15/05/2024).

533 At: https://www.fatf-gafi.org/en/countries/global-network/gabac.html (last visited 15/05/2024).

534 Article 2 of the Regulation (as amended). Also, ibid.

535 Ibid, Articles 22, 37, 39 and 53–54.

536 Ibid, Article 3.

8.8 *The Eurasian Group on Combating Money Laundering and Financing of Terrorism*

The EAG[537] was established in Moscow, on 6 October 2004, by the Declaration on the establishment of the EAG and the Terms of Reference of the EAG,[538] later, formalised through the Agreement on the Eurasian Group on Combating Money Laundering and Financing of Terrorism and Regulation on the Procedure for Forming and Implementing the Budget of the EAG, Moscow, 16 June 2011. These instruments together with the Agreement between the Government of the Russian Federation and the EAG on the Conditions of Stay of EAG Secretariat in the Territory of the Russian Federation (Paris, 14 February 2012) are the foundational documents of the organisation.

The EAG comprises 9 members which are: Belarus, China, India, Kazakhstan, Kyrgyzstan, Russian Federation, Tajikistan, Turkmenistan and Uzbekistan,[539] and its institutional framework includes a Plenary and Secretariat. The Plenary is the governing body meeting twice a year and decisions are made by consensus.[540]

The EAG is a regional intergovernmental organisation with indefinite term, headquartered in Moscow, Russia.[541]

8.9 *The Middle East and North Africa Financial Action Task Force*

The MENAFATF[542] was set up in Manama, Bahrain, on 30 November 2004, through the MoU between the Governments of the member States of the Middle East and North Africa Financial Action Task Force against Money Laundering and Terrorism Financing, which has been regularly amended.[543] This document together with the MENAFATF 2006 Accession Criteria and

537 At: https://eurasiangroup.org/en.

538 The initiative was announced by the Russian Federation at the FATF Plenary meeting in October 2003. At: https://eurasiangroup.org/ru/about-eag.

539 At: https://eurasiangroup.org/members' (last visited 15/05/2024). Observers: Afghanistan, Armenia, France, Germany, Italy, Iran, Moldova, Mongolia, Montenegro, Poland, Turkey, Serbia, Ukraine, USA, South Korea. At: https://eurasiangroup.org/ru/observers (last visited 15/05/2024).

540 Article 4 of the Agreement.

541 Ibid, Articles 1 and 12.

542 At: http://www.menafatf.org/.

543 Last amended 26 November 2013 (last visited 15/05/2024).

the annexed Memorandum of Accession (as amended),[544] form the core MENAFATF constitutional framework.

The MENAFATF is composed of 21 members that include: Algeria, Bahrain, Djibouti, Egypt, Iraq, Jordan, Kuwait, Lebanon, Libya, Mauritania, Morocco, Oman, Palestine, Qatar, Saudi Arabia, Somalia, Sudan, Syria, Tunisia, United Arab Emirates (UAE) and Yemen.[545]

The main bodies are the: Plenary Meeting of Representatives of member countries (decision-making body) which meets twice a year, and the Secretariat. Decisions are generally consensus-based.[546]

The MENAFATF headquarters are in Manama, Bahrain.

8.10 *Some Singularities*

From the preceding description, it is indisputable that there is value in joining jurisdictions that are located in the same geographic region, sharing "similar challenges in tackling money laundering and terrorist financing", and often sharing "a common working language".[547]

There are examples of jurisdictions moving from one FSRB to another due to language barriers or other obstacles, fostering better integration. This occurred with Comoros that withdrew from ESAAMLG's membership in 2015 to become a member of GIABA in 2016,[548] or the Dominican Republic that withdrew from CFATF's membership to become a member of GAFILAT in 2016,[549] or Guatemala that was a member both of CFATF and GAFILAT and became a sole member of GAFILAT in 2016,[550] or El Salvador that withdrew from CFATF's membership to become a member of GAFILAT in 2021.[551]

The possibility of dual membership was highlighted by the CFATF, underscoring "the geographic, cultural or linguistic periphery" advantages of being a member of more than one FSRB, which undeniably strengthens partnership

544 It establishes the criteria for membership, for holding an observer status, for assessing performance, proceedings and a mechanism of withdrawing or suspending the membership. It was adopted on 15/11/2006, and last amended on 26/11/2019 (last visited 15/05/2024).

545 At: http://www.menafatf.org/about/Members-Observers/members (last visited 15/05/2024).

546 Section 7, 8, 9 and 10 of the MoU.

547 2015–2016 FATF Report, 52; 2016–2017 FATF Report, 53.

548 2015–2016 FATF Report, 52.

549 2016–2017 FATF Report, 53.

550 Ibid.

551 At: https://www.fatf-gafi.org/en/countries/detail/El-Salvador.html and https://www.fatf-gafi.org/en/countries/global-network/financial-action-task-force-of-latin-america--gafilat-.html (last visited 15/05/2024).

ties across FSRBs.[552] The decision to choose and join a regional body exemplifies how jurisdictions are committed to be part of a regional or sub-regional network. It also reflects their diversity and adaptability, which are inherent qualities of the FSRBs's framework.

Another singularity is that one regional body can be observer of other regional bodies – either FSRBS are automatically entitled to participate as observers on a reciprocal basis, such is the case in the APG[553] or ESAAMLG,[554] or they need to apply to become an observer, such is the case in the EAG[555] or MENAFATF.[556]

There are other specificities: members of the FATF may also be members of the related regional body, such is the case of Australia, Canada, China, Hong Kong (China), India, Japan, Malaysia, New Zealand, Singapore, South Korea and the USA, which are members of the APG; Argentina, Brazil and Mexico, which are members of the GAFILAT; China, India and Russian Federation, which are members of the EAG; South Africa, which is a member of the ESAAMLG; Saudi Arabia, which is a member of the MENAFATF; and of Israel, which is a member of the MONEYVAL. This characteristic may be perceived as a positive aspect because it establishes a link between FATF's decision-making jurisdictions and those that do not have a seat in FATF's Plenary.

Moreover, sharing the same regional group may foster a sense of 'belonging and equal footing' among jurisdictions that have 'the region' as a common denominator. It may also promote an inter-change of views, knowledge, expertise, and familiarity with practical issues and, especially, enabling non-FATF members to address standards' implementation difficulties in the concerned region.[557] Further, it may allow a more accurate interpretation and application of the standards, as well as promoting criteria consistency and coherence in the FSRBs' ME process.

Alongside, non-FATF members have the opportunity to 'lobby' more effectively, explain their points of view, and even exert pressure for a better understanding of their concerns, constraints and contexts. But it may equally be understood as a means for FATF's members to exercise control and favour

552 At: https://www.cfatf-gafic.org/home/cfatf-news/87-cfatf-members-pioneer-fatf-new-policy-on-dual-membership-in-another-fsrb (last visited 15/05/2024).

553 At:http://www.apgml.org/members-and-observers/page.aspx?p=adbf954c-3fb5-415e-bc11-b333b61316d0 (last visited 15/05/2024).

554 At: https://www.giaba.org/about-giaba/index.html (last visited 15/05/2024).

555 At: https://eurasiangroup.org/ru/observers (last visited 15/05/2024).

556 At: http://www.menafatf.org/about/Members-Observers/observers (last visited 15/05/2024).

557 2007–2008 FATF Report, para. 6 and 46.

FATF's policies by influencing or 'manipulating' the agendas of the regional bodies. This could involve avoiding meaningful debates or boycotting decisions that may undermine or challenge FATF's authority.[558]

Offers of technical assistance by FATF members (as donors) to limited or low-capacity FSRBs jurisdictions by providing experts and capacity-building tools (eg. common law models in civil law jurisdictions and *vice-versa* or training)[559] or by financing AML/CFT programmes may also be viewed as a form of pressure. As a consequence, jurisdictions of the FSRBs may refrain from challenging the ideas of FATF members-donors within their regional group. This compromises the idea of a level playing field between FATF's members and non-FATF members, as well as the autonomy of the FSRBs.[560]

This is particularly notorious in regional groups where there is a significant economic differential among jurisdictions, such is the case, for instance of

558 Eg. MERs of jurisdictions who are members of both the FATF and FSRBs are often approved at the FATF Plenary and later at the FSRB Plenary. The fact that the FATF has three Plenary sessions per year and FSRBs bodies usually two (eg. ESAAMLG) or even one (eg. APG) originates a time-gap between the approval of the MER in the two *fora,* except when joint Plenary meetings are convened. This situation is unsettling: what is the benefit of considering and adopting the MER in the FSRB Plenary if it has already been approved by the FATF? Is the inclusion of non-FATF members to participate in the ME process merely an attempt to guarantee a certain level of transparency? Are FATF's decisions (ratings) susceptible to be challenged on the grounds of disagreement? Is the approval or ratification of a MER by an FSRB Plenary a mere formality (a 'rubber stamp')? Two examples, South Africa's MER was adopted at FATF's Plenary in June 2021 and at the ESAAMLG in September 2021. In October 2021, the report was published in FATF's website. The South Korea's case is even more peculiar. The FATF Plenary adopted the MER in February 2020 and subsequently published it on its website in April 2020. However, the report was only approved by the APG Plenary in July 2021.

559 Eg. Law on Anti-Money Laundering and Counter-Financing of Terrorism of 2014 of Lao PDR (at: https://amlio.gov.la/eng/files/regulation/Law%20on%20AML-CFT%2050.pdf) and Law on Countering Weapons of Mass Destruction Proliferation and Terrorism of 2019 (Revision) of Mongolia (at: https://www.unodc.org/uploads/icsant/documents/Legislation/Mongolia/Law_LCTP_law_English_Revised_1.pdf). Despite being civil law countries, both statutes were clearly influenced by common law drafting techniques, which may contribute to the fragmentation and incoherence of their domestic legal system.

560 The technical assistance can also be seen as a "lobbying effort" or a mean of "pooling of resources" from members, as mentioned by Shams, (n 47) 469. Jean d'Aspremont indicates several forms of exercising control in the decision-making process of IOs, including: i) aid and assistance; ii) coercion by economic pressure; or iii) policy pressure by the economic, political or military weight of certain States. The author refers to influential States and imbalance relations inside some IOs like SADC or ECOWAS. 'Abuse of Legal Personality of International Organizations and the Responsibility of Member States' (2007) 4 *International Organizations Law Review*, 97–112. Under this description, the APG may fall into that pattern.

the APG that joints members as China, USA, Canada or Japan together with eight of the least developed countries in the world – Afghanistan, Bangladesh, Cambodia, Lao PDR, Myanmar, Nepal, Timor Leste and Tuvalu.[561]

James Thuo Gathii explains the 'contingency' of developing countries in 'playing to the tune of the donors':

> The FATF has been very effective in developing countries like Kenya because its programs are tied to bilateral assistance programs of the United States Agency for International Development (USAID). Many developing countries welcome the kind of technical and capacity-building assistance that is promoted by bilateral aid agencies like USAID (...) Governments without the capacity to engage in the merits and demerits of a broad array of such programs are only too happy to play to the tune of donors.[562]

Additionally, it is crucial to consider the political agenda of certain jurisdictions that may influence the decision-making processes of the regional bodies and the FATF itself.[563] A depiction is the argument over Pakistan's nomination to the 'Black List' in October 2019, when the USA and India exerted pressure,[564]

561 There are 45 countries in the 2022 List of the WB of the Least Developed Countries (UN classification), at: https://data.worldbank.org/indicator/NY.GDP.PCAP.CD?locations=XL (last visited 06/05/2024). In the UN List of the Least Developed Countries (18/12/2023), out of 23 Countries, four are from APG (Afghanistan, Bangladesh, Cambodia and Lao PDR). at: https://www.un.org/development/desa/dpad/wp-content/uploads/sites/45/publication/ldc_list.pdf (last visited 06/05/2024).

562 'Financial Action Task Force and Global Administrative Law' (2010) *Journal of the Professional Lawyer, Forthcoming*, Albany Law School Research Paper Series No. 10, 16.

563 Jared Wessel refers the influence of the USA in FATF which "is widely reported (...) even though the organisation operates via consensus", (n 433) 113–114. Donnelly also acknowledges USA influence but underscores the power dynamics of the organisation (n 58), 202. Along these lines, Nance recalls that the USA and the EU are not always aligned and that the network itself "plays a much larger role in shaping actor preferences than has previously been acknowledged.", (note 46), 148. Ghoshray criticises the power exercised in the FATF by the great powers gravitating in a minority "global agenda paradigm" with lack of neutrality. As the author comments: "The FATF objectives have become a proxy for a handful of Western market economies", (n 401) 532–533. In this regard, De Oliveira points out the dichotomy of the 'great powers' and 'emerging powers' within FATF's governance, (n 2) 156–160.

564 'China Denounces FATF Members for Pursuing Political Agenda against Pakistan' (29/10/2019) *The Express Tribune*, at: https://tribune.com.pk/story/2089153/3-china-denounces-fatf-members-pursuing-political-agenda-pakistan; 'China Gives a Strong Snub to India over Nefarious Designs against Pakistan' (29/10/2019) *Daily Times*, at: https://dailytimes.com.pk/491338/china-gives-a-strong-snub-to-india-over-nefarious-designs-agai

while China openly reacted and criticised the situation. At the time, Mr. Yao Wen, Deputy Director General at the Department of Asian Affairs of China's Ministry of Foreign Affairs stated to the *media* that:

> China does not want the FATF to be politicised by any single country. There are some countries which want to include Pakistan in the blacklist. They have political designs which China is against (…) China stood with Pakistan and blocked any attempt to place it on the blacklist. We have made it clear to the United States and India that China cannot do this and it goes beyond the purpose of FATF. [565]

The need to maintain the reputation and credibility of the FATF requires a balanced and equitable political approach to all members and FSRB members. The FATF should be led by example and refuting an image of an organisation that favours members.

Lastly, some FATF members also have individual observer status in other FSRSBS, namely Australia (MENAFATF), Canada (COSUN/CFATF, MONEYVAL, GAFILAT), France (COSUN/CFATF, APG, EAG, MENAFATF, GAFILAT), Germany (APG, EAG, MENAFATF), Italy (EAG), Japan (MONEYVAL), Mexico (COSUN/CFATF, MONEYVAL), The Netherlands (COSUN/FATF), Portugal (ESAAMLG, GIABA, GAFILAT), Russian Federation (MENAFATF), Spain (COSUN/CFATF, MENAFATF, GAFILAT), South Korea (EAG), Turkey (EAG), UK (COSUN/CFATF, APG, ESAAMLG, MENAFATF, GIABA) and USA (COSUN/CFATF, MONEYVAL, ESAAMLG, EAG, MENAFATF, GIABA, GAFILAT). According to 2022 FATF's Status Report data, 75% of FATF members are members or observers of one or more FRSBS.[566]

---

nst-pakistan/; 'China Warns Members Not to Politicise the FATF' (29/10/2019) *Dawn Newspaper*, at: https://www.dawn.com/news/1513495.

565 Ibid, 'China Warns Members Not to Politicise the FATF'. In a Press Conference, Foreign Ministry Spokesperson Geng Shuang states, without contradicting Yao Wen that: the "FATF is an important platform for international cooperation in anti-money laundering and countering the financing of terrorist activities. Its purpose is helping countries better combat such illegal activities as money laundering and terrorist financing, rather than sanctioning or punishing any country". Foreign Ministry Spokesperson Geng Shuang Regular Press Conference (31/10/2019), China's MFA portal, at: https://www.mfa.gov.cn/mfa_eng/xwfw_665399/s2510_665401/2511_665403/201910/t20191031_692942.html.

566 At: 9.

9 External Relations

The FATF's external profile was designed to strategically address three domains: i) international and regional co-operation; ii) non-member jurisdictions (third countries); and the iii) private sector (later civil society). The institutional architecture, actions and outreach plans of the FATF were carefully conceived and adjusted throughout the years to reach its 'maturity state' as the "premier international body" to co-ordinate and set up the standards to counter ML/FT.[567]

As regards the first domain, the FATF established three main objectives: i) to be recognised as a global standard-setter; ii) to have the formal endorsement of the Forty Recommendations; and iii) to jointly co-operate in AML/CFT activities.

In the second domain, there are also three key objectives: i) to ensure the implementation of the Recommendations in third countries; ii) to assure that non-member jurisdictions become members of an FSRB; and iii) to provide technical assistance, if necessary.

In the third domain, the FATF mainly endeavours a partnership with the private sector to acquire information of the practical problems, challenges and possible solutions to counter ML/FT and PF, as well as to ensure standards' implementation in the sector. Such partnership would accordingly reflect an improvement of the Recommendations together with the development of informative and qualitative operational guidance and best practices papers.

9.1 *International and Regional Co-operation and Third Countries*

Since the start, the FATF has taken the necessary steps to develop close working relationships with international and regional organisations, as well as other international institutions or bodies involved in AML/CFT activities.[568] In the 1991–1992 FATF Report, the FATF highlights its pivotal role and need for global co-ordination:

> Perhaps in part as a result of the FATF's pioneering activity, the last year has seen a growth in the number of international bodies who have taken an interest in money laundering. Nevertheless, the key to a coherent and effective campaign against the menace of money laundering lies in the

567 1991–1992 FATF Report, para. 92–93; 1993–1994 FATF Report, para. 118–119; 2004–2012 Mandate, 1.

568 1995–1996 FATF Report, para. 65; 2009–2010 FATF Report, 14.

> effective co-ordination of the activities of all these bodies, and in ensuring that each has its own clearly identified role.[569]

Cognisant of the involvement of different organisations and bodies in AML matters, the FATF took the lead as the single international policy body to establish global standards on AML, and (subsequently) CFT and CPF. This was done leveraging its know-how and expertise,[570] while co-ordinating relevant international activities and *fora* to avoid overlapping or duplication of efforts.[571] The FATF takes a clear political stance in its 1991–1992 FATF Report:

> The FATF must lie at the heart of this process (...) the FATF has been able to take a lead in defining measures to combat money laundering. Other organisations have the structure and resources to disseminate good practice on the ground, but the FATF can provide the appropriate policy steer.[572]

FATF's mandate and *modus operandi* have been globally recognised by relevant IOs and international institutions,[573] including the UN/UNSC,[574] CoE,[575] EU,[576] IMF,[577] WB,[578] OECD,[579]

569 1991–1992 FATF Report, para. 92.

570 As mentioned in the 30 Years FATF Report: "As a member-driven organisation, the FATF has benefited from the experience of the experts involved in its work", 99.

571 1991–1992 FATF Report, para. 94; 1992–1993 FATF Report, para. 87, 104–105; 1994–1995 FATF Report, para. 99.

572 Para. 93.

573 30 Years FATF Report, 13. As highlighted in the 2012–2013 FATF Report: "The OSCE fully supports the 2012 Recommendations and the work of FSRBs and their observers to fully implement those standards", 33.

574 UNSCR 1617 (2005), op.para. 7; UNSCR 2462 (2019) Preamble, para. 12; UNSCR 2617 (2021), Preamble para. 27.

575 At: https://www.coe.int/en/web/moneyval/moneyval-brief/members/international-context-co-operation (last visited 25/02/2023). Also, CoE Explanatory Paper of the 2005 Warsaw Convention.

576 Para. 7 of the Preamble of the 2nd AML Directive 2001/97/EC recognises the FATF as the "leading international body devoted to the fight against money laundering" or para. 5 of the Preamble of the 3rd AML Directive 2005/60/EC that refers that the FATF "constitutes the foremost international body active in the fight against money laundering and terrorist financing".

577 2000–2001 FATF Report, para. 36; 2002–2003 FATF Report, para. 98.

578 Ibid.

579 At: www.oecd.org/tax and https://www.oecd.org/daf/anti-bribery/newanti-moneylaunderingstandardsreleased.htm (last visited 25/02/2023).

G-20,[580] or the Basel Committee.[581] These and other IOs and international institutions related to AML/CFT activities enjoy FATF's observers' status, as mentioned in Section 4 above.

As part of its co-operation programme, the FATF co-organises and/or promotes joint activities and projects with many of the refereed institutions, for example collaborating with the OECD's Committee on Fiscal Affairs to improve international and domestic co-operation to counter economic crimes, such as corruption, bribery and tax fraud tax associated with ML or with the Basel Committee to seek feedback from the private sector about AML/CFT challenges and how to address them.[582]

Since 2022, there has also been a stronger partnership with INTERPOL. As a means of combating transnational crimes associated with ML/FT/PF, the two organisations joined efforts to improve asset recovery. INTERPOL's know how and expertise are instrumental in terms of sharing of information in order to trace assets obtained illegally around the globe. The first FATF-INTERPOL Roundtable of Engagement (FIRE) was held in Singapore, September 2022 and the second in Lyon, September 2023, joining "more than 200 law enforcement, prosecutors, asset recovery, policy and regulatory experts, from both the public and private sectors".[583]

In this context, the relationship between the FATF with the IMF and WB, the UN/UNSC and the G-20 should be underscored. In the 2004–2012 FATF Mandate, the Ministers stressed the relevance of closer co-operation with these IOs:

> An important component of FATF's overall efforts is co-operation with other international bodies. The pilot programme, agreed with the IMF/WB, expired at the end of 2003. In order to achieve the best possible results, co-operation with the International Monetary Fund (IMF) and

580 G-20 Finance Ministers and Central Bank Governors Communiqué, Riyadh (February) 2020, 4; 2011–2012 FATF Report, 33; 30 Years FATF Report, 14.

581 Basel Guidelines on 'Sound Management of Risks related to Money Laundering and Financing of Terrorism' (February 2016), para. 3.

582 2011–2012 FATF Report, 33; 2016–2017 FATF Report, 25.

583 At: https://www.interpol.int/en/News-and-Events/News/2022/FATF-and-INTERPOL-intensify-global-asset-recovery; https://www.fatf-gafi.org/en/publications/Methodsandtrends/FATF-Interpol-partnership.html. Also, 2022–2023 FATF Report, 6. See 'Urgent action needed to fight money laundering and terrorist financing, say Heads of FATF, INTERPOL and UNODC' (Vienna, 13/05/2024), at: https://www.fatf-gafi.org/en/publications/Fatfgeneral/FATF-INTERPOL-UNODC-Call-to-action.html.

> the World Bank (WB) should continue and indeed become stronger (…) [T]he FATF should focus in particular on co-operation with other organisations, such as the United Nations and various donor organisations, and FATF should work with the International Financial Institutions (IFIS) to ensure that the pilot project becomes permanent.[584]

9.1.1 The IMF and the WB

The FATF's long-term alliance developed with the IMF and the WB dates back the early stages of the FATF, as mentioned (Section 4 above). However, the year 2000 marks the beginning of rounds of conversations between these organisations to deepen their collaboration (eg. granting access to meetings and the NCCT process)[585] and explore common ground and strategies.

On 29 April 2001, an IMF Press Release notes that "[the IMF and World Bank] generally agrees on the recognition of the FATF's Forty Recommendations as the appropriate international standards for combating money laundering".[586] Two years later, a pilot programme to develop a common methodology for evaluation was put into practice between these two IFIS and the FATF.[587]

This programme ended with an agreed methodology to conduct assessments, and the unequivocal endorsement of the FATF Recommendations as the standard.[588] It was equally agreed that the IMF and the WB could conduct assessments and their reports discussed at the FATF Plenary. Italy was the first FATF member jointly assessed by the FATF and the IMF in 2004–2005.[589] As explained in the 30 Years FATF Report:

> In addition to the FATF, the nine FATF-Style regional bodies (FSRBS), the IMF and the World Bank also assess their members' compliance with the

584 Para. 3.

585 2000–2001 FATF Report, para. 35 and 55; 2001–2002 FATF Report, para. 53–55.

586 IMF Press Release (29/01/2001): 'Communiqué of the International Monetary Fund and Financial Committee of the Board of Governors of the International Monetary Fund', at: https://www.imf.org/en/News/Articles/2015/09/14/01/49/pr0120. Also, 2000–2001 FATF Report, para. 36.

587 2002–2003 FATF Report, para. 99; 2003–2004 FATF Report, para. 17; 2004–2012 Mandate, para. 3.

588 2004–2005 FATF Report, para. 21; 25 Years FATF Report, 16; 2013–2014 FATF Report, 12.

589 2004–2005 FATF Report, para. 30. Reference to IMF and WB co-operation can be found in MONEYVAL or FATF ME process. Reference to WB's technical assistance in several MONEYVAL countries, at: https://www.coe.int/en/web/moneyval/moneyval-brief/members/international-context-co-operation (last visited 25/04/2024).

> FATF's anti-money laundering and counter-terrorist financing measures on the basis of the FATF's assessment methodology.[590]

This long-term partnership with the IMF and the WB has been crucial for the development of the FATF, both IFIs play an import role in FATF's life, just to name a few:

i) By adopting the FATF standards and methodology;
ii) In the development, implementation and dissemination of FATF standards;
iii) In promoting the effective implementation of FATF Recommendations and publication of assessment reports;
iv) By contributing in the drafting and revision of the standards;[591]
v) By providing technical assistance and capacity building on AML/CFT/CPF and other related threats;[592]
vi) By providing guidance and other policy for AML/CFT/CPF and other related threats to the integrity of the international financial system;
vii) By contributing to the elimination of the NCCT list;[593]
viii) In the participation of experts in joint assessments teams; and
ix) In the joint organisation of seminars and workshops, including assessors training.[594]

This partnership was highlighted in the 2024 Ministerial Declaration. Ministers commended the role of the IMF and WB "as qualified assessor bodies" and

590 At: 59.

591 In 2011, the IMF and WB argued that FATF's assessments "should adopt a more flexible, targeted approach", and proposed a number of changes, such as to identify areas where jurisdictions show a low compliance record or face particular risks, either domestically or cross-border. The inputs of both IFIs contributed to the revision of the standards and new methodology, as noted by Jackson, (n 6) 12–14.

592 Co-operation and burden-sharing arrangements on technical assistance and AML/CFT training programs were developed between the IMF, WB, FATF and FSRBs. The IMF created a donor-sponsor trust fund for on technical assistance on AML/CFT. 2011 IMF Paper AML/CFT Review (n 435) para. 11 and 18. Also, Jackson, ibid.

593 Ibid, para. 14–17. The Report addresses the ICRG process and the challenges that FATF's blacklisting process places on the "co-operative and voluntary nature of the IMF/WB (Risk-Based Reports on the Observance of Standards and Codes (ROSC) program, by involving 'the application of coercive elements'". IFIs must guarantee that the ICRG respects the ROSC principles, including: i) not publish statements before discussing with the jurisdiction to establish facts and to allow them to outline their plans to address the deficiencies; ii) statements should distinguish jurisdictions committed to action plans from those that have not; iii) public statements should encourage compliance with FATF's Standards, but also acknowledge jurisdictions' improvements (para. 16).

594 2009–2010 FATF Report, 21–22; 2017–2018 FATF Report, 47; 2019 Mandate, 6–7.

"technical assistance providers" in the ME, as well as as allies in the efforts to enhance, implement and reinforce FATF Standards.[595]

9.1.2 The UN/UNSC

In relation to the UN, this co-operation relationship has been continuous, in particular with the UNSC and its bodies, and the UNODC, especially following the 9/11 events that resulted in the adoption by the FATF of the SR targeting FT.[596] Nevertheless, it became noticeably more interactive in the second decade of 2000 with the imposition of targeted financial sanctions to individuals and entities (ISIL), *inter alia* UNSCR 2164 (2014),[597] UNSCR 2255 (2215),[598] UNSCR 2368 (2017),[599] UNSCR 2462 (2019),[600] UNSCR 2610 (2021)[601] or UNSCR 2617 (2021),[602] whereby UN bodies and Committees are called to work together or to consult FATF's expertise as regards countering FT or PF and emerging trends.[603]

The FATF has joint efforts with the UN Counter-Terrorism Committee Executive Directorate (CTED), the Counter-Terrorism Committee (CTC), the Analytical Support and Sanctions Monitoring Team to the Security Council Committee pursuant to Resolutions 1267 (1999) and 1989 (2011) concerning Al-Qaida and associated individuals and entities, the Expert Group to the Security Council Committee established pursuant to Resolution 1540 (2004), Panel of Experts to the Security Council Committee established pursuant to Resolution

595 Para. 12, 15–16. Tilahun mentions the influence of these bodies on the FATF's 'language' when introducing terms, such as "sustainability", "economic growth", "financial inclusion", (n 58) 9.

596 They were adopted by the FATF at an extraordinary Plenary meeting in Washington (30/10/2001). In 2004, a UN Report of the High-level Panel on Threats, Challenges and Changes entitled 'A More Secure World: Our Shared Responsibility', establishing a vision for collective security and international peace for the twenty-first century, exhorts all member States to sign and ratify the 12 international conventions against terrorism and to adopt the Eight SR of the FATF, as well as its Best Practices Papers, A/59/565 (02/12/2004) para. 150. On the role of the FATF within the wide range of adopted international measures following the 9/11, amongst others, Paul Eden, 'International Measures to Prevent and Supress the Financing of Terrorism' in P. Eden and T. O'Donnell (eds), *September 11, 2001: A Turning Point in International and Domestic Law?* (Brill Nijhoff 2005).

597 Op.para. 45 plus Annex.

598 Op.para. 53 plus Annex.

599 Op.para. 68 plus Annex.

600 Op.para. 14, 18, 33 and 35.

601 Op.para. 102.

602 Op.para. 27.

603 There is a six-year gap between the first and second Resolutions of the UNSCR referencing the FATF (2005 to 2011).

1718 (2006), Panel of Experts established pursuant Resolution 1929 (2010), the Al-Qaida and Taliban Sanctions Committee (1267 Committee) to assist countries how to better implement the obligations of the targeted financial sanctions against FT and PF.[604] Joint experts meetings,[605] typologies[606] and other activities[607] have been regularly carried out.

The inter-relationship between the UNSC and the FATF is noteworthy. The FATF offers expertise and know-how to develop the international obligations set forth in the Resolutions to counter terrorism and FT, in addition to providing feedback with regards to their implementation. The FATF and FRSBS MERS are reliable and valuable sources for the CTED in terms of jurisdictions' implementation of the Resolutions of the UNSC, as well as at identifying needs (gaps) and recommending technical assistance.[608]

The UNSC, on the other hand, provides political support to FATF, endorsing its mandate, Recommendations and *modus operandi*, including its Global Network.[609] As an illustration, the UNSC has taken note of the work developed by the FATF to counter emerging financing terrorists' threats, including the 2018 CFT Strategy and Operational Plan,[610] the development of risk indicators

604 2002–2003 FATF Report, para. 4; 30 Years FATF Report, 8.

605 Eg. Joint activities on targeting ISIL and on the PF of WMD (2015–2016 FATF Report, 20; 2016–2017 FATF Report, 13) or Joint Experts' meetings with the UN, IMF, WB and others in Tel Aviv (2018–2019 FATF Report, 35). On-line Experts Conference with the UN, IMF, WB and INTERPOL (2020), at: https://www.fatf-gafi.org/publications/methodsandtrends/documents/jem-2020.html.

606 Eg. 2016 Typologies jointly organised by the Eurasian Group, FATF and UNODC (2015–2016 FATF Report, 21) or the FATF/UNODC Workshop on Hawala and Similar Service Providers (2022–2023 FATF Report, 23).

607 Eg. In 2007, the FATF Secretariat offered a seminar to UN staff of the 1267, 1373 and 1540 Committees (2007–2008 FATF Report, para. 50); the 'No Money for Terror' Summit that was held in Paris in 2018 for the first time, followed by a second summit in Australia in 2019 (2017–2018 FATF Report, 13; 2019–2020 FATF Report, 19) or the High-Level Virtual meeting on UN Counter-Terrorism and Human Rights (2019–2020 FATF Report, 20).

608 UNSCR 2462 (2019), op.para. 33 and 35; UNSCR 2610 (2021), op.para. 102.

609 UNSCR 2482 (2019) op.para. 3: "Further stresses the importance of good governance and the need to fight against corruption, money-laundering and terrorist financing, in particular through the implementation of the United Nations Convention against Transnational Organized Crime (2000), the United Nations Convention against Corruption (2003), the International Convention for the Suppression of the Financing of Terrorism (1999) and the comprehensive international standards set forth in the FATF revised Forty Recommendations on Combating Money Laundering and the Financing of Terrorism and Proliferation". Also, UNSCR 2617 (2021), op.para. 27; UNSCR 2610 (2021), Preamble, para. 33.

610 Eg. FATF reports on the FT related to ISIL (2015) and Emerging TF (2015); Guidance on Criminalizing TF (2016); UNSCR 2368 (2017) op.para. 18; TF Risk Assessment; UNSCR 2462 (2019), op.para. 14.

related to FT,[611] the work on VA and VASPS (2019)[612] or FATF's Reports on ISIL, Al-Qaeda and Affiliates Financing (2021).[613]

The UNSC also encourages the study of new areas either in co-operation with its bodies or by directly suggesting it to the FATF:

- Encourages the FATF and FSRBS to consider financial flows analysis between trafficking in persons and FT in close co-operation with the CTED, the Analytical Support and Sanctions Monitoring Team and the UNODC;[614]
- Encourages the FATF to prioritise CFT, identifying and working with member States in AML/CFT deficiencies.[615]

The FATF's regular reporting and its ongoing involvement with the UNSC indicate that the UN/UNSC holds a unique position in FATF affairs, providing legitimacy to its mandate and implicitly overseeing its activities.[616]

9.1.3 The G-20

As regards the G-20,[617] the FATF relationship with G-20 has been strengthened following the 2008 world financial crisis, as mentioned. At the time, it was primordial to restore the trust and efficiency of the financial markets and to respond to the vulnerabilities identified in the system. To promote the integrity of the international financial market, the fight against ML had to be prioritised, and logically the work undertaken by the FATF had to be commended and boosted.

At the Washington Summit in 2008, the Declaration of the Summit on Financial Markets and the World Economy expressly recognised such work: "The Financial Action Task Force should continue its important work against money laundering and terrorist financing".[618] Later at the Pittsburgh

611 UNSCR 2368 (2017), op.para. 18.
612 UNSCR 2368 (2017), op.para. 25; UNSCR 2462 (2019), op.para. 21.
613 UNSCR 2610 (2021), op.para.18; UNSCR 2617 (2021), op.para. 31.
614 UNSCR 2331 (2016), op.para. 4.
615 UNSCR 2368 (2017), op.para. 19; UNSCR 2610 (2021), op.para. 21.
616 A/74/335 (29/08/2019) para. 46. Amongst others, Beekarry (n 61) 192; Turner (n 2) 557.
617 In 1999, the G-7 announced the creation of the G-20 to discuss matters of global economics and finance. Following the 2008 financial crisis, the USA proposed to increase the level of participation of the G-20 to Heads of State and Government. In the G-20 Leaders Statement: The Pittsburgh Summit 2009, the Heads of State and Government decided to institutionalise the G-20 as the "premier forum" for global economic and financial co-operation (Preamble, para. 19, 31 and op.para. 50).
618 Under the topic 'Promoting Integrity in Financial Markets'- 'Medium-term actions', 4.

Summit in 2009, the FATF was called to reform and act against non-cooperative jurisdictions in the light of the economic crisis (Section 7.2 above).[619]

At the Cannes Summit in 2011, the G-20, acknowledging FATF's mission, requests the presentation of the revised (new) standards in the following year. The Forty Recommendations were endorsed at the Los Cabos Summit in 2012 with the strong commitment of the G-20 members,[620] exhorting all countries in the world for "a swift and effective implementation of the FATF Standards".[621]

The increasing role of the G-20 in international affairs as the leading forum for international economic co-operation has had a direct impact in FATF's responsibilities and activities, as noted. As an example, the FATF has responded to G-20 calls on studies/papers, such as the 'White Paper on Global Standard-Setting Bodies and Financial Inclusion for the Poor – Towards Proportionate Standards and Guidance' (2011),[622] or on crypto-assets (2017),[623] or reporting on a consistent basis at several instances, namely to the G-20 Leaders' Summit, G-20 Finance Ministers and Central Bank Governors meetings and G-20 Anti-Corruption Ministerial meetings.[624]

At the Osaka Summit in 2019, the G-20 Leaders congratulated the FATF for regulating VA activities:

> We reaffirm our commitment to applying the recently amended FATF Standards to virtual assets and related providers for anti-money laundering and countering the financing of terrorism. We welcome the adoption of the Financial Action Task Force (FATF) Interpretive Note and Guidance.[625]

While in the FATF Public Statement on 'Virtual Assets and Related Providers' of 21 June 2019 related to the INote on VA, the organisation recognises the role of the G-20:

619 The G-20 Leaders Statement: The Pittsburgh Summit 2009, para. 15; 2009–2010 FATF Report, 28–29.

620 The G-20 Leaders Statement: Los Cabos Summit 2012, para. 48; 2011–2012 FATF Report, 33.

621 2015–2016 FATF Report, 16–17.

622 2011–2012 FATF Report, 19.

623 2017–2018 FATF Report 23; Riyadh Summit 2020 Declaration, para. 17.

624 Eg. FATF Report to the G-20 Leaders Buenos Aires Summit 2018; FATF Report to G-20 Finance Ministers and Central Bank Governors meetings in Washington in 2019; G-20 Leaders Statement: Riyadh Summit 2020, para. 17.

625 Para. 17.

> Today, the FATF has successfully delivered on the G-20 call to regulate and supervise virtual asset activities and related service providers for AML/CFT and to further clarify the FATF's expectations for how countries must develop robust AML/CFT frameworks in this regard.[626]

The FATF participates in joint meetings and expert activities under the aegis of the G-20 like the G-20 Anti-Corruption Working Group,[627] or G-20 Global Partnership for Financial Inclusion (GPFI),[628] or co-hosts special joint sessions with the IMF and G-20 on financial technology and AML/CFT.[629]

The G-20 is today one of the most influential political bodies guiding FATF's mission/actions, functioning as an external backing and oversight forum, as mentioned.[630] At the G-20 Finance Ministers and Central Bank Governors' meeting in Bali 2022, this political endorsement was openly expressed:

> We reaffirm our commitment to enhancing the capacity of the Financial Action Task Force (FATF) and its regional bodies to lead global action to respond to these threats. We support the effective implementation of FATF standards (…) and acknowledge their role in the fight against

626 Last paragraph of the Statement.

627 2012–2013 FATF Report, 15; 2016–2017 FATF Report, 26.

628 2017–2018 FATF Report, 39. On this *status quo*, also 2020–2021 FATF Report, 26.

629 2018–2019 FATF Report, 66; FATF Report to G-20 Leaders' Osaka Summit in 2019, para. 28.

630 The G-20 and the FATF have built a strong institutional relationship, where the G-20 endorses FATF's mission, encourages new studies and actions, makes recommendations, and follows their outcome. It provides political backup. Amongst others, Gathii commented that "The FATF is gaining visibility as a standard-setting international organisation. Its mandate is now formally incorporated in the agenda of the G-20 as well as in the work of the IMF and the Security Council.", (n 562) 17. Donnelly also concurs that the G-20 "drives institutional development and serves as the key political principal to which these bodies [FATF] are accountable (rather than all of the affected member States and the social partners). It therefore takes place outside the environment of the United Nations and other formal IOs, and outside any further accountability mechanisms", (n 58) 216–217. See, G-20 Leaders Statement: Riyadh 2020, para. 18: "We support the Anti-Money Laundering (AML)/Counter-Terrorist Financing (CFT) policy responses detailed in FATF's paper on COVID-19, and reaffirm our support for the FATF, as the global standard-setting body for preventing and combating money laundering, terrorist financing and proliferation financing. We reiterate our strong commitment to tackle all sources, techniques and channels of these threats. We reaffirm our commitment to strengthening the FATF's Global Network of regional bodies, including by supporting their expertise in mutual evaluations, and call for the full, effective and swift implementation of the FATF standards worldwide. We welcome the strengthening of the FATF standards to enhance global efforts to counter proliferation financing".

> grand and systemic corruption and environmental crimes, which gravely impacted economies and societies.[631]

At the New Delhi Summit in 2023, in addition to supporting recent developments of FATF Standards, G-20 Leaders addressed the resources needs of the FATF by declaring:

> We commit to supporting the increasing resources needs of the Financial Action Task Force (FATF) and FATF Style Regional Bodies and encourage others to do the same, including for next round of mutual evaluations.[632]

Considering that all G-20 countries are also FATF members, it is unsurprising that the G-20's influence and interconnectedness with FATF policy is increasing, and this is a relevant aspect that should be charted.

9.1.4 Third Countries

The international strategy towards non-members was initially focused on the implementation of the Forty Recommendations, preferably through the respective regional bodies, and in providing technical assistance, as explained (Section 7 above).[633] In the 1992–1993 FATF Report, it is affirmed:

> In its external relations work, the Task Force, in co-operation with other international bodies, must maintain the *momentum* of its efforts to persuade all financial centres to join the fight against money laundering. There are still some areas where the FATF's message has not penetrated and others where further work is needed to reinforce the process. The more widespread the action against money laundering, the more effective it will be.[634]

Members of the FATF also have a shared responsibility with the FATF to disseminate and encourage the implementation of FATF Recommendations, especially to "those dependent, associate or otherwise connected territories with which they have constitutional, historical or geographical links".[635] As Kenneth Blazejewski commented:

---

631 G-20 Chair's Summary: Third G-20 Finance Ministers and Central Banks, para 14.

632 Para. 75. Also, para. 22 and 75.

633 1991–1992 FATF Report, para. 85–89; 1992–1993 FATF Report, para. 89–103; 1993–1994 FATF Report, para. 119.

634 Para. 108. Also, 1991–1992 FATF Report, 20.

635 1991–1992 FATF Report, para. 85.

> The FATF has achieved a level of organisational complexity that allows it to preserve its own organisational structure and functional advantages while advancing the other functions that lie beyond its organisational reach (…) Specifically, through its institutional partners, the FATF is able to advance the universal implementation of the FATF Recommendations and assure that non-member States receive the capacity building and technical assistance they need to effectively enforce AML/CFT regulations.[636]

A plan with geographical and sectorial priorities for third countries was drawn up by the FATF, especially targeting small and low-capacity jurisdictions (heavily pressured to initiate AML/CFT measures). This plan involves the active participation of FATF members, including encouragement of bilateral initiatives and sponsorship programmes,[637] as well as collaboration of the regional bodies in a collective effort to provide third countries with adequate technical assistance and support.[638] In the 1994–1995 FATF Report, the FATF outlines its intentions:

> The FATF's goal remains to persuade all countries with significant financial centres to endorse and implement the FATF Recommendations. In co-operation with other international bodies, the FATF will continue to pursue an active programme of contacts with third countries to achieve this.[639]

In terms of FATF's external policy towards third countries, the expansion of the FSRBs and blacklisting (NCCT/ICRG) were influential in developing a systematic and comprehensive worldwide approach to FATF standards and securing the commitment of non-member jurisdictions.[640] After three decades, the

636 (n 60) 42.

637 1991–1992 FATF Report, para. 86: "Where the recommendations have been endorsed, the sponsor governments are continuing to encourage the territories to adopt appropriate legislation and introduce adequate institutional arrangements". Also, 1993–1994 FATF Report, para. 118–119.

638 1991–1992 FATF Report, para. 86–88; 1992–1993 FATF Report, para. 7, 86. The FATF also "seeks to involve financial institutions as well as government agencies in its contacts with non-member countries." (ibid, para. 88).

639 Para. 110.

640 1992–1993 FATF Report, para. 102–103; 1993–1994 FATF Report, para. 8; 2005–2006 Report, para. 16; 2007–2008 FATF Report, para. 5; 2008–2009 FATF Report, 24. More on Chapter 4, Section 4 and Chapter 5, Section 2.

overarching strategy has proven to be the right approach, leading to the establishment of a network of 206 jurisdictions (Section 7 above).[641]

9.2 *Private Sector and Civil Society Outreach*

9.2.1 Private Sector

The contribution and partnership of the private sector is essential to FATF's mission of successfully ensuring the integrity of the financial system. The insight of the financial services industry is extremely valuable due to its practical knowledge of problems or challenges that the industry faces when countering ML/FT/PF, and by identifying risk areas or new trends that are significant for the improvement of FATF's Recommendations, INotes and guidance papers. The same holds true for instance in relation to professionals in the legal and accounting sectors or trust and company service providers.[642]

The FATF organised its first Private Sector Consultative Forum in 1996, engaging in a constructive and permanent dialogue with the private sector in a spirit of co-operation that was built over time.[643] The Forum serves as a platform where representatives from national banking, the international financial services industry, and financial and accounting associations,[644] along with regulators and supervisors, holistically address the private sector's concerns and challenges.[645]

In 2004–2005, a comprehensive platform was built to improve the relations with the private sector via the dissemination of MERs and typologies reports

641 Amongst others, recognising the success of this strategy, Broome (n 6) 561; Turner (n 2), 556. Hülsse and Kerwer claim: "To date, FATF has successfully monopolised rule-making authority in this field, and a large number of States have started to implement its standards. Even some reluctant States seeking to preserve their role as tax havens have succumbed to FATFs' initiatives. Overall, FATF is, therefore, widely regarded as a successful rule-maker", (n 435) 63.

642 Eg. Consultation on the draft risk-based approach guidance for legal professionals, accountants and trust and company service providers. 1999–2000 FATF Report, para. 119; 2014–2015, 21–22; 30 Years FATF Report, 81.

643 1995–1996 FATF Report, para. 2, 28–29; 1997–1998 FATF Report, para. 111–112. The 30 Years FATF refers that following the 2017 terrorist attacks in London, FIs were "pro-actively reached" by FIUs and a "full financial picture of payments and spending patterns emerged rapidly, allowing investigators to confirm those involved in organising the attack", 80.

644 Wolfsberg Group, International Banking Federation, European Banking Federation, International Banking Security Association, European Insurance Committee, European Savings Banks Grouping, International Federation of Accountants, European Federation of Accountants and the Federation of European Stock Exchanges. 1999–2000 FATF Report, para. 119–120; 2004–2005 FATF Report, 31; 2012 Recommendations, 9.

645 Last meeting in April 2024. At: https://www.fatf-gafi.org/en/publications/Fatfgeneral/private-sector-consultative-forum-April-2024.html.

and establishing a regular consultation procedure of the standards (Section 6 above).[646] Some FATF Guidance and Best Practices Papers, which were initially used as reference tools by the private sector, began to be published with the private sector in mind, such as the Guidance for an RBA for Securities (2018), Life Insurance (2018), Accounting Profession (2019), Legal Professionals (2019) and Trust and Service Providers (2019), RBA to VA and VASP (2019), Trade-based ML: Risk Indicators (2021) or the webinar on ML through the Real Estate Sector (2022).[647] Nowadays, these documents are drafted using valuable and insightful input from the Private Sector Consultative Forum and public consultation procedure.

A number of initiatives involving the private sector have been carried out, including the establishment of the FATF FinTech and RegTech Forum (2017) to debate financial innovation (big data, data mining, artificial intelligence and machine learning),[648] the creation of the São José Principles (2017),[649] the launching of the FATF Business Bulletin (2018);[650] the creation of a one-stop-shop (2018)[651] and the launching of thematic editions (2019).[652]

Notable is the concurrent emergence of private sector participation in FATF affairs and the progressive consolidation of the organisation's institutional framework. This involvement also contributes to the publication of targeted and accurate guidance and best practices papers, an example is the 2019 FATF Guidance on Digital Identity Paper that offers guidance on how to determine if a digital ID is suitable to establish customer's identification. The FATF became the "first international body to produce comprehensive guidance on the use of digital identification".[653]

646 2004–2005 FATF Report, para. 32–34; 2015–2016, 43.

647 2011–2012 FATF Report, 33; 2012–2013 FATF Report, 6; 2018–2019 FATF Report, 42–43; 2021–2022 FATF Report, 35–37, 70–71, 2022–2023 FATF Report, 29.

648 The use of new technology that may pose a risk to AML/CFT/CPF investigations, on the other hand it may assist the identification of criminal activities. 2016–2017 FATF Report, 44–45; 2017–2018 FATF Report, 22–24, 65; 2018–2019 FATF Report, 40–41.

649 Partnership between the FATF, governments and FinTech and RegTech industries. The idea is to engage the private sector to counter FT/ML/PF and set clear regulatory expectations and *smart* regulation which address risks and allow innovation (2018–2019 FATF Report, 66). See: https://www.fatf-gafi.org/publications/fatfgeneral/documents/fatf-fintech-regtech-forum-may-2017.html.

650 2017–2018 FATF Report, 65.

651 Eg. Information on a particular sector or product (2018–2019 FATF Report, 67).

652 Eg. VA and Digital Identity (2019–2020 FATF Report, 49).

653 2019–2020 FATF Report, 12. The latest meetings focused on AML/CFT in the context of fighting corruption, de-risking, RBA guidance and emerging technologies, including VA and crypto-assets, digital identify, etc (2017–2018 FATF Report, 65; 2018–2019 FATF Report,

9.2.2 Civil Society Outreach

Aside from engaging the private sector, the FATF has enhanced its outreach activities to civil society, in particular refining its communication tools, most notably with the setting of its website in 1996[654] and the *enews* newsletter in 2007.[655] Both of which provide public access to FATF's policies, achievements and major actions on a regular basis, while given visibility to FATF's work.[656]

Like the private sector, the NPO sector actively participated in the review process of Recommendation 8 (Non-Profit Organisations) and respective INote,[657] as well in the improvement of the 2013 Best Practices on Combating the Abuse of NPOs, the 2014 Guidelines on Combating the Abuse of NPOs, the 2015 Best Practices on Combating the Abuse of NPOs, and the 2023 Best Practices on Combating the Terrorist Financing of Abuse of NPOs.

The tireless efforts of NPOs exposing the misinterpretation and misapplication of Recommendation 8, which have harmed NPOs with legitimate aims to pursue their objectives and work appropriately, were central in the recent review of Recommendation 8 and its INote in October 2023 (Chapter 5, Section 2 below). Both the 2023 Best Practice Paper and the Amendment to Recommendation 8 and its INote were subject of a broad public consultation process.[658]

The first Dialogue and Consultation meeting between the FATF and NPOs was held in London, in April 2013, gathering 20 NPOs, fostering an exchange of views on FT risks and vulnerabilities of the NPO sector,[659] while addressing the

---

67). The UNSC "*Highlights* the importance of strong relationships with the private sector in countering the financing of terrorism", UNSCR 2368 (2017), op.para. 25.

654 1996–1997 FATF Report, para. 89.

655 2006–2007 FATF Report, para. 51.

656 2007–2008 FATF Report, para. 61.

657 As stated in the 2015–2016 FATF Report: "NPOs provide an indispensable service to those in need, often in remote and dangerous areas. However, the same structure that allows NPOs to carry out their important work could make them attractive for terrorists or terrorist organisations to raise and move money to finance their atrocities. NPOs have been known to have been created for this purpose, or abused to support terrorism, often without the knowledge of management, donors, or staff", 45. Also, 2022–2023 FATF Report, 30. See: https://www.fatf-gafi.org/content/fatf-gafi/en/publications/Fatfrecommendations/protecting-non-profits-abuse-implementation-R8.html.

658 At: https://www.fatf-gafi.org/en/publications/Fatfrecommendations/FATF-BPP-Combat-Abuse-NPOs-Public-Consultation.html; https://www.fatf-gafi.org/en/publications/Fatfrecommendations/R8-public-consultation-jun23.html.

659 At: http://www.fatf-gafi.org/publications/fatfgeneral/documents/consultationanddialoguewithnon-profitorganisations.html.

unintended effects regarding the implementation of Recommendation 8 to the sector (Chapter 5, Section 2 below). The impact of this Recommendation (ex-SR VIII) is well noted by Ben Hayes:

> The FATF has taken a sledgehammer to crack the proverbial nut. Its approach appears both disproportionate and *ultra vires* with SR VIII going beyond its remit of reviewing the adequacy of laws to address potential vulnerabilities of NPO sectors to abuse by terrorism, to requiring States to regulate their NPO sectors as a whole.[660]

In 2014, the Global NPO Coalition on FATF was launched, joining more than 300 NPOs from around the globe, with the goal of monitoring the implementation of Recommendation 8 and its benchmarks. This Coalition is led by the Charity & Security Network, the European Centre for Not-for-Profit Law, the Philea on behalf of WINGS, and the Human Security Collective.[661]

In the 2015 Brussels meeting, the FATF President concurred to their claims on:

> [T]he need to avoid a "one-size-fits-all" approach to effectively combat terrorist abuse of NPOs given that not all NPOs are at high risk, and the importance of ensuring that misinterpretation or poor implementation of the FATF standards does not adversely impact legitimate charitable activities of NPO.[662]

660 2012 Hayes Report (n 293) 36. The author examined 159 MERs regarding the application of SR VIII.

661 At: https://fatfplatform.org/about-us/. The core group includes: Al-Hayat Center (Jordan), Al-Kawakibi Democracy Transition Centre (Tunisia), Community World Service Asia, Defenders Protection Initiative (Uganda), International Centre for Not-for-Profit Law (US), Islamic Relief Worldwide (UK), Muslims for Human Rights (Kenya), Norwegian Refugee Council (Switzerland), PINGO (Indonesia), Spaces for Change (Nigeria), UnidOSC (Mexico) (last visited 06/05/2024).

662 The second meeting was held in 2015 with 21 NPOs and the third in 2016 with 26 NPOs. At: http://www.fatf-gafi.org/publications/fatfrecommendations/documents/npo-consultation-march-2015.html; https://www.fatf-gafi.org/en/publications/Fatfgeneral/Outcomes-plenary-june2015.html; https://www.fatf-gafi.org/publications/financialinclusionandnpoissues/documents/consultation-non-profit-organisations-april-2016.html.

In addition to the interactive Dialogue and Consultation with NPOs, the FATF has created a direct link on its website to the Global NPO Coalition page, allowing direct input from the NPO community, building a closer and constructive forum for exchanging background information, experiences and suggestions, while enhancing transparency in FATF policy-making.

CHAPTER 3

International Organisations

1 Definitions and Criteria

There is no single definition of what an IO is in the international legal community.[1] The existing diversity of IOs with distinct aims, founding instruments, sizes, institutional structures, powers, functions, as well as membership, procedures and deliberation rules contributes unquestionably to such lack of consensus. As Klabbers astutely comments:

> [T]he question of when and whether an international organisation comes into existence is answered on the basis of general international law and there is widespread consensus among international lawyers that the criteria set by international law are neither strict or precise.[2]

Briefly, the origins of IOs trace back to the nineteenth century, the first ones being related to transport and communication, starting with the Rhine (1815) and Danube (1856) River Commissions, at the administrative co-operation level, and later, with a high-level of autonomy and an institutional framework of their own, with the International Telegraph Union (UIT) (1865), Universal Postal Union (UPU) (1874) and Intergovernmental Organisation dedicated to International Rail Transport (OTIF) (1893).[3]

---

1 The 'General Glossary' of the FATF defines IOs as "entities established by formal political agreements between their member States that have the status of international treaties; their existence is recognised by law in their member countries; and they are not treated as resident institutional units of the countries in which they are located. Examples of IOs include the UN and affiliated IOs, such as the IMO; regional IOs, such as the CoE, institutions of the EU, the OSCE and the OAS; military IOs, such as the NATO, and economic organisations such as the WTO or the ASEAN, etc.", FATF Recommendations (as amended), 131.

2 'Formal Intergovernmental Organizations' in J.K. Cogan, I. Hurd and I. Johnstone (eds), *Oxford Handbook of International Organzations* (Oxford University Press 2016), 140.

3 For a comprehensive historical overview and background of the origins and proliferation of IOs, among others, Amerasinghe, *Principles of the Institutional Law of International Organizations* (2nd rev ed, Cambridge University Press 2005), 1–13; Amerasinghe, 'International Institutional Law – a Point of View' (2008) 5 *International Organizations Law Review*, 143–147; Klabbers, *An Introduction to International Institutional Law* (2nd ed, Cambridge University Press 2009), 14–20; Schermers and Blokker, *International Institutional Law* (5th rev edn, Martinus Nijhoff Publishers 2011), 30–36; Klabbers, ibid, 139.

 | DOI:10.1163/9789004715134_004

IOs are factual realities. They are a 'construction' of the States focusing on mutual interests and common challenges to achieve better results through co-operation and inter-dependencies.[4] In a very pragmatic manner, Niels Blokker affirms that "international organisations are created in a particular field because there is some international problem that cannot be solved at national level alone".[5] From a more optimistic angle, Sofia Barros writes that "States' engagement in institutionalised forms of co-operation is premised on the existence of a common interest that is perceived as being best attained collectively".[6]

The International Court of Justice (ICJ) Advisory Opinion in *Reparation of Injuries Suffered in the Service of the United Nations 1949* recognises the birth of these new 'creatures' that are not States but have legal personality on the international plane:

> Throughout its history, the development of international law has been influenced by the requirements of international life, and the progressive increase in the collective activities of States has already given rise to instances of action upon the international plane by certain entities which are not States.[7]

Different areas of concern contribute to the development of IOs in world politics during the past two centuries. Volker Rittberger *et al* identify six prominent areas as a "stimulus for the establishment of IOs": i) war and power politics, such as the Concert of Europe (1815–1914), League of Nations (1919–1946), UN (1945), EU (1993) or African Union (AU) (2002); ii) industrial expansion, such as the Rhine River Commission, UPO, International Union of Railways (UIC) (1922), International Civil Aviation Organisation (ICAO) (1944) or

4 About the *raison d'être* of IOs, among others, D. Armstrong, L. Lloyd and J. Redmond (eds), *International Organizations in World Politics* (3rd ed, Palgrave Macmillan 2004), 1–10, 37; V. Rittberger, B. Zangl and A. Kruck (eds), *International Organizations* (2nd edn, Palgrave Macmillan 2012), 1–9, 35 *et seq*; Dapo Akande, 'International Organizations' in M. Evans (ed), *International Law* (3rd ed, Oxford University Press 2011), 252–253; Nicolae Purdă, 'Aspects on the International Legal Personality of International Organizations' (2012) 2, *Challenges of the Knowledge Society*, 891.

5 'Member State Responsibility for Wrongdoings of International Organizations: Beacon of Hope or Delusion?' in A.S. Barros, C. Ryngaert and J. Routers (eds), *International Organizations and Member State Responsibility: Critical Perspectives* (Brill/Nijhoff 2016), 36.

6 'Member States and the International Legal (Dis)order: Accounting for the Notion of Responsible Governance', in A.S. Barros, C. Ryngaert and J. Routers (eds), *International Organizations and Member State Responsibility: Critical Perspectives* (Brill/Nijhoff 2016), 48.

7 ICJ Reports 1949, 178.

International Maritime Organisation (IMO) (1958); iii) economic and trade, such as the IMF (1944), WB (1944), North American Free Trade Agreement (NAFTA) (1994), Southern Common Market (MERCOSUR) (1991) or World Trade Organisation (WTO) (1995); iv) human rights protection, such as the CoE (1949) or International Criminal Court (ICC) (1998); v) developmental disparities, such as the International Bank for Reconstruction and Development (IBRD) (1944) or ADB (1966); and vi) environmental concerns, such as World Meteorological Organisation (WMO) (1950), International Tribunal for the Law of the Sea (ITLOS) (1982) or International Tropical Timber Organisation (ITTO) (1983).[8]

According to the Union of International Associations 2022 database, there are an estimationed 7,846 IOs of the "intergovernamental type" in the world.[9]

The reasons behind the rise and proliferation of IOs and their predominance in the contemporary world as major actors in almost all fields of international affairs and global governance have been addressed by many authors in multiple perspectives and in different areas of knowledge, notably in international relations, international law and political science. As a result, a plethora of criteria, theories and classifications have been developed to analyse and understand this phenomenon.[10]

8 In parenthesis year of creation. Rittberger *et al* (n 4) 35–69. Also, amongst others, Amerasinghe, 'International Institutional Law – a Point of View' (n 3) 147.

9 It includes conventional international bodies (290), other international bodies (1,898) and special types (5,658). Yearbook of International Organisations 2022–2023, 27. The Yearbook gathers information on 75,000 IOs, including NGOs, from 300 countries and territories, around 42,000 of which are active organisations. At: https://uia.org/sites/uia.org/files/design/UIA_Sheet-04.pdf.

10 Amongst others, Kenneth Abbot and Duncan Snidal, 'Why States Act through Formal International Organizations' (1998) 42(1) *Journal of Conflict Resolution*, 23–29; Schermers and Blokker (n 3) 16–22; Klabbers, 'Contending Approaches to International Organizations: Between Functionalism and Constitutionalism' in J. Klabbers and A. Wallendahl (eds), *Research Handbook on the Law of International Organizations* (Edward Elgar 2011/2014); J. Samuel Barkin, *International Organisations – Theories and Institutions* (2nd ed, Palgrave Macmillan 2013). Anne M. Slaughter explains the three schools of thought that influence the conceptions of international law: realism, institutionalism, and liberalism, affirming that "the actual international system naturally contains realist, institutionalist and liberal elements. State behaviour is the product of a complex web of factors", 'Liberal International Relations Theory and International Economic Law' (1995) 10(2) *American University International Law Review*, 731. Klabbers debates conceptual approaches on how IOs operate and their checks and balances from a constitutionalist approach and a managerial concept, 'Two Concepts of International Organizations' (2005) 2(2) *International Organizations Law Review*. On the relation of States' power and the different schools of thought: functionalists, institutionalists, realists,

In international law, one of the conceivable classifications is to assemble IOs according to their purpose or field of action, legal character or geographical scope.[11]

IOs may have general and broad aims covering many aspects, including peacekeeping and security and economic and social development (eg. UN, OAS (1948), EU, AU), or specific aims. These can be of military (eg. North Atlantic Treaty Organisation (NATO) (1949), Southeast Asia Treaty Organisation (SEATO) (1954)), economic and financial (eg. IMF, WB, IBRD, European Free Trade Association (EFTA) (1960), OECD (1961), WTO), human rights and humanitarian (eg. CoE, International Organisation for Migration (IOM) (1951)), cultural and social (eg. International Labour Organisation (ILO) (1919), United Nations Educational, Scientific and Cultural Organisation (UNESCO) (1945), Food and Agriculture Organisation (FAO) (1945), World Health Organisation (WHO) (1948)), or scientific and technical nature (eg. ICAO, WCO (1953), International Atomic Energy Agency (IAEA) (1957), IMO).[12]

IOs may also be classified as inter-governmental (horizontal relation and co-ordination of the States *vis-à-vis* the organisation) or supranational (vertical relations and subordination of the States *vis-à-vis* the organisation), where the EU is the primary example of the latter.[13] They can also be categorised based on their geographical scope, such as universal (eg. ILO, UN, WHO or WTO), regional (eg. CoE, Arab League (1945), OAS, OSCE (1975), EU, Shanghai Co-operation Organisation (SCO) (2001), AU) or sub-regional (eg. BENELUX (1944), Andean Community (CAN) (1969)). IOs can be classified according to their membership criteria as open organisations (eg. UNESCO, WMO, WCO) or closed organisations (eg. Organisation of the Petroleum Exporting Countries (OPEC) (1960), Community of Portuguese Language Countries (CPLP) (1996)).[14]

These few examples echo the heterogeneity of IOs, highlighting the complexity of establishing a comprehensive definition that encompasses all existing types. On the other hand, there is a serious risk of creating stereotypes and

desegregationist, critical theories, constructivists, positivist, legalists, see José Alvarez, *International Organizations as Law-Makers* (Oxford University Press 2005), 17–44.

11 For IO classifications, amongst others, Amerasinghe, 'International Institutional Law – a Point of View' (n 3) 9, 11–13; Pierre Sands and Philipe Klein, *Bowett's Law of International Institutions* (6th ed, Sweet & Maxwell 2009), 17; Schermers and Blokker (n 3) 17–18.

12 In parenthesis year of creation.

13 The EU has the power to enact legislation which is automatically and directly applicable within member States' legal orders in certain policy domains, as well as to adopt binding decisions and to enforce them at domestic level.

14 In parenthesis year of creation.

misrepresenting their diversity. This is why, in codified international law, there are several terms or references to IOs without providing a definite definition.[15]

For instance, Article XI of UNESCO Constitution, Article 124 of the OAS Charter and Article 61 of the IMO Convention[16] all refer to IO as 'intergovernmental organisations'. Differently, Article 12 of the ILO, Article X of the IMF or Article 34 of the Statute of the ICJ use the term 'public international organisations' to refer to IOs. The term 'international organisations' is commonly employed, as is the case with Article 71 of the UN Charter, Article 33 of the WHO Constitution and Article 1(c) of the Statute of the CoE.

Article 2(1)(i) of the VCLT of 1969,[17] followed by Article 1(1) of the Vienna Convention on the Representation of States in their Relations with International Organisations of a Universal Character (1975, not yet in force) and Article 2(1)(i) of the Vienna Convention on the Law of Treaties between States and International Organisations or between International Organisations (1986, not yet in force), generally recognised as codified norms of customary international law, modestly define IOs as 'intergovernmental organisations'.[18]

The 2011 Draft Articles on the Responsibility of International Organisations (DARIO) of the International Law Commission (ILC), although marking an evolution from the previous sources, do "not intend to provide a definition [of an IO] for all purposes", rather attempt to delineate the proper meaning within the context of the DARIO.[19] This *rationale* is unequivocally explained in paragraph 7 of the General Commentary to DARIO:

15 Para. 1 and 3 of the Commentary to Article 2 of DARIO (ILC Report 2011). Amongst others, Kristen Boon, 'New Directions in Responsibility: Assessing the International Law Commission's Draft Articles on the Responsibility of International Organisations' (2011) *Yale Journal of International Law*, Seton Hall Public Law Research Paper No. 2011-01; Blokker, 'Preparing Articles on Responsibility of International Organizations: Does the International Law Commission Take International Organizations Seriously? A Mid-Term Review' in J. Klabbers and A. Wallendahl (eds), *Research Handbook on the Law of International Organizations* (Edward Elgar 2011/2014), 320–321, 323; Giorgio Gaja, 'Articles on the Responsibility of International Organizations' (July 2014) United Nations Audiovisual Library of International Law, 2, at: http://legal.un.org/avl/ha/ario/ario.html.

16 Originally named Inter-Governmental Maritime Consultative Organisation, changed in 1982 to IMO.

17 Para. 3 of the Commentary to Article 2 of DARIO refers that the VCLT is the first attempt to define what an IO is. Purdă and Gaja make the same comment, respectively (n 4) 891 and (n 15) 2.

18 If the word "intergovernmental" is narrowly interpreted, IOs could only be composed of States.

19 Para. 2 of the Commentary to Article 1 and para. 2 of the Commentary to Article 2 in DARIO. Gaja as the UN/ILC Special Rapporteur on the Responsibility of International Organisations also emphasises that "no attempt has been made" to establish a general definition

> There are very significant differences among international organisations with regard to their powers and functions, size of membership, relations between the organisation and its members, procedures for deliberation, structure and facilities, as well as the primary rules including treaty obligations by which they are bound. Because of this diversity and its implications, the draft articles where appropriate give weight to the specific character of the organisation, especially to its functions (…) Moreover, the diversity of international organisations may affect the application of certain articles, some of which may not apply to certain international organisations in the light of their powers and functions.

Although non-binding, the DARIO and related commentaries incorporate some norms of customary international law, making it an *authoritative reference* or as Blokker names it a 'quasi-legislative framework'[20] that can be taken into consideration.

---

of IO (n 15) 2. About DARIO, amongst others, Boon (n 15), Amerasinghe, 'Comments on the ILC's Draft Articles on the Responsibility of International Organizations' (2012) 9 *International Organizations Law Review*, 29–31; Chrysanthi Samara, 'International Responsibility of International Organizations (The Draft Articles of the International Law Commission)' (2017), at: https://papers.ssrn.com/sol3/papers.cfm?abstract_id=3480061. Blokker mentions the criticisms around DARIO, namely whether DARIO respects the "idiosyncrasy" of IOs and whether it is sufficient to embrace the wide variety of existing IOs, (n 15) 334–336. In this respect, James Crawford and Simon Olleson comment that DARIO follows closely the paradigm of States responsibility "and – yet precarious – international order", 'The Nature and Forms of International Responsibility' in M. Evans (ed), *International Law* (3rd ed, Oxford University Press 2011), 469. Blokker and Wessel provide an overview of the different views around DARIO's contribution, 'Introduction: First Views at the Articles on the Responsibility of International Organizations' (2012) 9(1) *International Organizations Law Review*. Stephen Bouwhuis also mentions the diversity of criteria to define an IO and that the Commission did "not intended a definition for all purposes". The author refers to the inclusion of DARIO in the 2015 Provisional Agenda of the UN General Assembly, but there are no developments since 2011. 'The International Law Commission's Definition of International Organizations' (2012) 9 *International Organizations Law Review*, respectively 452 and 465. On a critical note, Andrew Guzman comments: "The ILC, I must admit, stretches the definition of an international organisation, and by most definitions would surely not qualify as such", 'International Organizations and the Frankenstein Problem' (2013) 24(4) *European Journal of International Law*, 1019.

20 (n 15) 38. DARIO is based on the 'Articles on State Responsibility for Internationally Wrongful Acts' (2001) which incorporate many principles of customary international law (see para. 4 of the General Commentary to DARIO). Amongst others, Boon mentions that it "codifies some some principles of responsibility that are considered customary international law", (n 15) 9. Also, Kirsten Leube, 'Can the EU Be Held Accountable for Financing Development Projects that Violate Human Rights' (2017) 48 *Georgetown Journal of International Law*, 1253.

The ICJ Advisory Opinions, another important secondary source of international law, should also be acknowledged in this regard. The Advisory Opinions have addressed various aspects of IOs, such as their characteristics (personality), powers (legal capacity) and responsibilities under international law. However, they have been inconclusive in removing all questions about the criteria or elements that define or constitute an IO.[21]

This difficulty persists even among prominent scholars, who to this day struggle to provide a comprehensive definition. As an illustration, Finn Seyersted advocates that the criteria to define or elements to qualify an IO are:[22]

i) To have international organs of its own, ie. organs established by two or more sovereign States or communities, which are not subject to the authority of any one State or other organised community, except that of the participating communities acting jointly through their representatives on such organs;
ii) The organs are able to act in their own name, ie. to be able to perform 'sovereign' and/or international acts in their own name; and
iii) The organs must be sovereign (or self-governing) and not subject to the jurisdiction of any State or other organised community.

According to Chithatanjan Amerasinghe, the criteria or elements to be considered are:[23]

i) To be established through some kind of international agreement among States;
ii) To possess of what may be called a constitution;
iii) To possess organs separate from its members;
iv) To be established under international law; and
v) Generally, to have, but not always, an exclusive membership of States or Governments, but at any rate predominant membership of States and Governments.

The key elements for Henry Schermers and Blokker are:[24]

i) To be found on an international agreement;

21 Eg. ICJ Advisory Opinion on *Reparation for Injuries Suffered in the Service of the United Nations 1949*; ICJ Advisory Opinion on the *Interpretation of the Agreement of 25 March 1951 between the WHO and Egypt 1980*; ICJ Advisory Opinion on the *Legality of the Use by a State of Nuclear Weapons in Armed Conflict 1996*.

22 *Objective International Personality of Intergovernmental Organizations – Do Their Capacities Really Depend Upon Their Constitutions* (Krohns Bogtrykkeri (ed), København, Copenhagen 1963), 46–48; *Common Law of International Organizations* (Martinus Nijhoff 2008), 43–45, 64.

23 *Principles of the Institutional Law of International Organizations* (n 3) 10.

24 (n 3) 37–47.

ii) To have at least one organ with a will of its own; and
iii) To be established under international law.

Philippe Sands and Pierre Klein regard the following as essentials:[25]

i) Membership composed of States and/or other international organisations;
ii) To be established by treaty or other instrument governed by international law, such as a resolution adopted in an international conference;
iii) To have an autonomous will distinct from its members and be vested with legal personality; and
iv) To be capable of adopting norms (in the broadest sense) addressed to its members.

For Sands and Klein, the "requirement of international legal personality" is of paramount relevance because it endows the organisation with an identity of its own, separate from its members and distinctive from other entities, in which members are exempted from responsibility for the actions of the organisation.[26]

Amerasinghe has reservations about this understanding. This scholar considers that international personality and treaty-making capacity should rather be reckoned "as consequences of being an IO" than intrinsic elements of the concept of IO.[27] I concur with this scholar's viewpoint that these elements should not be seen as constitutive elements of legal personhood, but instead a result of such status.

For Ian Brownlie, the criteria to ponder are:[28]

i) To have a permanent association of States, with lawful objects, equipped with organs;
ii) To have a distinction, in terms of legal powers and purposes, between the organisation and its member States; and
iii) The existence of legal powers exercisable on the international plane and not solely within the national systems of one or more States.

Klabbers, in his writings, presents a sceptical viewpoint without offering a comprehensive definition of his own. However, he does enumerate the four prerequisites that are commonly acknowledged:[29]

i) To be created between States;
ii) To be based on a treaty;

25 (note 11) 15.
26 Ibid, 15 and 474.
27 *Principles of the Institutional Law of International Organizations* (n 3) 10.
28 *Principles of Public International Law* (6th ed, Oxford University Press 2003), 681–682.
29 (n 3), 6–12.

iii) To have at least one organ; and
iv) To have a distinct will (‘*volonté disctincte*’) from its members.

Klabbers also alludes to two other criteria that are occasionally mentioned:

v) The recognition of the organisation’s existence by third parties; and
vi) The public nature (*vel non*) of the organisation’s tasks.

José Alvarez also articulates the three elements that conventionally describe an IO, but adds that “these elements while useful for the purpose of characterisation, are not always easy to apply”:[30]

i) An international agreement between States;
ii) To have at least one organ distinct from member States and capable of acting; and
iii) To be created under international law.

Dapo Akande provides a succinct and contemporary description of the three elements mentioned above:[31]

i) Composed predominantly of States and/or other IOs;
ii) The entity must be established under international law, usually a treaty but can be other acts (Resolution of a Conference of States or by joint unilateral acts of States), and
iii) Possessing autonomous organs, ie. a separate legal personality and able to act on a majority basis.

In a different approach and referring to the dilemma around the conceptualisation of IOs, Angelo Golia Jr and Anne Peters offer a new insight that intends to reflect today’s reality: a patchwork of international actors deprived of legal personality that nonetheless play an important role in the international legal system.[32] The authors characterise IOs as “a cluster and open concept”[33] where autonomy (*volonté distincte*) is the core criterion combined with a permanent structure and the pursuit of a global public interest.[34]

Golia Jr and Peters contend that the idea of ‘autonomy’ for IOs is equivalent to ‘sovereignty’ for States. In this sense, the concept of ‘autonomy’ encompasses both a normative and a factual dimension. Autonomy is measured using the following criteria:

30 (n 10) 6.
31 (n 4) 254.
32 ‘The Concept of International Organization’ in J. Klabbers (ed), *The Cambridge Companion to International Organizations Law* (Cambridge University Press 2022) 48–49.
33 Ibid, 26.
34 The authors propose “replacing the outdated, obscure and even ‘metaphysical’ language of will with more modern concepts of autonomy and legal personality”, ibid, 34.

> [I]t concerns the scope of competences, the type of powers, especially lawmaking powers, decision-making procedures (especially majority voting or a requirement of unanimity), the procedures for amending the constituent act, the exit options for member States and more. We must thus examine the rules on these points and their application in practice – which will depend not only on the law but also on the factual constellation shaped for example by the overwhelming power of some member States, the degree of independence of the staff and the financial means of the organisation.[35]

According to the authors and based on the (criteria) degree of autonomy, structure and permanence, the OSCE is provided as an example at the top of the scale, whilst the G-20 at the lowest. The FATF and Basel Committee are described as organisations with a certain degree of autonomy in what concerns their lawmaking capacity and "less in the sense of independence from the participants", categorising FATF's acts as 'collective acts' of its members, for which they are "jointly accountable".[36]

The fact is that the FATF bears stronger resemblance to the OSCE as a full-fledged organisation as compared to the Basel Committee. The actions of the FATF have far-reaching implications beyond the realm of lawmaking. It operates on the international plane as a full and distinct legal person from its members (Chapter 4 below).

1.1 *'Common Characteristics', Nuances and Diversity of Design Patterns*

Notwithstanding the difficulties of ascertaining a simple and holistic definition, which all would agree upon,[37] it is nevertheless possible to distinguish 'common characteristics' that inter-cross the multiplicity of IOs and to identify nuances that divert from the conventional elements or criteria.

For instance, there are IOs whose members are not exclusively States but also consist of other IOs (eg. the UN is a member of the UPU and the EU is a

35 Ibid, 37–38.

36 Ibid, 46–47. Tilahun's views is that the FATF functions as a "permanent conference of its members". 'The Re-organization of the FATF as an International Legal Person and the Promises and Limits to Accountability' in A. Arcuri and F.C. Kund (eds) *Technocracy and Multi-level Governance: What Role for Accountability?* (Routledge 2021). On-line version, 2, at: https://papers.ssrn.com/sol3/papers.cfm?abstract_id=4127120. I do not share this opinion (Chapter 4 below).

37 Alvarez comments that drawing "definitions of IOs raise[s] more problems than they are worth.", (n 10) 4. Seyersted expounds the various attempts to define an IO, *Common Law of International Organizations*, (n 22) 41–42.

member of the Hague Conference on Private International Law and the FAO) or of other entities endowed with a certain degree of external autonomy (eg. the Hong Kong Special Administrative Region (HKSAR) and Macao Special Administrative Region (MSAR) are both members of the WCO and WTO, although not being sovereign States).[38] Or the case of the ILO that assembles Governments, employers and workers/trade unions as members.[39]

There are also IOs that are not created by a treaty (following the formal and traditional ratification procedure), but through other acts of international law,[40] such as Resolutions of the General Assembly (eg. the United Nations Conference on Trade and Development (UNCTAD)[41] or United Nations Industrial Development Organisation (UNIDO)[42]) or Declarations of the Parties (eg. the OPEC[43] or Association of Southeast Asian Nations (ASEAN) (1967)[44]).

These common characteristics or elements and these nuances, which have been acknowledged from reality and largely accepted, including in academic literature,[45] are reflected and enshrined in Article 2(a) of the DARIO. The given definition is as follows:

> For the purposes of the present draft articles: "International organisation" means an organisation established by a treaty or other instrument governed by international law and possessing its own international legal personality. International organisations may include as members, in addition to States, other entities.

However, controversy arises when certain organisations fail to meet the typical criteria and/or go beyond the 'acceptable' nuances. The line is even harder

38 Both Special Administrarive Regions enjoy external autonomy in economic and trade affairs (Articles 153 and 138 of HKSAR Basic Law and MSAR Basic Law, respectively).

39 At: https://www.ilo.org/about-ilo.

40 Ie. Acts governed by international law.

41 UNGAS Resolution 1995 (XIX) of 1964.

42 UNGAS Resolution 2089 (XX) of 1965.

43 The OPEC was created by the Conference of the Parties, in Bagdad, 1960, and its Statutes were adopted in the Second Conference, in Caracas, 1961.

44 The ASEAN was established in Bangkok with the signing of the ASEAN Declaration (Bangkok Declaration) in 1967.

45 Para. 1 of the Commentary to Article 2 of DARIO. Amongst others, Alvarez (n 10), 24; Klabbers (n 3) 7–8; Bouwhuis (n 19) 452; Guy Jones, 'Legal Personality and the Responsibility of International Organizations' (Dissertation for LLB (Hons), University of Otago, October 2013), 3, at: https://www.otago.ac.nz/law/research/journals/otago065260.pdf; Gaja (n 15) 2.

to draw, when looking at the broad and wide spectrum of organisations and different structural frameworks in the international contemporary landscape. Sands and Klein point out this reality when observing that "recent developments have called into question the traditional approaches to categories, functions and status of international organisations".[46]

Indeed, there are international courts that have been entrusted with independent legal status and international legal personality, such as the ITLOS, ICC or the Special International Tribunal for Lebanon carving away the traditional approach of international courts as treaty-organs, like the ICJ, European Court of Human Rights (ECtHR) or the European Court of Justice (ECJ).[47]

New forms of treaties supervision have also been instituted, such as the Conference of the Parties (COPs) within the framework of the 1992 UN Framework Convention on Climate Change and Kyoto Protocol[48] or the Preparatory Commission for the Comprehensive Nuclear-Test-Ban Treaty Organisation,[49] which are embodied with some decision-making powers,

46 (n 11) 13.

47 Ibid, 13–14. Independent judicial bodies *versus* judicial organs of the UN, at: https://research.un.org/en/docs/law/courts. Seyersted, *Common Law of International Organizations* (n 22) 9–14; Alvarez (n 10) 5 and 589; Klein and Sands, '(Re)Writing on the Law of International Organizations: Options and Challenges' (2008) 5 *International Organizations Law Review*, 220–221.

48 At: https://unfccc.int/ and https://unfccc.int/process/the-kyoto-protocol/compliance-under-the-kyoto-protocol. Amongst others, Akande raises the possibility of being qualified as IO (n 4) 254. Robin Churchill and Geir Ulfstein commented that these entities "talk and act like International Organisations: they conclude treaties and seem to enjoy 'implied powers' even though they were never formally established as an International Organisation or as international legal persons", 'Autonomous Institutional Arrangements in Multilateral Environmental Agreements: A Little-Noticed Phenomenon in International Law' (2000) 94(4) *American Journal of International Law*, 613. About shifting patterns, and the example of COPs in the context of multilateral environmental conventions, amongst others, Jutta Brunnée, 'Reweaving the Fabric of International Law? Patterns of Consent in Environmental Framework Agreements' in R. Wolfrum and V. Röben (eds), *Developments of International Law in Treaty-Making* (Springer 2005). Alvarez also describes the unusual capacities and practice of COPs and MOPs as compared with traditional IOs and the forum shifting of lawmaking in international law. The author comments on the "capacity of COPs and MOPs to conclude treaties as 'traditional IOs and States' and the development of 'implied powers' pursuant to the principle of effectiveness – even without the attributes of traditional IOs such as permanency or their own secretariats", 'International Organizations: Then and Now', 2006 (100)2 *American Journal of International Law,* 334–336.

49 At: https://www.ctbto.org/. Para. 7 of the Resolution establishing the Preparatory Commission for the Comprehensive Nuclear-Test-Ban Treaty Organisation (CTBT/MSS/RES/1, 19/11/1996) states that: "The Commission shall have standing as an international

institutional framework (a Secretariat) and certain legal capacities to adequately exercise their functions. These bodies are endowed with far reaching powers from those attributed to classic oversight bodies, such as the Human Rights (HR) Treaty Bodies or the International Narcotics Control Board.[50]

There are also organisations composed of States with informal frameworks or less structured forms of co-operation, which are not recognised as IOs. Schemers and Blokker or Felicity Vabulas and Duncan Snidal offer examples, such as the Quartet of the Middle East, BRIC, Group of Earth Observation, G-8 or G-20.[51]

These entities provide a positive and alternative room for international, regional or sectorial co-operation in fields like environment, finance and banking, as explained by Hartmut Hillgenberg in his theory of self-contained regimes on non-treaty multilateral agreements.[52]

Informal (or soft) organisations[53] may be an optimal solution from the cost-benefit *ratio* standpoint, wherein compromise is easily reached, and decisions

---

organisation, authority to negotiate and enter into agreements, and such other legal capacity as necessary for the exercise of its functions and the fulfilment of its purposes".

50 Amongst others, Amerasinghe, *Principles of the Institutional Law of International Organizations* (n 3), 1–12, Alvarez (n 10) 7, 136–137; Klein and Sands (n 47) 220, Schermers and Blokker (n 3) 34–35, 45, Klein and Sands (n 11) 12–13. Klabbers comments that: "others have pointed that treaty organs endowed with decision-making powers may well be IOs in disguise", (n 3) 9. Jana Petman claims that "[t]he diversification of the international institutional framework requires legal scrutiny. Lawyers should to a greater extent engage in the examination of the legal status and functions of new organs, such as treaty bodies", 'Deformalization of International Organizations Law' in J. Klabbers and A. Wallendahl (eds), *Research Handbook on the Law of International Organizations* (Edward Elgar 2011/2014), 445.

51 (n 3) 32–33; 'Informal Intergovernmental Organizations (IIGOs)' (International Political EcoNo.my Society Conference, University of Wisconsin 2011), 20, at: http://ncgg.princeton.Edu/IPES/2011/papers/S330_rm3.pdf.

52 'A Fresh Look at Soft Law' (1999) 10(3) *European Journal of International Law*. Amongst others, addressing the changing and sharing role of informal organisations or bodies and networks in global governance, Wessel and Evisa Kica, 'Political Economy and the Decisions of International Organizations: Choosing Governance Arrangements through Informality' in A. Fabbricotti (ed), *Political Economy of International Law* (Edward Elgar Publishing 2016), 130–131, 155–156.

53 About the differences between informal or soft organisations and formal or hard law organisations, amongst others, Angela Di Stasi enumerates the common elements of soft organisations: i) absence of an international treaty as a constituent instrument; ii) operativity and institutional effectiveness as evidence of their existence; iii) wide recourse to acts of 'soft law'; iv) frequent adoption of a top-down procedure (at the highest level) in decision-making activities. Di Stasi explains in an enlightening way that both soft and hard organisations have quantitative, evolutionary and normative elements that are manifested in both types of organisations or in similar ways, which "gives place to an element

can be obtained and changed according to circumstances in a rather smooth and cost-benefit manner in comparison to a classical IO format.[54]

Ramses Wessel emphasises the role of informal or hybrid organisations in his concept of *world legislation*. They are part of an *emerging reality of global governance* that cannot be denied in international lawmaking. The author refers to them as entities that "have as their main objective the crafting of rules for worldwide application".[55] This normative *forum shifting* process from States to organisations includes both traditional international lawmaking and *informal international lawmaking* (a concept developed by Joost Pauwelyn).[56]

of affinity" between then. But it also contributes to the difficulty in establishing a clear borderline between these two types of organisations beyond their "conventional nature". In fact, it seems that the formal element is the *only* element that clearly distinguishes both models. As the author remarks "the *summa division* separating those inspired by a model of so-called hard organisation (of a conventional nature) from those inspired by a model of so-called soft organisation (of a political-diplomatic nature)", 'About Soft International Organizations: An Open Question' in R. Virzo and I. Inagravallo (eds), *Evolutions in the Law of International Organizations* (Brill/Nijhoff 2015), 48.

54 A sign that formal IOs are becoming 'old-fashioned' and that their *modus operandi* is too bureaucratic, ineffective, and even unappealing to States. For a deeper understanding of soft organisations and informal international lawmaking, see, *Informal International Lawmaking*, J. Pauwelyn, R. Wessel and J. Wouters (eds), (Oxford University Press 2012). Pauwelyn, Wessel and Wouters also provide some reasons for saturation and change in the political preferences of States in an increasingly complex knowledge society with new inputs and outputs. This growing and diversified network society inevitably generates new actors and processes. The authors strongly criticise formal IOs or traditional lawmaking procedure, considering that parliamentary approval for ratification is a mere "domestic rubber-stamping", 'When Structures Become Shackles: Stagnation and Dynamics in International Lawmaking' (2014) 25(3) *European Journal of International Law*, 757–761. Di Stasi stresses the value of informal organisation for global governance in economic, financial and security matters, where "both great powers and weaker States" make use of them, ibid, 68.

55 'Informal International Lawmaking as a New Form of World Legislation?' (2011) 8 *International Organizations Law Review*, 254–256. Also, Wessel and Kica highlight that there are different and new informal bodies and networks with a role in global governance and that new approaches are needed ("normativity is different from imperativity"), (n 52) 130–131, 155–156.

56 It is 'informal' in the sense that it deviates from traditional lawmaking in relation to three aspects: *output*, *process* or the *actors involved*. Pauwelyn's definition of informal lawmaking is as follows: "Cross border co-operation between public authorities with or without the participation of private actors and/or international organisations, in a forum other than a traditional international organisation (process informality) and/or between actors other than traditional diplomatic actors (such as regulators or agencies) (actor informality) and /or which does not result in a formal treaty or traditional source of international law (output formality)", 'Informal International Lawmaking: Framing the Concept and Research Questions – Mapping the Action and Testing Concepts of Accountability

Vabulas and Snidal go even further, developing a model that may be useful for distinguishing (and classifying) formal IOs from informal ones, clarifying their legal status on the international plane. Formal IOs are established through treaties and have at least three-member States. They also have a permanent Secretariat or some other sort of institutionalisation, such as headquarters and permanent staff. Informal IOs are defined as groups of States that 'share expectations' about their purpose(s) and convene meetings without an independent Secretariat or any other significant institutionalisation.[57]

Based on the above criteria outlined by the authors – founding act (binding and non-binding agreement); members (States and others); mandate (formal treaty or shared expectations); organisation structure (regularised meetings and independent or non-independent/absence of a Secretariat); rules governing the organisation (treaty codified rules or spontaneous or implicit rules); duration (permanent or non-permanent); policy and lawmaking power; monitoring, compliance power and sanctioning power,[58] it is plausible to affirm that the FATF has most of the elements that characterise a formal IO.[59]

The proliferation of entities with distinct design-settings operating in the international arena, as well as the emergence of new frames of global governance, have been discussed in academic literature and categorised from many perspectives.[60]

---

and Effectiveness' (Project Framing Paper, February 2011) 11, at: https://www.researchgate.net/publication/228147656_Informal_International_Lawmaking_Framing_the_Concept_and_Research_Questions. Amongst others, Berman, S. Duquet, Pauwelyn, Wessel and Wouters, 'Introduction and Key Issues Surrounding Informal International Lawmaking' in A. Berman *et al* (eds), *Informal International Lawmaking: Case Studies* (Torkel Opsahl Academic EPublisher, The Hague 2012), 3.

57 (n 51) 6–7, 20.

58 Ibid.

59 Klabbers (n 2) 137. Also, Borlini and Montanaro raise such hypothesis. 'The Evolution of the EU Law against Criminal Finance: The 'Hardening' of FATF Standards within the EU' (2017) 48(4) *Georgetown Journal of International Law*, 1024–1026. With a different view, Tilahun categorises the FATF as soft organisation (an 'informal experts' body') due to the absence of a "formal legal existence", (n 36) 2–4.

60 Slaughter refers to a transnational society where the center-stage of the international system does not lie on States rather on individuals and groups that represent collective interests – epistemic communities, *A New World Order* (Princeton University Press 2004), 27–30, 261 *et seq*. Amongst others, Kaul Raustiala, 'The Architecture of International Cooperation: Transgovernamental Networks and the Future of International Law' (2002) 43(1) *Virginia Journal of International Law Association*; Sanjeev Khagram, 'Possible Future Architectures of Global Governance: a Transnational Perspective/Prospective' (2006) 12(1) *Global Governance*; Jonathan Koppell, 'Global Governance Organizations: Legitimacy and Authority in Conflict' (2008) 18(2) *Journal of Public Administration Research & Theory*; Rafael Domingo, *The New Global Law* (Cambridge University Press 2011);

Their heterogeneous nature challenges any uniform patterns or authoritative definitions. Within this context, diverse *epistemic communities*, transgovernamental networks, international agencies, public-private partnerships, *ad-hoc* global alliances and coalitions can be discerned.[61] All these *genera* reflect the "current hybridity of global governance", as rightly commented by Sanjeev Khagram.[62]

Transgovernamental networks and international agencies are regarded as two modern-day forms. The first type is described as networks of government officials (national regulatory authorities) in horizontal-loose structures, with peer-to-peer mechanisms, where technocrats co-ordinate actions and policies in an informal-consensual manner. These networks develop standards and best practices, such as the Basel Committee, the International of Securities Commission or the IOSCO.[63]

Ulfstein, 'Reflections on Institutional Design – Especially Treaty Bodies' in J. Klabbers and A. Wallendahl (eds), *Research Handbook on the Law of International Organizations* (Edward Elgar 2011/2014); Carol Harlow, 'Composite Decision-Making and Accountability Networks: Some Deductions from a Saga' (2012) Jean Monnet Working Paper 04/12, at: http://jeanmonnetprogram.org/paper/composite-decision-making-and-accountability-networks-some-deductions-from-a-saga/; Muldoon, 'New Types of Organizations and the Global Governance in the Twenty-First Century: The Case of ICANN' in J.E. Oestreich (ed), *International Organizations as Self-Directed Actors – a Framework Analysis* (Routledge 2012); Ranjay Gulati, Puranam Phanish, Michael Tushman, 'Meta-Organization Design: Rethinking Design in Inter-Organizational and Community Contexts' (2012) 33(6) *Strategic Management Journal*; Sandra Lavenex, 'Globalization and the Vertical Challenge to Democracy' in H. Kriesi *et al* (eds), *Democracy in the Age of Globalization and Mediatization* (Palgrave Macmillan 2013).

61 Amongst others, Kanishka Jayasuriya, 'Globalization, Law, and the Transformation of Sovereignty: The Emergence of Global Regulatory Governance' (1999) 6(3) *Indiana Journal of Global Legal Studies*, 453. Also, Slaughter, ibid; Klabbers (n 3) 9; Muldoon, ibid, 241, Lavenex, ibid, 108–109.

62 Khagram provides six models of global governance: i) multilateralism or polyarchic interstatism; ii) grassroots globalism; iii) multiple regionalisms; iv) world statism; v) networked governance (transgovernamental or multi-stakeholder); vi) institutional heterarchy, (n 60) 97.

63 Slaughter describes these networks as "informal institutions linking actors across national boundaries and carrying on various aspects of global governance in new and informal ways", (n 60) 3–4. Jayasuriya identifies three main features: (i) they are governed by networks of State agencies acting as independent actors rather than on behalf of the State; (ii) they lay down standards and general regulatory principles instead of strict rules; and (ii) they frequently contribute to the emergence of a system of decentralised enforcement or the regulation of self-regulation, (n 61) 453. An attempt to compare the FATF with other organisations such as the Financial Stability Board (FSB) and the Bank for International Settlements (BIS), or other types of institutions, such as the International Olympic Committee Board (IOC) and the Fédération Internationale de Football Association (FIFA)

The second type is featured as non-treaty-based bodies that are established by IOs rather than through inter-State regulatory co-operation. The rule-making capacity of these bodies and general compliance derive from their recognised technical expertise. This specialisation-factor is frequently acknowledged by granting the agency with public authority functions, such is the case of the Codex Alimentarius Commission, the Intergovernmental Panel on Climate Change or the Kimberley Scheme on Conflict Diamonds.[64]

The FATF exhibits attributes from both categories. The FATF may be described as a network of government officials, and an organisation with recognised technical expertise.[65] Its primary goal is to establish a global AML/CFT regime and ensure its compliance on a global scale. This comprises implementing a peer-to-peer mechanism that is associated with public functions and a position in global governance.

However, the FATF is neither a transgovernamental network nor an international agency. The institutional framework of the organisation is more

---

would be futile, because the first two are private organisations, established under Swiss law, with members of different legal nature (public and private), and the IOC and FIFA are two international NGOs, created under Swiss law with members that are individuals and national NGOs, respectively. By contrast, the FATF is an organisation with public international law features. It is composed of States and entities with international legal status under public international law, namely the HKSAR, EU and the Gulf Co-Operation Council. The FATF has been established by a series of acts of public international law nature that aim to regulate their relations on a matter of common concern (transnational crimes) that requires co-ordinated action in AML/CFT/CPF (national) policies. Therefore, it cannot be compared with the FSB, BIS, IOC or FIFA, based on: i) nature/mission, ii) membership and iii) source of law (domestic law).

64 Amongst others, Michael Livermore, 'Authority and Legitimacy in Global Governance: Deliberation, Institutional Differentiation and the Codex Alimentarius' (2006) 81 *New York University Law Review*, 81; Edoardo Chiti and Wessel, 'The Emergence of International Agencies in the Global Administrative Space: Autonomous Actors or State Servants?' in R. Collins and N. White (eds), *International Organiations and the Idea of Autonomy: Institutional Independence in the International Legal Order* (Routledge 2011). Berman and Wessel classify informal transnational entities as 'international agencies' or 'harmonisation networks'. Though recognising the role of these entities in global governance, both authors advocate the benefits of institutionalisation or formalisation. 'The International Legal Status of Informal International Lawmaking Bodies: Consequences for Accountability' in J. Pauwelyn, R. Wessel and J. Wouters (eds), *Informal International Lawmaking* (Oxford University Press 2012). However, the authors are unclear if the process of acquiring international legal personality necessarily requires a binding-legal instrument.

65 Amongst others, Slaughter (n 60) 54; Pauwelyn (n 56) 34; Nance, 'Re-Thinking FATF: An Experimentalist Interpretation of the Financial Action Task Force' (2018) 69 *Crime, Law and Socials Change*, 138.

complex and multi-layered than a mere network of regulators, and its regulatory and monitoring powers are more heterogeneous and multifaceted than international agencies (covering a wide range of fields and players). In addition, the FATF has the authority to blacklist a jurisdiction and recommend countermeasures against both its members and non-members. This capacity/power is archetypically associated with IOs that are treaty-based.[66]

In actuality, the international arena is teeming with a vast array of organisations characterised by distinct design patterns, fostering multilateral co-operation, transnational regulation, and establishing alliances in areas of international community interest or concern.

1.2 *Sui Generis* Cases

There are other organisations like the Inter-Parliamentary Union (IPU), INTERPOL, General Agreement on Tariffs and Trade (GATT), Commonwealth, Nordic Council, OSCE, Black Sea Economic Co-operation (BSEC) or even the EU, where categorisation is quite complex due to their *sui generis* characteristics and *modus operandi*.[67]

Some of these organisations have undergone legal changes to clarify their legal standing, while others are still in the process of (re)defining their status.

1.2.1 The Inter-Parliamentary Union

One example in dispute is the recognition of the IPU[68] as an IO. The singularity of this organisation is that the purpose of promoting peace, democracy, and

66 Eg. Articles 5, 6, 41, 42 of the UN Charter, Article 7 of the Constitution of the WHO, Articles XXIII, Section 2 and XXVI, Section 2 of the IMF Articles of Agreement. Amongst others, Nigel White and Ademola Abass state that "[i]n principle countermeasures must be available to any entity possessing international legal personality" and recall that "organisations possess a number of means to control their members: expulsion, suspension, and sometimes non-forcible measures, such as sanctions", 'Countermeasures and Sanctions' in M. Evans (ed), *International Law* (3rd ed, Oxford University Press, 2011), 536. On WB's sanctioning power, amongst others, Pascale Hé lè ne Dubois and Ailieen Elisabeth Nowlan, 'Global Administrative Law and the Legitimacy of Sanctions Regimes in International Law' (2010) 36 *Yale Journal of International Law*.

67 Amongst others, Seyersted, *Common Law of International Organizations* (n 22) 8, 21, 78, Slaughter (n 60) 109, 115–116, 137, 139; Alvarez (n 10) 5–6, Klabbers (n 3) 6–11; Schermers and Blokker, (n 3) 31–39; Jones (n 45) 7 and 36. Brownlie and Goodwin-Gill, G.S, 'Joint Opinion on the International Legal Personality of the Inter-Parliamentary Union (IPU)' 1999, at: http://www.ipu.org/finance-e/opinion.pdf. Anthony Aust describes the OSCE, Commonwealth and the EU as "special cases" in the topic related to IOs, *Modern Treaty Law and Practice* (3rd edn, Cambridge University Press 2013), 357–362.

68 At: http://www.ipu.org/english/home.htm.

sustainable development is achieved through parliamentary co-operation, as it was found by parliamentarians.[69]

Initiated in 1889 as the Inter-Parliamentary Conference, the organisation changed its name to the Inter-Parliamentary Union in 1899, placing its headquarters in Berne, Switzerland, and creating the position of Secretary General (on a volunteer basis) in 1902.

The headquarters of the IPU was formally established with the Agreement between the Swiss Federal Council and the Inter-Parliamentary Union to Settle the Juridical Status of the Organisation in Switzerland, on 28 September 1971, and the IPU's Statutes were later adopted in 1976.[70] Presently, in addition to its headquarters in Geneva, the IPU also has offices located in New York (USA) and Vienna (Austria).

According to Article 1(1) of the IPU Statutes of 1976, the organisation is explicitly defined as an "international organisation of the Parliaments of sovereign States".[71] However, the legal standing of the IPU has been called into question on two grounds: i) it is composed of national parliaments and ii) its Statutes are not treaty-based.[72]

Brownlie and Guy Goodwin-Gill in their legal opinion on IPU's legal status uphold the recognition of the organisation as an IO under international law.[73] The scholars structure essential criteria and provide an analytical analysis of the ICJ Advisory Opinion in *Reparation of Injuries* that supports their perspective, ultimately concluding that "[t]he IPU possesses international legal personality and is an international organisation *sui generis*, that is, it is an international parliamentary, political and representative organisation".[74]

The scholars point out that:

69 At: https://www.ipu.org/about-us.

70 The Statutes of the IPU have been regularly revised in 1983, 2003, 2013, 2016, 2017, 2018, 2019, 2020, 2021 and last amended March 2023 (last visited 15/05/2024).

71 Ibid.

72 (n 67) para. 8–9.

73 "The IPU is unique in its combination of aims and purposes with a representative character. It is distinguishable from non-governmental organisations and private voluntary organisations in its membership of parliaments, the public, legislative organs of States, rather than of private or personal interests." (para. 11 of the Statement). Ibid.

74 Ibid, para. 1 of the Statement. To demonstrate IPU's international legal status under international law, both scholars undertake a functional approach analysing the criteria and characteristics of an IO *vis-à-vis* the IPU, focusing on member's intent and on the functional activities/responsibilities of the IPU (para. 9).

> In those countries where it is physically located, the IPU is recognised and treated as an international organisation. In the 1971 Agreement between the Swiss Federal Council and the IPU on the latter's juridical status, the former expressly 'recognises the personality and legal capacity' of the IPU, 'due to it by virtue of its status', and 'guarantees (...) the independence and freedom of action belonging to it as an international institution'. The status, privileges and immunities extended to the IPU and its staff parallel those due to other international organisations and, indeed, those generally accorded in the context of diplomatic relations.[75]

In October 2018, a new paragraph was added to Article 1 of the IPU Statute clarifying the nature of the organisation:

> IPU has legal personality and has the authority to enter into international agreements, including co-operation agreements with national parliaments and inter-parliamentary organisations, as well as with international intergovernmental and non-governmental organisations.[76]

This amendment although elucidating (and underpinning) that the organisation views itself as an international legal person, does not address the concerns of those who defend a more conservative-formal approach, namely that an IO must be treaty-based and concluded by States.

However, Brownlie and Goodwin-Gill rightly explain that the premise that "traditionally international representation of the State is vested in the Head of State and carried out by his or agents (diplomats)" is being contested, since the "world has evolved, and international relations are no longer merely diplomatic".[77] And, as both scholars remarked, parliaments are also "a supreme organ of the State as much as the Government or the Executive".[78]

This understanding is also supported and further substantiated and mirrored in the DARIO with Commentaries. In this document it is emphasised that a narrow interpretation of the term 'intergovernmental' may exclude a number of IOs given the fact that many of them "have been established with the participation also of State organs other than Governments".[79] The ambivalence of the term is also acknowledged, as it may be interpreted as referring

75 Ibid, para. 30 and 32.
76 Article 1(4).
77 (n 67) para. 66.
78 Ibid.
79 Para 3. of the Commentary to Article 2.

to the founding instrument of an IO or as referring to the quality (legal nature) of the member.[80]

There is also compelling evidence of political commitment of States towards the IPU. Governments' explicit or implicit endorsement of their parliaments in the work of the IPU, applications for membership, allocation of funds from national budgets for IPU activities, and use of official channels, including diplomatic communication with the organisation, all provide unequivocal evidence of practical recognition of the institutional and legal nature of the IPU.

1.2.2 The International Criminal Police Organisation

The above debate and conceptual interpretation are also discernible in relation to the INTERPOL.[81] The INTERPOL began as the International Criminal Police Commission in 1923, although the idea of an IO for criminal police and legal co-operation dates to 1914 (the first International Criminal Police Congress, held in Monaco, 14 to 18 April).

A number of Resolutions concerning the operation of the organisation were subsequently approved, and later revoked with the adoption of the Constitution of the INTERPOL in 1956,[82] establishing the main principles and rules of the organisation, including its funding, and changing its name to the present one.[83]

The INTERPOL is set up in Lyon as determined in the Agreement between the Government of the French Republic and the International Criminal Police Organisation concerning the Headquarters of INTERPOL and its Privileges and Immunities in French territory (3 November 1982), where the organisation is recognised as an international legal person, enjoying the necessary privileges and immunities "for the exercise of its functions and the achievement of its aims",[84] including extraterritorial and diplomatic mission status.

The organisation understands that it is an "intergovernmental organisation" endowed with "legal personality separated from that of the member countries, and that it is governed by international

80 Ibid.

81 At: https://www.interpol.int/en.

82 Last amended by the General Assembly at its 91st Session, in Vienna 2023 (last visited 02/05/2024).

83 At: https://www.interpol.int/en/Who-we-are/Our-history. For a comprehensive historical background and evolution, amongst others, Giulio Calcara, 'A Transnational Police Network Co-Operating Up to the Limits of the Law: Examination of the Origin of INTERPOL' (2020) 11(4) *Transnational Legal Theory*.

84 Articles 1 and 2.

law".[85] However, the lack of a traditional agreement (a treaty), subject to ratification procedure, and the fact that is established between high-ranking police officers as opposed to representatives of the State raised doubts about its legal status on the international plane.[86]

These doubts are well-addressed in the 1982 Legal Opinion of the UN Office of Legal Affairs regarding the status of INTERPOL with the UN, making it clear that there is "no authoritative definition in international law of the term 'intergovernmental organisation'".[87] The Legal Opinion confronts the arguments of INTERPOL not being treaty-based, defending that its founding instrument – the Constitution of the INTERPOL – "may be considered an international agreement in the simplified form" and that the term 'intergovernmental' should be broadly interpreted to include Government agencies. Accordingly, the claim that the Constitution of the INTERPOL, because signed by high-ranking police officers, is not an international treaty, should not be valid.[88]

In an International Law Roundtable about the INTERPOL, chaired by David Bentley, at the Chatham House in December 2012, Tim Tyler and Yaron Gottlieb comprehensively described the controversy over the legal nature of INTERPOL and the grounds for INTERPOL to assert its legal standing:

> Both academics and practitioners have raised questions concerning INTERPOL's status under international law. It is the view of INTERPOL

85 Para. 4 of the Executive Director of INTERPOL, Written submission to UK Foreign Affairs Parliament Committee, October 2020. At: https://committees.parliament.uk/writtenevidence/12772/html/.

86 Eg. Written Answer E-011707-13, 'The Status of INTERPOL as an International Organisation' under Commission Rule 117, EU Parliamentary Question (15/10//2013) at: https://www.europarl.europa.eu/doceo/document/E-7-2013-011707_EN.html. In favour of the recognition of INTERPOL as an IO, amongst others, Ljubo Runjic, 'The Legal Nature and Status of INTERPOL in the Context of Contemporary International Law' (22nd International Scientific Conference on Economic and Social Developments – Legal Challenges of Modern World, Split 2017). The author addresses the controversy of not being treaty-based and being composed of police bodies. At: https://papers.ssrn.com/sol3/papers.cfm?abstract_id=3166171.

87 Extracts UN Juridical Yearbook of 1982, Chapter VI, Selected Legal Opinions, 179–180. The Legal Opinion refers that during the drafting of the VCLT, the proposal to establish as a "requirement a constituting treaty, was not retained because this criterion was not always met in practice", 180. See ECOSOC Decision 109 (LIX) of 30/07/1975 on the Observer Status of IOs; A/RES/51/1 of 15/10/1996 on INTERPOL Observer Status in the General Assembly. Also, https://www.interpol.int/en/Our-partners/International-organization-partners/INTERPOL-and-the-United-Nations.

88 Ibid (Legal Opinion). The Legal Opinion also responds critically to those who advocate INTERPOL's non-governmental character.

> that it is an independent and autonomous international organisation established by international law. It has its own organs and its own rules of operation; it has headquarters agreements on privileges and immunities with several countries, and also has agreements with other international organisations. In addition, INTERPOL is party to the UN Vienna Convention on the Law of Treaties between States and International Organisations or between International Organisations, and its tools and channels are mentioned in international conventions related to transnational organised crime. It is also subject to the jurisdiction of the International Labour Organisation Administrative Tribunal (in relation to cases concerning INTERPOL staff). It is recognised as an international independent organisation in many decisions by national courts around the world. Member States fund it from their national budget. And finally, in the annual meeting of the INTERPOL General Assembly, each delegate presents official credentials provided by its State.[89]

Along these lines, Ljubo Runjic classifies INTERPOL as an internatiomal transnational organisation. This author makes a distinction between intergovernmental and transnational organisations. Membership of intergovernmental organisations is composed primarily of sovereign States, while membership of transnational organisations is composed of public legal persons of the national law, such as national police forces.[90]

---

89 'Policing INTERPOL' (International Law Roundtable Summary, Chatham House, 05/12/2012), 4–5. At: https://www.chathamhouse.org/sites/default/files/public/Research/International%20Law/051212summary.pdf. The UK was one of the countries that did not recognised INTERPOL as an IO. During the debate of the International Criminal Police Organization (Immunities and Privileges) Order 2023 in the House of Lords, Lord Goldsmith of Richmond Park (Minister of State, Foreign, Commonwealth and Development Office) explains the merit of such statutory act, particularly the need to "enable Interpol to function effectively in the UK in the longer term, including by providing it with legal personality in this country" (Section 4 stipulates that INTERPOL has legal personality). UK Parliamentary debate of 05/06/2023, House of Lords, at: https://hansard.parliament.uk/lords/2023-06-05/debates/05E1207C-222D-4373-9AFF-10CC860BBA3C/InternationalCriminalPoliceOrganisation(ImmunitiesAndPrivileges)Order2023. The act was approved on 19/07/2023. The Order gives effect to the Agreement signed on 20/02/2023 between UK and the INTERPOL on Privileges and Immunities. Paragraph 2 of the Preamble of the Agreement states that INTERPOL is an IO, and Article 3 recognises legal personality to INTERPOL in the territory of the UK, including capacity to conclude contracts, to acquire and dispose of movable and immovable property and to institute and be a party to legal proceedings (see Explanatory Report and the Agreement).

90 Runjic argues that by being holder of certain rights and obligations in the international legal order, the INTERPOL has achieved international *capacitas iuridica,* and consequently

Similar to the IPU, State or Governments' commitment can be inferred from several provisions of the INTERPOL Constitution[91] and at a practical level.[92] The political engagement of Governments is evidenced, for instance, at the institutional level, when Ministers attend INTERPOL's annual assemblies, or at the diplomatic level, when INTERPOL travel documents are recognised as being akin to diplomatic passports, and at the financial level, with contributions from Governments budgets.

Another example consistent with INTERPOL legal status is the recognised role of INTERPOL in bilateral[93] or multilateral[94] extradition agreements, as the entity responsible to transmit international arrest warrants between States or the use of INTERPOL Red Notices.[95]

1.2.3 The General Agreement on Tariffs and Trade

The GATT is another example. In the aftermath of the II World War, there was a need to restore financial and trade relations and to promote socio-economic growth. The idea of building a new international economic order founded on

---

international legal personality, (n 86) 169–172, 176–177. Calcara conceptualises INTERPOL as an independent transnational police network where there is a "struggle of the organisation in balancing between functionality and legality", (n 83) 17. See, Schermers and Blokker (n 3) 40.

91 Eg. Articles 4 and 7 stipulate that States are the members of INTERPOL, however they may delegate representation in any official police body; Article 38 regarding member States' financial contributions to the organisation; Article 41 on the external relation powers conferred to the organisation.

92 See EU Commission Reply to Question E-011457/2013 (17/12/2003) mentioning that: "INTERPOL, formally, is not based on an international treaty but is, in practice, treated as an international organisation with a legal personality both by countries and international organisations. This is derived notably from: the way national authorities apply for INTERPOL membership; the fact that the United Nations has a general co-operation agreement with INTERPOL; the fact that the United Nations General Assembly has awarded INTERPOL permanent observer status; the fact that INTERPOL has agreements with countries and international organisations and a headquarters agreement with France. INTERPOL is not accountable to an international court, being a *sui generis* organisation". at: https://www.europarl.europa.eu/doceo/document/E-7-2013-011707-ASW_EN.html?redirect.

93 Eg. Article II (2) of the Extradition Treaty between Canada and India; Article 12(3) of the Agreement between HKSAR and Czech Republic on Surrender of Persons; Article 13(3) of the Extradition Treaty between Portugal and Uruguay.

94 Eg. Article 8 of the Third Additional Protocol to the European Convention on Extradition; Article 6 of the Agreement on Extradition between the EU and USA. See, Article 20 of the UN Model Law on Extradition (2004).

95 The Red Notice is a notification system circulated among members informing that an arrest warrant was been issued by one of them.

three key institutions – the International Trade Organisation (ITO), IMF and WB – began to materialise.[96]

During the negotiations of the ITO Charter (1946–1948), under the aegis of the United Nations Conference on Trade and Employment (UNCTE), the GATT principles and rules were framed.[97] The Final Act that established the GATT was signed in Geneva on 30 October 1947, however it never entered into force.[98]

Nonetheless, the organisation operated on the basis of the Protocol of Provisional Application and other accession Protocols since 1 January 1948, developing an undisputable international trade regime aimed at reducing and eliminating trade barriers, along with a mechanism for dispute settlement.

The non-creation of the ITO has potentialised the role of the GATT as the leading multilateral organisation for trade co-operation for 47 years. In its efforts to reduce trade barriers, the GATT continued to craft an international trading system, improving its rules through periodic rounds of multilateral negotiations. During these rounds, the GATT also improved its institutional apparatus according to its operational needs, becoming rather complex and diverse.[99] The GATT had eight trade rounds, the last one culminated with the establishment of the WTO.[100]

---

96 *An Anatomy of the World Trade Organization* – The Anatomy Series of International Institutions in K. Adamantopoulos (ed) (Kluwer Law International 1997), 1.

97 See Preamble, para. 2–3. Eg. Principles of non-discrimination, Most Favoured Nation and reciprocity.

98 As explained in the WTO website: "What is perhaps less known is that the GATT, as an international treaty, never entered into force either. Unknown to the 23 delegations celebrating 70 years ago, it was the signature of the PPA ['Protocol of Provisional Application'], by those six 'key' countries, and not the 23 signatures of the 'Final Act' of the GATT that ultimately provided the legal hook that saved the multilateral trading system. The PPA allowed for the provisional application of the GATT for almost 50 years, and was finally terminated on 1 January 1996, one year after the entry into force of the Marrakech Agreement establishing the WTO". At: https://www.wto.org/english/tratop_e/gatt_e/task_of_signing_e.htm.

99 Eg. WTO organisational chart in the 2023, WTO Annual Report, 200. The WTO absorbed GATT's structure, see the Transitional Arrangements: Avoidance of Procedural and Institutional Duplication, Decision of the Preparatory Committee at the Implementation Conference and the Contracting Parties of 08/12/1994, para. 2.

100 The Geneva (1947), Annecy (1948) Torquay (1950), Geneva (1956), Geneva/Dillon (1960–1961), Geneva/Kennedy (1964–67), Geneva/Tokyo (1973–79) and Geneva/Uruguay (1986–94) Rounds. Eg. The adoption of the GATT Anti-Dumping Agreement in the Kennedy Round or the non-tariffs measures and "framework agreements" in the Tokyo Round or the birth of the WTO at the Uruguay Round. At: https://www.wto.org/english/thewto_e/whatis_e/tif_e/fact4_e.htm. Also, Table A-Chronology of the GATT Rounds, (n 96) 3.

The GATT's main bodies were the meeting of the Contracting Parties (plenary),[101] the Council of the Representatives (executive body),[102] and the Secretariat (led by the Interim Commission for the International Trade Organization (ICITO)).

Although the ITO never entered into force, the ICITO assumed the functions of GATT's Secretariat during its existence, within the organisations' budget. The GATT was led by a Director-General (since 1948) and assisted by Deputy Director-Generals.[103]

Other Committees were established, including the Committee on Trade and Development,[104] Committee on Balance-of-Payments Restrictions, Committee on Anti-Dumping Practices, Committee on Customs Valuation, Committee on Import Licensing, Committee on Subsidies and Countervailing Measures, Committee on Technical Barriers to Trade; The Committee on Tariff Concessions and the Technical Group on Quantitative Restrictions and Other Non-Tariff Measures, as well as other bodies and WG, each one with its terms of reference and/or procedural rules.[105]

GATT headquarters were located in Geneva and the Secretariat staff enjoyed the privileges and immunities in the host State based on the Agreement on the Privileges and Immunities of the United Nations concluded between the Swiss Federal Council and the Secretary-General of the United Nations, on 19 April 1946. This agreement was applied by analogy pursuant an agreement between

101 Article XXV (Joint Actions by the Contracting Parties). Parties shall meet and act collectively on a regular basis. Today equivalent to the WTO Ministerial Conference.

102 It was established on 04/06/1960 replacing the Intersessional Committee, which was an operational body created in early date to deal with matters expressly referred to it by the Parties and with other matters requiring urgent action. Today is the WTO General Council.

103 In September 1948, an arrangement was made with the ICITO Secretariat to permanently assist the GATT and the costs to be borne by the Contracting Parties from of 01/01/1951. Before 1965, the Director-General was referred to as the 'Executive Secretary', its designation changed to 'Director-General' on 23/03/1965. On 15/04/1987, the appointment of 'Deputy Directors-General' was approved. In 1993, a third Deputy Director-General was appointed. *Institutions and Procedures*, WTO documentation, 1127–1129, WTO website, at: https://www.wto.org/english/res_e/booksp_e/gatt_ai_e/intitu_proced_e.pdf, and https://www.wto.org/english/thewto_e/dg_e/exdgs_e.htm.

104 It was established on 26/11/1964, replacing the functions of Committee III, of the Action Committee, and its subsidiary bodies and of the Working Party on Preferences. Today is the WTO Trade Policy Review Body.

105 Some were instituted on a temporary basis, later becoming permanent bodies. Eg. Prior to 1958, the Committee on Balance-of-Payments Restrictions functioned as the Working Party on Balance-of-Payments Restrictions. Before 1962, the GATT budget was examined by an *ad hoc* working party appointed each year by the Contracting Parties. In May 1962, the Committee on Budget, Finance and Administration was appointed.

the Swiss Federal authorities and the Director-General of GATT, acting in the name of and on behalf of the Contracting Parties, signed on 18 August 1977.[106] The relationship of GATT with other IOs included the UN/ECOSOC and IMF, among others.[107]

The GATT performed its functions and exercise its powers similarly to an IO, and that was a general perception among many stakeholders.[108] This perception and conviction that the GATT is an IO is manifested in Schermers and Blokker's comment that GATT has "gradually transformed into an international organisation". These scholars point out a statement of a former Director of the Legal Affairs Division of GATT mentioning the organisations' perspective:

> [J]urists may differ on the question whether GATT is also an international organisation in a formal legal sense (...) The fact that counts for them [administrators of the organisation] is that the GATT has been acting consistently as an entity legally separate from its Contracting Parties and has been treated as having legal capacity.[109]

Later on, as an outcome of the Uruguay Round Agreements, the GATT gave rise to the WTO, which was established on 15 April 1994 by a formal agreement signed by 123 jurisdictions in Marrakesh.[110] The new organisation improves GATT model responding to new developments of the international trade and

106 This Agreement was applied by analogy to ICITO and ICITO staff by decision of the Swiss Federal Council of 20/05/1948. The same reasoning was later applied to GATT, the agreement signed by the Swiss authorities and GATT was approved by the Council of Representatives on 26/07/1977, (n 103) 1130.

107 GATT's status at the UN was controversial, however "arrangements of a practical nature have developed over the years covering exchange of information and documents, resolutions of the United Nations, reciprocal representation and coordination". The GATT never had a formal agreement with the IMF, but the organisations managed to establish a partnership co-operation over the years. About the status of GATT in the UN and IMF, ibid, 1131–1133.

108 Seyersted, *Objective International Personality of Intergovernmental Organizations – Do Their Capacities Really Depend Upon Their Constitutions* (n 22) 55; Marco Odello, 'The Developing Legal Status of the Organisation for Security and Co-operation in Europe' (2006) XXII *Anuario de Derecho Internacional*, 361.

109 Quotation of F. Roessler in relation to the Agreement establishing the WTO in J.H.J. Bourgeois, F. Berrod & E.G. Fournier (eds), *An Agreement establishing the World Trade Organisation* – The Uruguay Round Results – A European Lawyer's' Perspective 1995, footnote 128 (n 3) 33–34.

110 For an historical background, 'The GATT Years from Havana to Marrakesh', WTO website, at: https://www.wto.org/english/thewto_e/whatis_e/tif_e/fact4_e.htm.

globalisation challenges, broadening the scope to include services and intellectual property.[111]

However, the absence of a formal treaty shadowed its legal nature, making it quite controversial.[112] Donald McRae comments that: “Notwithstanding its tentative and interim nature, GATT operated for almost 50 years before being subsumed within the WTO”.[113] In this vein: “[i]t seemed well-established, but throughout those 47 years, it [the GATT] was a provisional agreement and organisation”.[114] There are also references to GATT as a *de facto* organisation as noted by Klabbers:

> GATT’s status as an IO has been debated which has led some scholars to the question-begging conclusion that if was not a *de jure* organisation, it would at least a *de facto* organisation.[115]

For Nguyen Quoc Dinh, Patrick Daillier and Alain Pellet, the GATT is an IO born from an international legal agreement in a simplified form that was progressively institutionalised.[116] The complexity of the GATT’s institutional structure and *modus operandi* is revealed in the transition period that occurred between the GATT and the WTO.

During the Marrakesh Ministerial Meeting, a Preparatory Committee for the WTO was created with a mandate *inter alia* to ensure a smooth transition from GATT to WTO. The Preparatory Committee was entrusted with administrative, budgetary, and financial matters, as well as with institutional, procedural, and

111 Eg. General Agreement on Trade in Services and the Agreement on Trade-Related Aspects of Intellectual Property Rights.

112 In this regard, Claudio Zanghì comments that “[s]ulla personalità giuridica del GATT, la dottrina non è unanime” (free translation: “regarding the legal personality of the GATT, the doctrine is not unanimous”). *Diritto delle Organizzazioni Internazionali* (3rd ed, G.Giappichelli Editore 2013), 108–110.

113 ‘General Agreement on Tariffs and Trade’ (United Nations Audiovisual Library of International Law, 22/09/2021 – This Introductory Note was written in June 2021), 6. The “GATT was not intended to be a fully independent body. Its function was to act as an interim measure to put into effect the commercial policy provision of the ITO”, (n 96) 2.

114 Under the topic ‘GATT: ‘Provisional’ for Almost Half a Century’, WTO website, at: https://www.wto.org/english/thewto_e/whatis_e/tif_e/fact4_e.htm.

115 (n 3) 6, footnote 20.

116 *Droit International Public* (3rd ed., L.G.D.J. 1987), 931 or *Direito Internacional Público* (4th ed, Fundação Calouste Gulbenkian 1999) 946. Also sharing this view, Zanghì (n 112) 108–110.

legal matters (ie. to make the necessary arrangements to transfer GATT's institutional structure, budget, staff, assets, liabilities, records, etc, to WTO).[117]

In the Transitional Arrangements: Avoidance of Procedural and Institutional Duplication, it is clearly stated that the GATT and WTO are two "legally distinct" organisations with members of their own,[118] and that the transition:

> [S]hall be conducted in a manner which ensures that the enjoyment of the rights and the performance of the obligations under the GATT 1947, the Tokyo Round Agreements and the WTO Agreement and the exercise of the competence of the Contracting Parties to the GATT 1947, the Committees established under the Tokyo Round Agreements and the bodies of the WTO are unaffected.[119]

The arrangements described above provide empirical evidence that GATT's nature and institutional framework are analogous to an IO than to a basic and informal organisation. They also show that, while GATT's founding instruments divert from the conventional model of creating IOs, GATT has evolved into a self-governing and autonomous organisation separate from its members.[120]

1.2.4 The Commonwealth

The Commonwealth has also been the subject of diverging views regarding its legal status. Although dating back to the British Empire, the 'modern' Commonwealth was created with the 1949 London Declaration[121] as an organisation aiming at maintaining peace and security.[122]

The Commonwealth sees itself as a non-formal organisation, ie. "a voluntary association" of independent States.[123] Nevertheless, in July 1964, the

117 Eg. Transitional Arrangements: Avoidance of Procedural and Institutional Duplication; Agreement on the Transfer of Assets, Liabilities, Records, Staff and Functions from the Interim Commission of the International Trade Organisation and the GATT to the World Trade Organisation.

118 Preamble, para. 1 of the Transitional Arrangements: Avoidance of Procedural and Institutional Duplication (n 99).

119 Ibid, op.para 4.

120 The WTO framework incorporates the GATT original text on trade in goods with the amendments of 1994 (as GATT 1994), and it is known as 'the GATT *acquis*'. The WTO is an independent organisation with international personality (Article VIII Status of the WTO).

121 At: https://thecommonwealth.org/about-us/history.

122 Commonwealth Charter (14/12/2014) and Commonwealth Declarations and Principles setting the values and main principles that govern the organisation in the different fields of action.

123 At: https://thecommonwealth.org/about-us (last visited 02/05/2024).

Commonwealth Prime Ministers decided to set up a Secretariat which was formalised through the Agreed Memorandum on the Commonwealth Secretariat (1965).[124] The Secretariat was established to "assist in supporting and building the Commonwealth association", with a budget of its own and autonomy to adopt the appropriate internal rules.[125]

The Memorandum urges Commonwealth Governments to accord legal personality, privileges and immunities, and taxes exemption privileges to the Secretariat, while it is established that the UK will give legal personality to the Secretariat and the required immunities and privileges to perform its functions.[126] A Commonwealth Secretariat Arbitral Tribunal was established on 1 July 1995.[127]

The absence of a treaty and the explicit reference in the Memorandum to the informality and flexibility of the organisation are the primary arguments for those who argue that the Commonwealth cannot be classified as an IO.[128] Others contend that a "written constitution" is not a prerequisite, and that the existing institutional framework, privileges, and immunities provide the conditions or requisites deemed necessary for the Commonwealth to perform its functions as any formal IO.[129]

124 Last amended in 2022 (last visited 15/05/2024). Bouwhuis explains in detail the powers of the Secretariat, (n 19) 460–463.

125 Eg. The Secretary-General represents the Commonwealth and directs its office in accordance with the strategic guidance of the Heads of Government. The costs of the Secretariat are borne by Commonwealth Governments. See also, Annex B (Commonwealth Secretariat Arrangement).

126 Para. 44–47 of the 2022 Further Revised Agreed Memorandum on the Commonwealth Secretariat and Annex A (Commonwealth Secretariat Propose Scale of Immunities and Privileges).

127 The court has jurisdiction in the following cases: (a) a staff member of the Commonwealth Secretariat; (b) the Commonwealth Secretariat; (c) any person who enters into a contract with the Commonwealth Secretariat. The Tribunal may also exercise jurisdiction over disputes involving other commonwealth international or intergovernmental bodies or organisations under certain conditions. See Annex C (Statute of the Commonwealth Secretariat Arbitral Tribunal (as amended)).

128 Para. 4 of the Agreed Memorandum: "At the same time the Commonwealth is not a formal organisation. It does not encroach on the sovereignty of individual members. Nor does it require its members to seek to reach collective decisions or to take united action. Experience has proved that there are advantages in such informality. It enables its members to adapt their procedures to meet changing circumstances; conversely there would be disadvantages in establishing too formal procedures and institutions in the association". Amongst others, Schermers and Blokker (n 3) 38.

129 Seyersted makes a compelling comment: "But the most striking evidence may perhaps be found in those Organisations which have been established on the basis of conventions which pretend that no Organisation is being set up, or which even say explicitly

Furthermore, it is suggested that the practice of the Commonwealth's external relations with other IOs and States, as well as the practices of States in respect to the organisation align with the understanding that the Commonwealth is indeed an IO.[130]

In light of the above and supporting the theoretical approach that an IO may be established through acts of international law other than a treaty, Stephen Bouwhuis argues:

> This instrument [Memorandum] is not a treaty status instrument, although it certainly is not an instrument governed by domestic law. In particular, it is an instrument concluded by States concerning the establishment of the Commonwealth Secretariat and the relations which are to exist between the organisation and its member States as well as what relations are to exist between each of these States as concerns the organisation. As such the Agreed Memorandum does appear to be an instrument intended to be governed by international law.[131]

1.2.5 The Nordic Council

The Nordic Council is another example. It started, on 15–16 March of 1952, as a consultation body for Nordic parliamentarians to meet regularly, following a Danish proposal.[132] This initiative was consolidated with the signing of the

that no Organisation shall be set up, but which, nevertheless, have the same organs and perform the same 'sovereign' and international acts as other intergovernmental organisations", *Objective International Personality of Intergovernmental Organizations – Do Their Capacities Really Depend Upon Their Constitutions* (n 22) 55. Brownlie and Goodwill-Gill comment that "[l]ikewise, the Commonwealth Secretariat did not start as an international organisation but may have evolved into one after adoption of the Declaration of Commonwealth Principles at the 1971 Singapore Meeting", (n 67) para. 64 and 78. Amerasinghe mentions the Commonwealth Secretariat as an example of an organisation of State's common background, *Principles of the Institutional Law of International Organizations* (n 3) 12. Bouwhuis sustains that the Memorandum "appears to be an instrument governed by international law" and develops a theory based on the indicators of legal personality, contending that the Commonwealth Secretariat is an IO, (n 19) 458–465.

130 Eg. MoU on Co-operation between the Commonwealth Secretariat and the Office of the UN High Commissioner for Human Rights (1998); MoU between the IMO and the Commonwealth Secretariat with respect to the Co-operation on Sustainable Maritime Development (2022); participation in observer missions, such as the general elections of Pakistan (08/02/2024). At: https://thecommonwealth.org/news/commonwealth-group-observe-pakistan-elections (last visited 15/05/2024).

131 (n 19) 464.

132 At: https://www.norden.org/en/news/70-years-nordic-council-still-delivering-nordic-synergies or https://www.norden.org/en/information/history-nordic-council. The Nordic Council is composed of five sovereign States (Denmark, Finland, Iceland, Norway,

Helsinki Treaty (the 'Nordic Constitution') on 23 March 1962, which changed its status into a forum for permanent co-operation.[133]

The initial informal nature and parliamentary basis of the Nordic Council was noted among scholars. Seyersted questioned the need of a convention to establish an IO, giving as an example the Nordic Council.[134] In this respect, Klabbers comments that:

> The Nordic Council itself originated as a form of co-operation between parliaments of the five States concerned (Denmark, Finland, Iceland, Norway and Sweden), rather than being clearly treaty-based.[135]

In 1971, the institutional framework of the Nordic Council was strengthened and redesigned with the creation of the Nordic Council of Ministers, and the Helsinki Treaty amended accordingly.[136] The addition of this intergovernmental political body signals and confers official empowerment to the Nordic Council. Nevertheless, like prior examples, there were still uncertainties over its international legal status.

As commented by Schermers and Blokker:

> The Nordic Council was established by parallel decisions of the parliaments of Denmark, Iceland, Norway and Sweden, the governments of these States demonstrate their approval by co-operating with the organisation (...) The borderline may be vague. Government participation in the Nordic Council has been so active that this Council can be classified as an international organisation.[137]

The Nordic Council has a complex institutional structure. It comprises a Presidium (plenary), four committees, five party groups and the Nordic

---

Sweden), which are full members, and of three associate members, which are non-sovereign States (the self-governing regions of the Faroe Islands, Greenland, and Åland).

133 As last amended on 02/01/1996 (last visited 15/05/2024).

134 *Objective International Personality of Intergovernmental Organizations – Do Their Capacities Really Depend Upon Their Constitutions* (n 22) 48–50. In the same vein, para. 4 of the Commentary to Article 2 in DARIO.

135 (n 3) 10.

136 At: https://www.norden.org/en/information/history-nordic-council-ministers. The Nordic Council Secretariat was established in Stockholm in 1971, and the Nordic Council of Ministers was created in Oslo, in 1972; both have been based in Copenhagen since July 2010.

137 (n 3) 38.

Council Secretariat.[138] The Council of Ministers is organised in 10 ministerial councils covering different sectors and one *ad hoc* Council of Ministers for Digitalisation, being represented by a Secretary-General.[139] There is also a considerable number of satellite organs and institutions.[140]

Members have decided to grant legal capacity to both Secretariats, including the capacity to acquire and dispose of real estate, to be a party to legal proceedings, as well as immunities and privileges in the Agreement concerning the Legal Status of the Nordic Council of Ministers' Secretariat and Nordic Council's Secretariat (signed on 13 May 1987).[141] Equal capacities were granted to other satellite institutions of the Nordic Council and their staff with the Agreement between Denmark, Finland, Iceland, Norway and Sweden concerning the Legal Status of the Nordic Institutions and Their Staff (signed on 9 December 1988).[142]

The Nordic Council is a regional inter-parliamentary consultative organisation that brings together representatives of the members of parliament. And although composed of parliamentary representation, the Nordic Council has set up and broadened its treaty co-operation areas to include legal, cultural, economic, social, environmental protection, transport and communications co-operation and other areas of co-operation.[143] External relations with European and other IOs and international co-operation in foreign affairs, security and defence policy are also considered major strategic points.[144]

The complex institutional structure and functional methods of the Nordic Council, on the one hand, and the political commitment, behaviour, and financial support of its members, on the other, point to an organisation parallel to a formal IO.

138 At: https://www.norden.org/en/organisation/nordic-co-operation.

139 At: https://www.norden.org/sites/default/files/2022-11/Organisationsdiagram.pdf (last visited 15/05/2024).

140 At: https://www.norden.org/en/nordic-council (last visited 15/05/2024).

141 Articles 1 and 2, last amended 29/12/2005 (last visited 15/05/2024).

142 Articles 1 and 2, last amended 03/07/2002 (last visited 15/05/2024).

143 Articles 1 and 2 of the Helsinki Treaty (as amended). A landmark example of such co-operation is the 'Nordic Passport' a document that permits the freedom of movement of the citizens across the Nordic countries.

144 At: https://www.norden.org/en/political_areas and https://www.norden.org/en/information/official-nordic-co-operation (last visited 03/05/2024).

1.2.6 The Organisation for Security and Co-operation in Europe

Another case also involved in profound controversy is the legal status of the OSCE.[145] According to Blokker and Wessel, the "OSCE still struggles with its legal status",[146] while Isabelle Pingel adds that the "questions surrounding the Organisation's status and the strengthening of its legal framework continue to prompt debate".[147]

The organisation started as a high-level conference, the so-called Conference on Security and Co-operation in Europe (CSCE), an informal forum fostering peace, justice, and co-operation on security matters in the region. It was set up through a political agreement – the 1975 Helsinki Final Act.[148]

Mindful of Europe's particular *momentum* and envisaging the role that CSCE could play in the peacebuilding, security, and disarmament in Europe, following the aftermath of the dissolution of the Warsaw Pact, the unification of Germany, and the dissolution of the Soviet Union, a comprehensive plan was adopted at the 1990 Paris Summit: The Charter of Paris for a New Europe. The initiative reached its zenith with the 1994 Budapest Summit.[149]

---

145 This controversy is well displayed in the 7th Report of the Special Rapporteur (A/CN.4/610), ILC Sixty-first Session Report (2009) concerning the DARIO. In the Report it is stated that the definition "is intended to include instruments, such as resolutions adopted by an international organisation or by a Conference of States. Examples of international organisations that have been so established include (…) OSCE", 45. However, the 2011 Final Draft omitted any allusions to OSCE. Amongst others, Tufan Höbek mentions that "[t]he case of the OSCE is not a success story in terms of transforming a political entity into a legal one", 'Legal Attributes of International Organizations in the Absence of a Constituent Legal Document. The Case of the OSCE' (2011) University of Vienna, 2. At: https://backend.univie.ac.at/fileadmin/user_upload/s_rechtswissenschaft/Doktoratsstudium_PhD/Expose1/Europarecht/Legal_Attributes_of_International_Organizations_in_the_absence_of_a_constituent_legal_document.pdf. Odello also comments that "[t]he risk is that the OSCE, not being a proper international organisation with legal personality, would be in a sort of limbo, outside the realm of international law.", (n 108) 354.

146 'Revisiting Questions of Organisationhood, Legal Personality and Membership in the OSCE: The Interplay between Law, Politics and Practice' (final draft to be published in M.S. Platise, C. Moser and A. Peters (eds), *Revisiting the Legal Status of the OSCE* (Cambridge University Press 2018)), 1.

147 'Privileges and Immunities of the Organisation for Security and Co-operation in Europe (OSCE)' (2018) *Max Planck Institute for Comparative Public Law and International Law*, MPIL Research Paper Series No. 2018–37, 2.

148 At: https://www.osce.org/whatistheosce.

149 Para. 3 of the Budapest Summit Declaration strengthening the CSCE (version of 21/12/1994) states that "[t]o reflects this determination; the CSCE will henceforth be known as the Organisation for Security and Co-operation in Europe (OSCE)".

The Budapest Summit introduced significant institutional reforms, including a new name for the organisation, though maintaining its original informal nature:

> The change in name from CSCE to OSCE [Organisation for Security and Co-operation in Europe] alters neither the character of our CSCE commitments nor the status of the CSCE and its institutions. In its organisational development the CSCE will remain flexible and dynamic.[150]

Over time, the OSCE became the world largest regional security organisation, with a complex and broad institutional framework and *modus operand* akin to any formal IO, addressing a wide range of subjects covering three dimensions: politico-military, economic and environmental, and human rights.[151]

The legal status of the OSCE has been extensively debated at institutional[152] and doctrinal levels,[153] as underlined by the 2017 Austria Chairmanship of OSCE:

150 Ibid, para. 29.

151 It comprises Summits, the Ministerial Council, the Permanent Council, the Forum for Security and Co-operation, an OSCE Secretariat in Vienna, the OSCE Parliamentary Assembly in Copenhagen, the OSCE Court on Conciliation and Arbitration in Geneva, three institutions (the Office for Democratic Institutions and Human Rights in Warsaw, the High Commissioner for National Minorities in The Hague and the Representative of the Freedom of Media in Vienna) and more than 14 field operations. At: https://www.osce.org/whatistheosce and https://www.osce.org/where-we-are (last visited 15/05/2024).

152 Eg. The 1993 Rome Council Decision that attempts to harmonise the rules regarding the legal capacity of the CSCE institutions and privileges and immunities; 2007 Draft Convention on the International Legal Personality, Legal Capacity, and Privileges and Immunities of the OSCE; 2009 Informal WG on Strengthening the Legal Framework of the OSCE; 2013 Report to the Ministerial Council on 'Strengthening the Legal Framework of the OSCE; 2015 Report of the Legal Services of the OSCE Secretariat at the Helsinki + 40 Project', Food-for-Thought Paper: 'The OSCE Lack of an Agreed Legal Status – Challenges in Crisis Situations'; 2015 'The Question of Legal Status for the OSCE and Implications for Ukraine'; 2015 Helsinki Declaration; 2015 Resolution on Helsinki + 40: Building the OSCE of the Future; and the 2017 Report of the Ministerial Council on 'Strengthening the Legal Framework of OSCE under Austria Chairmanship' (2017 OSCE Austria Chairmanship Report).

153 Amongst others, Brownlie and Goodwill-Gill (n 67) para. 63; Alexander Matveev, 'The OSCE Identity Crisis' in IFSH (ed), *OSCE Yearbook 1999* (Baden-Baden 2000); Klabbers, '(I Can't Get No) Recognition: Subjects Doctrine and the Emergence of Non-State Actors' – Essays in International Law for Martii Koskenniemi 2003 *Nordic Cosmopolitanism,* 352; Odello (n 108) 717; Höbek (n 145) 738; Jana Arsić-Đapo, 'Another Brick in the Wall – Building Up the OSCE as an International Organization One Agreement at a Time' (2017) 14 *International Organizations Law Review*, 14; Blokker and Wessel (n 146); Pingel (n 147) 740.

> The legal status of the OSCE, in particular its enjoyment of international legal personality, has been a longstanding discussion in the CSCE/OSCE for more than forty years (…) In contrast to the ongoing internal debate on the legal status of the OSCE, other international organisations recognise the international legal personality of the OSCE by routinely concluding agreements with it on an equal basis.[154]

Academics have attributed the absence of a legally binding document (treaty-based) and to the lack of strong political will, particularly that of the original participating States who envisioned an organisation with a flexible, dynamic, and low-profile diplomatic action,[155] as the main reasons for the OSCE's ambiguous legal status.[156]

As Jasna Arsić-Đapo explains:

> Though the progression from the Conference to Organisation was effected through a number of politically binding instruments, including summit-level and ministerial decisions, the fact that the OSCE has evolved considerably but is not (yet) a treaty-based organisation has left open for interpretation the issue of the international legal personality of the OSCE and the status of the OSCE as an international organisation.

154 Para. 1 and 35 of the 2017 OSCE Austria Chairmanship Report.

155 Amongst others, Matveev (n 153) 74–75; Höbek (n 145) 2'; Arsić-Đapo (n 153) 415. Klabbers mentions that: "a discernible tendency is to remain nebulous about intentions when creating international institutions. Organisations such as OSCE (…) [h]ave been established, but it remains unclear whether they are all to be regarded as full-blown organisations rather than, say, frameworks for occasional diplomacy, and even whether their constituent agreements constitute treaties or not.", (n 3) 10. Loïc Simonet and Hans Georg Lüber argue that "[w]hile the OSCE has managed to assert itself as an active and dynamic player on the international stage, it does not enjoy the attributes of an international organisation. Its *sui generis* status, the result of a unique legal and political process, leaves it in an unclear position under international law, for three main reasons". The authors founded their arguments mainly in the DARIO definition: i) not treaty-based and the non-registration condition; and ii) does not possess its own legal personality that "most constitutive documents provide [for an IO] to exercise its functions", 'The OSCE and Its Legal Status: Revisiting the Myth of Sisyphus', OSCE Yearbook 2016, 278.

156 Matveev (n 153) 74; Simonet and Lüber, ibid, 312. The uncertainty of OSCE's legal status is being questioned by the UK as regards the role of the organisation in the region because of the war in Ukraine. The role of OSCE is emphasised as the "only cooperative security organisation that brings together all NATO allies, Ukraine, Russia, Central Asian States and others with a diverse agenda", 'Current state of the Organization for Security and Co-operation in Europe' House of Lords, UK Parliament, 19/09/2023, At: https://lordslibrary.parliament.uk/current-state-of-the-organization-for-security-and-co-operation.

> The assertion that the OSCE needs a constituent treaty as a precondition to recognition of its international legal personality and the ongoing debate was an obstacle.[157]

Others like Marco Odello uphold that the OSCE "matches the main criteria required by general international law related to IOs".[158] Blokker and Wessel adopt a pragmatic approach, observing that the current impasse creates an "international legal *vacuum*" from which for the OSCE it is "difficult to escape the application of international rules".[159] Seyersted is more straightforward; based on his objective criteria theory, OSCE is undoubtedly an IO since 1994.[160]

The argument that there is a lack of political motivation because both the Charter of Paris and 1994 Budapest Summit Declaration stipulate that their texts "are not eligible for registration under Article 102 of the UN Charter"[161] is debatable. Both instruments are translated into six languages,[162] have depository entities[163] with the responsibility, *inter alia* to transmit the texts to the UN Secretary-General and circulate them among members and other IOs as an official UN document.[164]

---

157 (n 153) 415.

158 Odello's reasoning is based on soft law, customary law and general principles of international law, (n 108) 392–393. Also supporting this view, amongst others, Blokker and Wessel (n 146) 3–7, 13–14 and Arsić-Đapo (n 153) 429. Shermers and Blokker comment that "[w]hile States originally decided that the Organisation for Security and Co-operation in Europe should not be structured as an international organisation, in practice this Conference has become a fully-fledged organisation", (n 3) 1212.

159 In a metaphorical manner Blokker and Wessel state that: "According to the duck test (if it looks like a duck, swims like a duck, and quacks like a duck, it probably is a duck) this seems fully justified.", ibid, 20–21.

160 *Common Law of International Organizations* (n 22) 21. Also sharing this view, Zanghì (n 112) 106–108. According to Lisa Tabassi, the conclusions of the ICJ "can easily be assimilated word-for-word to the situation of the OSCE", Update on the Operational Consequences of the Lack of a Clear Legal Status of the OSCE, Open-Ended Informal WG on Strengthening the Legal Framework of the OSCE, 29/04/2016, attached to SEC.GAL/67/16, 06/05/2016 (para. 2.2.).

161 At: 13 and para. 21–22, respectively.

162 English, French, German, Italian, Russian and Spanish.

163 French and Hungarian Government, respectively.

164 Moreover, each participating State must receive an authentic copy of both instruments and must publish domestically and disseminated widely. Host countries must enable OSCE institutions to function fully, including to enter into contractual and financial obligations and be accorded diplomatic status. Dinh, Daillier and Pellet suggest that the Charter of Paris and Budapest Summit Declaration can be recognised as agreements in simplified form, (n 116) 354–355 or 353–354.

On the other hand, the recognition of the OSCE by Austria and Poland, respectively with the conclusion of the Agreement between the Republic of Austria and the OSCE regarding the Headquarters of the Organisation, signed on 14 June 2017,[165] and the Arrangement between the OSCE and the Government of the Republic of Poland regarding the Status of the OSCE, signed on 28 June 2017,[166] provides a solid basis for consolidating the position of those who favour the OSCE as an international legal person.[167]

1.2.7 The Black Sea Economic Co-operation

The BSEC, today a regional economic organisation, is an illustration of a classical evolution of a joint multilateral political initiative that progressively evolved until the participating States agreed to institute a formal IO.

The Black Sea initiative began with a high-level meeting in Istanbul of the Heads of State and Government of the countries of the Baltic region[168] with the aim of promoting economic co-operation, particularly to address the priorities and needs of countries that were "in transition to market economy".[169]

Co-operation was predominantly envisioned in the finance, trade and economic areas, where consideration was given as to establish a Black Sea Foreign Trade and Investment Bank (BSTDB).[170] In addition, and whilst desiring a flexible and informal format, there was a common understanding that Ministers for Foreign Affairs should hold annual meetings to assess progress and define new priority areas, and to set up *ad hoc* and permanent WGs of experts in the different fields of co-operation, whenever necessary.[171]

The high-level meeting ended with the signing of the Summit Declaration on Black Sea Economic Co-operation and the 'Bosporus Statement' on 25 June

165 Article II – Legal Capacity, Section 2.

166 Arsić-Đapo (n 153) 414, 416 *et seq* and 2017 OSCE Austria Chairmanship Report, 20.

167 Ibid, 420. Para. 41 of the 2017 OSCE Austria Chairmanship Report concludes: "[e]ven if the original intention of the participating States was not to create an international legal person, the acts of the CSCE/OSCE decision-making bodies have had the consequence of creating one, as its operations and its treatment are otherwise not explainable in legal terms" (the same reasoning as the ICJ applied to the UN in *Reparation of Injuries*).

168 Albania, Armenia, Azerbaijan, Bulgaria, Georgia, Greece, Moldova, Romania, Russia, Turkey and Ukraine. Today 13 countries with North Macedonia and Serbia. At: https://www.bsec-organization.org/member-states (last visited 09/05/2024).

169 Summit Declaration on Black Sea Economic Co-operation, para. 9–10.

170 Ibid, para 16. See the Agreement establishing the Black Sea Trade and Development Bank of 30/06/1994 established the BSTDB. It is endowed with legal personality (Article 44) and its headquarters are located in Thessaloniki, Greece (Headquarters Agreement between the Government of the Hellenic Republic and the BSTDB of 28/10/1998).

171 Summit Declaration, para. 7.

1992, marking the beginning of this new multilateral partnership. Two years later, a Permanent International Secretariat is established on 10 March 1994 and BSEC's headquarters placed in Istanbul.[172]

The Statement of the high-level meetings of the BSEC, in Bucharest, on 30 June 1995, refers to a growing number of bodies and a higher degree of formalisation being designed.[173] The creation of the BSTDB is acclaimed, and a deeper political commitment of the participating States is envisioned. Countries are urged to allocate domestic "co-ordination structures entrusted with the implementation of BSEC projects and decisions"[174] and to expand co-operation areas (eg. system of transportation and communication, co-operation programmes on energy resources and environment).[175]

The degree of political engagement and multilateral co-operation in multiple domains led to a geostrategic decision to establish a more formal institutional setting. In the Moscow Declaration of the Heads of State or Government of the participating States of the Black Sea Economic Cooperation, dated 25 October 1996, members agreed:

> [T]hat one of the priorities at present is the strengthening of the institutional and legal basis of the BSEC which will contribute to enhancing effectiveness of the Black Sea Economic Co-operation and ensuring better interaction in all its dimensions including intergovernmental, interparliamentary, business, finance, academic and public ones (…) consider it appropriate that the process of transformation of the BSEC into a regional economic organisation be continued.[176]

On 5 June 1998, in Yalta, the BSEC became a formal IO with the signing of the Charter of Organisation of the Black Sea Economic Co-operation, maintaining the same acronym. In the Yalta Summit Declaration, the participating States affirm BSEC's new status:

172 At: https://www.bsec-organization.org/bsec-at-glance; https://www.bsec-organization.org/faq.

173 The Bucharest Statement mentions BSEC Subsidiary Bodies and the BSTDB (para. 2) and the 1996 Moscow Declaration refers to various bodies such as the BSEC Parliamentary Assembly, the BSTDB, the Business Council as well as the Centers affiliated to the BSEC, involving a complex structure.

174 Para. 6.

175 Para. 5.

176 Item 2 'Strengthening of the Institutional and Legal Framework of the BSEC', 3.

> To that end we signed the Charter of the Organisation of the Black Sea Economic Co-operation, an act which transforms the existing intergovernmental mechanism into a fully-fledged regional economic organisation. [177]

The Charter of BSEC also recognised the "need to (…) consolidate the international legal personality" of the organisation, transforming into a more formal standing.[178]

Notwithstanding the significance of the Charter, the value of the previous legal instruments, high-level statements, decisions, and rules of procedure is undisputable and constitutes an *acquis* of the organisation, where principles and objectives of co-operation were laid down as well as proceedings. All instruments should, therefore, be read in a comprehensive manner.[179]

1.2.8 The European Union

The last controversial example is the legal status of the EU until the signing of the Treaty of Lisbon in 2007. The absence of an explicit provision in the EU Treaty (1992 Maastricht Treaty) conferring legal personality to the EU sparked a divisive debate, especially considering that its predecessor treaties – the Treaty establishing the European Coal and Steel Community (1951), Treaty establishing the European Economic Community (1957) and the Treaty establishing the European Atomic Energy Community (1957), all contemplated a provision granting international legal personality to the organisations (Articles 6, 210 and 184, respectively).

In this respect, Gabriel Pascu and Caius Tudor Luminosu commented that:

> The ratification of the Maastricht Treaty triggered ample debates in German literature, both regarding the legal nature of the EU and the existence of a legal personality of the Union. The German Federal Constitutional Court qualified the Union as 'a confederation of States', a notion that was widely accepted.[180]

177 Yalta Summit Declaration, para. 1. The Charter entered into force on 01/05/1999.

178 Preamble para. 11–12, Article 1. See Article 27 (Legal Capacity), Article 28 (Privileges and Immunities). Additional Protocol on the Privileges and Immunities of the BSEC signed on 30/04/1999 and the Headquarters Agreement between the Organisation of the Black Sea Economic Co-operation and the Government of Turkey signed on 27/04/2002.

179 Eg. Istanbul Summit Declaration (07/11/1999), para. 1.

180 'The Legal Personality of the European Union – between the Maastricht Treaty and the Draft Treaty Establishing a Constitution for Europe – Reality and Perspectives' (2006) 6(3) *Romanian Journal of European Affairs*, 55.

The above situation was acknowledged and debated internally, some countries expressed reluctance to recognise the EU as a legal person, others advocated the need for clarification of its legal status.[181] Even so, neither the Amsterdam Treaty (1997) nor the Nice Treaty (2001) resolved this ambiguous *status quo*. The 2004 EU Draft Constitution attempted to settle this 'constitutional impasse' by including a provision, but the Constitution was never adopted.[182] As Philippe de Schoutheete and Sami Andoura noted:

> European treaties are notorious for legal ambiguities and internal contradictions resulting from precarious compromises between opposing views. The matter of the legal personality of the European Union is a good example.[183]

Paradoxically, the Maastricht Treaty granted *ius tractum* capacities (to negotiate and conclude treaties) in common foreign affairs and defence policy, as well as in legal and police co-operation in criminal matters,[184] while the Amsterdam Treaty created the figure of the High Representative for Common Foreign and Security Policy.[185] These features favoured the supporters of EU's personhood.

The fact is, as correctly observed in the 2002 Final Report of the European Convention WG III on Legal Personality, an "explicit conferral of a single legal personality on the Union does not *per se* entail any amendment".[186]

181 See the European Parliament Report on the Legal Personality of the EU (2001/2021(INI)); 2002 Final Report of the European Convention WG III on Legal Personality. About the diverging opinions and fears of some member States, amongst others, Wessel, 'Revisiting the International Legal Status of the EU' (2000) 5(4) *European Foreign Affairs Review*; Pascu and Luminosu, ibid; Philippe de Schoutheete and Sami Andoura, 'The Legal Personality of the European Union' (2007) LX(1) *Studia Diplomatica*.

182 The Treaty establishing a Constitution for Europe (2004) adopted by the European Council was rejected by France and The Netherlands in their national *referenda*. At: https://www.europarl.europa.eu/about-parliament/en/in-the-past/the-parliament-and-the-treaties/draft-treaty-establishing-a-constitution-for-europe. Amongst others, Schoutheete and Andoura, ibid, 8; Joxerramon Bengoetxea, 'The EU as (More Than) an International Organization' in J. Klabbers and A. Wallendahl (eds), *Research Handbook on the Law of International Organizations* (Edward Elgar 2011/2014), 461.

183 Ibid, 1.

184 Articles 24 and 38.

185 Articles J.8(3) and J.16.

186 Para. 20. Even so, the Report also acknowledges that "[c]ertain amendments, however, do seem desirable in order to enhance the effectiveness of the Union's external action and simplify existing procedures", (para. 21).

International personality can be inferred, following the *ratio* expressed in the ICJ Opinion in *Reparation of Injuries* (to be addressed further below).

The debate about the legal status of the EU extended to academia.[187] Some scholars categorically opposed to recognise the legal personality of the EU,[188] while others like Wessel, defended the "inherent status of the EU as an international legal entity".[189] In the same lines, de Schoutheete and Andoura stressed that there is a general acceptance "in international public law that legal personality can be implicitly conferred to an IO".[190]

Wessel argues that "legal persons are legal facts" derived from the constitutive legal rule that creates them.[191] In this case, the EU is an *institutional legal fact* and, consequently, a legal person because it arises from the Maastricht Treaty (constitutive rule) that was precisely designed to create the organisation. Thus, the EU is a subject of international law with a distinct will from its founding members, wherein its legal capacities (explicit and implicit) are a corollary of EU's legal personality.[192]

For de Schoutheete and Andoura "there is little doubt that the European Union has implicitly acquired international legal personality" under international law.[193] The authors analysed the EU case in light of the *rationale* of the ICJ Opinion in *Reparation of Injuries* (purposes and functions of the EU), of the criteria adopted by doctrine (Brownlie criteria) and EU practice, particularly its "treaty-making power which is one of the main characteristics of international

187 Amongst others, Klabbers (n 153) 352; Klabbers (n 3) 6, footnote 20; de Schoutheete and Andoura (n 181) 792; Seyersted, *Common Law of International Organizations* (n 22) 52; Schermers and Blokker (n 3) 991. In this regard, see in particular, points C, E, I and L of the European Parliament Report on the Legal Personality of the EU (2001/2021(INI)).

188 At the time, the majority of German doctrine refused to accept the EU as a subject of international law, and consequently as an IO. Pascu and Luminosu (n 180) 59–60.

189 Wessel analyses the concept of legal personality, the EU's treaty-making capacity and implied external capacities as a whole (n 181) 507 *et seq.*

190 (n 181) 3. The authors explain that "[i]n 1996, the Reflection Group preparing the Amsterdam negotiations said that the Union 'did not exist' on the international scene. That would no longer be true today. The Union is a recognised actor in its own right", 7–8.

191 (n 181) 513–515.

192 Ibid, 553.

193 As the authors explain: "The absence of a treaty clause would of course in no way diminish the existing implicit legal personality of the Union, now recognised worldwide and disputed only by a small minority of member States. The situation would develop as it has done in the past few years with additional evidence in the form of new treaties concluded with more partners. But the situation would be much less satisfactory than that resulting from the constitutional treaty", (n 181) 9.

legal personality".[194] External recognition among its counterparts, which is visible in multiple joint missions and the fact that enjoys diplomatic representation are additional persuasive factors.[195]

Despite some political opposition to formally recognising the international legal personality of the EU, reality has proven that the EU is seen as an international on par with its peers.[196] As Schermers and Blokker perceptively remarked, the "EU experience is an example of how practice can be more powerful than politics".[197]

This controversy was resolved with the inclusion of an explicit mention regarding the legal character of the EU in Article 47 of the Treaty of Lisbon: "The Union shall have legal personality".[198]

1.3 *Finding Common Ground among International Organisations*

Notwithstanding the foregoing, there is a *common ground* that may be found among IOs, and this common ground has been a central focus of international institutional law.[199] Although it is true that there is no "unique blueprint for

194 Eg. Agreements concluded with countries for the crisis management in the Balkans or for peacekeeping operations in the Democratic Republic of Congo, or with other IOs, such as, NATO or ICC (Article 34 of the TEU). Agreement between the EU and Iceland and Norway on the application of certain provisions of the Convention of on Mutual Assistance in Criminal Matters (Article 38 of the TEU) or with the USA on Extradition and Mutual Legal Assistance in Criminal Matters (Articles 24 and 38 of the TEU).

195 Eg. The accreditation of two EU Council representations to the UN in New York and Geneva; taking the floor in the UNSC; participation in diplomatic activities and crisis management missions; appointment of Special Representatives of the EU in specific regions, such as: Middle East, Great Lakes, Macedonia, Kosovo, Moldova, Afghanistan, South Caucasus.

196 As Bengoetxea commented: "No two organisations are alike: they are all *sui generis*. But some international organisations (IOs) are more *sui generis* than others. The European Union (EU), formerly including the European Community (EC), is clear one of them", (n 182) 448.

197 Schermers and Blokker (n 3) 993. As affirmed by Judge Allan Rosas: "Today there are no uncertainties regarding EU's legal nature. It is a subject of international law, with legal personality and bound to international law", 'The European Court of Justice and Public International Law', Speech at the CoE Committee of Legal Advisers on Public International Law on 23/03/2018. At: https://rm.coe.int/statement-delivered-by-judge-allan-rosas-at-the-55th-cahdi-meeting-55t/16807b3b04.

198 The Treaty of Lisbon amends the EU Treaty and adopts a set of 'constitutional norms', replacing the EC and EURATOM Treaties (Protocols). It comprehends the Treaty on the Functioning of the EU. More at: https://european-union.europa.eu/principles-countries-history/principles-and-values/founding-agreements_en.

199 About the emergence of IOs and international institutional law, amongst others, Alvarez (n 10) 4–8; Amerasinghe, 'International Institutional Law – a Point of View' (n 3) 149–150. Amerasinghe speaks of the concept, aims and nature of international institutional

the institutional law of all international organisations",[200] IOs share a certain 'unity in diversity'.

Common institutional frameworks, as well as common practices and general principles can be discerned among the different IOs.[201] As Sands and Klein properly observed:

> [E]ach organisation of course has its own governing law deriving from its constituent instrument and decisions and resolutions it adopts, as well as its established practice. Each organisation may therefore be considered as something of a sub-system. However, that plainly does not preclude the possibility that there may exist a common law of international organisations and that a degree of cross-fertilisation of basic principles might occur.[202]

Each IO develops its own *modus operandi* and law-creating practices, which bear no binding character on other IOs, but may offer direction for analogous or comparable situations.[203] The production of internal norms, rules of procedure, practice standards and guidelines, which generate systematic behaviour patterns and common solutions usually leads to precedents and the emergence of uniform principles within the organisation.[204] As Seyersted commented:

> The common law of intergovernmental organisations is not normally found in the constitutional or other conventions between the member

law as *lex specialis* in *Principles of the Institutional Law of International Organizations* (n 3) 15–17, 33; Amerasinghe, 'The Law of International Organizations: A Subject which Needs Exploration and Analysis' (2004) republished in E. Kwakwa (ed), *Globalization and International Organizations* (Ashgate Publishing 2011). Golia Jr and Peters critically comment the narrow scope of international institutional law since there are aspects of IOs which are not regulated or governed by international law but by domestic legislation (eg. law of the host State) or by chosen domestic law (eg. contracts or dispute resolution), (n 32) 26.

200 Blokker 'Comparing Apples and Oranges? Reinventing the Wheel?' (2008) 5(1) *International Organizations Law Review*, 200.

201 Alvarez (n 10) 4, 8, 15–17.

202 Sands and Klein (n 11), 16.

203 Amongst others, Amerasinghe speaks about the individuality and uniqueness of each IO and that there is no general law or general principles applicable to all IOs, *Principles of the Institutional Law of International Organizations* (n 3) 15–17; same author (n 199). Seyersted describes basic aspects and provides examples of common rules and practices developed by IOs, *Common Law of International Organizations* (n 22) 21–29.

204 Amerasinghe, ibid, 17–19.

> States, but in the customary law developed in common by numerous IGOs.[205]

There is a classic design among IOs as regards their institutional structure. In general, it consists of a plenary body (General Assembly, Parliamentary Assembly, Conference of Parties, Council of the member States or Ministers) as the policy-making and authority organ, an executive body (Executive Council or Committee, Council or Board of member States) responsible to implement, administer and supervise the decisions of the plenary and an administrative body (Secretariat or sort of secretariat) responsible for the administrative and bureaucratic part.

Depending on the powers, scope, size, composition and financial resources of the IO, its structure may be more or less complex. It may have subsidiary bodies (Committees, WG, Panels) within the Secretariat edifice or separately, a court-like body (eg. ICJ or WTO Dispute Settlement Mechanism) and a liaison mechanism with NGOs (eg. UN, CoE, WTO).

The size and complexity of the Secretariat also mirrors the size and complexity of the IO. Some are composed of a Secretary-General and Deputy Secretary Generals and a paraphernalia of committees and sub-committees, administrative employees and staff members such as political appointees and experts designated by members.[206] For example, the WTO has one Director-General and four Deputy-Director Generals with around 620 staff members and more than 20 divisions,[207] and the ICAO has one Secretary General who runs five divisions, seven Regional Offices and four other departments, involving around 671 staff members.[208]

---

205 Ibid, 21.

206 The exceeding number of committees and sub-committees in some organisations to assist in decision-making gives rise to the concept of 'comitology'. This concept has been used as a reference to the 'system of committees' developed in the EU. Klabbers raises some concerns about this phenomenon: where are the Parties' decision-making and the objectives effectively taking place? These concerns interlink with: i) checks and balances; ii) democracy and transparency; iii) composition of these committees. (n 3) 161–163. This phenomenon is not exclusive to the EU, it is patent in many IOs, raising the question of who really runs the IO: Parties or these committees full of bureaucrats?

207 At: https://www.wto.org/english/thewto_e/whatis_e/tif_e/org4_e.htm and https://www.wto.org/english/thewto_e/secre_e/intro_e.htm (last visited 15/05/2024).

208 2022 ICAO Annual Report of the Council to the Assembly (6.3 Human Resources Management), 30; ICAO Chart, at: https://www.icao.int/DownloadDocsFix/Organigramme_en.pdf (last visited 05/05/2025).

The decision-making process is usually driven by three modes: unanimity, consensus or majority basis, and sources of income are usually funding through member Parties mandatory and voluntary contributions.

IOs carry out many activities in order to fulfil their mandate. Lawmaking is one of the major functions fostering intergovernmental co-operation among the Parties.[209] However, they have a number of operational activities that go beyond rule-making and legal harmonisation, *inter alia* scientific and research activities, technical standards and best practices, implementation and monitoring compliance, generating and collecting information, exchanging and publishing information, adjudicating conflicts and applying sanctions, if necessary.

Generally, the 'life of IOs' is usually conducted and guided by the application of the following sources of international law:

i) Conventional law, *ie.* constitution or constitutional texts, statutes, regiments, internal regulation, as well as interpretation of these texts generating general principles and practices, in particular in areas concerning membership, privileges and immunities;
ii) Customary law in areas regarding the responsibility of and to IOs; and
iii) General principles of law, in particular in areas related to administrative matters, *ultra vires* doctrine and employment relations.[210]

As subjects of international law, all IOs possess rights and obligations under international law and are subject to the general principles and rules of international law.

2 IOs as Subjects of International Law and Theoretical Approaches

2.1 *International Personality and Capacity*

It is unquestionable that IOs are subjects of international law. They are secondary[211] or derivative[212] subjects of international law since they are *legal*

209 The acts of IOs can be of many sorts, such as recommendations, decisions, resolutions and are in general non-binding (soft law). Some exceptions are the UNSC Resolutions (Articles 24 and 25 of the UN Charter) and EU Regulations (Article 249 of EU Treaty), which bind all member States. See Alvarez (n 10) or Klabbers (n 3).

210 Schermers and Blokker commented that "the general development of the institutional structure of international organisations over time represents in some measure an *acquis institutionnel*, an institutional achievement or *status quo* that has been accepted and is used and further developed.", (n 3) 1219. Amongst others, Amerasinghe, *Principles of the Institutional Law of International Organizations* (n 3) 15–21; Akande (n 4) 258.

211 Sands and Klein (n 11) 474; Purdă (n 4) 891.

212 Purdă, ibid, 22; Jones (n 45) 11–12, 27.

constructions[213] of the international legal system. IOs are created under and by international law, originally and traditionally by States, the primary subject of international.[214]

The acknowledgement of the emergence of new subjects of international law in the dynamics of the international scene is well noted by Lauterpacht in 1970:

> [B]ear in mind that the range of subjects of international law is not rigidly and immutably circumscribed by any definition of the nature of international law but is capable of modification and development in accordance with the will of the States and the requirements of international course.[215]

The theoretical debate over the legal status of IOs dates back to early twentieth century,[216] when admitting that entities other than States can be subjects of international law. Again, Lauterpacht wrote:

> As in any other legal system, so also in the international sphere the subjects of law are the persons, national and juridical, upon whom the law confers rights and imposes duties. In international law, these persons are normally States; but they are not so exclusively. Organisations of States,

213 Klabbers (n 3) 6–7; Wessel (n 181) 513–514.

214 Amerasinghe, *Principles of the Institutional Law of International Organizations* (n 3) 20–21, 92–99; Alvarez (n 10) 140–141; Schermers and Blokker (n 3) 995–1007.

215 'The Subjects of International Law' (1970), republished in A. Bianchi (ed), *Non-State Actors and International Law* (Routledge 2009), 137.

216 In 1945, Wilfred Jenks commented that: "There has in the past been a considerable amount of controversy on the question whether public international organisations can be regarded as possessing legal personality. In the absence of any clear definition of the position recourse has been had, in order to avoid practical inconvenience of an analogous legal status, to agreements with the States where such organisations have had their headquarters recognising that the organisation enjoy legal personality and to such doubtful expedients as securing legal personality for public organisations by incorporation of analogous action under some system of municipal law". The author provides the dispute about the recognition of the international personality of the BIS under Swiss law as a good example. 'The Legal Personality of International Organizations' (1945), republished in F. Johns (ed), *International Legal Personality* (Routledge 2010), 229–230. David Bederman provides a brief historical context and evolution of the theoretical debate around the subjects of international law and legal personality, 'The Souls of International Organizations: Legal Personality and the Lighthouse at Cape Sparte' (1995–1996), republished in F. Johns (ed), *International Legal Personality* (Routledge 2010), 265–268, 332–354.

> having a different juridical personality from the States composing them, may and have become subjects of international law.[217]

The well-known ICJ Advisory Opinion in *Reparation of Injuries* stands as a landmark in expressly recognising the existence of other subjects of international law other than States, by affirming that "[t]he subjects of law in any legal system are not necessarily identical in their nature or in the extent of their rights, and their nature depends upon the needs of the community".[218]

The case in this Advisory Opinion was whether the UN had capacity to bring an international claim against a non-member (Israel) for the death of Count Folke Bernadotte, an appointed UN mediator for the Israeli-Palestinian conflict.[219] Before ruling on the claim's right, the Court had first to determine whether the UN enjoyed international legal personality, however, the absence of an explicit *provisio* in the UN Charter conferring such quality caused an extensive debate.[220]

Although this circumstance was neither unusual nor understood as problematic,[221] as other IOs like the IMO, WHO or WMO have no reference to it in their founding treaties;[222] all the same, it remained a controversial

217 (n 215) 136. Lauterpacht lectures on the concept and provides examples of different subjects of international law apart from States, such as individuals, belligerents, insurgents, colonies and other dependencies and the Holly See. For an understanding on the initial thoughts about the idea and conceptualisation of legal persons and legal personality, Hans Aufricht, 'Personality In international Law' (1943), republished in F. Johns (ed), *International Legal Personality* (Routledge 2010).

218 ICJ Reports 1949, 178. Lauterpacht mentioned that by affirming the international legal personality of the UN, the ICJ clarifies that there is life beyond States in the international arena, ibid, 140–141.

219 Count Folke Bernadotte was a Swedish diplomat. He and his French aide were killed in Jerusalem, in 1948, while acting on behalf of the UN. At: https://nl.wikipedia.org/wiki/Folke_Bernadotte.

220 The UN Charter only refers to legal capacity and privileges and immunities (Articles 104 and 105).

221 As Jones comments: "But, despite an early plea to include express personality articles in the interests of clarity, most constituent treaties do not do so. Indeed, prior to the 1990s they were extremely rare and it is only in more recent times they have become more conspicuous. There is, therefore, a curious lack of relevant practice to support the assertion that express constitutional provisions are, or ought to be, determinative of legal personality", (n 45) 28. Along these lines, Blokker (n 200) 200.

222 Article 64, Articles 66–68 and Article 27, respectively, only refer to legal capacity and privileges and immunities.

matter. As it happens, this topic was discussed when the UN Charter was being crafted.[223]

Some delegations supported a clear provision in the UN Charter to avoid misunderstandings, others had serious reservations, fearing the emergence of a 'super-State'.[224] In the end, the Drafting Committee left the subject from the UN Charter, deeming it a "superfluous matter". The legal personality of the UN would be inferred "from the provisions of the Charter as a whole" (interpretation) and developed in practice.[225]

In its Advisory Opinion in *Interpretation of the Agreement of 25 March 1951 between the WHO and Egypt 1980*, the ICJ ruled unequivocally that "international organisations are subjects of international law".[226] And, in the Advisory Opinion in *Legality of the Use by a State of Nuclear Weapons in Armed Conflict 1996*, the Court noted that it "need hardly point out that international organisations are subjects of international law".[227]

Even though not providing, as stated earlier, a comprehensive definition or identifying the general requirements to qualify an IO, the ICJ acknowledged that IOs are subjects of international law and governed by international law:

> International organisations (...) are bound by any obligations incumbent upon them under general rules of international law, under their constitutions or under international agreements to which they are parties.[228]

As different subjects of international law, their powers, rights, and obligations will differ from those of States, as asserted by the Court:

> That is not the same thing as saying that it is a State, which it certainly is not, or that its legal personality and rights and duties are the same as those of a State. Still less is it the same thing as saying that it is a 'super-State', whatever that expression may mean. It does not even imply that all its rights and duties must be upon the international plane, any more than

223 The Court also commented: "Does the Organisation possess international personality? This is no doubt a doctrinal expression, which has sometimes given rise to controversy", ICJ Report 1949, 178.

224 Ibid, 179.

225 Jenks (n 216) 231–232; Amerasinghe 'International Legal Personality Revisited' (1995), republished in F. Johns (ed), *International Legal Personality* (Routledge 2010), 241–242; Shermers and Blokker (n 3) 988.

226 ICJ Reports 1980, 89–90.

227 ICJ Reports 1986, para. 25, 78.

228 ICJ Reports 1980, 89–90.

> all the rights and duties of a State must be upon that plane. What it does mean is that it is a subject of international law and capable of possessing international rights and duties, and that it has capacity to maintain its rights by bringing international claims.[229]

As the Court emphasised, being a subject of international law means to be embodied with international legal personality, capacity, and responsibility,[230] ie. to be vested in powers, rights and obligations under international law.[231] As Amerasinghe explains:

> Having international personality for an IO means possession of rights, duties, powers and liabilities, etc, as distinct from its members or its creators on the international plane and in international law. What these rights, etc, are and how they are established is the subsequent question.[232]

The characteristic of having international responsibility is equally a sign of the organisation's factual independence on the international plane as an international legal person (Chapter 5 below).

In tune with the theoretical understanding of Wessel, Amerasinghe and Seyersted, I consider that international legal personality is associated with the *being*, the existence of a legal person *in* and *under* international law, while international legal capacity comprehends the *means* and *powers* that are granted to such organisation to perform its functions and purposes.

Some of these capacities may be categorised as *general capacities*, 'inherently' enjoy by all IOs (common to all), and others as *specific capacities,*

229 ICJ Reports 1949, 179.

230 On international legal personality, amongst others, Brownlie (n 28) 680–689; Amerasinghe, *Principles of the Institutional Law of International Organizations* (n 3) 92 *et seq*; M.N.S. Sellers, 'International Legal Personality' (2005) 11 *IUS GENTIUM*; Klabbers, 'The Concept of Legal Personality' (2005) 11 *IUS GENTIUM*; Sands and Klein (n 11) 477, Akande (n 4) 255–256; Tarcisio Gazzini, 'The Personality of International Organizations' in J. Klabbers and A. Wallendahl (eds), *Research Handbook on the Law of International Organizations* (Edward Elgar 2011/2014).

231 Amongst others, Amerasinghe, ibid, 92–104 or 'International Institutional Law – a Point of View' (n 3) 147. In a straightforward manner, Sellers affirms: "personality concerns the possession of rights and duties", ibid, 74.

232 (n 225) 243. As Sands and Klein commented: "It should be clearly understood that legal personality has no pre-determined content in international law (…) [T]he attribution of international legal personality simply means that the entity upon which it is conferred is a subject of international law and that it is capable of possessing international rights and duties.", (n 11) 477.

capacities that are specifically attributed to that particular IO in accordance with its constituent instrument(s) (purposes and functions)[233] and/or developed through practice.

Within the general capacities, one can identify *inter alia* the right to conclude treaties (*ius tractum*), the right to enjoy privileges and immunities (*ius legationis*), the right to have active and passive responsibility (ie. the right to bring international claims and to be internationally accountable), the right to recognise other subjects of international law, the right to own property, the right to have financial autonomy and capacity to have its own budget, the right to establish its internal rules, and be exempt from taxes.[234]

Wessel distinguishes between legal personality and legal capacity in a clear and distinct manner. For the scholar, IOs are legal persons (*institutional legal facts*),[235] therefore legal personality cannot be subject to a *quantum* or measured. An organisation either exists or does not, either it has legal personality or does not.[236]

Diversely, legal capacity may be subject to variations depending on the functions and purposes assigned to a particular IO in its founding instrument(s) and according to the explicit and/or implicit rights, duties, and competences conferred upon that legal person.[237] Among these, I understand that the explicit and/or implicit rights, duties, and competences developed through practice for the organisation to properly perform its functions and achieve its purposes should also be considered.

Schermers and Blokker also concur that an IO either has personality or not, while its powers and capacities may vary:

> While the first question, relating to the personality of the organisation, needs an absolute, 'black and white' answer (yes or no), the answers to

233 Amongst others, Wessel (n 181) 511–512, 518, 533–534; same author (n 55); Seyertested, *Common Law of International Organizations* (n 22) 32–33; Purdă (n 4) 895.

234 Purdă explains in detail the forms of manifestations related to international personality of IOs, ibid, 895–900. Also, Wessel, idid, 511–512; Alvarez (n 10) 134; Amerasinghe *Principles of the Institutional Law of International Organizations* (n 3) 15–23, 68–69, 80–82, 100–102; Schermers and Blokker (n 3) 1139–1149; Akande (n 4) 258; Jones (n 45) 6–7, 27–28.

235 As the author explains: "The institutional fact as such is something of which the existence cannot be denied (being *a fact*) once a constitutive rule decides on its existence. This also underlines the view that *partial* legal personality is impossible", ibid, 514.

236 Ibid, 508–514.

237 Ibid, 511–512. However, there is a close and inseparable link between the 'being' and the 'exercise of capacities', wherein the legal person is only 'successful' if there is a relation "between the institutional fact (*being* a legal person) and the rights, powers and responsibilities attached to the existence of that institutional fact (the 'legal capacities')", 514–515.

> the second question, more relative, and vary from organisation to organisation (…) because organisations exercise only those powers that have been attributed to them.[238]

In this respect, a critical note to the ICJ Opinion in *Reparation of Injuries* where the two concepts – personality and capacity – are mixed. The absence of a clear distinction between them and the fact that the Court did not resort to domestic law to drawn up such distinction, contributed to the uncertainty and debate surrounding the concept of personality.

On this topic of characterising an international legal person, Runjic makes a compelling observation that deserves reflection, remembering that the dynamics of the international system is at the *heart* of the emergence of (new) subjects of law, as well as to the 'relativeness' of the concept:

> Who is a subject of international law, ie. who is an international legal person, is one of the fundamental and most controversial issues of international law. The answer to this question is to be sought at the very heart of international law, where subjects of international law represent both the starting point and the end point of international law. Moreover, to this day no single definition of a subject of international law has been adopted at the level of positive international law, delegating the definition of this concept to the international legal doctrine. The cause for this can be traced back to the fact that the dynamics of international relations is driven by the needs of the international community at a given point in time, resulting in the emergence of a wide range of different subjects of international law. Consequently, international legal subjectivity is a relative concept which varies from one subject of international law to another.[239]

2.2 *Theoretical Approaches to International Personality*

The ICJ Opinion in *Reparation of Injuries* has led to many interpretations and different theoretical approaches regarding the acquisition of international legal personality by IOs.[240] The two contending theoretical approaches or

238 (n 3) 993.

239 (n 86) 173.

240 Amongst others, Wessel (n 181) 515; Alvarez (n 10) 134; Amerasignhe, *Principles of the Institutional Law of International Organizations* (n 3) 79–82, 86–91; Odello (n 108) 361–364; Sands and Klein (n 11) 474–480; Schermers and Blokker (n 3) 988–989; Jones (n 45) 1.

schools of thought are the subjective or will of founder's personality theory and the objective personality theory.[241]

The subjective personality theory holds that the acquisition of international legal personality by an IO depends solely on the *subjective intention* of its founding States. This intention should be *expressis verbis* in the constituent (binding) legal instrument. According to this theory, the functions and powers of an IO are conferred and limited to the sovereign will of the founding States and State members.[242] This theoretical approach, as Guy Jones refers:

> [A]ligns with a positivist view of the international legal system where the rules binding upon States emerge, primarily, from their consent (...) It is also compatible with a restrictive conception of the powers of international organisations, whereby all such powers are conferred by the State members and are limited to those necessary for the organisation to fulfil the purposes set out in its constituent instrument.[243]

Schermers and Blokker comment that "[t]oday this view has little if any support. In the past, it has supported mainly by socialist writers".[244] The major shortcoming of this theory is that, as observed, not all founding instruments have an explicit provision attributing legal personality to an organisation.[245]

241 In this respect, Sands and Klein commented that "the concept of legal personality and its implications are not always easy to grasp", ibid, 473. About these theories, amongst others, Seyersted, *Objective International Personality of Intergovernmental Organizations – Do Their Capacities Really Depend Upon Their Constitutions* (n 22) 15 and 45; Schermers and Blokker, ibid, 988–993; Gazzini (n 230) 35. Also, para. 8 and 9 of the Commentary to Article 2 of DARIO.

242 Alvarez argues that "International Organisations inherent powers must be premised on specific powers affirmatively granted in their Charters and that the functionality principle must be delimited to what is strictly necessary for each organisation to fulfil its functions", (n 10). 137.

243 (n 45) 9–10. Jones refers that this approach is close to the legalist approach theory and with the realism school of thought "where States are the primary actors of the international system".

244 (n 3) 988–989. Jones also refers the soviet writers as supporters of the theory that IOs could only acquire international personality through treaties, ibid, 9–11.

245 In 1945, Jenks commented how this matter was dealt: "It is of interest that in certain cases in which the instrument constituting an International Organisation does not specify that the organisations will enjoy legal personality it has been found necessary for the organisation to recommend governments to take any action required under their national law to enable it to discharge its functions effectively, and governments have found it convenient to take such action in a form tantamount to the recognition of the legal personality of the International Organisation (...) whenever such capacities are expressly conferred by or can reasonably be implied from the constituent instrument of the organisation

Based on this requisite, the EU would have not been considered an international legal person from 1993 to 2007.

By contrast, the objective personality theory contends that once an organisation meets a set of objective elements or criteria, it will automatically acquire international legal personality under general and customary international law.[246] IOs are therefore subjects of international law irrespective of their founders' intention. Such independent entity will be a bearer of rights and duties *per se* under international law.

Seyersted is identified as the original proponent of this theory:

> Once an organisation or a State has been established, no matter how, it is *ipso facto* a general subject of international law. All that is required is that it possesses the objective characteristics of a State or organisation, respectively. These necessary and sufficient characteristics are, in the case of States, generally considered to be: territory, population and a sovereign government. In case of IGOs the facts required are submitted to be: International organs (ie. organs established by two or more sovereign States), which (1) are not all subject to the authority of any one State or other organised community (except that of the participating States/communities acting jointly through their representatives on such organs); (2) perform 'sovereign' and/or international acts in their own name and (3) are not authorised by all their acts to assume obligations (merely) on behalf of the several participating States or communities.[247]

concerned; and that the same principle is probably also applicable whenever such capacities are recognised by the law of the country where the organisation has its seat, or are exercised by the organisation on the basis of well-established custom", (n 216) 233–234. In this regard, Amerasinghe explains that "whether there is explicit provision in constitutions for the recognition of personality in municipal law [in treaties] or not, municipal systems will have their own methods of dealing with the problem and in general finding a way to recognise such personality if necessary", (n 225) 241. An express provision in the founding instrument became more common since the '90s'. Amongst others, Odello (n 108) 362; Sands and Klein (n 11) 475; Schermers and Blokker (n 3) 988–989; Jones (n 45) 28.

246 As Odello remarked: "The 'objective theory', based on Seyersted's work, provides a simpler way to determine the personality in international law. It is based on some objective criteria that would attribute legal personality to a specific organisation. These criteria must be matched with the structure of the organisation and see if they constitute relevant elements to provide the organisation with international legal personality", ibid, 362.

247 *Objective International Personality of Intergovernmental Organizations – Do Their Capacities Really Depend Upon Their Constitutions* (n 22) 46–48 and *Common Law of International Organizations* (n 22) 43–44, 64. In the latter, the author adds a reference to "participating communities".

This theory makes an analogy with the acquisition of 'statehood'.[248] Statehood is an assertion of the international legal system (on the basis of general international law) through the acknowledgment of three objective elements or criteria – territory, population and government.

The acquisition of 'organisationhood' follows the same reasoning. IOs are general subjects of international law as soon as specific objective elements or criteria, as enumerated in Seyersted's theory, are met.[249] As Jones outlines:

> [S]tatehood is not a fact transcending the legal system, but rather a status bestowed if particular objective criteria are met. State sovereignty is a quality imparted by the international legal system and not an absolute, pre-existing power.[250]

There are obvious differences between these two (general) subjects of international law, embodied with different features and distinctive nature,[251] however, as Jones explains, "these distinctions do not necessarily suggest that the source of their legal personality should also be different".[252] Both result from the operation of the international legal system, their source of creation (and acquisition of personality) derives from general and customary international law.[253]

---

248 As Amerasinghe clarifies: "conceptually, the attributing of legal personality to organisations is not problematic. They would be juridical persons, just as States are artificial, and not natural persons", 'International Institutional Law – a Point of View' (n 3), 149. See, Jones (n 45) 12–13, 26–27.

249 *Objective International Personality of Intergovernmental Organizations – Do Their Capacities Really Depend Upon Their Constitutions* (n 22) 29, 54–55, 60–61 and *Common Law of International Organizations* (n 22) 64. As recalled by Alvarez: "[Seyersted] argues that all International Organisations by virtue of customary law and not because of a specific authority granted in their Charters, have powers analogous to those enjoyed by States, including exclusive jurisdiction over organs, capacity to conclude treaties, active and passive personality and ability to settle disputes", (n 10) 137.

250 (n 45) 26.

251 As well-noted by Amerasinghe (in relation to the ICJ Opinion in *Reparation of Injuries*) "comparison with statehood cannot be ignored". The court rejected the 'super-statehood' to IOs yet it recognized that there is a general acceptance of inherent rights, duties and capacities of organisations, even independently of their constitutions, which may be "not as numerous or extensive as those of States" or even "identical", 'International Institutional Law – a Point of View' (n 3), 249–250.

252 (n 45) 26–27. Amongst others, d'Aspremont, 'The Multifaceted Concept of the Autonomy of International Organizations and International Legal Discourse' in R. Collins and N. White (eds), *International Organizations and the Idea of Autonomy: Institutional Independence in the International Legal Order* (Routledge 2011).

253 Jones, ibid. Seyersted compares several ambivalent and analogous situations between IOs and States and the practical differences between these two subjects of international

In light of the above, Seyersted strongly criticised those who maintain that IOs only possess personality if it is drawn solely from their founding instrument and the will of their founders, as their assertion is clearly dissociated with reality. This criticism extends to those who defend the inductive or implied personality theory.[254]

It is widely agreed that the founding instruments of IOs are not exhaustive. IOs perform numerous acts on the international plane that are not explicitly contemplated in the founding instrument *but are essential to the extent* of the organisation's needs to fulfil its *purposes* (pragmatic and functional approach).[255] The above scholar underscores:

> Practice demonstrates that, contrary to what is usually assumed in legal theory, such organisations have an inherent capacity to perform any sovereign and international act which they are in a practical position to perform, even if their constitution contains no relevant provision and even if there is no evidence of any relevant intention of their drafters or of any previous practice by or in respect of the organisation.[256]

Any 'sovereign' or international act that organisations are in a practical position to do, means *all the decisions and actions* taken by the IOs' *sovereign organs* to fully exercise their functions ("inherent and exclusive organic jurisdiction"), within the *limits* set forth in their constitutive instruments and in the principle of speciality.[257] The factual existence of such capacities and the capacity/

law and concludes that IOs are created and interact in the international law on the basis of general and customary international law, similar as States, *Objective International Personality of Intergovernmental Organizations – Do Their Capacities Really Depend Upon Their Constitutions* (n 22) 100.

254 Ibid. As the scholar argues that "[i]t is not the convention (if there is one) or the intention of the contracting parties thereto which establish the international personality of intergovernmental organisation, and determines its extent, but general international law",100.

255 Acts usually not contemplated in the founding instruments can be *inter alia* technical assistance, *ius tractum*, missions and permanent representatives, privileges and immunities, international claims, peacekeeping and peacebuilding operations, other unilateral acts (eg. as depositories).

256 *Objective International Personality of Intergovernmental Organizations – Do Their Capacities Really Depend Upon Their Constitutions* (n 22) 99. The scholar considers that IOs enjoy *inherent* 'international capacities' as States, which are "not *delegated* by (or *implied* in) the provisions of their constitutions", 45 and 100.

257 According to Seyersted, IO's external actions capacity and corresponding limits should be specified in the constitutive instrument. If the IO has the power to issue binding decisions upon its member States or exercise jurisdiction over their territory or nationals, or to act

ability to exercise them is an undeniable objective fact. Therefore, the argument that legal personality must be expressly enshrined in the constitutive instrument should not be decisive.

A more moderate approach to the objective school is supported by other scholars, such as Brownlie[258] or Jones.[259] IOs are derivative subjects of international law (*factual existence*), but they are not confined to a specific treaty provision to acquire legal personality or to specific prerequisites, nor must all their powers and competences be expressly ascribed in the constituent or founding instrument.

The presence of certain criteria showing that the organisation has a will distinct from its members, such as having its own organs, administrative apparatus and financial resources, confers legal personality to the organisation under international law. As with States, their source of *legal existence* arises from the international system: "international organisations may acquire rights and duties under both their founding treaties and general international law".[260]

Moreover, regardless of exercising a distinct will from its members (*volonté distincte*), such a fact does not preclude members' control of the functioning and competences of the IO or "their ability to terminate the organisation's existence".[261] States are still the *ultimate decision-makers*.

The basic idea can be summed up as follows: the founding treaty or other constituent instrument(s) of international law constitute the legal foundation of the organisation but are not the decisive source of personality, which instead arises from international law, ie. from the operation and recognition of such organisation in the international legal system.

Another personality theory emerged, the so-called 'third school of thought' or the implicit (implied) personality theory, referred to by Schermers and Blokker as "currently the prevailing one".[262]

on behalf of them, these acts should be expressly enshrined in the constitutive instrument. Ibid, 28–29, 45, 100.

258 (n 28) 681–682. Jones indicates Brownlie's formula as the most appropriate, absorbing the key features of the objective personality approach, (n 45) 38.

259 Ibid, 24, 34, 37–38. As the author explains: "On a conceptual level, the function of the concept of personality indicates that it ought logically to derive through operation of the rules of the relevant legal system, rather than being bestowed by particular actors. This would make the granting of personality analogous to the acquisition of statehood, even though the factual reality of an organisation remains derivative", 37.

260 Ibid, 26–27.

261 Ibid.

262 (n 3) 989. Bederman mentions Schermers and others (n 216) 356. Akande also associates Schermers and Blokker and Sands and Klein to this theory (n 4) 257.

This theory argues that IOs are *not ipso facto* international legal persons, such quality is provided to them either explicitly in the founding instrument or implicitly when, in the absence of an explicit provision, certain powers/capacities are granted.[263] This approach is closely aligned with the will of the founders' theory.

Legal personality is implicitly inferred if the founders confer a number of powers and capacities, such as the right to conclude treaties (*ius tractum*), the right to enjoy privileges and immunities (*ius legationis*) or the capacity to bring international claims. A functionalist test is conducted to demonstrate that an organisation has a separate will from its founders through the exercise of some functions and capacities developed in practice.

There is also a legal presumption that an organisation cannot be deprived of personality unless an explicit contrary intention is declared. In other words, if the founding instruments expressly state that the organisation is not to be considered an international legal person, then the organisation is devoid of international personality. Based on this premise, for example, the OSCE or FATF would never be considered international legal persons.

A major preliminary difference between these three theories is that the objective theory advocates that IOs have *original* legal personality as States, both are subjects under general international law, while the subjective and implied theories maintain that States have *original* legal personality and IOs have *derived* legal personality.

The implied or inductive theory is criticised for ignoring the *objective reality* of organisations, which I concur. It is contended that the capacities in which the underlying theory supports the legal presumption of personality of an organisation are nothing more than *manifestations* of its factual existence, ie. *indicia* that such an organisation exercises a distinct will from its founders.[264]

By focusing on the capacities of an organisation, the implied theory is departing from the centre-stage of the analysis, ie. the elements or criteria that characterise the existence of an organisation – the 'being'.

Klabbers elaborated another theory, known as the presumptive legal personality theory. The scholar claims that "when an organisation performs acts which can be only explained on the basis of international legal personality,

263 Amongst others, Klabbers (n 230) 49; Odello (n 108) 361–363; Schermers and Blokker (n 3) 989.

264 Amongst others, Klabbers, ibid, 49 and 53; same author (n 153) 368; Akande (n 4) 30; Jones (n 45) 29 and 37.

such organisation will be presumed to be bestowed with international legal personality".[265]

From Klabbers' perspective, the reasons for debating personality in international law are correlated with the external-political nature of the relationship between the different subjects of international law, ie. more a 'plea' for external recognition, then to other factors.[266] As Klabbers observes:

> Legal personality has relevance. Its relevance resides, not in forming a threshold for action in any given legal system (as is often thought) but as a matter of politics. It is relevant in two ways: personality forms recognition of the group's legitimate existence and it shields that existence from possible interference by outside authorities.[267]

Klabbers' reasoning has merit because, despite legal considerations, international relations are fundamentally political in nature, and the matter of international personality involves nothing less than a political recognition and the political positioning of the several subjects of international law on the international plane. At the same time, this political recognition signals the autonomy and independence of the organisation in relation to its members.

A new approach to legal personality is the existence personality theory, developed by Wessel in relation to the legal status of the EU.[268] This theory was later applied by Odello to assess the legal status of the OSCE under international law.[269]

For Wessel, the critical feature that characterises an IO in the international legal system is the possibility of *demarcating itself* from its founders, the so-called '*volunté distincte*'. 'Autonomy' is thus the essential element to ascertain

265 'The Concept of Legal Personality' (n 230) 59; same author (n 153) 369; (n 3) 49–50.

266 (n 229) 38, 63, 65.

267 Ibid, 64–65. The presumption of personality theory has been pointed out in some literature as problematic or unclear in what concerns international responsibility or the international standing between the different subjects of international law – who is internationally accountable and liable for breaching international law – the organisation or its members (?). On this subject, see Odello (108) 361–362; Jones (n 45) 30.

268 (n 181) 508–516.

269 As Odello remarked: "The central point of Wessel's analysis for determining the existence of legal personality is based on the 'autonomy' of the institution, with regard to member States. This element is usually required by definitions of International Organisation as provided by most authors as one of the characteristics of International Organisations", (n 108) 364. Wessel elaborates more on the concept of 'autonomous' or at least 'separate' will of an international entity, as the core element of personality", ibid.

whether an organisation has an independent and autonomous will *vis-à-vis* its founders/members.[270]

This element or criterion is also the *common core denominator* among the several international law sources, and well underscored by academics. As Golia Jr and Peters commented "autonomy is a key feature of international organisations not only as a marker of independence from the member States but also as a marker of their power to govern individuals and, more generally, to shape reality".[271]

To evaluate the EU's level of autonomy – to determine its '*volunté distincte*', Wessel develops his theory based on Ruiter's analysis of the legal conditions required for institutions to act as 'legal persons' (as subjects of law) in domestic legal orders.[272] The legal conditions are:

i) Existence of decision-making processes;
ii) Practices of the institutions conceived as external behaviour; and
iii) Existence of external behaviour of other subjects towards the legal person.[273]

Odello uses Wessel's theory to demonstrate that OSCE has organs of its own, entrusted with decision-making capacity, ability to operate, and representation power. Moreover, the organisation's bodies act on behalf of the OSCE's interests and decisions rather than those of of its members, in accordance with the internal rules of the organisation.[274] The relationship of the OSCE with other organisations and *vice-versa* (external relations) is another factor that is considered to ascertain *the autonomous will* and *legal capacity of the organisation*.[275]

Odello conducts an analysis of the expressed powers attributed by the OSCE's constitutive documents, of the *inherent* and *implied powers* of the

270 (n 181) 516 *et seq.*

271 (n 32) 42.

272 There is this sort of analogy (transposition of the reasoning) in relation to 'legal persons' as a legal construction of the domestic legal order and 'IOs' as a legal construction of the international law system.

273 (n 181) 516–517. Three elements have to be demonstrated: an *organ* that acts on behalf of the organisation, *membership* (in contrast to 'participation') which underlines a distinctiveness with the international entity and *decision* from the organisation implying a distinction between the participating States (collectivity of States) and the international entity.

274 (n 108) 364–365.

275 Ibid. Also, Wessel (n 181) 516 *et seq.*

organisation, and of its *body of practice* to determine the organisation's level of autonomy.[276]

Wessels' existence theory and Seyersted's objective theory are not that different from one another; both attempt to identify the elements or legal conditions that validate the factual existence of an organisation.

The reasons behind the emergence of all these different theories are explained in a very compelling manner by Jones:

> The doctrinal disagreement over the source of an international organisations' personality can partly be traced to differing conceptions of the organisation itself. An organisation may be viewed in an 'open' light as a forum for inter-State co-operation or alternatively as a 'closed' independent actor in its own right. Because international organisations effectively serve both functions, perspectives tend to oscillate between these two images (…) [I]f international organisations are distinct legal actors, then it is natural for their personality to derive from general international law. If viewed as an open structure, however, the will of the member States assumes much more importance and might therefore be seen as constitutive of personality.[277]

2.3 The ICJ Opinion in *Reparation of Injuries Suffered in the Service of the UN*

All the above theories and debate emerge essentially from the analysis and interpretation of the ICJ Opinion in *Reparation of Injuries*. Each theoretical approach to the legal personality of IOs extracts arguments from the ICJ Opinion to substantiate its reasoning, being the subjective, objective, inductive, presumptive, or existence theory.[278]

---

276 Soft law and customary law are sources of OSCE's legal personality and the 'constitutional' documents of the organisation, documents and decisions taken by organs of the OSCE, as well as States' commitments within the OSCE's policies and activities provided relevant *indicia* as regards its status. Ibid, 371–374.

277 (n 45) 15. There are also scholars who tried to connect the different schools of thought, Jones mentions the 'Gazzini synthesis' as an attempt to reconcile the implied or inductive personality theory with the objective personality theory. This idea is also mentioned by d'Aspremont, 'Abuse of the Legal Personality of International Organizations and the Responsibility of Member States' (2017) 4 *International Organizations Law Review*, 91–93. Also, Akande (n 4) 257.

278 Seyersted, *Objective International Personality of Intergovernmental Organizations – Do Their Capacities Really Depend Upon Their Constitutions* (n 22) 99–102; Klabbers (n 230) 53; same author (n 156) 367; Odello (n 108) 361–365; Amerasinghe, 'International Institutional

In the ICJ Opinion in *Reparation of Injuries*, the Court relied on several elements. It not merely considered the treaty provisions but also the functions and purposes of the organisation and its *modus operandi* (an objective functionalist approach), while considering the founders' intention (will of the members approach) by attributing certain capacities to the UN.[279]

If founders conferred rights to the organisation, such as the possibility of *ius tractum* or of granting privileges and immunities to UN staff that are necessary for it to perform and achieve its purposes, then it can be inferred that there is a legal assumption of the organisation having legal personality (implied or presumption theories).[280] The ICJ Opinion held:

> This development culminated in the establishment in June 1945 of an international organisation whose purposes and principles are specified in the Charter of the United Nations. But to achieve these ends the attribution of international personality is indispensable.[281]

But the ICJ Advisory Opinion also relied on objective facts. If the UN carries out certain actions, even not provided for in the UN Charter, in an independent and autonomous manner, ie. detached from its founders, to functionally operate on the international plane, then there is an *objective assumption* of legal personality. As the Court argues:

Law – a Point of View' (n 3) 245–247; Schermers and Blokker (n 3) 989–990; Jones (n 45) 23–24.

279 The court analysis the intention of the founders from an objective perspective: "To answer this question, which is not settled by the actual terms of the Charter, we must consider what characteristics it was intended thereby to give to the Organisation", ICJ Reports 1949, 178. As Amerasinghe comments: "It is not some subjective intention of the minds of the founders but an objective that was to be found in the circumstances of creation and constitution of the UN", (n 225) 246.

280 For Schermers and Blokker, the implied theory interprets the ICJ opinion as follows: i) the attribution of legal personality is indispensable for its purposes, ii) to have organs of its own and attributed with special tasks, iii) members agree to provide assistance to the organisation and certain powers; iv) practice as demonstrated the character of the organisation, in particular its detachment *vis-à-vis* its members. The attribution of certain functions and powers by member States for the organisation to act in the international sphere means an implicit attribution of personality, (n 3) 989–990. Amongst others, Bederman (n 216) 356; Amerasinghe (n 225) 256; Odello (n 108) 367. For Klabbers, the ICJ Opinion has as basis the presumed international personality of the UN. The author extracts from the Opinion that "you can only have rights and obligations when you are a subject of international law, and you can only be a subject of international law when you have rights and obligations under international law", (n 153) 366–368.

281 ICJ Reports 1949, 178.

> Practice – in particular the conclusion of conventions to which the Organisation is a party – has confirmed this character of the Organisation, which occupies a position in certain respects in detachment from its Members, and which is under a duty to remind them, if need be, of certain obligations (…) [I]t is difficult to see how such a convention could operate except upon the international plane and as between parties possessing international personality.[282]

The Court equally notes that the existence of such characteristics (developed in practice) cannot be disregarded (objective and existence theories):

> In the opinion of the Court, the Organisation was intended to exercise and enjoy, and is in fact exercising and enjoying, functions and rights which can only be explained on the basis of the possession of a large measure of international personality and the capacity to operate upon an international plane.[283]

The ICJ recognised the *international legal personhood* of the UN and affirmed that the UN has *objective legal personality* towards third countries, when questioned in relation to whether the UN has the capacity to bring an international claim against a non-member:

> [The UN] had the power, in conformity with international law, to bring into being an entity possessing objective international personality, and

282 Ibid, 179.

283 Ibid. The ICJ seems to affirm the objective existence of the UN as detached from its members. As Jones explains: "the founders' intentions will establish the competences of the UN but if the factual entity created requires legal personality then personality must follow through the objective operation of international law", (n 45) 18. Also, Bederman (n 216) 359; Amerasinghe (n 225) 243–245. Odello (also Wessel) criticises the expression "a large measure of international personality". An IO cannot have layers of personality, differently is capacity. As the author correctly points out, it "shows the overlapping of two concepts, personality and capacity. In fact, personality is the fact of being a subject of the legal system, and this fact cannot be measured. A legal or natural person is either a subject or it is not. It cannot have a 'large' or a 'small' amount of 'subjectivity'. What can vary is the amount of legal capacity. Subjects in all legal system may have different rights and duties that depend on their legal capacity, but not on their legal personality", (n 108) 363–364.

> not merely personality recognised by them alone [members], together with capacity to bring international claims.[284]

As the source of all personality theories, the ICJ Opinion in *Reparation of Injuries* has been thoroughly examined by numerous authors. David Bederman acclaims the ICJ Advisory Opinion because it signals "the final days of the 'law of nations' in international law",[285] the end of the State-centric system of international law and the beginning of the modern age:

> The significance of the *Reparation* Opinion can hardly be overestimated (…) [T]he Court's opinion conclusively ushered in a new era of international law, fully diversified with multiple subjects and objects. Indeed, what the *Reparation* Opinion achieved was a fusion between the subjects and objects of international law. Any entity, thing or person bound by international legal rules was an international legal person. The distinction between active subjects and passive subjects of the law was no longer relevant. This was the first formalism to be eschewed by postwar international jurists.[286]

In a different mode, Tarcisio Gazzini comments that the topic of IOs having legal personality was not resolved with the ICJ Opinion in *Reparation of Injuries* and continues to be an open matter:

> However, many questions still remain unsettled or controversial, including how an international organisation acquires international legal personality; in what way such a personality is different from that of States; and how the responsibility for internationally wrongful acts is to be allocated between the organisation and its members.[287]

---

284 Ibid, 177–178, 185. Seyersted concludes from the ICJ Opinion that third States must treat IOs in their external relations in the same manner as States, because both are entrusted with objective international personality, *Objective International Personality of Intergovernmental Organizations – Do Their Capacities Really Depend Upon Their Constitutions* (n 22) 102. Akande also affirms that "[t]he personality of international organisations derives from the effect that customary international law (which is binding on all States) ascribes such characteristics. Thus, once international law ascribes personality of an organisation, a subject of international law is created with its own rights and its own duties", (n 4) 259.

285 (n 216) 267.

286 Ibid, 355.

287 (n 230) 33; Jones (n 45) 17.

Seyersted, Amerasinghe or Jones argue that "the court did not go beyond that is necessary to arrive a 'cautious' opinion'"[288] or "did not commit itself"[289] to one of the contending theories or "did not take a clear stance on the source of personality",[290] with which I concur.

Some scholars, like Odello, consider that the ICJ used the different theoretical approaches in its reasoning and "provided a sort of mixed solution".[291] I also share this understanding.

Similarly, Jones comments that there are parts of the ICJ Opinion "compatible with a search for implied founding intention", while there are other parts that give emphasis to functions and rights and other parts where the "objective existence of the UN detached from the founding members is underlined".[292]

Wessel also supports this reasoning:

> In doing so, the Court did not rely on either the so-called 'will theory' (in which the will of the States is conclusive) or the 'objective theory' (in which international legal personality simply follows from the existence of an international organisation). Rather, a combination of both elements was used to justify the possession of legal personality by the United Nations (UN).[293]

Jones goes further and affirms:

> The ICJ reference to a mixture of an intention-based and objective criteria justifications, whether because the Court was seeking a pragmatic middle-ground or because it was not cognisant of the debate, has led to the judgment being cited in support of two fundamentally incompatible positions (...) It certainly sparked much of subsequent scholarly

288 Seyersted, *Objective International Personality of Intergovernmental Organizations – Do Their Capacities Really Depend Upon Their Constitutions* (n 22) 17 and 99–102.

289 Amerasinghe (n 225) 245–246.

290 Jones (n 45) 23.

291 Odello considers the ICJ Opinion a mix of "law and fact". This may be the reason why international legal personality has been considered "a nebulous concept in international law". The author outlines that it "provides a sort of mixed solution, as the case argued on objective, subjective and inductive criteria" and why the three "theories have emerged", (n 108) 361 and 364.

292 (n 45) 19.

293 (n 181) 521-522. As the author claims that "[t]he will of the Member States was not instrumental in establishing the legal personality of the organisation, but rather in determining the *capacities* of the organisation", 522.

> discussion, but has equally constrained the search for a sound juristic basis for international personality by requiring consistency with its (somewhat unclear) reasoning.[294]

Also, in this footpath, Bederman concludes:

> In one sentence the Court combined the most radical intellectual tradition for these organisations. It recognised not only the notion of implied powers for entities, unchaining the institution from the literal text of its constituent instrument. It also acknowledged that these organisations were evolving creations, capable of expanding their rights and duties and living their international life to the fullest.[295]

From a different perspective, Akande considers that there is "no radical difference" between the implied and objective schools of thought in the ICJ Advisory Opinion:

> What the court seemed to be saying was that the intention of the members to ascribe certain rights, functions and characteristics to the UN, could only be given effect if the organisation possessed its own legal personality. This is not inconsistent with saying that the members ascribed characteristics to the organisation which satisfied the criteria required for conferring international personality. While the key factor is the possession of those characteristics, they necessarily arise out of the will of the members.[296]

The DARIO with Commentaries concluded that the ICJ Opinion favoured the objective personality theory;[297] a perception that is also shared by several scholars.[298]

---

294 (45) 19. Klabbers concurs that the ICJ Opinion "leaves room for different interpretations", (n 230) 53.

295 (n 216) 357.

296 (n 4) 257.

297 Para. 9 of the Commentary to Article 2 of DARIO. With a different view from the ILC, Jones comments that "contrary to the ILC's claims, ICJ judgments furnish very limited guidance in the search for a convincing juristic and practical basis for the legal personality of international organisations", (n 45) 21.

298 Berdeman (n 216) 356; Akande (n 4) 257; Jones (n 45) 37. Alvarez comments that from ICJ's findings "many conclude that legal personality emerges not from the explicit or 'implicit' intent of IO creators but from the operation of general customary international law; that is, the personhood of IO s results from their existence as an 'objective fact'", being

Regardless of scholars' views, the fact remains that, notwithstanding addressing a concrete case – the UN, the *rationale* of the ICJ Advisory Opinion in *Reparation of Injuries* and the functionality test have been (and continue to be) a source of theoretical argumentation for organisations whose legal personality remains uncertain.[299] As accurately observed by Alvarez in this regard:

> [T]the Courts' implied functional necessity test for the rights and duties accompanying legal personality is regarded as generally applicable to all IOs, even those with far different purposes and structures that the United Nations.[300]

Some scholars have suggested however the reconceptualisation of the international personality, considering the "changing sociological circumstances on the international scene", stressing the role of other actors on the international plane, including non-State actors.[301]

---

recognised as 'principles of international institutional law', (n 10) 134. The author points out three grounds to substantiate the application of the objective international personality criteria (to the UN): i) necessity, ii) members' intent and iii) practice of the organisation (the UN had concluded treaties with States), criteria that may be applied to defend the legal personality of other IOs, such as GATT, EU, INTERPOL, IPU, OSCE, 131. Bouwhuis questions "whether the test for international legal personality should not be a test more akin to the sort of test that one would find in domestic law, namely an ability to enter into legal relations on the international plane", (n 19) 455.

299 Seyersted, *Objective International Personality of Intergovernmental Organizations – Do Their Capacities Really Depend Upon Their Constitutions* (n 22) 102. As Sands and Klein remarked: "legal personality has no pre-determined content in international law reason why functionality test has to be undertaken", (n 11) 476.

300 (n 10) 134. The author states that: "[a]ll International Organisations have benefited at least this much from the *Reparation* Opinion, regardless of the intent of their creators, although as addressed below, the specific rights and duties that can be inferred from legal personality remain under dispute", while critically pointing out the questions left unanswered by the court, 132–135.

301 Karsten Nowrot underpins the discrepancy between theory and practice where the "traditional prerequisites for international legal personality can no longer be regarded as an adequate approach for the allocation of community interests", particularly when they are non-State actors in the international scene. 'Reconceptualising International Personality of Influential Non-State Actors: Towards a Rebuttable Presumption of Normative Responsibility' (2006), republished in F. Johns (ed), *International Legal Personality* (Routledge 2010), 374–388. Janne Nijman calls for the reconceptualisation of international legal personality linked to the idea of responsibility, wherein "international legal personality as an aspect of our ethical-juridical identity, in other words, is not merely having rights; it also includes a responsibility to fight against exclusion and misrecognition on the global scale (...) international legal personality, in short, concerns the life in global institutions", 'Paul Ricoeur and International Law: Beyond 'the End of

3 Summary

Needleless to say, the debate over defining or classifying an IO may go on *ad infinitum*,[302] given that not all IOs embrace the typical or traditional elements, meaning that a case-by-case analysis is always required before classifying an organisation.

Each IO is unique and may differ in its characteristics in relation to others, as different solutions (may and) have been found on the international plane to answer collective needs. There is no 'one-size fits all'. As Alvarez wisely, comments:

> International Organisations are too complex to reduce to typologies, their normative impact too broad to be limited to specialised branches of domestic or international law, their evolving nature too difficult to pin from one character type.[303]

Nevertheless, certain elements can be identified as fundamental for ascertaining such a quality. An IO must be established under international law, ideally through an international agreement (treaty),[304] but it may be instituted through other acts of international law like Resolutions, Declarations, Final Acts, which are also governed under international law and not regarded as national law. Although, as highlighted by Klabbers, a treaty-based organisation provides a higher degree of legal certainty:

the Subject' – Towards a Reconceptualization of International Legal Personality' (2007), republished in F. Johns (ed), *International Legal Personality* (Routledge 2010), 515. In this respect, Bederman also refers to *epistemic communities,* new centers of functional cooperation and harmonisation, (n 216) 360–362, 364. Klabbers stresses the "organic bond between State and international law", and how international law system is still a 'State centric-system', (n 153), 353–356. And, Jones mentions the tension between these competing views and the difficulty of incorporating IOs into a traditional State-centric context of international law, (n 45) 15.

302 As Runjic correctly explains: "In the international legal order exists organisations about whose legal nature there is no agreement neither in international legal doctrine nor in practice. According to the understanding of the respective authors, these organisations are classified among intergovernmental organisations or among international non-governmental organisations, and in certain cases their nature is determined as *sui generis*", (n 86) 169.

303 (n 10) 12.

304 Sands and Klein (n 11) 43, 46–47; Schemers and Blokker (n 3) 37.

> The importance of this characteristic, then, is above all to indicate that the creation of an international organisation is an intentional act. Organisations rest upon conscious decisions of the States involved; they do not come out of the blue, and are not created by accident.[305]

Yet, several practical examples have been underlined that challenge such a paradigm, proving that not all IOs meet the traditional criteria, paraphrasing Andrew Guzman's commentary:

> Like Alvarez, I adopt a pragmatic approach and take the above criteria as *indicia* of an IO, but not adhere to a rigid formalism that demands that all three be present in every cited example.[306]

Klabbers comments that among the three elements: treaty-based, created by States and having at least one organ "are formal in nature", while the "element or requirement that taps on substance" is the organisation having an organ with a distinct will. Often mentioned as '*volonté distincte*' – the "quintessential characteristic".[307]

Although I acknowledged the categorisation of 'to have at least an organ' as a formal element, I believe that it should be equally regarded as a material element because it is the body through which the organisation expresses its distinctive will (*volonté distincte*). The 'organ' is the centre stage of the organisation's policy and decision-making processes, whereas its identity is formed and affirmed. Consequently, it is formal and material in nature.

Nevertheless, I share the views of Klabbers, Wessel and others that the core element at the heart of characterising an IO is the *volonté distincte* – autonomy: an organ with a distinct will from its members.

For an organisation to be recognised as an IO in the international realm, it must have an autonomous and separate will from its members and act in an independent manner. To this end, the organisation must demonstrate that it possesses an *identity of its own*, in other words, that there is a clear distinction between the organisation and its members in terms of legal powers and purposes. As Golia Jr and Peters properly commented, "[t]o be autonomous, the organisation must not only be 'willing' but it must also be 'able'".[308]

305 (n 3) 10.

306 (n 19) 1002.

307 (n 3) 12. Also, Schermers and Blokker (n 3) 44–45.

308 (n 32) 38.

An IO is created for specific functions/purposes (principle of speciality and *ultra vires* doctrine), with the attribution of certain powers, either explicit (attribution of powers doctrine) or implicit (implied powers doctrine),[309] to achieve its purposes. It is designed with a specific institutional framework as well as policy and lawmaking powers, allowing to adopt acts of its own and to act on its own.[310]

Based on the criteria addressed in this Chapter and the relevant theoretical approaches, I will argue that the FATF is an IO[311] and, therefore, a subject of international law, bearing international rights, duties, and responsibilities.

Looking at all 'attempted' definitions and criteria to categorise an IO provided by the various international law sources discussed above, it is possible to assert that there is a general consensus around IOs that reunite the basic elements of being treaty-based, created by States and 'with an organ of its own' with a distinct will (*volunté discincte*). It is also possible to acknowledge that these basic elements have evolved and expanded, as well as that there are nuances in the institutional setting of IOs.

For an organisation whose legal personhood is uncertain, this author outlines a coherent, structured, and comprehensive reasoning consisting of five elements. This reasoning provides a rational conceptual basis when the organisation is unable to meet the previously specified agreed-upon basic requirements, and the separate and autonomous will (*volunté discincte*) of the organisation must be established.

As it happens, theories on the personality of IOs emerge due to the absence of a founding treaty or a treaty with an express provision conferring legal personality to the organisation. These international personality theories or

309 As the ICJ states: "the Organisation must be deemed to have those powers which, though not expressly provided in the Charter are conferred upon it by necessary implication as essential to be performance of its duties", ICJ Opinion 1949, 182.

310 The powers, capacities and duties are expressed in the founding instrument or implied through interpretation. As Amerasinghe explains, if there is no "express or implicit prohibitions in constitutional elements", there is a presumption that such powers are necessary for the organisation to perform its functions, *Principles of the Institutional Law of International Organizations* (n 3)100–102.

311 Habibi and Zanershan argue that FATF's role, positions and recommendations comply with international and customary law. I cannot offer more information as to the arguments of the authors as this article is written in Arabic, 'The Role & Position of FATF in International Law System' (2021) 20 (45) *Journal of Legal Research*, (Abstract) – Arabic/Persian.

approaches seek to illustrate *how* the *autonomy* and *distinct will* of an organisation can be 'assessed' (manifestation), particularly in cases where the constitutive and formal instrument (a treaty) fails to explicitly mention that the organisation is a separate legal person.

In light of the foregoing, a comprehensive and contemporary categorisation of elements to characterise an IO is conceptualise. These elements are as follows:

i) To be constituted by States or other entities with recognised status under international law;
ii) To be created under international law, a treaty or other acts of international law with constitutive effect, acts that are not part of domestic law;
iii) To have a separate and independent organ with a will distinct from that of its members, ie. manifestations must be according to the aims and interests of the organisation;
iv) The organisation operates on the international plane according to international law;
v) The organisation interacts with other subjects of international law, ie. it operates on the international plane as an autonomous entity and it is acknowledged by other international actors as acting in such capacity.

The first three elements can be categorised as basic requirements, whereas the last two are sub-elements or sub-criteria. These sub-elements will be employed whenever the organisation's distinct will (*volonté distincte*) must be proven in order to establish the legal nature of the organisation.

In this scenario, understanding *how* the organisation operates on the international plane, both internally and externally, *how* it relates with other international actors, and *how* it is perceived by other subjects of international law is of the utmost relevance to ascertaining the core criterion: whether the organisation has a *separate identity* from its members. These sub-elements (iv) and (v) are particularly relevant because they reflect the practical aspect of the exercise and recognition of an IO's acting capacity as a separate and autonomous entity.

These five criteria derive from the international legal system (source), ie. from the operation and recognition of such organisation in the international legal system.

In order to determine the legal status of the FATF, I consider the various conceptual approaches to defining an IO, as well as the theoretical understanding and testing models associated with the objective and existence personality theories. These theories seek to prove the material existence of IOs when the traditional elements that qualify an IO are not fully met (eg. Seyersted, Brownlie and Goodwin-Gill, Wessel, Odello, Jones). The author presents a rational conceptual basis and evidence to determine the core criterion, concluding that the FATF is a separate entity with its own will.

CHAPTER 4

The Financial Action Task Force as an International Organisation

As mentioned in Chapter 2, the FATF considers itself an *intergovernmental policy-making* body, playing a key role in global governance matters to counter ML, FT, and PF and to ensure the integrity and security of the global financial market. It was originally set as a flexible and informal organisation, ie. with no treaty foundation and unintended legal personality, though it gained permanent status in 2019.

The FATF's institutional framework and mandate evolution allied with the facts of international life contributed to the growing functions/powers of the FATF and gradual development (and recognition) as a global standard-setter and a leading world organisation. The exercised functions and general acquiescence (explicit and implicit) of FATF's Recommendations and action plans by members, FSRBs jurisdictions and other stakeholders, such as the UN, CoE, EU, IMF, WB, G-20, have legitimised FATF's role with public authority (*public auctoritas*).[1]

Ghoshray comments about this 'superior binding' authority:

1 On the endorsement of FATF's work and Recommendations by the UN/UNSC, WB, IMF, G-20, Basel Committee, amongst others, Blazejewski, 'The FATF and Its Institutional Partners: Improving the Effectiveness and Accountability of Transgovernamental Networks' (2008) 22(1) *Temple International* and *Comparative Law Journal*, 59; Gathii, 'Financial Action Task Force and Global Administrative Law' (2010) *Journal of the Professional Lawyer, Forthcoming*, Albany Law School Research Paper Series No. 10, 2–3; Turner, 'The Financial Action Task Force: International Regulatory Convergence through Soft Law' (2014) 59 *New York Law School Law Review*, 557; Romaniuk and Keatinge, 'Protecting Charities from Terrorists ... and Counterterrorists: FATF and the Global Effort to Prevent Terrorist Financing through the Non-Profit Sector' (2018) 69(2) *Crime, Law and Social Change*, 268; A/74/335, 29/08/2019, para. 46. Beekarry comments the incorporation of the FATF Recommendations within the framework of the IMF, WB, UNODC, and the Commonwealth as well within IOSCO, Basel Committee, IAIS and the Egmont Group, enabling FATF not only "to reach out to most countries of the world" but also to legitimise its own actions. 'The International Anti-Money Laundering and Combating the Financing of Terrorism Regulatory Strategy: A Critical Analysis of Compliance Determinants in International Law' (2011) 31(1) *Northwestern Journal of International Law & Business*, 192.

 DOI:10.1163/9789004715134_005

> Is there an ordering advantage within the FATF? What is the origin of such ordering? The FATF, interconnected via loosely coupled sources, might look isolated and disjointed. Yet, its broader trajectory forms a *corpus* of an ordered regulatory landscape. As the central determinant of these norms and procedures, the FATF acts as the glue that has exhibited a superior binding ability with all associated stakeholders. Such stakeholders include the constituent members, targeted jurisdictions, and its associated supranational bodies, such as the IMF, United Nations, and various regional AML/CFT organisations.[2]

The nature, complexity, and impact of FATF's mission on the international plane go well beyond that of a mere informal or soft organisation. The FATF not only establishes universal standards (policy and lawmaking capacities) but also ensures their application through solid compliance and supervisory mechanisms, being able to blacklist and call for countermeasures, impacting even non-members (Chapter 2, Sections 7.2. and 9 above).

It is possible to contend that the FATF has a stronger normative dimension and intervention capacity than the large majority of IOs formally established. In this respect, Xinyuan Dai, when describing IOs, mentions that "few treaty organisations have the resources and authority to carry out the entire monitoring procedure", and notably, the ability to detect non-compliance, bring it to light and to impose sanctions.[3] Following this logic, it may be argued that, though not formal in the traditional meaning, the FATF possesses all of these capacities together.

Furthermore, informal organisations do not encompass *all* the features (capacities) that currently distinguish the FATF and are attributable to formal IOs. Such circumstance lead us to question the legal nature of the FATF – is it a hybrid organisation (?), is it a *tertium genus* (?) or a new *species* of IO (?).

This inquiry is important because the FATF's uncertain legal standing raises concerns at various levels, in particular:

i) The legal value of FATF's actions under international law, ie. legitimacy, including accountability, transparency, and rule of law;
ii) States' sovereignty matters (within the decision-making processes at international and domestic levels);

---

2 'Compliance Convergence in FATF Rulemaking: The Conflict Between Agency Capture and Soft Law' (2014/2015) 59(3) *New York Law School Law Review*, 542.

3 *International Institutions and National Policies* (Cambridge University Press 2007) 108, 100 *et seq.* In FATF's case, enforcement of the sanctions (blacklisting) is delegated in jurisdictions and other stakeholders, such as FIs.

iii) To which principles of international law the FATF should be bound; and
iv) International responsibility, particularly, when exercising public power functions.

In Chapter 3, the elements or criteria believed to be essential to define an IO, whenever its legal status is unclear, are outlined as follows:

i) Membership – to be constituted by States or other entities with recognised status under international law;
ii) Created under international law, treaties or other acts of international law, such as Resolutions, Declarations, and Final Acts of a constitutive nature;
iii) To have an organ with a distinct will (*volunté disctincte*), ie. to have a separate and independent organ; an organ that ensures a distinct and autonomous will of the organisation *vis-à-vis* its members (manifestations must be according to the aims and interests of the organisation);

and sub-criteria:

iv) To operate on the international plane according to international law; and
v) External recognition by other subjects of international law.

With these criteria or elements in mind, the hypothesis is whether the gradual evolution of the mandate, institutional setting and *modus operandi* of the FATF on the international plane has changed its *modus constituendi*, in other words, whether it has changed the FATF's informal nature, overtaking members' initial intention and the absence of a founding treaty, into a formal IO. In this analysis, the interaction between the different international actors on the international plane plays a crucial role as a manifestation of the general practice and acquiescence of FATF's legal standing.[4]

This Chapter discusses the legal status of the FATF in the current international legal system and argues that the FATF satisfies all the fundamental elements to be qualified as an IO under international law. The Chapter endeavours to provide new insights and a deeper understanding of FATF's complex legal nature.

4 How the organisation interacts with other subjects of international law? Does it operate on the international plane as an autonomous entity and is it acknowledged by other international actors as acting in such capacity?

1 A New Perspective on the Legal Status of the FATF

To analyse the practical hypothesis of whether the FATF satisfies all the essential criteria identified for an organisation to be qualified as an IO, several factors and indicators, including the FATF's existing constitutive elements (*modus constituendi*), FATF's overall internal framework and body of practice (*modus operandi*) in the international legal system, need to be taken into consideration.

2 Membership

The FATF's membership assembles different types of members, being all subjects of international law. It is composed of States, two regional IOs (the European Commission/EU and Gulf Co-operation Council) and Hong Kong (China), an entity with recognised international legal status.[5]

Although referred to by some as a 'club-member',[6] the FATF strives for a balanced geographical representation with delegates from America, Europe, the Middle East, Africa, Asia and Oceania.

The FATF is a closed membership organisation wherein members are admitted only if they fulfil specific criteria. Since 1999, all the new members were invited to join the organisation in line with the 'limited membership expansion' policy, as explained in Chapter 2, Section 4 above.

Regarding the IO's membership requirement, it is possible to avow that the FATF meets such a criterion: all its members (the above-mentioned) are subjects of international law under international law.

5 Hong Kong is a SAR of China with a high degree of autonomy, enjoying external autonomy in economic and trade affairs (see Articles 2, 12, 13 and 153 of HKSAR Basic Law).

6 Amongst others, Hülsse, 'Even Clubs Can't Do Without Legitimacy: Why the Anti-Money Laundering Blacklist Was Suspended' (2008) 2(4) *Regulation & Governance*, 466; Beekarry (n 1) 190; Hülsse and Kerwer, 'How International Organizations Rule the World: The Case of the Financial Action Task Force' (2011) 2(1) *Journal of International Organisations Studies*, 27; Romaniuk and Keatinge (n 1) 276. Blazejewski features FATF's membership as "small and relatively homogeneous", and the FATF as being "run by like-minded experts" (n 1) 11. Borlini categorises the FATF as an elite of technocrats with a specific mandate and specialised competence. 'Soft Law, Soft International Organizations e Regolamentazione 'Tecnica' di Problemi di Sicurezza Pubblica e Integrità Finanziaria' (2017) 2 *Rivista di Diritto Internazionale*, 365, 368–369, 405.

3 Created under International Law

As expounded, it is consensual among the diverse sources of international law (Chapter 3, Section 1 above) that a founding treaty is not a *sine qua non* condition to constitute an IO. Amongst the most known scholars, it is possible to withdraw the following observations.

Seyersted speaks of IOs established under "some other form of understanding", such *understanding* would be inferred from a member's behaviour, whether by explicit or implicit acceptance of a resolution or decision related to the organs and work of the organisation or "any other text which embodies certain basic organisational provisions, in such a manner that it may be said to constitute an international agreement".[7] The author provides the OSCE as an example.

Brownlie mentions that IOs may be instituted through Resolutions of a Conference (it is inferred that it can be either an International Conference of States by their initiative or under the umbrella of an IO, such as the UN) or a "uniform practice".[8] However, the scholar does not define *uniform practice* and offers the GATT as an example.

Odello, though acknowledging the preference for a treaty-based organisation, goes further by providing examples of other forms of agreements:

> [U]sually, international treaties constitute the basic norms of new international entities, but other forms of agreement, such as memorandums of understandings, exchange of notes, and final acts can be envisaged. The different names used may be of little importance when dealing with the creation of an entity, but generally authors consider that an international agreement is required for the coming into existence of an international organisation.[9]

Schermers and Blokker argue that an international agreement is essential, although accepting a broad interpretation of this term and the *eventual evolutionary character of the IO*. Both scholars recognise that "UN and EU practice

---

7 *Common Law of International Organizations* (Martinus Nijhoff 2008), 6.

8 *Principles of Public International Law* (6th ed, Oxford University Press 2003), 683. Also, Bronwlie and Goodwin-Gill, 'Joint Opinion on the International Legal Personality of the Inter-Parliamentary Union (IPU)' (1999), para 62.

9 'The Developing Legal Status of the Organisation for Security and Co-operation in Europe' (2006) XXII *Anuario de Derecho Internacional*, 359.

has demonstrated, sooner or later, organisations will act as international legal persons, because they simply cannot function without such capacity".[10]

Akande asserts that IOs can be created through international acts other than treaties, such as a Resolution of a Conference of States, or "by joint actions of States",[11] citing OSCE or OPEC as examples.

Notwithstanding the treaty-based requirement the prevailing practice, Article 2(a) of DARIO's definition reflects the general understanding that an IO may be established by other instruments governed by international law, offering as examples the Nordic Council or OPEC.[12] Notably, what is materially relevant is that the organisation is founded by an instrument governed by international law.[13]

It is thus possible to argue that although not treaty-based, the instruments that created the FATF (founding instrument) and other instruments of a constitutional nature, were *all created under* and *by international law*. All these legal instruments constitute FATF's constitutional framework and serve a parallel function as treaties or statutes of a formal IO.[14]

In Wessels' reasoning of a *constitutive rule,* the constitutive rule determining the existence of the EU as an *institutional legal fact* is treaty-based (Maastricht Treaty), I contend that such a constitutive rule may be broadly interpreted to include any given international legal act (hard or soft law) that reflects the *objective intention* of the members (explicit or implicit) to create an organisation, as long as it satisfies certain features and criteria.

3.1 *The Constitutional Framework of the FATF*

The FATF was established through a G-7 Declaration, which is an international act, albeit of a soft law nature (Chapter 2, Section 1 above). However, its

10 *International Institutional Law* (5th rev edn, Martinus Nijhoff Publishers 2011), 1212. For the authors, a treaty is essential not only to assure the commitment of the Parties through parliamentary approval (ratification procedures and legitimacy), but also to unmistakably establish the organisation own separate legal personality. The scholars contend that "[o]rganisations which are not created by treaty will have to prove the existence of an inter-State agreement when they claim a public, intergovernmental status", 40–43, 46–47.

11 'International Organizations' in M. Evans (ed), *International Law* (3rd ed, Oxford University Press, 2011), 254.

12 Para. 4 and 5 of the Commentaries to Article 2 of DARIO.

13 Sands and Klein, *Bowett's Law of International Institutions* (6th ed, Sweet & Maxwell 2009), 15, 218–222, 694.

14 The reasoning of Brownlie and Goodwin-Gill in relation to the IPU's Statutes when the scholars claim that the IPU Statutes have been adopted and amended by members playing an "equivalent constitutional role" to a treaty (para. 11 of the Statement) is applied *mutatis mutandis.*

constitutional skeleton is wider as it comprises other fundamental documents, including the successive Mandates that govern the FATF's institutional framework and *modus operandi,* describing its functions, powers and strategic internal rules, as well as Ministerial Declarations and statements.

The current Mandate comprises four Chapters and 50 paragraphs related to key aspects of FATF's institutional framework. Chapter 1 establishes the objectives, functions and tasks of the organisation The main functions and tasks are to: i) identify risks and threats of the international financial system; ii) develop standards (the FATF Recommendations); iii) assess and monitor compliance (MERs and FURs); iv) identify high-risk non-co-operative jurisdictions (blacklisting); v) co-ordinate action on strategic deficiencies in national regimes, and within the Global Network (FSRBs); vi) assist jurisdictions; vii) provide guidance, training and outreach activities; and viii) engage with other international organisations and bodies, in particular the UN (external relations).

Chapter 2 on 'Composition and Participation' addresses membership, affiliation criteria (members, associate members, observers), conditions of approval as well as duties and some rights (eg. participation). Paragraph 10 of the Mandate refers that the rules governing the relationship between the FATF and its associate members are "set by high-level principles" (HLPOs).

Chapter 3 designs the internal legal framework of the organisation by defining the structure of the FATF – its bodies, composition, criteria, responsibilities, decision-making, and budgetary matters. This Chapter also covers some members rights, such as representation, participation and voting rights, as well as members duties (eg. membership fee).

Chapter 4 on the 'Legal Effect of the Mandate; Accountability' mentions the 'open-ended' mandate of the FATF and the legal effect of its actions, as well biannual and extraordinary meetings of ministers, accountability and annual reports. Reference is also made to the officials, experts, and the FATF Secretariat in charge of upholding the FATF's Mandate.

The FATF's Mandate can be qualified as the organisation's Charter. However, as underlined, there are other legal instruments that complement the Mandate and are also relevant in this context, including the Ministerial Declarations (eg. 2019, 2022 and 2024), which provide politico-institutional support, as well as FATF's Statements, HLPOs, Universal Procedures and Procedures for the 4th Round of ME or even FATF Reports.

The FATF Statements pertaining to the Russian Federation on membership issues, addressing FATF's core principles, the 2022 and 2024 Ministerial Declarations endorsing such principles and the 2022–2023 FATF Report reaffirming them - all these acts play an important role in shaping FATF's constitutional framework and establishing its core principles.[15]

In the 2024 Ministerial Declaration, under the topic of 'Promoting Robust and Inclusive Governance', FATF Ministers mention, for the first time, that the organisation must fulfil its mission based on the values of "integrity, accountability, and transparency", as well as the matters of "equality and diversity" and women's empowerment in the FATF. This declaration bears significance because it is now part of the FATF *acquis*.[16]

As regards to the Universal Procedures and Procedures for the 4th Round of ME, both documents mention: i) the role of the ICRG (referred to only in Annex D of the Mandate in the FATF WG list); ii) brand concerns; iii) ratings: and iv) the consequences for low ratings, ie. enhanced follow-up measures: the issuance of public statements and the possibility of suspension or termination of FATF membership.

Some of FATF Reports also address matters of an institutional nature. By way of example, the 2004–2005 FATF Report explains and refers to the new FSRBS status (associate member) and Annexes 5 and 6 of the 2007–2008 FATF Report, respectively, disclose the 'FATF Membership Criteria' and the 'FATF Policy on Observers'. Additionally, Annex I of the 2009–2010 FATF Report establishes the 'Rights & Obligations of Associate Members'. The ICRG role and review process are also fairly explained in the FATF's annual reports. The new procedures for the next round of ME also contribute to the clarification of the internal functioning of the ICRG by publicly providing information on its composition and responsibilities and on the ICRG process.[17]

These concerted acts are intentional and aim at establishing, sustaining, and developing the FATF. They are not national acts, but *unilateral declarations* and *collective decisions* of members who are subjects of international law. The international legal system categorises these acts as acts of international law.[18]

15 See Chapter 2, Section, 2.4; 2024 Ministerial Declaration, para. 4 and 21; 2022–2023 FATF Report, 9.

16 Para. 21.

17 'Procedures for the FATF AML/CFT/CPF Mutual Evaluations, Follow-Up and ICRG' (April 2024).

18 About the different unilateral and collective acts performed by States, amongst others, Dinh, Daillier and Pellet, *Droit International Public* (3rd ed., L.G.D.J. 1987), 328–358 or *Direito Internacional Público* (4th ed, Fundação Calouste Gulbenkian 1999) 328–358. The authors mention different categories of *actes concertés non conventionnels*, as well of blurred cases where it is difficult to distinguish *actes concertés non conventionnels* from conventional ones, citing ICJ Opinion in *Aegean Sea Continental Shelf Case 1978* where the court observed that there is "no rule of international law which might preclude a

Ministers of FATF's members have consistently and in a systematic manner upheld the FATF's existence, while providing directions, setting priorities, and endorsing its mandates, including changing its status from temporary to permanent.

As proclaimed at the 2019 Ministerial Meeting, Ministers "agreed to enhance the FATF's capacity to respond to these threats all countries face".[19] This political endorsement has been reaffirmed and strengthened in subsequent Ministerial Declarations.[20] Ministers Declarations are also international acts recognised under international law.

Supporting the view that the absence of a formal international treaty does not preclude the character of the organisation as an IO, as long as the substance of such constituent instruments performs the basic functions of a founding treaty, is the aforementioned 1982 Legal Opinion of the of the UN in relation to the status of the INTERPOL. According to the Legal Opinion:

> It had gradually been recognised that the substance of the constitution or statute of an organisation may be more relevant to the determination of the intergovernmental character of the organisation that the form in which was cast. Even if its constitution does not qualify as a formal international treaty, an international organisation may well be called intergovernmental as a result of the role which that constitution ascribes to Governments with regard to such matters as membership, representation, financing, etc.[21]

3.2 *The High-Level Principles and Objectives for FATF and FATF-Style Regional Bodies*

Adopted in October 2012, the HLPOs on the relationship between the FATF and its FSRBs[22] is another instrument that integrates the constitutional framework of the FATF, enshrining the high-level principles and reciprocal rights and obligations of the FATF and FSRBs.

The HLPOs are an intriguing document, deserving forethoughtful consideration as it touches matters of international institutional law. From one standpoint, the HLPOs are not ground-breaking or even original. They *codified* the

---

joint communiqué from constituting an international agreement", 355 or 353. In fact, such determination depends on the legal nature of the act, language, circumstances of the acts.

19 Para. 2.

20 2022 and 2024 Ministerial Declarations.

21 Extracts UN Juridical Yearbook of 1982, Chapter VI, Selected Legal Opinions, 180.

22 Last amended February 2019 (last visited 15/05/2024).

FATF and FSRBS *status quo*, reaffirming the rules of the associate membership status and the partnership terms developed over the years:

i) FATF and the FRSBS are independent organisations;
ii) Sharing of common goals and interests;
iii) FSRBS' endorsement of FATF Recommendations and methodology;
iv) Usage of the Universal Procedures for AML/CFT Assessments;
v) Reciprocal participation in Plenary meetings, WG meetings and others;[23]
vi) Reciprocal access to documents (confidential and non-confidential);
vii) Reciprocal participation for comments on the final draft of ME Reports;
viii) Joint Plenary meetings;[24]
ix) Joint mutual evaluations;[25]
x) Reciprocal provision of assessors and reviewers (peer review process);
xi) Joint typologies, seminars, workshops, training, and studies;[26]
xii) Provision of technical assistance;
xiii) Co-operation between FATF and the FRSBS Secretariats;[27]
xiv) Promotion of FATF's Recommendations and support of FATF's activities at a regional level.[28]

Yet, the same cannot be said about the 'governance' theme, which addresses institutional setting and design, financial procedures and budgetary matters of the regional bodies and FATF.

In an unprecedented manner, the HLPOS provide *strong guidance* on membership issues (eg. a minimum of six jurisdictions for an FSRB to be established, observership criteria, member's rights and obligations); on regional bodies' institutional framework (eg. mandate,[29] institutional setting modalities,[30] Secretariat's status, hierarchy and selection criteria of Secretariat's staff); and

23 2017–2018 FATF Report, 61.

24 The first Joint Plenary Meeting was with the APG in Singapore 2005 (2004–2005 FATF Report, para. 26).

25 The first Joint ME between the FATF and an FSRB was with the APG, and the jurisdiction was Australia (2004–2005 FATF Report, para. 28).

26 One of the first joint typologies meetings was with MONEYVAL in December 2004 and GAFISUD in November 2005 (2004–2005 FATF Report, para. 28). Also, 30 Years FATF Report, 36.

27 2019–2020 FATF Report, 13–44.

28 At: 1–5 of the HLPOS.

29 "The FSRB should not have functions in other areas that are substantially outside the scope of AML/CFT matters or that would seriously hinder performing its effective functioning as an FSRB", ibid, 5.

30 "The body should observe its written agreement, such as a mandate, memorandum of understanding or terms of reference, which sets out the objectives of the body and commits the member governments to implementing the body's principles and programs for

on decision-making process (authority of the Plenary, number of meetings and procedural norms).[31]

At finance and budgetary levels, the HLPOs provide specific guiding principles and objectives, determining that the: "body [FRSBs or FATF] needs to have in place adequate and transparent budgetary arrangements, including proper budgeting and independent auditing functions".[32]

Although non-binding under international law (soft law), the HLPOs address matters of an international institutional law nature in an unparalleled manner. This circumstance raises several concerns, particularly with regard to: i) autonomy *rationale*; ii) FATF's genuine intention; iii) practical effects; and iv) legitimacy.

In relation to the first concern, it seems that there is a contradiction between the autonomy *rationale* endorsed in the HLPOs and the true scope of the guidelines given the level of detail on governance issues.

The FATF and its FSRBs are described in the document as "free-standing organisations" with no "organisational hierarchy".[33] However, considering the subjects touched upon, the HLPOs are effectively limiting the institutional freedom and scope of the regional bodies, creating a veil of institutional hierarchy, given the fact that the FATF is the sole decision-maker regarding the content and terms of the HLPOs.

As regards the second concern, it may be questioned why governance issues (structure and finance) are included in the HLPOs. If the purpose of the document is to set up norms that govern the relationship of the FATF with its FSRBs, why does it address matters that should be freely designed by the members of each regional body in their founding instruments, such as the number of members, membership rules or institutional model?

What is the genuine intention of this document? It may be contended and reasoned that, in the absence of a formal agreement, the FATF is using the HLPOs to self-establish a *minimal set* of codified institutional (constitutional) rules.

---

combating ML/TF, to undertake mutual evaluations and follow-up, and to promote international co-operation among its members and with other FATF/FSRB members". Ibid.

31 Ibid, 1–6. Eg. number of annual meetings and political backing.

32 Ibid, 6–7 and 9–10. See Annex I 'Principles on Financial Governance for FATF/FSRBs'.

33 Ibid, 1. The 2016–2017 FATF Report states that: "The FATF and FSRBs are interdependent partners", 53. Also, the 30 Years FATF Report underpins that: "The FATF and FSRBs are independent organisations that meaningfully contribute to each other's projects and share the common goal of protecting the integrity of the financial system by addressing new and emerging threats and through mutual evaluation and follow-up processes", 70.

Regarding the third concern, it can be argued that these guiding principles and objectives have only rhetorical value. They are a mere collection of each FSRB institutional characteristics without immediate implication or even practical effect, considering that all FSRBs have been founded before 2012. Nevertheless, the HLPOs are valid for guiding (and potentially constraining) the establishment of future sub-regional bodies or any institutional reform that the existing regional bodies wish to engage in.

As to the fourth concern, it can be questioned on what legal grounds an organisation establishes, through 'high-level principles and objectives', a number of rules governing matters of international institutional law pertaining to other organisations? In terms of legitimacy, it is highly questionable that a 'members-club' (consisting of 40 members) approves and extends a set of HLPOs to its regional bodies and respective members (accounting 166 jurisdictions) without voting rights on its content.

In fact, these rules confine the autonomy and independence of the regional bodies,[34] raising the question of where members' free will lies on their own. Hence, the content of the HLPOs appears to be an abusive interferencc in jurisdictions' sovereign authority.

From an ethical standpoint, it is somewhat paradoxical that an organisation with an informal legal standing is issuing guidelines (rules) on institutional configuration models to its regional bodies when the vast majority of its FSRBs are formal IOs or have adopted more formal foundational instruments than the FATF itself (Chapter 2, Section 8 above).

This unique piece of soft law – HLPOs – merits careful consideration and should not be taken lightly. It leaves a few questions unanswered and, ultimately, it creates a tacit hierarchy between the FATF and its FRSBs, especially considering that the HLPOs were drafted to frame the FSRBs' institutional design, thus reinforcing my idea of an *octopus-effect network*.[35]

At the same time, it provides the FATF with some sort of formal institutional support by ascribing several institutional rules that were missing from previous constitutive instruments, especially its mandates (Chapter 2, Section 2 above).

---

34 The term 'body' means both the FATF and FRSBs, otherwise the term 'FRSB' or 'FATF' is used.

35 For instance, in relation joint ME, para. 48 of the 4th Round of ME Procedures establishes a clear hierarchy by stating that when FATF members are also FSRB members by stating that: "[t]he first discussion of the MER should take place in the FATF" and that "the presumption is that the FATF's view would be conclusive". In other words, there is no equal standing.

In short, the G-7 Declaration, FATF's Mandates, Minister's Declarations, HLPOs, some reports and statements, and other internal regulations (eg. the Internal Governance Principles (IGP)) form the constitutional *corpus* of the FATF. They incorporate the core rules that govern the organisation and the relationship of the FATF with its members, FSRBs and third parties.

This combined normative framework, which constitutes the FATF's *acquis*, gives substance to the factual and legal existence of the FATF, satisfying Wessels' *constitutive rule* and classifying the FATF as an institutional legal fact.

Therefore, it is possible to argue that a considerable number of intentional collective acts of an international law nature jointly build the legal foundations of the FATF, fulfilling the criterion of being created under international law.

4 An Organ of Its Own with a Distinct Will

For the FATF to be recognised as a separate and independent organisation with a distinct and autonomous will from its members (*volonté disctincte*), a *certain level of detachment* of the organisation *from* and *towards* its members needs to be demonstrated, ie. FATF's *material* independence from its members needs to be proven.

First, it must be shown that the organisation has organs of its own and the capacity to take autonomous decisions. This condition is underlined in the definition of Seyersted, Amerasinghe and Wessel, with the latter author designating it as *decision-making processes*.

The FATF's Plenary is the main governing political body vested with decision-making capacity, meeting Seyersted's *self-governing* requirement. All decisions take place on a consensual basis, where members enjoy equal legal status, represented by their high-ranking officials.

Decisions are made to meet the functions and purposes of the organisation and are not subject to the authority or on behalf of the members, but of the organisation itself, where affairs are conducted in its own name, as 'sovereign acts'.[36]

36 The concept is developed by Seyesterd. Organisations have an *inherent* capacity to perform certain acts that are strictly within their jurisdiction, such as organic acts (establishment of internal rules and procedures) and others acts that they are in a "practical position to perform", as long as they do not contravene with their founding instruments or the purposes of the organisation. *Objective International Personality of Intergovernmental Organizations – Do Their Capacities Really Depend Upon Their Constitutions* (Krohns Bogtrykkeri (ed), København, Copenhagen 1963) 28, 44–45, 54, 99–100.

The FATF is represented by its President and Vice-President that, together with the assistance of the FATF Secretariat, form the 'executive body' of the organisation under the Plenary's instructions. All FATF officials are duty-bound to exercise their office with total independency, autonomy, and impartiality (Chapter 2, Section 3 above).[37]

As previously mentioned, the FATF has another political body equivalent to a Conference of Ministers, the FATF Ministerial meeting, which convenes on a biannual basis for high-level political and strategic decisions.[38] It provides political backing and exercises supervisory functions. In the 2019 Ministerial Declaration, Ministers agreed as follows:

> We will increase our engagement as Ministers of the FATF by meeting every two years, starting from 2022, to discuss strategic issues and to take stock of FATF progress in its mandate. We will continue to support the decision-making role and member-led process of the FATF Plenary.[39]

Ministers have reiterated this political compromise in the following biannual meetings.[40] During the 2024 biannual meeting, the Ministers vow to grant human and financial resources for the FATF to carry out its new round of assessments under the new methodology.[41]

At the last meeting, Ministers also addressed new topics:

> We reiterate our commitment to promote robust governance within the FATF, based on integrity, accountability, and transparency. The FATF is also committed to promoting equality and diversity in the Global Network, including through the development of the Women in FATF and the Global Network initiative.[42]

Resembling other IOs, the FATF has two layers of policy decision-making: the political decision-making body – the Plenary, and the high-level political body – the Ministerial meetings, engaging Governments at the highest level (Chapter 2, Section 3 above).

37 2019 Mandate, para. 34.
38 Before (normally) every 8 years with the renewal of the mandate or mid-term reviews.
39 Para. 16.
40 2022 Ministerial Declaration, para. 2; 2024 Ministerial Declaration, para. 1.
41 Ibid, para. 12.
42 Ibid, para. 21.

In Chapter 2, a diversity of elements (*indicia*) was provided illustrating FATF's decision-making capacity and autonomous will, in line with Sands and Klein, Schermers and Blokker or Klabbers' definition. The FATF is able to adopt decisions *from* and *for* its members, and to act on its own, in line with Sands and Klein or Alvarez's definition. There is also a clear distinction of legal powers and purposes between the organisation and its members, how they are exercised in the international realm, and who represents and speaks on behalf of the organisation, in line with Brownlie and Odello's definition.[43]

In this Chapter, a detailed overview of some decisions and actions taken at the political and policy levels is provided, as is distinctive of the autonomous character of the FATF. These acts demonstrate that the FATF acts on its own (*volonté disctincte*) and in the interest of the organisation.

4.1 *FATF's Reports and Action Plans*

Every MER or FUR of the FATF, although resulting from a peer-review mechanism, after approval of the FATF Plenary, is a report of the organisation. Recommendations therein lay down to improve national AML/CFT/CPF regimes are exclusively from the FATF. Both the MERs and FURs are examples of the autonomy and independence of the FATF, expressing its detachment from its members.

The FATF also highlights priority actions, key findings and recommendations, and major deficiencies. All these are manifestations unveiling an independent institutional, political and technical stand of the organisation *vis-à-vis* its members.

For instance, in the MER of Israel (December) 2018 under the 4th Round of ME Procedures, the FATF concluded that the country relied on general CDD obligations, mostly related to money service businesses (MSBs), "whose business model (…) to a large extent the provision of wire transfers is not subject to specific obligations". The lack of specific requirements for wire transfers resulted in Israel being rated as 'PC' under Recommendation 16 (Wire Transfers).[44]

In May 2022, Israel was subject to its first Follow-up Report & Technical Compliance Re-Rating, where the FATF acknowledged that:

> Israel has implemented specific obligations for wire transfers, particularly in relation to higher risk sectors such as MSBs. Israel has amended

43 Eg. Brand concerns, specific public statements towards members like Brazil, Turkey and Russian Federation, Grey and Black Lists and technical assistance.

44 At: 13.

> the legislation that applies to MSBs and Credit Service Providers (including [Money Value Transfer Services] (MVTS) which now includes a new section regarding wire transfers that is substantially in line with the requirements in R.16.[45]

In the MER of China (April) 2019, some shortfalls were pointed out by the FATF; Recommendation 29 (Financial Intelligence Units) was one of them. China was rated as 'PC' because its FIU did not perform the national agency role to receive, analyse Suspicious Transaction Reports (STRs) and disseminate its results. Furthermore, China's FIU had limited operational powers and autonomy, for instance, it could not "request from the reporting institutions any additional information".[46] As an outcome, the FATF recommended China to:

> [R]eview the functioning of its FIU to ensure that all information received, analysed and disseminated by all three FIU components is readily available and accessible both at the central and provincial levels (…) to ensure the operational independence of the FIU.[47]

China's progress was later recognised in China's 2nd Enhanced Follow-up Report and Technical Compliance Re-Rating, in October 2021, in virtue of the creation of a database for information sharing (2nd Generation AML Monitoring and Analysis System) and the establishment of a co-ordination mechanism within its FIU.[48]

In the MER of South Africa (October) 2021, a joint assessment of the FATF/ESAAMLG, the FATF concluded that:

> However, pursuing TF [terrorist financing] investigations is not very well integrated with strategies to combat terrorism in South Africa and authorities are failing to produce results reflective of the country's identified TF risk. The low level of viable investigations and prosecutions into

45 At: 2.

46 At: 5–6, 240–244. About the influence of FATF's standards in shaping the AML framework in China after being granted observer status, Nicole Schulte-Kulkmann, 'The Architecture of Anti-Money Laundering Regulation in the People's Republic of China – Shortfalls and Requirements for Reform' (2006) 14(4) *European Journal of Crime, Criminal Law and Criminal Justice*.

47 At: 14.

48 At: 4.

> TF in South Africa is not consistent with the countries recognised TF risk profile.[49]

The jurisdiction's vulnerability to laundering of domestic and foreign crime proceeds from the region, where FT risks are deeply associated with domestic terrorism, foreign terrorism and foreign terrorist fighters, was identified as one major shortcoming. South Africa was rated 'PC' under Recommendation 5 (Terrorist Financing Offence).[50]

Notwithstanding South Africa's steps to overcome its deficiencies, including its CFT regime,[51] the jurisdiction is still under FATF's monitoring exercise. On 6 June 2023, the Department of National Treasury announced:

> President Cyril Ramaphosa has recently signed into law two key Acts of Parliament, namely the General Laws (Anti-Money Laundering and Combating Terrorism Financing) Amendment Act, 2022 ('General Laws Amendment Act') and the Protection of Constitutional Democracy Against Terrorism and Related Activities Amendment Act, 2022 ('POCDATARA Amendment Act'). This is a significant step towards addressing the deficiencies in South Africa's AML/CFT measures that were identified in the 2021 Mutual Evaluation Report (…) These amendments also address two key findings of the mutual evaluation by refining the offence of terrorist financing and improving the processes for the implementation of financial sanctions against supporters of terrorist organisations. (…) The General Laws Amendment Act and POCDATARA Amendment Act address 15 of the 20 deficiencies relating to the adequacy of laws and legal frameworks related to the 40 FATF Recommendations that were identified in the mutual evaluation report.[52]

Another indicator of FATF's autonomy sphere is its detailed action plans to countries that show strategic vulnerabilities in their AML/CFT regimes. These action plans or roadmaps are tailor made. They are specifically designed to a particular jurisdiction addressing the main deficiencies in its legal, regulatory

49 At: 9.

50 Ibid, 2–3, 9 and 14.

51 FATF's acknowledgment at: https://www.fatf-gafi.org/en/publications/High-risk-and-other-monitored-jurisdictions/Increased-monitoring-february-2024.html.

52 'Enactment of Key Money-Laundering and Combating Terrorism Financing Laws' (06/06/2023) Media Statement, Department of National Treasury of South Africa, at: https://www.fsca.co.za/Regulatory%20Frameworks/Pages/AMLCFT.aspx.

or operational frameworks, establishing benchmarks, targeting measures and concrete timelines.

Progress is strictly monitored by the ICRG (FATF) regardless of the jurisdiction's regional group and, as stated, any jurisdiction placed on the 'Grey List' is subject to this mechanism (Chapter 2, Section 7.2. above).

Even though not publicly available, FATF's action plans are referred to or briefly described on FATF website (Jurisdictions under Increased Monitoring – February 2024)[53] or addressed in the declarations of jurisdictions or in the *media*.

Examples can be extracted from FATF's website, such as Cambodia, which has been subject to ICRG's review after the results of its MER (September) 2017. Cambodia was rated with one 'NC', 19 'PC', 19 'LC' and two 'C', and ten 'low or moderate level of effectiveness' out of eleven Immediate Outcomes, hence placed in enhanced (expedited) follow-up.[54]

Cambodian authorities have committed to FATF's action plan,[55] working together with its regional body – the APG, however, in June 2022, the FATF expressed concern with the lack of progress:

> The FATF again expresses significant concern that Cambodia failed to complete its action plan, which fully expired in January 2021. The FATF strongly urges Cambodia to swiftly complete its action plan by October 2022 or the FATF will consider calling on its members and urging all jurisdictions to apply enhanced due diligence to business relations and transactions with Cambodia.[56]

In October 2022, the FATF Plenary acknowledged the Cambodian Government's efforts in "substantially" completing is action plan and engaging in concrete

53 At: https://www.fatf-gafi.org/en/publications/High-risk-and-other-monitored-jurisdictions/Increased-monitoring-february-2024.html.

54 APG MER Cambodia (September) 2017, 13.

55 Actions required: (1) enhancing disseminations of financial intelligence to law enforcement authorities in connection with high-risk crimes; (2) demonstrating an increase in ML investigations and prosecutions in line with risk; (3) demonstrating an increase in the freezing and confiscation of criminal proceeds, instrumentalities, and property of equivalent value; (4) demonstrate that implementation of TFS [targeted financial sanctions] related to PF is occurring by providing training to strengthen the skills of competent authorities to implement TFS related to PF, and enhance the understanding of sanctions evasion. At: https://www.fatf-gafi.org/en/publications/High-risk-and-other-monitored-jurisdictions/Increased-monitoring-march-2022.html.

56 At:https://www.fatf-gafi.org/en/publications/high-risk-and-other-monitored-jurisdictions/documents/increased-monitoring-june-2022.html#Cambodia.

AML/CFT reforms, nevertheless the jurisdiction remained under monitoring pending an on-site visit and additional analysis.[57] Cambodia was later removed from the 'Grey List' in February 2023.

In a similar position the UAE. In the MER of UEA (April) 2020, a joint assessment FATF/MENAFATF, the jurisdiction was rated with nine 'low or moderate level of effectiveness' out of 11 Immediate Outcomes and rated 'PC' for Recommendations 6 (Terrorist Financing Offence) and 7 (Target Financial Sanctions related to Terrorism and Terrorist Financing), amongst others.[58]

At time, the UAE expressed its political commitment to work with the FATF and MENAFATF to improve its AML/CFT regime, namely to follow FATF's action plan.[59] In its official *media* channel the UAE stated that:

> The UAE, the region's financial capital and a gold trading hub, will work to implement a FATF action plan to strengthen the effectiveness of its anti-money laundering and counter terrorism financing regime (…) In response to the listing, the UAE government said it had a 'strong commitment' to working closely with FATF on areas for improvement.[60]

57 At: https://www.fatf-gafi.org/publications/high-risk-and-other-monitored-jurisdictions/documents/increased-monitoring-october-2022.html#Cambodia.

58 At: 16.

59 Action required. (1) demonstrating through case studies and statistics a sustained increase in outbound MLA requests to help facilitate investigation of TF, ML, and high-risk predicates; (2) identifying and maintaining a shared understanding of the ML/TF risks between the different DNFBP sectors and institutions; (3) showing an increase in the number and quality of STRs filed by FIs and DNFBPs; (4) achieving a more granular understanding of the risk of abuse of legal persons and, where applicable, legal arrangements, for ML/TF; (5) providing additional resources to the FIU to strengthen its analysis function and enhance the use of financial intelligence to pursue high-risk ML threats, such as proceeds of foreign predicate offenses, trade-based ML, and third-party laundering; (6) demonstrating a sustained increase in effective investigations and prosecutions of different types of ML cases consistent with UAE's risk profile; and (7) proactively identifying and combating sanctions evasion, including by using detailed TFS guidance in sustained awareness-raising with the private sector and demonstrating a better understanding of sanctions evasion among the private sector. At: https://www.fatf-gafi.org/en/publications/High-risk-and-other-monitored-jurisdictions/Increased-monitoring-june-2022.html.

60 'UAE continues progress and reconfirms its deep commitment to AML/CFT following FATF decision' (05/03/2022) Abu Dhabi Media Office, at: https://www.mediaoffice.abudhabi/en/economy/uae-continues-progress-and-reconfirms-its-deep-commitment-to-AML-CFT-following-FATF-decision/.

The UAE was removed from the 'Grey List' in February 2024. In a public declaration, the Chairman of the Abu Dhabi Department of Economic Development, comments:

> The FATF announcement acknowledges the efforts exerted by various UAE authorities, led by the Executive Office of Anti-Money Laundering and Counter Terrorism Financing, to meet the Action Plan requirements. We remain committed to collaborating with our partners and stakeholders to fulfil our long-term sustainable AML/CFT strategy.[61]

4.2 *High-Level Missions or Letters to Governments*

A validation of FATF's individual political will and independent institutional position on the international plane are its high-level missions and letters to Governments. The missions are carried out either to assess a candidature of membership/observership or to bring the attention of members to their inadequate AML/CFT/CPF regime, or to call the attention of jurisdictions from the Global Network to their inadequate AML/CFT/CPF regime.

For example, in the EAG Bulletin of July 2010, reference is made to a joint FATF/EAG mission, in April, to Turkmenistan, aiming at outlining "recommendations on developing the national AML/CFT system". After two months, Turkmenistan became a full member of the EAG.[62]

Following its application of observership, the FATF conducted a high-level mission to the Kingdom of Saudi Arabia, as reported by the Saudi Central Bank:

> To achieve this [observer] status, considerable efforts to implement legal, regulatory and operational measures for combating money laundering, terrorist financing and other related threats to the integrity of the international financial system have been recognised by the FATF high-level mission that visited the Kingdom in early June 2015 (…) The positive impressions gained by the high-level mission were echoed at Plenary meeting of FATF (…) based on the above and results of previous assessments, the Kingdom of Saudi Arabia was voted as an Observer Member in the international FATF organisation.[63]

61 'Chairman of ADDED Statement on FATF Resolution' (23/02/2024) Department of Economic Development, at: https://www.added.gov.ae/en/news-and-highlights/media-announcement/chairman-of-added-statement-on-fatf-resolution.

62 At: https://eurasiangroup.org/files/uploads/files/Bulletens/en/2bulletinjul2010eng.pdf.

63 'The Kingdom of Saudi Arabia's Accession to Observer Member in FATF' (08/02/2015) Saudi Central Bank website, at: https://www.sama.gov.sa/en-us/news/pages/news08022015.aspx.

In 2018, the EAG also announced a high-level mission of the FATF to Indonesia as a procedure for its membership application candidature:

> At the same time, following the completion of the high-level mission to Jakarta in May 2018, whose participants, including from Russia, certified Indonesia's commitment to the speedy fulfilment of its obligations, Indonesia became the latest country to be granted observer status in the FATF.[64]

Another act with significance and demonstrative of FATF's independence are its letters addressed to Governments. On 23 January 2019, the FATF President wrote to the Minister of Justice and Public Security of Brazil to encourage effective action against its long-lasting shortages. In this letter, the FATF President recalls a high-level mission to Brazil and the action plan that was drawn up.

> As we discussed, I am concerned about Brazil's lack of progress to enact legislation that would address long-standing deficiencies in its implementation of targeted financial sanctions. (…) The FATF first identified the deficiencies in Brazil's legal regime in 2010. Since then, FATF has engaged extensively with Brazil (including a high-level mission in 2015) to encourage improvement in this area. In November 2017, Brazil committed to a clear action plan and timeline for enacting the necessary legislation to improve its legal regime by June 2018. (…) However, despite these efforts, the necessary legislation has not been enacted which means that Brazil is now in breach of its action plan on deficiencies that have been outstanding for over eight years.[65]

4.3 *Public Interventions and Statements*

Public interventions and statements by the FATF President, as well as the Vice-President or Executive Secretariat on behalf of the organisation, are equally evidence of FATF's capacity to make stands of political nature in the international realm. The FATF President intervenes in a considerable number of events, as mentioned in Chapter 2, Section 3 above.

At the 2020 Chairmanship OSCE-Wide Counter-Terrorism Conference, the FATF President stressed the uniqueness of this organisation as a *global*

64 'Participation in the Joint FATF/MENAFATF Plenary' (02/07/2018) EAG website, at: https://eurasiangroup.org/en/ob-uchastii-v-sovmestnom-plenume-fatf-menafatf.

65 Letter of the FATF President (ref. 20190123VS01), 23/01/2019, at: https://legis.senado.leg.br/sdleg-getter/documento?dm=7919389&ts=1551098724610&disposition=inline.

standard-setter and *global keeper,* as well as the source for legal authority of the AML/CFT standards.

> [The standards] are backed-up in many areas by the legal authority of the UN Conventions and Security Council Resolutions and by strong political support from the G-20. But we are not only a standard setting body, but we also evaluate jurisdictions against these standards assessing whether they have implemented the standards technically by introducing the necessary legal and regulatory requirements, but – even more important – assessing whether they have implemented the rules effectively on the ground.[66]

At the 'Joint Special Meeting of the Counter-Terrorism Committee and the 1267/1989/2253 ISIL (Da'esh) and Al-Qaida Sanctions Committee of the UNSC', in November 2021, the FATF President emphasised that "FATF's role is to complement and reinforce the UN's counter-terrorism framework" by giving "practical effect to the relevant UN Conventions and Security Council Resolutions", while the ME process allows to assess how well States are implementing their international obligations.[67]

At the 2022 AML Intelligence Summit, the FATF President's distinguishes the singularity of the ME process:

> The mutual evaluation process is at the heart of the FATF's mandate. This peer-review exercise assesses countries' compliance with the FATF standards and the effectiveness of their actions in tackling money laundering, terrorist and proliferation financing. Each mutual evaluation also provides the country with a roadmap and priority actions to strengthen their systems (…) the unique feature of the FATF: it is not just about having the legal frameworks in place – countries actually have to be effective in fighting money laundering and terrorist financing. Often this means going beyond the minimum requirements to have a system in place that is fit for purpose, and one that can address the risks we all face.[68]

66 FATF's President Speech (15/09/2020), at: https://www.fatf-gafi.org/publications/fatfgeneral/documents/2020-osce-counter-terrorism-conference.html.

67 FATF's President Speech (18/11/2021), at: https://www.un.org/securitycouncil/ctc/sites/www.un.org.securitycouncil.ctc/files/financial_action_task_force.pdf.

68 Intervention of the FATF President (28/04/2022), at: https://www.amlintelligence.com/2022/04/exclusive-fatf-presidents-phenomenal-speech-at-amli-ppp-summit/.

The FATF public statements are another crystal example of FATF's individuality as a full-fledged organisation in the international system. The FATF has made general public statements in relation to matters of international relevance associated with its mission, as it occurred in the case of the Pandora Papers. In October 2021, the FATF commented on the findings, and recalled its warnings about the risks of anonymous shell companies, and legal arrangements, recognising that there are still gaps:

> Tougher global standards to promote transparency of beneficial ownership information and the more effective use of that information to hold to account those who hide behind the corporate veil or other structures, will be major steps forward. By taking collective action against illicit financial flows, we can help prevent and combat financial crime, curb corruption and tax evasion and support sustainable economic growth.[69]

In another sphere, the FATF Public Statements in relation to the Russian Federation clearly attest to the autonomy of the organisation *vis-à-vis* its members, bearing significant relevance (Chapter 2, Section 4 above). This is the first time that the FATF has taken a public and political stance against a member for violating the FATF's principles of mutual co-operation and dialogue, and for violating the territorial integrity of an FSRB member.

On 4 of March 2022, in a Public Statement, the FATF declares that the Russian Federation's membership is under review "and will consider what future steps are necessary to uphold these core values", such as being subject to sanctions, including membership suspension for placing the global financial system at risk and vulnerable to transnational crime and cyber-attacks, thereby potentiating ML/FT/PF activities.[70]

The FATF's institutional and public position was endorsed by the FATF Ministers at the 2022 biannual meeting by declaring: "We recall the March 2022 FATF Public Statement on the situation in Ukraine and reaffirm that the ongoing Russian invasion runs counter to the FATF".[71]

The Public Statement of March is, in essence, a political condemnation with reputational impact. It marks and distinguishes the FATF as an independent and autonomous organisation from its members, particularly knowing that some of its members have strong views as regards the Russian Federation

69 At: https://www.fatf-gafi.org/publications/fatfgeneral/documents/pandora-papers.html.

70 At:https://www.fatf-gafi.org/en/publications/Fatfgeneral/Ukraine-2022.html;https://www.fatf-gafi.org/en/publications/Fatfgeneral/Outcomes-fatf-plenary-march-2022.html.

71 Para. 4.

invasion, such as is the case of the USA, Canada, or the EU, while others have maintained a neutral position like China. It also represents a major individual international stance of the FATF in parallel with other IOs (eg. CoE, EU, OECD, OSCE or UN), which released similar statements.[72]

On 17 June 2022, at the Plenary meeting, the FATF reiterated the previous statements while recognising the Russian Federation's role in the FATF and EAG. The FATF decided, without suspending the Russian Federation's membership, to limit considerably its powers as a member.[73] However, at the Plenary meeting of 21 October 2022, the membership rights of the Russian Federation are further restricted,[74] as described in Chapter 2, Section 4 above.

On 24 February 2023, by a ground-breaking decision, the membership of the Russian Federation was suspended at the Plenary meeting, and a specific statement was issued. This is the first time that a FATF member has had its membership suspended in the three decades of the organisation. This decision was upheld at the FATF Plenary in February 2024.

The grounds for the suspension are not the ones provided for in the Mandate, but are implicit in FATF's aims and functional model:

72 Eg. Statement by the President of the CoE Congress and CoE Secretary General condemning the Russian Federation military attack against Ukraine (24/02/2022); Decision to suspend Russian Federation rights of representation in the Committee of Ministers and Parliamentary Assembly of the CoE (25/02/2022); and Resolution on the cessation of the membership of the Russian Federation in the CoE (16/03/2022), at: www.coe.int/en/web/cdcj/-/russian-federation-excluded-from-the-council-of-europe. EU Joint Statement by the members of the European Council condemning Russia's military aggression against Ukraine and agreeing on sanctions against the Russian Federation (24/02/2022), at: https://www.consilium.europa.eu/en/press/press-releases/2022/02/24/joint-statement-by-the-members-of-the-european-council-24-02-2022/; and https://www.consilium.europa.eu/en/meetings/european-council/2022/02/24/. The OECD after issuing a statement on 24 February condemning Russian Federation's large-scale aggression against Ukraine, the OECD Council decided to suspend the participation of Russian Federation from all OECD bodies (08/03/2022), at: https://www.oecd.org/en/about/news/speech-statements/2022/03/statement-from-the-oecd-council-on-further-measures-in-response-to-russia-s-large-scale-aggression-against-ukraine.html. Joint Statement of OSCE Chairman-in-Office and OSCE Secretary General condemning military operation in Ukraine (24/02/2022), at: https://www.osce.org/chairmanship/512890. The UN General Assembly adopted Resolution on the aggression against Ukraine condemning Russian Federation military intervention (A/RES/ES-11/1, 02/03/2022) and Resolution on the suspension of the rights of membership of the Russian Federation in the Human Rights Council (A/RES/ES-11/3, 07/04/2022).

73 At: https://www.fatf-gafi.org/publications/fatfgeneral/documents/ukraine-june-2022.html.

74 At: https://www.fatf-gafi.org/en/publications/Fatfgeneral/Outcomes-fatf-plenary-october-2022.html.

> The Russian Federation's actions unacceptably run counter to the FATF core principles aiming to promote security, safety, and the integrity of the global financial system. They also represent a gross violation of the commitment to international cooperation and mutual respect upon which FATF Members have agreed to implement and support the FATF Standards. Considering the above, the FATF has decided to suspend the membership of the Russian Federation.[75]

FATF's decision to continue to suspend membership rights of the Russian Federation received political support from Ministers at the 2024 Ministerial biannual meeting.[76]

The above decision is significant because it surpasses the interests of individual members, aims at protecting the organisation's interests, and expresses the organisation's will.

These public statements against a member illustrate and reinforce the position that the FATF has the ability to act on its own, ie. that the FATF has international legal capacity and independence on the international plane. In this sense, it is fair to conclude that the FATF meets the criterion of having autonomous organs and the ability to express the will of the organisation.

5 To Operate on the International Plane According to International Law

Another element to consider is how the FATF operates on the international plane, ie. how it conducts its affairs, if actions undertaken are conducted in an independent and autonomous manner, and how such actions are understood by its members, associate members (FSRBs) and other jurisdictions from the Global Network.

Pursuant to Wessel's autonomy test, one must identify the *practices of the FATF conceived as external behaviour.* To this end, it is necessary to ascertain how the FATF engages externally to pursue its objectives and implementing its policies? Do the FATF's external actions or positions indicate the possession of legal capacities? Is there a clear distinction between the FATF and its members as separate subjects of international law at external level? Are the

75 At:https://www.fatf-gafi.org/en/publications/Fatfgeneral/outcomes-fatf-plenary-february-2023.html.

76 2024 Ministerial Declaration, para. 4.

competences and capacities of the organisation perceived by its members as of the organisation?

The answers to these questions have been partially provided in Chapter 2 in a systematic manner in line with Brownlie and Goodwin-Gill approach when assessing the legal nature of the IPU. The Brownlie and Goodwin-Gill criteria are:

i) Character and purpose;
ii) Membership criteria and affiliation;
iii) Structure and functions;
iv) Representation and voting;
v) Budgetary matters;
vi) Internal legal order; and
vii) External relations.[77]

A detailed description and critical analysis of the FATF's institutional, regulatory and operational frameworks, including at the external level, have therefore been covered in that Chapter. This description also highlights the evolving nature of the FATF.

Odello's methodology presupposes an analysis of the legal powers conferred (express, inherent and/or implied) and body of practice of the FATF, ie. the relation between the powers that are conferred, how they are exercised and how they are perceived by members (closely in line with Wessel's approach).[78]

Based on the cited scholars, this Section discusses some decisions and actions that explicitly and/or implicitly indicate FATF's capacity to operate on the international plane and the mechanisms and tools developed by the organisation through time within the international legal system to effectively pursue its goals. It also explores how jurisdictions have responded to FATF's *modus operandi* and how its legal position is perceived.

Emphasis is given to some important institutional decisions and actions, including the relationship between the FATF and the FSRBs, the relevance of the Global Network and brand, some regulatory and operational actions and their external impact in jurisdictions, and how these aspects relate to FATF's external capacities and self-sufficiency, ie. how these practices are conceived and perceived as FATF behaviour.

77 The 'primary test' is functional – autonomy and function are reflected in the IPU: "It is an entity, universal character, having the task of realising common goals, where participation and functional activities have the implicit consent of States and which are recognise by other international organisations", (n 8), para. 9 of the Statement.

78 (n 9) 365.

5.1 *Key Institutional Decisions and Actions*

The FATF has made several relevant decisions related to its initial institutional design to improve its functional performance and to better achieve its purposes in accordance with the dynamic nature of money laundering and associated transnational crime and trends, as well as in accordance with the demands of the international community.

The encouragement of setting FRSBs, creation of the associate membership status, creation of the ICRG, position of Vice-President, adoption of the HLPOs and Universal Procedures, 'institutionalisation' of a Global Network, protection of a brand, two years term of President and Vice-President and the biannual ministerial meetings are just a few examples.

5.1.1 Core Institutional Change

In 2019, the FATF underwent a core institutional change, transitioning from its initial conception as a non-permanent body with successively renewed terms of eight years to a permanent organisation.

Interestingly, in 2011, Beekarry had already mentioned that the FATF did not fit within the concept of an '*ad hoc* group':

> Moving beyond conventional theory which limits analytical focus of IO to the establishment process, the FATF institutional set up has now evolved into a separate and autonomous organic entity, molding itself as it interacts with the environment in which it is located. It no longer fits the traditional description of a mere 'ad hoc grouping of governments and others with a complex single issue agenda', but it resembles more of a permanent and fully functional international organisation managing a set of legally, albeit non-binding norms. Although the FATF has developed some level of autonomy in its operations and management, its initial 'programmed purpose' allows it to maintain the link with the states that created it.[79]

79 (n 1) 168–169. Amongst others, UK House of Lords – European Union Committee, Nineteenth Report-Money Laundering and the Financing of Terrorism (2008–09) (2009 House of Lords Report), para 17; Ghoshray (n 2) 542. With a different viewpoint, the HR Special Rapporteur notes that: "In 2019, the mandate of the Financial Action Task Force was changed into an open-ended one, marking the evolution of the Task Force from a temporary forum into a standing body. The change has not led to the formal establishment of the Task Force as an international organisation", A/74/335, 29/09/2019, para. 30.

Different statements with distinctive terminology have been provided over three decades regarding its character: a task force with specific goals and projects (1989), an *ad hoc* group (1990), an inter-governmental body (2006), an inter-governmental policy-making body (2007), an international organisation (30 Years FATF Report) or an independent inter-governmental body (2008–2024).

Nonetheless, FATF's 'decision-making role and member-led process' have consistently remained intact across its various mandates, even when its institutional nature changed progressively from a technical and temporary forum to a policy and long-standing organisation.

In fact, its decision-making capacity and is mission to review and update the standards in response to global trends and threats have been broadened and consolidated without being challenged. The evolution of the FATF's mandate until it reaches its current status is explained in Chapter 2, Section 2 above.

5.1.2 The Relationship between the FATF and the FSRBS

This is one of the FATF's most significant strategic politico-institutional decisions, if not the 'game-changer' of the FATF's position in international affairs. The incentive to set up FSRBS and at the later decision to only recognised FSRBS that *satisfy certain criteria* determined by the FATF as associate members created a high-pressure environment that was difficult to escape. This pressure became even higher when the FATF decided that jurisdictions around the world "should" be part of a regional group.[80]

In short, jurisdictions were/are individually compelled to be members of an FSRB.[81] Jurisdictions are collectively compelled to create regional or sub-regional bodies (FSRBS), and FSRBS are compelled to be associate members. A system ingeniously conceptualised that I call the *octopus-effect network*.

The concept of the *octopus-effect network* provides a faithful image of the internal and external *modus operandi* of the FATF's creative framework. The 'octopus head' resides in the FATF, governed by 40 members who dictate the AML/CFT/CPF standards and procedures, and the 'octopus arms' are the nine FSRBS, which comply with the rules set by the 'octopus head' and

80 As Hülsse and Kerwer stressed the "FATF's regionalisation strategy, aimed at including non-FATF member states in the global AML network (…) Hence, FATF remains largely in control over the regional AML bodies. And, while FATF now grants FSRBS the status of associate members, it has no intention of making them full members", (n 6) 57.

81 Belonging to an FSRB is a *condition sine qua non*. A jurisdiction will be immediately under the ICRG Review Process if it is not a member of an FSRB (2018–2019 FATF Report, 57).

guarantee that the remaining 166 jurisdictions under their monitoring capacity follow these rules.[82]

By encouraging the expansion of regional groups, the FATF has found an optimal solution that, simultaneously, enables the implementation of its policies within an interconnected network and allows the organisation to uphold its limited membership policy and the *status quo* of a 'club'.[83] In the 1993–1994 FATF Report, it affirmed:

> There was agreement that a significant increase in the size of the FATF would prejudice its flexibility and efficiency. Hence it was decided that there should be no more than a very limited expansion. However, the FATF will be examining further the possibility of setting up additional regional Task Forces on the lines of the Caribbean FATF.[84]

Corroborating such strategy, the 2008–2009 FATF Report states:

> To successfully combat money laundering and terrorist financing requires a consistent approach on a global scale. The FATF has worked closely with the FSRBs for more than ten years to establish a global network to ensure effective implementation of FATF standards in all regions of the world.[85]

Initially, the establishment of regional bodies was *impromptu*. It started spontaneously in the early 1990s, more precisely, with the initiative of some

82 FATF Report to the G-20 Antalya Summit in 2015: "The FATF-Style regional bodies (FSRBs) create an interconnected international network to combat money laundering and the financing of terrorism based on a strong commitment to follow the FATF standards, principles and methodologies as well as to enforce effective ML/FT countermeasures", 3. At: http://www.fatf-gafi.org/publications/fatfrecommendations/documents/terrorist-financing-fatf-report-to-g20.html. Also, about this "unequal relationship", amongst others, Tilahun, 'The Re-organization of the FATF as an International Legal Person and the Promises and Limits to Accountability' in A. Arcuri and F.C. Kund (eds) *Technocracy and Multi-level Governance: What Role for Accountability?* (Routledge 2021). On-line version, at: https://papers.ssrn.com/sol3/papers.cfm?abstract_id=4127120.

83 2000–2001 FATF report, para. 32. As commented by Blazejewski: "Through a strategy of building institutional partnerships, the FATF has managed to maintain the functional advantages that derive from its limited membership while advancing universal implementation of the Recommendations.", (n 1) 23.

84 1993–1994 FATF Report, para. 23. Daniel Drezner also mentions the encouragement of setting FSRBs and the value of such strategy. 'On the Balance between International Law and Democratic Sovereignty' (2011) 2(2) *Chicago Journal of International Law*, 330.

85 2008–2009 FATF Report, 21.

jurisdictions of the CFATF and of the APG by acknowledging the Forty Recommendations and the advantages of regional co-ordination. Hereafter, it became a logical phenomenon with spill-over effects to other regions of the world.

As noted, the CFATF resulted in two meetings held in Aruba and Jamaica in 1992 aiming at implementing the 1988 Vienna Convention and the Forty Recommendations of the FATF, culminating with the Kingston Declaration in 1992, which institutes a regional body based on the FATF model.[86]

The origins of the APG started in the early 1990s, when Australia launched a FATF-Asia Secretariat to raise awareness in the Asia-Pacific region of FATF activities and to encourage the adoption of sound AML regimes. Symposia convened in Hong Kong (China), and Japan between 1995 and 1996, and the last one, in Thailand in 1997, ended with the signing of the 1997 Bangkok Terms of Reference establishing the APG, mirroring the FATF model.[87]

The FATF quickly understood (1997–1998) that these bodies could play a crucial role in its intention to be a global standard-setter, so the idea of an *interconnected international network* (*octopus-effect network*) evolved as a natural and obvious step.

However, to be recognised as a global standard-setter, the FATF needed to cover all the following dimensions:

i) Universal adoption/implementation of the Recommendations, common compliance (monitoring),
ii) World co-ordination, and ultimately,
iii) Collective harmonisation or uniformisation of AML/CFT regimes.

Henceforth, the creation of FSRBs became of prime relevance and a priority for the FATF.

These regional bodies were successively created all over the world: the CFATF in 1992, the APG and MONEYVAL in 1997, the ESAAMLG and GIABA in 1999, the GAFILAT and GABAC in 2000 and the EAG and MENAFATF in 2004 (Chapter 2, Section 8 above).

Several reasons can explain why the FATF encouraged the creation of regional bodies (FSRBs). Firstly, it allows the FATF to maintain its limited

86 Blazejewski comments that "[b]y copying the FATF model, the Regional Bodies are able to utilise the same soft and persuasive means of advancing compliance with the recommendations that the FATF has found so effective internally", (n 1) 23. Anthony Smellie, 'The Work of the Caribbean Regional Division of the Financial Action Task Force' (1993) 19(2) *Commonwealth Law Bulletin*.

87 See Chapter 5, Section 1.

membership policy, while ensuring the adoption of its standards on a global scale in a more efficient, comprehensive, and low-cost manner.[88]

Secondly, the regional bodies, who attempt to balance the characteristics and particularities of each region *vis-à-vis* the FATF Standards, play the role of encouraging the implementation of the standards, as well as assessing and monitoring their compliance in the region.[89]

This last feature is openly recognised by the FATF President at the 2021 Joint Special meeting with the Counter-Terrorism Committee:

> The role of the Global Network of FATF-Style Regional Bodies, or FSRBS, is crucial in this regard. FSRBS evaluate 80% of the world's jurisdictions – around 160 countries – including some of the highest risk. We need these bodies to lead in understanding the methods used by terrorists to raise, move and deploy funds, the state of measures to prevent these risks, and the action needed that will make a difference on the ground.[90]

Thirdly, the FATF controls the decision-making process (ie. Recommendations, methodology and blacklisting)[91] and the outcome – the 'brand' (ie. quality and consistency), indirectly overseeing the work of the FSRBS.

This *co-operative but not reciprocal relationship* is well-defined in the HLPOS stating that: "Each FSRB is an autonomous body. They share the common goal with the FATF (...) but the FATF is the only standard-setting body".[92]

88 1997–1998 FATF Report, para. 21: "The medium to long term objectives of the FATF are the development of credible and effective FATF-style regional bodies and an adequate expansion of its membership to include strategically important new members. At the beginning of 2005, the FATF should ideally have achieved its objective of promoting the establishment of a worldwide anti-money laundering network".

89 2008–2009 FATF Report, para. 5: "The mutual evaluation process which is an essential and long-standing core activity of the FATF. This peer review process has now been extended through the FATF-Style Regional Body (FSRB) network to more than 170 countries and is the critical mechanism for promoting timely and effective implementation of FATF Recommendations and for contributing to the creation of a level playing field throughout the membership and beyond. Countries that are not FSRB members will be encouraged to join the relevant regional body".

90 FATF's President Speech (18/11/2021), at: https://www.un.org/securitycouncil/ctc/sites/www.un.org.securitycouncil.ctc/files/financial_action_task_force.pdf.

91 Eg. FATF's validation of the ME process of other bodies like the CFATF, CoE or OGBS (1996–1997, para. 5 and 92–93) Also, 1997–1998 FATF Report, para. 127–128.

92 2018–2019 FATF Report, 62. The 2017–2018 FATF Report mentions that "[t]he FATF and FSRBS are independent partners (...) While the FATF is the only standard-setting body, FATF and FSRBS each assess how effectively their respective members implement the FATF standards, based on the consolidated processes and procedures for mutual

Remarkably, this institutional hierarchy is well discerned among the regional bodies:

> The CFATF is an international/inter-governmental organisation, a regional style body like FATF which follows and ensures its members comply the FATF Recommendations. It does not issue standards on its own.[93]
>
> Within the international network for fight against money laundering and terrorist financing, MONEYVAL's role is as one of the eight FATF-style regional bodies (FSRBS). As such, MONEYVAL is autonomous and independent from the FATF, but closely cooperates with it, as well as with other FSRBS.[94]
>
> The Eastern and Southern Africa Anti-Money Laundering Group (ESAAMLG) is a Regional Body subscribing to global standards to combat money laundering and financing of terrorism and proliferation (…) The Purpose of The Eastern and Southern Africa Anti-Money Laundering Group (ESAAMLG) is to combat money laundering by implementing the FATF Recommendations.[95]

The relationship between the FATF and the FSRBS enters in a new phase with the creation of the associate membership status (2005–2006) (Chapter 2, Section 4 above).[96] The new position recognises the value and relevance of the work carried out by the FSRBS, particularly their contribution to the improvement of standards, and promotes *closer institutional engagement* with the regional bodies within the operational framework of the FATF. As underlined in the 2007–2008 FATF Report:

evaluations and follow-up ('Universal Procedures')", 59. As Hülsse and Kerwer summarise: "the FATF remains largely in control over the regional AML bodies", (n 6) 57.

93 At: https://www.cfatf-gafic.org/what-is-the-relation-between-the-fatf-and-the-cfatf-does-the-cfatf-issue-its-standards (last visited 15/05/2024).

94 At: https://www.coe.int/en/web/moneyval/moneyval-brief/members/international-context-co-operation (last visited 15/05/2024).

95 At: www.esaamlg.org/index.php/about_what_we_do (last visited 15/05/2024).

96 2003–2004 FATF Report, para. 21: "The *Ad Hoc* Group also prepared concrete proposals to strengthen the relationships between the FATF and the FATF-style regional bodies (FSRBS). Through increased dialogue with the regional bodies, the FATF hopes that it will enhance relationships with them and will demonstrate its desire for a better understanding of the problems outside its membership".

> The FSRBS, several of which are now associate members of the FATF, play an important leadership role in their respective regions and provide important regional expertise and input into the FATF policy-making function. The FATF and FSRBS will continue to strengthen their working relationships, as well as extending outreach at a regional level with key partners.[97]

FSRBS' participation in FATF's affairs as associate members is a sign of inclusiveness by providing a 'voice' in the FATF Plenary meetings and in the setting of FATF's policies, even if it falls short of ideal (Chapter 5, Section 2 below).

The relationship of the FATF with its FSRBS has been widely acknowledge and praised by counterparts, such as the UN/UNSC, IMF, WB, or G-20, where express references can be found.[98] This external recognition of the network legitimises and strengthens FATF's political and institutional framework and *modus operandi*.

FATF's interconnectedness and normative authority are emphasised by Ghoshray:

> Thus, the dynamics of social connectivity and peer relationships have allowed the FATF to develop a predictable trajectory of expected behaviour. This in turn has enabled the FATF Recommendations' soft prescriptions to attain the scope and characteristic of hard law within global finance. The FATF's mandate-driven enforcement paradigm empowers the FATF to formulate legal, financial, and law enforcement policies.[99]

As noted, currently all FSRBS are associate members of the FATF. The first FSRBS to benefit from such status were the GAFILAT and the MONEYVAL in 2006[100] and the last one was GABAC in 2015.[101]

---

97 Para. 17.

98 Eg. UNSCR 2482 (2019) and UNSCR 2610 (2021), para. 20 and 33 of the Preamble, respectively. Also, G-20 Leaders' Statement on Countering Terrorism: The Hamburg Summit 2017, para 11; G-20 Chairs' Summary, Third G-20 Finance Ministers and Central Bank Governors Meeting in Bali 2022, para. 14. FATF and FSRBS partnership with WB, at: http://web.worldbank.org/archive/website01075/WEB/0__CO-22.HTM. And close co-operation with IMF, at: https://www.imf.org/en/About/Factsheets/Sheets/2016/08/01/16/31/Fight-Against-Money-Laundering-the-Financing-of-Terrorism (last visited 15/05/2024).

99 (n 2) 530.

100 2005–2006 FATF Report, para. 21.

101 2015–2016 FATF Report, 51. The FATF created a new liaison with the FSRBS via a regular high-level meeting between the FATF and the FSRBS Chairs, 2022–2023 FATF Report, 4.

5.1.3 The Global Network

The architectural design of a global network began to take shape with the gradual number of associate members, expressing their undertaking to FATF's mission of countering ML and FT in the international financial system, and assuming each one of them the role of supervisor in their respective regional space. This architectural design is emphasised in the 2007–2008 FATF Report:

> Currently, the FATF is focusing on the accession of and on ensuring the best possible partnership with the associate members and other FSRBs. Once these initiatives are completed, the FATF will next consider the structure of the global AML/CFT architecture, including the enhanced role played by associate members and FSRBs, and FATF membership.[102]

FATF's *octopus-effect network* is more than a regular network as it involves co-ordination, common interpretation and application of the Recommendations, common compliance, and articulated supervisory mechanisms.

FATF's goal and ambition is for all jurisdictions to implement the same standards, adopt similar regimes in their national systems, share identical compliance mechanisms, and be supervised at regional and FATF's levels through uniform methods and core common values.[103]

At the 2022 Ministerial Declaration, Ministers highlighted such accomplishment:

> The Global Network, comprising the FATF and the nine FATF-Style Regional Bodies (FSRB), is an inclusive framework bringing together more than 200 governments and 20 observer international organisations, united by a shared commitment to tackle illicit finance and applying a single set of standards and a universal system of mutual evaluations.[104]

New soft law instruments were developed to ensure co-ordinated global governance and to certify quality and consistency with regards to the implementation of FATF's Recommendations. Within this context, the HLPOs and the

102 Para. 45.

103 The 2016–2017 FATF Report states that: "Each assessment is conducted in accordance with the FATF assessment methodology. FATF and FSRBs each have a certain amount of flexibility in determining the procedural arrangements for their mutual evaluations, but there is a set of core elements that apply to all assessment, regardless of the assessing body", 53. Also, 2015–2016 FATF Report, p. 51.

104 Para. 9.

Universal Procedures are two fundamental and structural documents, both playing a decisive part in the architecture of the FATF Global Network, contributing to consolidate FATF's position as the sole policy-making body.

A Global Network Co-operation Group was founded in 2012 as a forum for the FSRBS and the FATF to exchange views and work together.[105] In the 2014–2015 FATF Report, this synergy is explained:

> Through the Global Co-operation Network Group (GNCG), the FATF and FSRBS collaborate on equal terms to share experiences from their respective regions, work on typologies research into money laundering and terrorist financing trends and develop guidance. This collaboration between FATF and FSRBS is especially important in the mutual evaluation process. FSRBS assess the effectiveness of their members' AML/CFT measures and how well they have implemented the technical requirements of the FATF Recommendations.[106]

In short, the FATF has managed to perform an outstanding deed. It has managed to establish a common methodology to ensure a minimum common denominator (principles and objectives) for all bodies, as well as adopting common core procedures, and foremost, the acknowledgement and support of all FSRBS that the organisation is *the* AML/CFT "standard-setting body", "guardian" and "arbiter".[107]

FATF's leadership capacity to exert jurisdictions around the world in implementing its policies and standards is thus remarkable, even unique. It also demonstrates in a substantive and objective manner the FATF's decision-making capacities and the related external impact.

In this respect, Wessel and Dekker make an interesting observation about the exercise of sovereign powers entrusted to certain organisations:

> [T]hese days it is undisputed that many organisations 'exercise sovereign powers' in the sense that they do not only contribute to lawmaking by providing a framework for negotiations but also take decisions that legally bind – or otherwise exert legal force on – their members States.[108]

105 2012–2013 FATF Report, 32. The WG is co-chaired by a representative from FATF and another from an FSRB.

106 At: 23.

107 HLPO, 1.

108 'Identities of States in International Organizations' (2015) 12(2) *International Organizations Law Review*, 24. Examples are provided of IOs that issue binding decisions, such as the UNSC, WHO, EU, ICAO, OAS, NATO, UPU, OECD, WMO, IMF, as well of standard setting,

5.1.4 The Brand and Reputation Issues

Another decision that underscores FATF's autonomous identity and its ability to make decisions with external impact, showing a clear cleavage between the organisation, its members, and associate members, is the protection of FATF's brand.

The risk of undermining the credibility of the FATF, both as a 'global standard-setter' and a 'global keeper' through incorrect interpretation or misapplication of the FATF standards or of the 2013 Methodology in the ME process of the FSRBs was explicitly admitted with the HLPOs and, for the first time, in 2012.[109]

The reasons behind such 'brand concerns' are described in the Universal Procedures, when:

i) The ratings are clearly inappropriate and not consistent with the analysis;
ii) There has been a serious misinterpretation of the standards, methodology and/or procedures;
iii) An important part of the methodology has been systematically misapplied; or
iv) Laws that are not in force and effect have been considered in the analysis and ratings of a report.[110]

The HLPOs go further by elucidating that the protection of FATF's image extends to all FSRBs:

---

such as IMO, FAO, ICAO, ILO, IAEA, UNEP. Also, Wessel, 'Towards World Legislation? The Exercise of Public Authority by International Institutions', (2010) Conference World Legislation: Perspectives from International Law, Legal Theory and Political Philosophy (First draft), 2–4, at: https://ramseswessel.eu/Publications/Conference-papers/. Wessel and Steven Blockmans also address this topic and commented on the impact that informal intergovernmental co-operative structures, such as G-20, FATF, Basel Committee have in EU law, as well as formal IOs, such as WHO, IMF or WB. 'The Legal Status and Influence of Decisions of International Organisations and Other Bodies in the European Union' in P. Eeckhout and M. Lopez-Escudero (eds), *The European Union's External Action in Times of Crisis* (Hart Publishing 2016) 228, 234, 247.

109 The HLPOs were adopted in October 2012, see 2. As stated in the 2014–2015 FATF Report: "If one of the organisations is functioning poorly and not delivering rigorous assessments for example, then this can have an impact on all organisations in the FATF Global Network and the credibility of their work and the FATF brand", 23. Also, 2015–2016 FATF Report, 51.

110 Universal Procedures, para. 34. The 'Key Principles for Mutual Evaluations and Assessments' developed by the FATF in co-operation with the FSRBs, IMF and World Bank are at the origin of this document (2009–2010 FATF Report, para. 21).

> Since the FATF and FSRBs are part of a larger whole and the success or failure of one organisation can have an effect on all organisations, protection of the FATF brand is therefore in the common interest of both the FATF and FSRBs. The FATF brand is not limited to FATF output, but also extends to any FSRB output based on the FATF Recommendations, assessment methodology, best practices and guidance papers, mutual evaluations and follow-up.[111]

Another institutional decision that should be underlined, together with the decision to safeguard FATF's reputation, is the procedural requirement that all MERs must be submitted to FATF's Secretariat.

Based on the 'brand argument', the FATF Secretariat reviews all MERs of the FRSBs for Q&C and may likewise raise doubts regarding the application of the methodology and ratings.[112] As stated in the 2013–2014 FATF Report:

> [T]he Secretariats of the FATF, FSRBs, World Bank and IMF have worked closely to achieve a level of consistency in the approach to conducting a mutual evaluation. Each assessment body will have a robust review mechanism in place that will follow the FATF's quality and consistency review. In addition, prior to adoption, all mutual evaluation reports will be submitted to the FATF Secretariat for possible inclusion in the global quality and consistency review process.[113]

It is reminded that although a certain flexibility is given to the regional bodies to develop their own operational methods, FSRBs must pay attention to brand concerns during their ME process to guarantee "that the results of peer reviews – mutual evaluations – remain of high quality and consistency".[114]

111 At: 2 and 7–8.

112 As stated in the 2017–2018 FATF Report: "For this reason, the FATF Secretariat reviews all draft assessments of members of the Global Network at various stages in the process", 60. Also, HLPOs mention that "the review aims to identify any serious or major issues with the potential to affect the credibility of the FATF brand", para. 35–36.

113 At: 12.

114 As stated in the 2016–2017 FATF Report: "Each assessment is conducted in accordance with the FATF assessment methodology. FATF and FSRBs each have a certain amount of flexibility in determining the procedural arrangements for their mutual evaluations, but there is a set of core elements that apply to all assessment, regardless of the assessing body", 53. Also, 2017–2018 FATF Report, 59.

The result is that the FATF has always had an 'indirect say' in the final MER of each individual jurisdiction in the world and oversees all core aspects of the FSRBS' 'life'.

5.2 *Key Regulatory and Operational Actions and Their External Impact*

This part looks at FATF's practice as a regulator, in which its framework and operational methods have been gradually strengthened to enable it to properly perform its functions (functionality test). These key regulatory and operational actions provide *indicia* that the FATF possesses the legal capacities to operate on the international plane, ie. to externally pursue its objectives and implement its policies. It also demonstrates the inter-relations between the different subjects of international law and how FATF's members respond to FATF as a regulator (global keeper and arbiter).

The FATF's regulatory framework can be studied from the perspective of the FATF as an organisation, enacting acts that govern the life of the organisation and its relations with its members and third parties, or from the perspective of the FATF as a global standard-setter by establishing international standards.[115]

FATF's policy and lawmaking powers comprehend internal and external acts, as mentioned in Chapter 2, Section 6 above. The internal acts (*stricto sensu*) are the internal rules that regulate the functioning of the organisation (ie. voting rules, rules governing the Plenary and the WGS, election of chairs and other operational aspects).[116] There are also internal acts that are exclusively aimed at its members, such as MERS, FURS or individual statements.[117]

There are internal acts that regulate the relationship between the FATF and its FRSBS. These acts intentionally intend to have an external impact within the FATF Global Network to ensure the integrity and coherency of the system, such as the methodology, HLPOS or Universal Procedures.

115 Amongst others, Ryder, 'The Financial Services Authority and Money Laundering, a Game of Cat and Mouse' (2008) 67(3) *Cambridge Law Journal*; Hülsse and Kerwer (n 6) 53 *et seq*. Golia Jr and Peters underline the organisations rule-making power as a core manifestation element of autonomy, as it "distinguishes the collective actor not only from its members but is also crucial for shaping affected individuals' normative status", 'The Concept of International Organization' in J. Klabbers (ed), *The Cambridge Companion to International Organizations Law* (Cambridge University Press 2022), 44.

116 Eg. IGP, ICRG Procedures (not publicly available until 2024).

117 Eg. Confidential 2018 FATF Report on Terrorist Financing Disruption Strategies (2018–2019 FATF Report, 14). The 30 Years FATF Report also states that: "While the majority of the FATF's typologies research is published on the FATF's public website to maximise the reach of the findings, FATF's work in this area has also resulted in a number of internal reports", 39.

There are internal acts that regulate the FATF's relationship with its members. These include the ME procedures and other internal rules that may have an external impact on the regional bodies and concerned jurisdictions, such as by analogously modelling their procedures.[118]

There are also internal acts like the Forty Recommendations that have a widespread effect that goes far beyond the FATF Global Network by having an impact in the international arena, either by being recommended or endorsed by other international actors (eg. UNSC or G-20), by shaping their AML/CFT regimes (eg. CoE and UE), or by modelling their practices (eg. Basel Committee or OECD Tax Global Forum).[119] The same may be held about Guidance Papers that before addressing specifically the private sector, they were used as a reference.[120]

External acts (*stricto sensu*) are the ones adopted or undertaken by the FATF on its own on the international plane, including FATF's statements and reports in international fora (eg. to the UN/UNSC, CoE, OSCE and G-20) and joint activities and partnerships with other IOs or international institutions. Also, within this spectrum are calls for actions (countermeasures) against non-FATF members or jurisdictions outside of the FATF Global Network. The Best Practices and Guidance Papers for the private sector and civil society can also be underlined as external acts considering the target audience (Chapter 2, Sections 7 and 9 above).

5.2.1 The FATF Recommendations and Their Normative Dimension

The FATF Recommendations are recognised as soft law.[121] As the name expressly indicates they are *recommendations* that do not intend to have any

118 Eg. CFATF or APG assessment procedures.

119 See Chapter 5, Section 1.

120 Eg. FIs, accountants and lawyers.

121 A/74/335, para. 39. The role, relevance and controversy of the use of soft law in the context of countering terrorism is addressed in detail in para. 8–27. Amongst others, Rémy Davison, "Soft Law' Regimes and European Organizations' Fight against Terrorism and Money Laundering' in L. Holmes (ed), *Terrorism, Organised Crime and Corruption – Networks and Linkages* (Edward Elgar Publishing, 2007); Jaye Ellis, 'Shades of Grey: Soft Law and the Validity of Public International Law' (2012) 25(2) *Leiden Journal of International Law*, 333–334; Cheong-Ann Png, 'International Legal Sources III – FATF Recommendations' in W. Blair, R. Brent and T. Grant (eds), *Banks and Financial Crime – the International Law of Tainted Money* (2nd eds, Oxford University Press 2017), 61; Borlini (n 6). Michelle Gallant, referring to the traditional and proper mode of multilateral negotiations and conventions making, mentions that: "the recommendations (...) by the FATF are not authoritative sources of law in any traditional sense. No principle of international law acknowledges or confers any particular status into the FATF to prescribe global norms or to set global standards. The recommendations proffered by the FATF fall under the rubric of soft-law

binding effect rather to "set minimum standards for action for countries to implement them in detail according to their circumstances and constitutional frameworks.".[122] The soft law nature of the Recommendations facilitates their general and voluntary acceptance.[123]

In FATF's role as a policy-lawmaker, the Forty Recommendations provide a holistic and systematic regime to counter ML/FT/PF aiming for universal observance. Their evolution and degree of normative and regulatory activity

(…) that lack the qualities of hard binding international law", 'Promise and Perils: The Making of Global Money Laundering, Terrorist Finance Norms' (2010) 13(3) *Journal of Money Laundering Control*, 178.

122 2003 Forty Recommendations, 2. Klabbers mentions that the concept of 'soft law' may be understood in different forms, and may "[give] rise to legal effects, but do not (or not yet, perhaps) amount to real law". In a sceptical manner, the author affirms that the "self-contained nature of the soft legal order (so to speak) is not just a by-product of the soft law thesis, but is one of its essential foundations. For, if it could be claimed that soft law leads in its application, to either hard law (hard responsibility, hard sanctions) or to non-law (no responsibility and no sanctions), soft law loses its distinctiveness, and therewith its reason of existence". 'The Redundancy of Soft Law' (1996) 65 *Nordic Journal of International Law*, 169. D'Aspremont also criticises the supporters of soft law calling attention to the risk of this trend undermining the "consistency of the international legal system", 'Softness in International Law: A Self-Serving Quest for New Legal Materials' (2008) 19(5) *European Journal of International Law*, 1088 *et seq.* The HR Special Rapporteur describes soft law as "those international norms, principles and procedures that are outside the formal sources of Article 38(1) of the Statute of the ICJ and lack the requisite degree of normative content to create enforceable rights and obligations but are still able to produce certain legal effects." (A/74/335, para. 8).

123 The Recommendations cover all the measures that national systems should have in place within their criminal justice and regulatory systems; the preventive measures to be taken by financial institutions and certain businesses and professions; and international co-operation. Amongst others, Broome, *Anti-Money Laundering – International Practice and Policies* (Sweet and Maxwell Asia 2005), 561. On the role of the FATF Recommendations in the EU and in the harmonisation of substantive norms for the FIs and DFNBPs (eg. CDD, STRs, record keeping, tipping of, internal policies), amongst others, Melissa Van den Broek, 'Harmonization of Substantive Norms in Preventive AML policy' in B. Unger, J. Ferwerda, M. Van den Broek and I. Deleanu (eds), *The Economic and Legal Effectiveness of the European Union's Anti-Money Laundering Policy* (Edward Elgar Publishing 2014). Turner underpins FATF's success in "harmonising national legal and regulatory systems without explicit, formal authority under international law". The author believes that in this field "highly formalised approaches to lawmaking, such as treaties, are dispensable", particularly if considered three aspects: 1) global financial crisis require expeditious actions; ii) domestic constraints (some economically powerful countries are reluctant in ceding control or sovereignty); and iii) difficulty in reaching a consensus on technical issues and ratification procedures. 'The Governance of the Financial Action Task Force: An Analysis of Power and Influence throughout the Years' (2018) 69 *Crime, Law and Social Change*, 549–551.

in the past three decades are in line with the dynamics of society and the constant trends and threats related to transnational financial crime.

FATF's statements about the nature of the Recommendations are also illustrative of the organisation's evolutionary character. In 1997–1998, the FATF assumed that the Recommendations "have gained some international prominence";[124] whereas in 2001–2002 the FATF stated that the Recommendations "are now widely accepted as the global anti-money laundering standard".[125] In 2019, the FATF declared that the Recommendations "are recognised as the global anti-money laundering (AML) and counter-terrorist financing (CFT) standard".[126]

This aspect is equally perceived in the language of the Recommendations, where it is possible to identify terminological changes from "should consider", reflecting a discretionary archetype by granting countries flexibility as regards regulation methods, to "should be required by law or regulation" or "should be required by law", substantiating a mandatory requirement.

This modification of language and, consequently, of the requirements throughout the years can be seen, for instance, in FATF's Recommendations related to international co-operation.[127] In the 1990 Forty Recommendations, it is stated:

- Recommendation 34: International co-operation *should be supported* by a network of bilateral and multilateral agreements and arrangements (...);
- Recommendation 35: Countries *should encourage* international conventions such as the draft Convention of the Council of Europe on Confiscation of the Proceeds from Offenses.

In the 1996 Forty Recommendations, it is stated:

- Recommendation 34: International co-operation *should be supported* by a network of bilateral and multilateral agreements and arrangements (...);

124 Para. 14. The Forty Recommendations' initial scope was to assist States counter ML from illicit production and trafficking of drugs and to promote information sharing and inter-State co-operation. In 1996, it evolved into a policy-making body.

125 Para. 84.

126 Colophon page of the 30 Years FATF Report.

127 The same exercise can be done for instance in relation to Recommendation 3 (Money Laundering) former Recommendation 1 (2003), Recommendation 4 (1996) and Recommendations 4 and 5 (1990); Recommendation 10 (CDD) former Recommendation 5 (2003), Recommendation 10 (1996) and Recommendation 12 (1990); Recommendation 20 (Reporting STRs) former Recommendation 13 (2003), Recommendation 15 (1996) and Recommendation 16 (1990); or Recommendation 19 (High-risk Countries) former Recommendation 21 (2003), Recommendation 14 (1996) and Recommendation 15 (1990).

- Recommendation 35: Countries *should be encouraged to ratify and implement* relevant international conventions on money laundering such as the 1990 Council of Europe Convention on Laundering, Search, Seizure and Confiscation of the Proceeds from Crime.

In the 2003 Forty Recommendations, it is stated:

- Recommendation 35: Countries *should take immediate steps to become party* to *and implement fully* the Vienna Convention, the Palermo Convention, and the 1999 Convention for the Suppression of the Financing of Terrorism;
- Recommendation 36: Countries *should rapidly, constructively, and effectively* provide the widest possible range of mutual legal assistance in relation to money laundering and terrorist financing investigations, prosecutions, and related proceedings.

In the 2012 Forty Recommendations, it is stated:

- Recommendations 36: Countries *should take immediate steps to become party to and implement fully* the Vienna Convention, Palermo Convention, 2003 United Nations Convention against Corruption (Merida Convention) and the Convention for the Suppression of the Financing of Terrorism (…) Countries are *also encourage to ratify and implement* other relevant international conventions, such as the 2001 Council of Europe Convention on Cybercrime, the 2002 Inter-American Convention against Terrorism and the 2005 Council of Europe Convention on Laundering, Search, Seizure and Confiscation of the Proceeds from Crime and on the Financing of Terrorism.
- Recommendation 37: Countries *should rapidly, constructively and effectively provide* the widest possible range of mutual legal assistance in relation to money laundering, associated predicate offences and terrorist financing investigations, prosecutions, and related proceedings (…).

From the preceding, it is discernible that the FATF has been gradually changing the language of the Recommendations, setting higher and stronger standards, leaving little room to national policy and decision-making.[128]

128 As Doron Goldbarsht mentions that the FATF Recommendations "[d]o not delegate authority to interpret or implement law, although they do enjoy enforcement in the way of Mutual Evaluation Reports (MER) and follow-up procedures, which no government or regulator sector can shirk, in addition to sanctions for non-compliance in the dorm of blacklisting and economic sanctions", 'Who's the Legislator Anyway: How the FATF's Global Norms Reshape Australian Counter Terrorist Financing Laws' (2017) 45(1) *Federal Law Review*, 129.

It also attests the evolution of FATF's lawmaking power underlining its decision-making capacity as an autonomous organisation with a will of its own.[129] Furthermore, it highlights the increasing normative dimension of the FATF Recommendations. In the beginning, the Forty Recommendations were considered mere guidelines, good practices and shared principles, developing progressively into standards, and from standards to *mandatory requirements* (the normative dimension).[130]

5.2.1.1 *Normative Dimension of the Forty Recommendations*

The normative dimension of the Forty Recommendations is an important feature that merits careful consideration. The Forty Recommendations, INotes and Glossary (the FATF Standards) are understood within the ME process as binding (superior normativity), while other documents enacted by the FATF are considered as auxiliary to better comprehend and/or implement the Recommendations.[131]

Due to a complex and robust compliance mechanism, empirical evidence shows that the FATF Recommendations have a substantial impact on national systems, shaping their domestic legal orders and operational aspects, regardless of jurisdictions' distinct legal and financial backgrounds and frameworks.

As Shawn Donnelly comments:

> [T]he FATF is a world apart from the rest of what we see in intentional financial market regulation (…) it can not only generate broad principles, as the OECD does, or detailed rule as IOSCO and the Basel Committee do to differing degrees, but to push them down into the national level where they will affect the real laws and institutions that are at the sharp end of regulation and policy-making, with strong isomorphism as a result. Both

129 As Wessel and Dekker affirmed "an international entity to be regarded as existing separately from its member States, the entity must have a decision-making organ that is able to produce a 'corporate' will, as opposed to a mere 'aggregate' of wills of the member States", (n 108) 20.

130 As explained by the HR Special Rapporteur: "The Task Force currently has 40 recommendations, which are intended to be implemented at the national level through legislation and other legally binding measures, and are complemented by interpretative notes, a set of best practices". A/70/371, para. 18.

131 2018–2019 FATF Report, 20–21; 2012 FATF Recommendations, 7–8. Blazejewski highlights the advantages of an informal nature, particularly absence of the ratification process or other formal procedures, reduction of transaction costs and facilitation of quick policy responses focused on expertise and comments that "[a] more traditional international agreement fashioned by diplomats with little working knowledge of AML/CFT systems would be unlikely to provide equally effective recommendations", (n 1) 0–13.

> also require consensus, but the dynamic of decision-making makes them relevant and forceful, to the extent that the member States concur.[132]

The FATF Recommendations have built a *paradigm* or *model* to be universally followed. Indeed, FATF members and the FSRBs jurisdictions undertake significant changes in their legislative, regulatory, operational, and international co-operation fields to be in conformity with the Recommendations. This normative character fits into Beekarry's *hard-type obligations theory of soft norms* and his concept of *soft law legalisation.*[133]

> The increased 'legalisation' and 'judicialisation' of the FATF process with the mandatory obligations, compliance monitoring mechanism, and sanctions, contributed greatly to its institutionalisation, ensuring greater compliance. Although it does not have a treaty-based formation, it nevertheless enjoys sufficient legal authority over the creation of the norms and their implementation across the world.[134]

In this context, Hülsse and Kerwer attempt to reconcile two perspectives: the FATF as a coercive body and the FATF as a voluntary rule-maker, using both functions according to the circumstances. The FATF generates standards that are non-binding for voluntary compliance, and, on the other hand, creates 'incentives' for compliance through strong enforcement mechanisms that include monitoring and blacklisting processes. The Forty Recommendations have a normative character in terms of general and voluntary compliance among jurisdictions with a *quasi*-coercive dimension.[135]

---

132 'Informal International Lawmaking: Global Financial Market Regulation', A. Berman *et al* (eds), *Informal International Lawmaking: Case Studies* (Torkel Opsahl Academic EPublisher 2012), 201–202.

133 The author stresses the creation of an AML/CFT international regime, which is based on hard and soft norms complemented with strong compliance mechanism, and a sanction system that puts 'on hold' countries' reputation. This regime, according to Beekarry's theoretical approach, tests previous assumptions that soft law is mere programmatic without a normative character. The author develops the concept of *soft law legalisation*, however it does not clearly distinct the notion of hard law *versus* soft law, nor the requirements for the theory of *hard-type obligations of soft norms*, (n 1). Also, about the increasing number of lawmaking and recourse to non-binding norms, their impact, compliance and nature, Dinah Shelton, 'International Law and 'Relative Normativity'' in M. Evans (ed), *International Law* (3rd edn, Oxford University Press 2011).

134 Ibid, 169.

135 The authors focus on the role of the FATF as a global and international standard-setter (global governance) and the use of soft law, and mentions that FATF's Recommendations are part of a "broader shift in global regulation from coercive public international law to

Measuring the external impact of FATF's policy and lawmaking powers, especially how national systems have changed and been shaped in accordance with the FATF Standards, is a challenging task. This would require an in-depth analysis of jurisdictions' 'state of play' before joining a regional body and after being assessed (in accordance with the 2004 and 2013 Methodologies) to clearly understand to what extent the FATF's regulatory power and *modus operandi* have affected the institutional, legal, and operational frameworks of every single jurisdiction. This phenomenon is commented by Ebikake:

> [A] unique aspect of the FATF Recommendations is the emphasis on their implementation through mutual evaluations undertaken by the FATF and assessments undertaken by the IMF and the World Bank. Essentially, whilst the FATF Recommendations are not binding, the focus of their implementation, particularly through mutual evaluations and assessments, has meant that they have had supranational influence over the development of preventive national AML laws and practice around the world.[136]

In this context, I would like to provide some examples of changes in domestic systems covering criminalisation of conducts (eg. tax evasion), establishing new regimes (cross border declarations, freezing regimes, BO requirements or VA regulation) and new institutions (eg. the FIU).

5.2.1.1.1 Tax Crimes as Predicated Offences

In the 2012 Forty Recommendations, the FATF expanded the list of designated predicate offences of ML to include the crime of fiscal evasion or fiscal fraud in Recommendation 3 (Money Laundering Offence).[137]

Canada was one of the countries that reviewed its domestic law to comply with the Recommendation 3. The Income Tax Act and Excise Tax Act was

---

global standards", exploring the idea of acquisition of rule-making authority (the FATF as *coercive* and *voluntarist rule maker*), (n 6) 53 *et seq.*

136 'Money Laundering: An Assessment of Soft Law as a Technique for Repressive and Preventive Anti-Money Laundering Control' (DPhil Thesis, Liverpool John Moores University, 17/05/2021), 211. The author emphasises the relevance of FATF Recommendations for national courts though "not legally binding", they "contain a relatively high-level of specificity", which "can be relevant in constructing domestic law and practice, which gives effect to them", 212.

137 FATF Recommendations, General Glossary, 122. It is worth mentioning the impact in EU law, namely EU Directive 2018/1673 that introduces tax crimes as a predicate offence of ML in accordance to FATF Recommendations (para. 1, 3, 4, 7 of the Preamble and Article 2(1)(q)).

amended to "introduce the offence of tax evasion as a predicate offence to money laundering and terrorist financing offences", in compliance with the designated predicate offence introduced in the 2012 FATF Recommendations.[138] In March 2011, at the Standing Committee of Finance on Tax Evasion and Offshore Bank Accounts, the Canadian Assistant Director of the Financial Analysis and Disclosures, Financial Transactions and Report Analysis Centre explained:

> [T]he FATF defines money laundering as the processing of the proceeds of criminal acts to disguise their illegal origin (…) In this context, a designated offence means most serious offences under the Criminal Code or any other federal act. It includes, but is not limited to, those relating to illegal drug trafficking, bribery, fraud, forgery, murder, robbery, counterfeit money, stock manipulation, and, since very recently, tax evasion.[139]

In relation to FATF's influence in Canadians' domestic law, Jacqueline Shinfield and Mena Bellofiore comment:

> Although not legally binding, FATF Recommendations are considered the foundation for Canadian AML Legislation. As a founding member of the FATF, the Government of Canada has, over the years, made significant changes to strengthen Canada's Anti-Money Laundering

138 At: https://canadagazette.gc.ca/rp-pr/p2/2011/2011-02-16/html/si-tr13-eng.html. As mentioned in the 2010–2011 Evaluation of the Integrated Proceeds of Crime Initiative Final Report (30/03/2011): "recent legislative amendments to the Criminal Code to include all of the offences under the Income Tax Act as predicate offences for money laundering, were introduced in 2010", 20. The Report makes several references to the FATF, namely that the "first two steps to effectively implementing FATF recommendations [in the Integrated Proceeds of Crime strategy] are as follows: successfully investigate and prosecute money laundering and terrorist financing; and deprive criminals of their criminal proceeds and the resources needed to finance their illicit activities", 16. At: https://www.publicsafety.gc.ca/cnt/rsrcs/pblctns/vltn-ntgrtd-prcds-crm-2010-11/vltn-ntgrtd-prcds-crm-2010-11-eng.pdf. On the relation between tax evasion, terrorism and money laundering, amongst others, Gallant, 'Tax and Terrorism: A New Partnership?' (2007) 14(4) *Journal of Financial Crime*; same author 'Money Laundering Consequences – Recovering Wealth, Piercing Secrecy, Disrupting Tax Havens and Distorting International Law' (2014) 17(3) *Journal of Money Laundering Control*.

139 The Canadian Assistant Director also refers that "with the recent adoption of Bill C-9, we are now permitted to use tax evasion as a predicate offence from which to build a case disclosure. The Criminal Code regulations were amended to make tax evasion a predicate offence to money laundering", (08/03/2011), Canadian Parliament portal, at: https://www.ourcommons.ca/DocumentViewer/en/40-3/FINA/meeting-62/evidence.

> (AML) and Anti-Terrorist Financing (ATF) regime in response to FATF Recommendations and it is therefore very likely that a number of notable changes in the revised Recommendations will impact future developments in the Canadian AML/ATF legal landscape including recent changes proposed in the November and December Consultation Papers.[140]

Likewise, tax crimes became a money laundering predicate offence in Switzerland in 2015.[141] According to a Press Release of the Swiss Government of April 2015, the Federal Council enacted a Federal Act to implement the new 2012 FATF Recommendations, stating that the said law would be implemented in two stages and amends would be made to the Criminal Code.

> On 12 December 2014, Parliament approved the Federal Act for Implementing the Revised Financial Action Task Force (FATF) Recommendations of 2012 (…) The enactment will take effect in two stages (…) [the second stage] On 1 January 2016, the following will enter into force: the provisions on tax predicate offences (amendment of the Swiss Criminal Code and the Administrative Criminal Law Act).[142]

In 2021, the Philippines also reviewed its AML legislation to add tax crimes as designated predicate offences of ML. In a study conducted by the Anti-Money Laundering Council of Philippines it is underscored that:

> In the Financial Action Task Force's (FATF's) 'Methodology for Assessing Technical Compliance with the FATF Recommendations and the Effectiveness of AML/CFT Systems' (…) The threat of tax crimes to ML is considered as high-risk in various jurisdictions, including the Philippines (…) The recent amendment per RA 11521, titled 'An Act Further Strengthening the Anti-Money Laundering Law, Amending for the Purpose of Republic Act No. 9160', otherwise known as the 'Anti-Money Laundering Act of 2001', as Amended, expanded the list of unlawful

140 'Canada: Revised FATF Recommendations: What Effect Will They Have in Canada?' (2012), at: http://www.mondaq.com/canada/x/168544/Financial+Services/Revised+FATF+Recommendations+What+Effect+Will+They+Have+In+Canada Tax Crimes.

141 Article 305 bis (Money Laundering) of the Swiss Criminal Code, at: https://www.fedlex.admin.ch/eli/cc/1998/892_892_892/en.

142 Press Release of the Swiss Government (29/04/2015): 'Entry into Force of Federal Act for implementing Revised FATF Recommendations of 2012', at: https://www.admin.ch/gov/en/start/documentation/media-releases.msg-id-57064.html. Also, https://www.finma.ch/en/finma/international-activities/policy-and-regulation/fatf/.

> activities covered by the AMLA (…) This section of the Tax Code pertains to the 'Attempt to evade or defeat tax' or tax evasion.[143]

5.2.1.1.2 Cash Couriers

Similar examples can be provided in relation to Recommendation 32 on 'Cash Couriers' (former SR IX). For instance, Malaysia was rated 'NC' in SR IX in its MER (August) 2007 due to a deficient cross-border declaration system.[144]

Considering FATF Recommendations, the Government of Malaysia amended its AML/CFT regime in order to introduce a travel declaration system for those entering or leaving Malaysia with cash and/or negotiable bearer instruments (eg. traveller's cheques, bearer cheques); this system entered into force on 1 January 2010.[145] As observed by the Central Bank of Malaysia:

> This is a requirement under Section 23 of the Anti-Money Laundering and Anti-Terrorism Financing Act 2001 (AMLATFA) and is in line with the Special Recommendation IX by the Financial Action Task Force which requires countries to have measures in place to detect the physical cross border transportation of cash and negotiable bearer instruments. Travellers could be fined up to RM1 million and/or face imprisonment not exceeding a term of one year if they fail to declare or make a false declaration.[146]

Like Malaysia, Macao (China) was rated 'NC' in SR IX in its APG MER (August) 2007,[147] and as an outcome specific legislation, Law 6/2017 to Control Cross-Border Transportation of Cash and Bearer Negotiable Instruments was enacted to conform with the new Recommendation 32. The respective Explanatory Note addresses the reasons why Macao (China), as an APG member, is required to introduce a cross-border system:

> The FATF established the Forty Recommendations being its implementation mandatory to all countries and jurisdictions. Recommendation 32 is one of these recommendations (…) The implementation of a control system is therefore necessary for the Macao SAR, and this is especially

143 'An Analysis of Suspicious Transactions Reports with Possible Links to Tax Crimes', Anti-Money Laundering Council, April 2021, 3.

144 APG Malaysian MER (August) 2007, 218.

145 At: https://www.bnm.gov.my/declaration-requirement-for-currency.

146 Ibid.

147 At: 218.

> pertinent given that the Macao SAR will shortly be evaluated, including in this domain by the APG.[148]

Hong Kong (China) also adopted the Cross-boundary Movement of Physical Currency and Bearer Negotiable Instruments Ordinance in 2018 to comply with Recommendation 32 after its MER (June) 2008.[149] A public consultation was held in 2015, where Hong Kong authorities explained the grounds for such reporting system deemed to be necessary and possible consequences in case of failure to implement:

> At present, Hong Kong is the only FATF member jurisdiction, among 34, which has yet to establish the R32 System. In practice, R32 is the only area where Hong Kong was still rated as 'non-compliant' in the last round of ME. This suggests that Hong Kong would need to accord priority to establishing the R32 System as soon as possible, since it would inevitably be one of the major foci of the fourth ME on Hong Kong. Past experience suggested that major deficiencies in fulfilling FATF's recommendations would result in a more intensive follow-up process and enhanced scrutiny by FATF and would have a negative impact on Hong Kong's reputation as an international financial centre.[150]

5.2.1.1.3 Freezing of Assets

Recommendation 6 on 'Target Financial Sanctions related to Terrorism and Financing of Terrorism' (former SR III) requires jurisdictions to have in place a system that freezes without delay funds or other assets, and that ensures that no funds or assets are made available to any person or entity designated by the UNSC Sanctions Committees or designated by a country pursuant to Resolution 1373 (2001) of the UNSC.

In 2014, Japan approved legislation establishing a freezing mechanism in accordance with the international requirements. This was a recommended action after the conclusion of the MER of Japan (October) 2008, which identified SR III as a major legal gap.[151] The adoption of Act No. 124 on Special Measures concerning Asset Freezing, etc, of International Terrorists by Japan

148 At: 1–2 (free translation), at: https://www.al.gov.mo/uploads/attachment/2016-12/66509585dee675c120.pdf.

149 At: 16.

150 Para. 1.7, at: https://www.gov.hk/en/residents/government/publication/consultation/docs/2015/R32.pdf.

151 At: 240.

took into consideration the recommendation of the FATF, as announced in the Japanese *media*:

> The Diet on Wednesday enacted a law to freeze financial and real estate transactions in Japan by organisations and individuals involved in terrorism, including al-Qaida and the Islamic State group (...) The government had been urged by the Financial Actions Task Force – an intergovernmental body aimed at eliminating terrorist financing – to block the transfer of funds used to sponsor terrorism.[152]

Also, in the official website of the Japan Financial Intelligence Center, it is stated that in June 2014, the "FATF requested Japan to take prompt response to insufficient parts of AML/CFT measures". The Japanese FIU highlights the "enforcement in October 2015 of the International Terrorist Assets Freezing Act" as a response.[153]

In the APG MER of Macao (China) (August) 2007 the jurisdiction was rated 'PC' due to the lack of a comprehensive system to freeze funds or assets without undue delay under SR III, and it was advised to adopt a freezing regime.[154] As a consequence, Law 6/2016 was adopted, establishing the Assets Freezing Regime aiming at complying with FATF's international standards.[155] This aspect is explicitly recognised in its Explanatory Note:

> In the FATF's President Statement of 25–27 February in Paris, 2015, it is affirmed: Those jurisdictions with significant deficiencies in the implementation of Recommendations 5, 6, or former SR II and SR III, need immediately to put such requisites legal and, as required, to have regulatory frameworks in place to meet these Recommendations (...) The Macao SAR will be reassessed by the APG in 2016 on countering money laundering and financing of terrorism, where one of the focus

152 'Diet Enacts Law to Freeze Terrorist Assets in Japan' (19/11/2014) *The Japan Times*, at: https://www.japantimes.co.jp/news/2014/11/19/national/crime-legal/diet-enacts-law-freeze-terrorist-assets-japan.

153 History of the AML Measures, Japan Financial Intelligence Center portal, at: https://www.npa.go.jp/sosikihanzai/jafic/en/maneron_e/manetop_e.htm.

154 At: 217.

155 Law 6/2016 expressly specifies that its purpose is to freeze the assets of targeted-designated persons and entities under Resolutions of the UNSC to counter FT and PF of WMD, to which China is internationally bound in relation to the Macao SAR and under Resolution 1373 (2001) of the UNSC.

> of this assessment will be whether [Macao SAR] is in compliance with Recommendation 6.[156]

On the same grounds, Brazil had to enact specific legislation to establish an asset freezing mechanism to guarantee the inaccessibility of assets and funds to designated persons and entities and to set up a national designation system for persons under investigation or accused of terrorism, FT, or co-related acts, in accordance with international standards.[157]

In the Senate, during the debate of Law 13,810/2019 to Enforce an Immediate Freezing Mechanism of Terrorist Assets and Funds, it was emphasised that:

> FATF granted Brazil until February 2019 to enact laws that meet the requirements recommended by the organisation. It also mentioned that Brazil is the only one of the 35 members' countries of the FATF that, according to the organisation, has not yet adopted anti-terrorism measures. We run the risk of being blacklisted by the FATF if this bill is not approved.[158]

5.2.1.1.4 Beneficial Ownership Requirements

In relation to Recommendation 24 (Transparency and Beneficial Ownership of Legal Persons) and Recommendation 25 (Transparency and Beneficial Ownership of Legal Arrangements), jurisdictions are requested to revise their legislation on legal persons and trusts pursuant to new and stringent BO requirements. Singapore, Luxembourg, and the USA are some examples of jurisdictions that have made legislative amendments.

Singapore amended the Trustees (Amendment) Act 2017 (No. 14 of 2017) to add 'Part VII on Transparency and Effective Control' – Sections 83, 84, 84-A, where it defines BO and the requisites to properly identify the ultimate BO. In an interpellation to Parliament, the Senior Minister of State for Law explains:

> Singapore is one of the leading financial centres in the world (…) as a member of FATF and GF, Singapore has regard to the standards promulgated

156 At: 1–3 (free translation), at: https://www.al.gov.mo/uploads/lei/leis/2016/2016-06/nota_justificativa.pdf.

157 MER of Brazil (June) 2010, 267.

158 Senate News Agency (20/02/2019), at: https://www12.senado.leg.br/noticias/materias/2019/02/20/bloqueio-imediato-de-bens-de-terroristas-e-aprovado-em-comissoes-e-segue-ao-plenario. See FATF's Statements on Brazil, at: https://www.fatf-gafi.org/publications/mutualevaluations/documents/brazil-statement-june-2019.html.

> by these international bodies and participates in the peer assessment exercises conducted by these bodies on its members. In September 2016, the National Steering Committee for Combatting Money Laundering and Terrorism Financing announced that Singapore will follow-up on certain areas of improvement recommended by the FATF assessors (…) To this end, the Bill introduces a framework for the Minister for Law to prescribe the necessary regulations, so as to give effect to the FATF recommendations and GF requirements concerning beneficial ownership and identity information and/or the keeping of accounting records in relation to trusts.[159]

Luxembourg is a good example within the EU context. EU jurisdictions also need to revise their legislation on this subject matter, not only as members of the FATF, but in light of the EU Directives to counter ML/FT, which in turn mirror the Forty Recommendations and have been enacted to be consistent with them.

The Luxembourg Law of 10 July 2020 on the Register of Fiducies and Trusts (or Fiduciary Contracts), as amended, establishes an obligation to obtain and keep BO information, and creates a register system (ie. fiducies and trusts subject to registration, registration authority, conservation of and access to BO information). This new law although 'transposing' Article 31 of EU Directive 2015/849, as amended by EU Directive 2018/843, responds to Recommendations 24 and 25 of FATF and corresponding methodology criteria.[160]

Another jurisdiction that, based on the international standards, has also undertaken reforms is the USA. The May 2021 Public Consultation to amend the Corporate Transparency Act (CTA) of 2019 explains that the country needs to impose new standards to obtain BO information (of the individual natural persons who ultimately own or control the legal persons or legal arrangements), to

159 Second Reading Speech by Senior Minister of States Law, Indranee Rajah SC, on the Trustees (Amendment) Bill (10/03/2017), at: https://www.mlaw.gov.sg/news/parliamentary-speeches/second-reading-speech-by-senior-minister-of-state-for-law--indra5. Also, https://www.mlaw.gov.sg/files/NoteonTrusteesAmendmentBill.pdf/. It is noteworthy that Section 83 (Interpretation) points out FATF and FATF Recommendations, and Section 84-A (Regulations) prescribes that ministers may adopt regulations to implement FATF's Recommendations on transparency and BO.

160 MER of Luxembourg (September) 2023, 10 and 22. Andres Knobel and Markus Meinzer, 'Don't Forget the Trust: Amendments Needed in FATF's Recommendations and in EU's AML Directive', Tax Justice Network, Drilling Down to the Real Owners – Part 2 (28/06/2016). At: https://www.taxjustice.net/wp-content/uploads/2016/06/TJN2016_BO-EUAMLD-FATF-Part2-Trusts.pdf.

introduce new rules on maintenance and disclosure on BO, and to strengthen reporting duties. In the Consultation Paper, the US Government states:

> The 2016 FATF Mutual Evaluation Report of the United States underscored the seriousness of this deficiency as the lack of beneficial ownership transparency was one of the main reasons for the United States' failing grade regarding the effectiveness of the transparency of its beneficial ownership regime (…) the CTA, which Congress enacted on January 1, 2021, establishes a new framework for the reporting, maintenance, and disclosure of beneficial ownership information to: Bring the United States into compliance with international AML/CFT standards.[161]

5.2.1.1.5 Virtual Assets and Virtual Assets Service Providers

More recently, Recommendation 15 on 'New technologies' and its INote on the use of VA and VASPs (June 2019 and 2021) determines that this sector needs to be regulated,[162] ie. jurisdictions are required to conduct a self-risk-based assessment of this phenomenon, including the eventual misuse of VA/VASPs for FT/PF purposes, and to elaborate a policy-strategy.

Depending on the assessment, jurisdictions may either criminalise or license the use of VA/VASPs, as long as both solutions ensure adequate supervision and enforcement measures. Some jurisdictions of the Asia-Pacific region, Australia, Hong Kong (China), Japan, Mongolia, New Zealand, Philippines, South Korea, Thailand and USA have chosen to regulate VA/VASPs accordingly,[163] others as China, Indonesia, Bangladesh or Chinese Taipei have chosen to criminalise VA/VASPs.[164]

---

161 'Beneficial Ownership Information Requirements – a Proposed Rule by the Financial Crimes Enforcement Network' (04/05/2012), Financial Crimes Enforcement Network, Treasury, at: https://www.federalregister.gov/documents/2021/04/05/2021-06922/beneficial-ownership-information-reporting-requirements.

162 This Recommendation started to be reviewed in October 2018. The FATF self-proclaims as "the first body to develop global standards for virtual assets", see FATF President's remarks (22/10/2020) to the G-20 Anti-Corruption Ministerial Meeting, at: http://www.fatf-gafi.org/publications/corruption/documents/g20-anti-corruption-2020.html. See, FATF Report to the G-20 Finance Ministers and Central Bank of Governors on the so-called 'stablecoins'. At: http://www.fatf-gafi.org/publications/virtualassets/documents/report-g20-so-called-stablecoins-june-2020.html?hf=10&b=0&s=desc(fatf_releasedate).

163 At: https://en.wikipedia.org/wiki/Legality_of_cryptocurrency_by_country_or_territory (accesed on 25/02/2023). Also, Report on the 'Status of Implementation of Recommendation 15 by FATF Members and Jurisdiction with Materially Important VASP Activity'.

164 Ibid. Also, www.cryptimi.com/guides/a-list-of-countries-where-bitcoin-and-or-crypto-is-banned#:~:text=Bitcoin%20and%20other%20crypt (acceded on 25/02/2023).

The FATF undertook a two-year review on this matter, concluding in July 2021 that:

> In April 2021, 128 jurisdictions (38 FATF members and 90 members of FATF-Style Regional Bodies (FSRBs)) advised on their progress in implementing the revised FATF Standards. 58 jurisdictions (28 FATF members and 30 FSRB members) reported that they had introduced the necessary legislation to implement the revised FATF Standards. 52 of these jurisdictions advised that they had a regulatory regime permitting VASPs, while 6 of these jurisdictions advised that they had prohibited VASPs. The other 70 jurisdictions (10 FATF members and 60 FSRB members) have not yet implemented the revised Standards into their national law.[165]

The FATF has recently enacted two reports on this subject: the 'Target Update Implementation of the FATF Standards of Virtual Assets Report' (June 2023) and the 'Status of Implementation of Recommendation 15 by FATF Members and Jurisdiction with Materially Important VASP Activity' (March 2024) that show how jurisdictions are addressing Recommendation 15 and the challenges they face. Both reports stress the difficulties with the implementation of the 'travel rule' requirement under Recommendation 16 (Wire Transfers).[166]

According to the first Report of 98 MERs and FURs, "since the revised R.15/INR.15 was adopted, 75% of jurisdictions are only partially or not compliant with the FATF's requirements".[167] Based on these reports, a roadmap has been designed to follow the proper and effective implementation of this Recommendation in the context of VASPs.[168]

5.2.1.1.6 Establishment of a Financial Intelligence Unit

The 2003 Forty Recommendations set as mandatory that "countries should establish a FIU" under Recommendation 26 on 'Financial Intelligence Units', now Recommendation 29. This requirement is reiterated under Resolution

165 'Second 12-Month Review on the FATF Revised Standards on VA and VASPs', para. 2. In the first year, 33 jurisdictions (25 FATF and 8 FSRBs' members) reported that they had an AML/CFT regulatory regime for VASPs and three prohibiting VASPs.

166 The 'travel rule' demands VASPs and FIs to obtain, hold, and transmit basic originator and BO information immediately and securely when transferring VA. 'Target Update Implementation of the FATF Standards of Virtual Assets Report', 16–26; 'Status of Implementation of Recommendation 15 by FATF Members and Jurisdiction with Materially Important VASP Activity', 5-10.

167 Ibid, 2.

168 Ibid, 6.

2462 (2019) of the UNSC by urging "Member States which have not yet done so to establish operationally independent and autonomous financial intelligence units".[169]

FIUs are responsible for receiving and analysing STRs and relevant information related to ML, associated predicate offences and FT, as well as disseminating the findings of their investigations. The institution should also be able to obtain information from reporting entities and have access on a timely basis to any financial, administrative, or law enforcement record.

According with the Egmont Group, a network founded in 1995 that promotes co-operation and information sharing among FIUs worldwide,[170] there are presently 174 FIUs.[171]

Examples of the most recently instituted FIUs are the FIU of Liberia, which started its operation as an autonomous central government agency with the Financial Intelligence Unit Act 2012; the FIU of Cuba, which was instituted by Decree-law 317 of 2013 on the Prevention and Detection of Operations of Money Laundering, Financing of Terrorism and Proliferation of Weapons and Movement of Illicit Capital and Decree 322 of 2013 of the Council of Ministers on the functions and structure of the FIU; and the FIU of Nigeria, which was established by Nigeria Financial Intelligence Unit Act of 2018.

Based on the above examples, it is fair to conclude that there is a remarkable level of commitment and degree of compliance with the FATF's Recommendations, especially considering the 'informal institutional character' of the organisation and the non-binding nature of its Recommendations. The FATF Consolidated Table of Assessment Ratings of May 2024 also exemplifies in an elucidative manner such compliance levels.[172]

The recognised expertise of the FATF[173] and the normative dimension of the

---

169 Op.para. 15.

170 The Egmont Group provides a secure platform to exchange financial intelligence related to AML/CFT/CPF among FIUs and promotes co-operation especially as regards information exchange, training, and sharing of expertise. At: https://egmontgroup.org.

171 It is divided in regions: Europe I (29 FIUs), Europe II (24 FIUs), Eurasia (7 FIUs), Middle East and North Africa (15 FIUs), West and Central Africa (14 FIUs), Eastern and Southern Africa (13 FIUs), Asia and Pacific (30 FIUs) and Americas (40 FIUs). At: https://egmontgroup.org/about/ and https://egmontgroup.org/members-by-region/ (last visited 15/05/3024).

172 Table of 07/05/2024, at: https://www.fatf-gafi.org/content/dam/fatf-gafi/Global-Network/4th-Round-Ratings.pdf.coredownload.inline.pdf (acceded on 10/05/2024).

173 Hülsse and Kerwer comment that when experts are at the center stage of decision-making processes, rules on complex technical problems become more comprehensive and efficient, hence more effective, (n 6) 55–56, 59–60.

Recommendations,[174] combined with a strong monitoring mechanism, generate extreme pressure on jurisdictions at the domestic level to comply with the standards, which represents a high degree of effectiveness regarding the organisations' mission.[175]

Some jurisdictions, such as Canada,[176] Switzerland,[177] UK[178] or Hong Kong

---

174 Beekarry notes that: "The mandatory nature, as opposed to being mere 'programmatory', of the AML/CFT international obligations provides the strongest basis for understanding recent compliance impact. The substantive rules embodied in the FATF Recommendations constitute the minimum international mandatory standards that have shaped and constrained countries' regulatory practices in the fight against ML/FT", (n 1) 157.

175 Amongst others, Chibueze Valentine Ezewudo, 'The Money Laundering and Terrorist Financing: An Insight into the Money Laundering (Prohibition) Act of 2004, Laws of Nigeria' (Dissertation LLM 2011-2012, Institute of Advanced Legal Studies, School of Advanced Study, University of London, 03/09/2012), at: http://sas-space.sas.ac.uk/4736/1/Chibueze_Ezewudo_LLM_ICGFREL_dissertation.pdf. Also, Elise Whitaker, 'Compliance among Weak States: Africa and the Counter-Terrorism Regime' (2010) 36 *Review of International Studies*.

176 Canada MER (September) 2016 and the plans to review Canadian AML/CFT legislation in 2018. "Released in 2016, a Mutual Evaluation Report by the Financial Action Task Force (FATF) found that Canada has strong anti-money laundering and anti-terrorist financing legislation and Regulations but noted there are several areas where action could be taken to ensure the framework meets technical standards and is even more effective", 'Reviewing Canada's Anti-Money Laundering and Anti-Terrorist Financing Regime' (07/02/2018) Department of Finance Canada, 5, at: https://www.canada.ca/content/dam/fin/migration/activty/consult/amlatfr-rpcfa-eng.pdf.

177 MER of Switzerland (December) 2016 and the plans to review Swiss AML/CFT legislation in 2021, see the Federal Council Press Release (01/10/2021): 'Federal Council Initiates Consultation on Amendments to Anti-money Laundering Ordinance' states that "Parliament approved the revision of the Anti-Money Laundering Act on 19 March 2021. This strengthens Switzerland's toolkit to combat money laundering and terrorist financing and includes the most important recommendations from the Financial Action Task Force's (FATF) mutual evaluation report on Switzerland of 2016". Some of the measures included provisions, in the area of AML reporting system, licencing for purchasing precious metal scrap, an AML oversight authority for precious metal control, and the transparency of associations that pose a higher FT risk. At: https://www.admin.ch/gov/en/start/documentation/media-releases.msg-id-85324.html.

178 MER of the UK (December) 2018 and the plans to review UK AML/CFT legislation in 2022. The Review Policy Paper states that "[t]he UK's AML supervision regime received a rating of 'moderate' effectiveness in its 2018 MER; indicating the FATF identified 'major' deficiencies in the UK's regime. The FATF noted deficiencies including the need for all supervisors other than the Gambling Commission to improve their risk-based approach, the importance of applying proportionate, dissuasive, and effective sanctions, and ensuring all supervisors provide effective guidance and engagement to their supervised populations. The recommendations of the MER were included in the actions of the

(China)[179] have started their internal process of re-examining national assessments following their most recent round of ME and revising their domestic regime, contemplating the main recommendations and looking ahead to the future ME process.

The external impact of the FATF Recommendations is indeed incommensurable. Leonardo Borlini underlines, for instance, the impact of the Forty Recommendations in the context of the EU's legal framework:

> Despite the limited membership of the FATF and the soft law nature of its Recommendations, the FATF standards constitute one of the most successful cases of international co-operation in penal and regulatory matters. They are the basis of the existing anti-money laundering (AML) and counter terrorism financing (CFT) paradigm and have been extensively mirrored in the laws of both members and non-member countries. They also have been translated into international binding instruments such as the European Union AML Directives.[180]

5.2.2 Emergence of Customary International Law

The preceding examples and commentaries, seconded by the FATF Consolidated Table of Assessment Ratings of May 2024, which reflect States' compliance behaviour, trigger the question about the normative dimension and perception of FATF Recommendations *vis-à-vis* its members and FSRBS jurisdictions, and whether they have been studied to their core, including the possible emergence of customary international law.[181]

---

first Economic Crime Plan", Policy Paper 'Review of the UK's AML/CFT Regulatory and Supervisory Regime' (June 2022) para. 4.21, at: https://assets.publishing.service.gov.uk/government/uploads/system/uploads/attachment_data/file/1085407/MLRs_Review_Report_-_2.5_for_publication.pdf.

179 MER of Hong Kong (September) 2019 and the plans to review Hong Kong AML/CFT legislation in 2022. The Executive Summary of the NRA Report – 'Enhancing the AML/CFT Legal Framework' mentions: "To address gaps identified in the AML/CFT in fulfilment of Hong Kong's obligations under the FATF, the Government has pursued the following legislative exercises, which will further strengthen the AML/CFT capability of Hong Kong: [(c)] Address a number of technical issues relating to the AMLO, identified in the FATF's ME report on Hong Kong and other FATF contexts", AML/CFT NRA Report of Hong Kong (China) (July 2022) para. 31, xi, at: https://www.fstb.gov.hk/fsb/aml/en/risk-assessment.htm

180 'The Financial Action Task Force: An Introduction' An Introduction' (2015) 2 *Anti-Corruption Research Center* (U4 BRIEF), 2, at: https://papers.ssrn.com/sol3/papers.cfm?abstract_id=3834449; same author (n 6).

181 Gallant raises this hypothesis when commenting on how States "regularly heed the voice of the FATF, do regularly seek to comply with the recommendations", when "no principle

This development would not be surprising in international lawmaking as Roberto Adorno[182] or Abbot and Snidal emphasise.[183] The 'normative weight' of soft law may *catalyse* the emergence of customary international law.[184]

Borlini and Francesco Montanaro signalled this uncommon widespread behaviour of obedience to FATF's *dicta* as a form of *legitimisation*:

> FATF standards have determined the evolution of hard law on the AML/CFT field. On the other hand, hard law consequently adopted within domestic jurisdictions around the world or by other international organisations, like the EU, have, in turn, reinforced the legitimacy and relevance of the FATF Recommendations.[185]

of international law mandates that they comply with the FAFT recommendations'". The author recognises the extent of States' compliance to FATF's Standards as well as its AML/CFT monitoring mechanism, shaping AML/CFT domestic frameworks, concluding that "[FATF] recommendations tend to calcify into a form of hard law", (n 121) 179. Drezner also refers this possibility of producing customary international law when mentioning that "as of May 2020 over 10 international bodies, representing over 140 countries and territories, acknowledge the FATF 40 as the accepted international standard to prevent money laundering", (n 84) 330–332.

182 'The Invaluable Role of Soft Law in the Development of Universal Norms in Bioethics' (2007), at: http://www.unesco.de/wissenschaft/bis-2009/invaluable-role-of-soft-law.html?&L=0. Also, A/74/335, para. 8–27.

183 'Hard and Soft Law in International Governance' (2000) 54(3) *International Organization*.

184 Evidence of customary international law: diplomatic correspondence, policy statements, press releases, opinions of official legal advisers, official manuals on legal questions (eg. military law), comments or statements by governments, executive decisions and practices, State legislation, international and national decisions, recitals, pattern of treaties, practice of international organs, resolutions relating to legal questions in the UN General Assembly, judicial decisions, publications by international law commentators. See Article 10 of the 2018 Draft Conclusions on Identification of Customary International Law with Commentaries, at: https://legal.un.org/ilc/texts/instruments/english/commentaries/1_13_2018.pdf. Some Resolutions of the UN General Assembly or Declarations may be considered as binding or reflecting States' practice, as well as a "vehicle to propound their *opinio juris*, thereby suggesting that the Assembly is a forum for pronouncing on rules of custom" and general principles of law. Alvarez addresses this topic in 'International Organisations and the Rule of Law: Challenges Ahead', forthcoming in The International Legal Order: Essays Commemorating the 10th Anniversary of the Xiamen Academy of International Law 2016, 21. The HR Special Rapporteur also acknowledges that some Resolutions of the UN General Assembly may have contributed to the creation of customary international law, A/74/335, para. 15, 26. The same reasoning may be applied in relation to Resolutions of the UNSC.

185 'The Evolution of the EU Law against Criminal Finance: The 'Hardening' of FATF Standards within the EU' (2017) 48(4) *Georgetown Journal of International Law*, 55.

A combination of factors may have contributed to this course: i) the relevance of the FATF Recommendations in the contemporary and inter-dependent global scenario involving political commitment; ii) the endorsement of the Recommendations by relevant IOs (such as the UN/UNSC, EU, CoE, IMF and WB);[186] and iii) the establishment of monitoring and enforcement mechanisms.

These factors, along with serious reputational and sovereignty costs, drive jurisdictions towards compliance that signals a reiterated common practice. Furthermore, the circumstance that implementation and compliance with FATF's Recommendations are used as a reference for the WB and IMF to fund money also contributes to their "crystallisation into domestic law".[187]

The general acquiescence of jurisdictions changing and shaping their domestic systems not only demonstrates the effective impact of the FATF Recommendations on jurisdictions' legal orders, but may also reveal their true legal nature. As to this 'general compliance', Anja Jakobi writes:

> The FATF is thus at the centre of a highly complex regulatory framework that shows universality as well as hierarchies (some States decide for other actors). The regulations are formally non-binding for States, but followed by most of them. Moreover, States made them compulsory for non-State actors related to finance. Although it has never moved from a network structure to become a more formalised international organisation, FATF recommendations are perceived as standard in the UN and EU regulations on money laundering and counter-terrorism financing. Unlike many other global regulations, the AML regime is rarely questioned in politics.[188]

186 Gathii comments that: "the soft law of the FATF is hardened by its direct incorporation in UN Security Council Resolutions or IMF conditionality.", (n 1) 3. Turner also refers to the incorporation of several FATF Recommendations into Resolutions of the UNSC, (n 1) 557. Romaniuk and Keatinge speak about the endorsement of FATF Recommendations by the EU, WB, IMF, Egmont Group, Basel Committee, UNSC and several UN bodies "elevating their status into international law", (n 1) 268.

187 Ebikake (n 136) 201. The author comments that "whilst the substance and drafting of the FATF Recommendations ultimately reflect a consensus among the FATF members (and the scope and language of individual Recommendations are often heavily negotiated in view of members' positions), they nevertheless contain a relatively high-level of specificity as to what is expected in this area. In this respect, although FATF Recommendations are not legally binding in domestic courts, they can be relevant in constructing domestic law and practice, which gives effect to them", 211–212.

188 'Governing Illicit Finance in Transnational Security Spaces: The FATF and Anti-Money Laundering' (2018) 69 *Crime, Law and Social Change*, 176. Markus Forsman comments that the "FATF [is] the most powerful organisation you have ever heard of" and although being the central authoritative organisation in AML/CFT field, is probable that individuals

The cited US Government Consultation Paper makes an interesting observation on this matter corroborating that there is a general conviction that the FATF Recommendations are imperative:

> Many countries, including the United Kingdom and all member States of the European Union, have incorporated elements derived from these [FATF] standards into their domestic legal and/or regulatory frameworks.[189]

This assumption is also perceptible at the level of the FSRBS. For instance, an evolution may be witnessed from the initial version of the APG Terms of Reference and successive amendments about the role of the FATF Recommendations. In the beginning, FATF's Recommendations were understood as guiding principles and were subject to the approval of the regional group.[190] During successive years, the APG has either formally endorsed (eg. 2006 and 2020) or adopted (eg. 2012) the FATF Recommendations.

In July 2021, following a decision of the members, the Forty Recommendations members are accepted as universal standards and incorporated directly into APG's framework. The amendment to the APG Terms of Reference stipulates that the FATF Recommendations and methodology are automatically inserted into the constitutional framework of the APG without needing members' prior approval or any other prerequisite.[191]

The FATF emphasises this perception of being imperative in its 2018–2019 Report, unequivocally affirming that: "countries need to transpose the new binding requirements into their national legal, regulatory and operational framework".[192] This understanding is reiterated by the FATF President at the G-20 Finance Ministers and Central Bank Governors' Meeting in Bali 2022,

never heard about the organisation. '30 Years of Combating Money Laundering in Sweden and Internationally – Does the System Function as Intended?' (2020) 1 *Sveriges Risbank Economic Review*, 26.

189 (n 161).

190 In Section 2.2. of the Terms of Reference, it is mentioned that in the 1997 Beijing meeting, it was agreed that "the 40 Recommendations are the guiding principles for action for the creation of an effective anti-money laundering framework. Members will implement the 40 Recommendations according to their cultural values and constitutional frameworks thus allowing them a measure of flexibility rather than prescribing every detail".

191 Ibid, Section 2.13.

192 At: 22.

declaring that the "FATF introduced the first binding AML/CFT global standards on crypto assets in 2019".[193]

FATF's ME process and the fear of reputational damages resulting from being blacklisted are undoubtedly responsible for the impressive levels of compliance, as noted by the FATF President at the 2020 Chairmanship OSCE-Wide Counter-Terrorism Conference:

> If a jurisdiction is assessed below certain thresholds, we publicly identify this jurisdiction on a Grey or Black List. This sword is a strong motivator for countries to adhere to our standards.[194]

Several authors questioned the non-binding character of the Recommendations and the enforcement mechanisms that are in place. Shams comments that the "elaborated and stringent character of the enforcement system that supports the recommendations renders this non-binding characterisation illusory".[195] In the same line of thought, Kern Alexander underscores that "the non-binding nature of the standards has been called to question in recent years because FATF has on several occasions threatened to impose sanctions against States deemed FATF as having failed to adopt national legislation".[196]

John Broome notes the inconsistency of FATF Recommendations as advisory standards "with the notion that non-members countries who have not met the requirement of the Recommendations should be subject to a naming and shaming policy and the imposition of economic sanctions".[197] While, Alejandro Rodiles comments on the inherent paradox of the informal nature of the FATF Recommendations, "which claim to be deprived of legal intent but interact so closely with hard obligations that it becomes increasingly difficult to categorically distinguish between the two".[198]

---

193 FATF's President Speech (16/07/2022), at: https://www.fatf-gafi.org/publications/fatfgeneral/documents/speech-g20-fmcbg-july-2022.html.

194 (n 66).

195 'Club Multilateralism and Global Supranationalism: The Case of FATF' in J.B. Attanasio and J.J. Norton (eds), *Multilateralism v Unilateralism: Policy Choices in a Global Society* (British Institute of International and Comparative Law and SMU Dedman School of Law 2005), 471.

196 *Economic Sanctions – Law and Public Policy* (Palgrave Macmillan 2009), 324.

197 (n 123) 67.

198 'The Design of UN Sanctions through the Interplay with Informal Arrangements' in L. van den Herik (ed), *Research Handbook on UN Sanctions and International Law* (Edward Elgar Publishing 2017), 187. As the author claims the standards "although legally non-binding they are attached to economic and political incentives or adverse economic and political

Nathanael Tilahun comments that notwithstanding the FATF's informal character:

> [T]he FATF's rules (known as 'Recommendations') are legally non-binding but practically observed nearly universally – in fact, by more States than the total membership of the United Nations. The FATF states that 205 jurisdictions have so far made high-level political commitment to its Recommendations, and, by February 2020, in-depth assessment of compliance (known as 'mutual evaluation report') have been conducted in 98 States.[199]

The above exposes in an indisputable manner the extension of the internal and external impact of FATF's decisions and policies, indicating capacities conventionally associated with formal IOs.

The UNSC's role in countering FT/PF under Chapter VII of the UN Charter is an additional argument to support the changing legal nature of the Forty Recommendations that should be carefully considered.

In the beginning, the Resolutions of the UNSC urged member States "to implement the comprehensive, international standards embodied in the FATF Recommendations",[200] but through time, the Resolutions started to reproduce the language of FATF's Standards, and the language of the benchmarks and criteria set out in FATF's methodology.[201]

The Resolutions also began to indicate specific Recommendations and/or INotes[202] and to recommend FATF's Best Practices and Guidance

effects in case of non-compliance (like naming and shaming; exclusion from trade privileges, etc)", 181.

199 (n 82) 2.

200 Eg. UNSCR 1615 (2005) op.para. 7; UNSCR 1989 (2011) op.para. 41; UNSCR 2083 (2012) op.para. 43; UNSCR 2161 (2014) op.para. 10; UNSCR 2166 (2014) op.para. 10; UNSCR 2195 (2014) op.para. 5; UNSCR 2253 (2015) op.para. 16; UNSCR 2255 (2015) op.para. 10; UNSCR 2368 (2017) op.para. 17; UNSCR 2462 (2019) op.para. 4; UNSCR 2617 (2021), op.para. 31.

201 Eg. UNSCR 2083 (2012) op.para. 44; UNSCR 2161 (2014) op.para. 11 as regards Recommendation 6; UNSCR 2166 (2014) op.para. 12 on preventing the abuse of NPOs, use alternative remittance systems and physical trans-border movement of currency; UNSCR 2331 (2016) op.para. 5 on FIU's operation; UNSCR 2462 (2019) op.para. 14, 16, 21, 22 as regards FT risks and vulnerabilities, FIU, and regulation of VA and a RBA to VA; UNSCR 2368 (2017) op.para. 22 on financial transparency and the use of a RBA; UNSCR 2610 (2021), op.para. 17 on Immediate Outcome 10, op.para. 26 on registries and BO or para.28 on ransom as a FT source.

202 Eg. UNSCR 2253 (2015) op.para. 17, UNSCR 2322 (2016), op.para. 6 and UNSCR 2368 (2017) op.para. 17 on Recommendation 5 and its INote; UNSCR 2255 (2215) op.para 11 and UNSCR 2462 (2019) op.para. 23 on Recommendation 8 and its INote; UNSCR 2610 (2021), op.para.

Papers,[203] leaving no doubts as to their content being clearly inspired, if not replicating, FATF's Standards. This fact should not go unnoticed, as it bears substance as to the legal nature of the Forty Recommendations.

From 2015 onwards, these FATF Recommendations were not just standards; some had *become legal obligations* under the umbrella of the UNSC. A few examples are provided below:

– Resolution 2253 (2015):

Strongly urges all member States to implement the comprehensive international standards embodied in the Financial Action Task Force's (FATF) revised Forty Recommendations on Combating Money Laundering and the Financing of Terrorism and Proliferation, particularly Recommendation 6 on targeted financial sanctions related to terrorism and terrorist financing; to apply the elements in FATF's Interpretive Note to Recommendation 6, with the final objective of effectively preventing terrorists from raising, moving and using funds, in line with the objectives of Immediate Outcome 10 of the FATF methodology;[204]

– Resolution 2462 (2019):

*Urges m*ember States which have not yet done so to establish operationally independent and autonomous financial intelligence units with a view to strengthening their framework to prevent and counter the financing of terrorism, in line with FATF standards,[205] and (…) *calls on m*ember States to periodically conduct a risk assessment of its non-profit sector or update existing ones to determine the organisations vulnerable to terrorist financing and to inform the implementation of a risk-based approach;[206]

– Resolution 2610 (2021):

Strongly urges all member States (…) to consider elements in FATF Recommendation 15 on virtual assets as "property," "proceeds," "funds," "funds or other assets," or other "corresponding value" and apply the relevant

17 on Recommendation 6 and its INote and op.para. 18 on Recommendation 5 and its INote.

203 Eg. UNSCR 1989 (2011) op.para. 41; UNSCR 2083 (2012) op.para. 25; UNSCR 2161 (2014) op. para. 11 and 49; UNSCR 2166 (2014) op.para. 11; UNSCR 2253 (2015) op.para. 16; UNSCR 2368 (2017) op.para. 17 on FATF's Best Practices on Targeted Financial Sanctions; Preamble of UNSCR 2347 (2017) on Guidance to Recommendation 5; UNSCR 2610 (2021), op.para. 27 on FATF's risk indicators.

204 Op.para. 16.

205 Op.para. 15.

206 Op.para. 23.

measures under the FATF Recommendations to virtual assets and virtual asset service providers (VASPs).[207]

The FATF also refers to the Resolutions of the UNSC in its reports and to the relevance of its standards in the international legal system. In the 2015–2016 FATF Report, it is stated that Resolution 2253 (2015) of the UNSCR "integrated FATF Standards in international law".[208]

The 2018–2019 FATF Report notes that the Resolution 2462 (2019) of the UNSCR "has embedded an FATF Standard in international law";[209] and in the 30 Years FATF Report, the FATF claims that its Recommendations give effect to member's States legal obligations under international law,[210] complementing the Resolutions of the UNSCR by providing "clear measures to assist countries in fulfilling their legal obligations".[211]

At the 2021 Joint Special Meeting of the Counter-Terrorism Committee and the 1267/1989/2253 ISIL (Da'esh) and Al-Qaeda Sanctions Committee, the FATF President declared the consolidation of FT standards "for the first time in a UN instrument" referring to Resolution 2462 (2019).[212]

The evolution of the content of the Resolutions of the UNSC adopted under Chapter VII of the UN Charter to counter FT/PF contributes materially to the transformation of the legal nature of FATF's Recommendations by shaping and shifting the behaviour of States (practice and *opinio iuris*) resulting in an implicit and/or explicit general perception that FATF's Recommendations are binding.[213]

207 Op.para. 17.

208 At: 16.

209 At: 15.

210 At: 89. It is also a fact that some of the Recommendations reproduce some of the UNSCRs' operative paragraphs which impose legal obligations, for example, the requirement to be part of the Convention for the Suppression of the Financing of Terrorism (Recommendation 36), to criminalise TF (Recommendation 5), to implement targeted financial sanctions to PF (Recommendation 7), or to confiscate and freeze assets without undue delay (Recommendations 4, 6 and 7). However, some of its INotes and methodology apart from providing guidance go a little beyond.

211 At: 40.

212 FATF's President Speech (18/11/2021), at: https://www.un.org/securitycouncil/ctc/sites/www.un.org.securitycouncil.ctc/files/financial_action_task_force.pdf.

213 In this regard, Blazejewski notes "[p]erhaps no other institutional partnership reinforced the FATF's claim to substantive legitimacy as much as the UN Security Council through Resolution 1617. By formally endorsing the FATF Recommendations, Resolution 1617 arguably raises these rules as close to international law as possible without imposing direct legal obligations. International law is commonly viewed as one of or perhaps the primary source of legitimacy in international relations", (n 1) 59.

Furthermore, amendments and new international legal instruments adopted under the auspices of other IOs, international institutions or bodies (Section 6 bellow), as well as national legislation or regulation reflecting the FATF Recommendations, INotes or even the methodology criteria, support the understanding of a common and universal practice with a general belief in their imperativeness.

The normative dimension of the FATF Recommendations – nature and effects – is another crucial aspect that should be underscored to characterise the legal nature of the FATF, in the context of the evolutionary character of the organisation at *political* (policy and lawmaking) and *institutional* levels.

5.2.3 Mutual Evaluation Process and Blacklisting

A strong example of FATF's external dimension within its operational decision-making capacity is the overall ME process that covers implementation and assessment mechanisms and the blacklisting process, as explained in detail in Chapter 2, Section 7 above. As highlighted by Nance:

> [I]f blacklisting operates more in line with the notion of a penalty default rather than more standard conceptualisations of material enforcement, then it stands to reason that the role of extensive monitoring within the FATF system should be more diagnostic than punitive. The mutual evaluations are among the most extensive monitoring of any international organisation and imperfect compliance is well documented, yet enforcement remains rare. This stands in stark contrast to standard approaches to monitoring and enforcement within political science, which see monitoring as necessary to detect defections and to provide the evidence needed to overcome the collective action problem associated with enforcement. Without strict monitoring and enforcement, compliance with standards that require meaningful change from States will be lacking.[214]

The adoption of a common methodology in 2004 and its increasing complexity in the 2012 revision (combined with chirurgical amendments), including the shift in emphasis from technical compliance to effectiveness, along with

---

214 'Re-Thinking FATF: An Experimentalist Interpretation of the Financial Action Task Force' (2018) 69 *Crime, Law and Socials Change*, 143. Nance provides a brief and clear overview of the evolution of the FATF's monitoring process.

the introduction of the RBA, have had a cascading impact on jurisdictions' domestic frameworks.[215]

National policies, mechanisms and measures are challenged and measured in a meticulous monitoring process with a prospect of being referral to the ICRG and blacklisted.[216] This considerable amount of pressure starts with the ME process (see, for instance, earlier remarks by Brazil, Hong Kong (China) and Macao (China)). As Borlini comments:

> The FATF mutual evaluation process is an unusual case of international oversight designed to encourage compliance with international rules (...) the mutual evaluation process has been set up to provide a framework for a global, unified, and methodical approach to assessments.[217]

In fact, as stated in the 30 Years FATF Report, the FATF prides itself as being the "first international body to assess its members on effectiveness".[218] This declaration is echoed by the FATF Executive Secretariat at the 2019 RUSI meeting about the FATF Strategic Review:

> The FATF become the first global standard-setter to assess not only the existence of law, regulations, institutions, etc. – so called 'technical compliance' – but to also attempt to assess the use of those measures and the impact of them.[219]

The power that the FATF self-entrusted to identify those jurisdictions that undermine or pose a threat to the international financial system and, if necessary, to call for actions to safeguard it is another clear-cut example of the

215 The work of "two decades of identifying high risk and non-cooperative jurisdictions" allowed the development of sound AML regimes all over the world, 30 Years FATF Report, 66. Along these lines, Borlini comments that: "Although the FATF's membership is limited and its standards do not have the binding force of a treaty, the mutual evaluation process provides incentives for member as well as non-member countries to improve their AML/CFT regimes. The mutual evaluations help member countries identify areas where ML and FT risks are high, thereby assisting them in prioritising interventions and allocating resources efficiently", (n 180), 4.

216 2009–2010 FATF Report, 28–29; 2016–2017 FATF Report, 39–40.

217 (n 180) 2.

218 At: 53.

219 FATF's Executive Secretariat Speech (18/11/2019), at: http://www.fatf-gafi.org/publications/fatfgeneral/documents/rusi-fatf-strategic-review.html.

FATF's policy-making and decision-making capacities, wherein operational tools to ensure the success of its goals were/are developed.

As described in Chapter 2, Section 7.2. above, in the year 2000, the FATF initiated the 'naming and shaming' policy or blacklisting process, known as the NCCT list, on its own, which was later replaced in 2007 by the 'Grey and Black Lists'. In the 2007 NCCT Review Report, the FATF stressed the potential reputational damages of being blacklisted, but also the underlined pressure placed on jurisdictions to undertake reforms.

> Being identified by the FATF as an NCCT and being the target of the FATF's application of Recommendation 21 were also viewed by countries as harmful to their reputation, requiring steps to address the identified anti-money laundering (AML) deficiencies. Also, in some jurisdictions, there were already *stimuli* for moving forward with AML reforms such as through feedback from mutual evaluations conducted by FSRBs.[220]

During the NCCT mechanism, some listed jurisdictions were able to address the deficiencies and make amendments, avoiding the call for countermeasures by showing substantial progress, like the Russian Federation,[221] Hungary, Israel, and Lebanon.[222] Others, like Ukraine[223] or Philippines,[224] warnings were issued that countermeasures would be applied if the identified deficiencies were not efficiently addressed. Other cases, like Nauru, the failure to enact adequate AML legislation and measures to cease the operation of shell banks caused the application of countermeasures. Nauru was de-listed in 2005 with a continuous follow-up monitoring process.[225] Nigeria[226] and Myanmar[227]

220 Para. 7.

221 2001–2002 FATF Report, para. 75; 2002–2003 FATF Report, para. 123.

222 2001–2002 FATF Report, para. 77.

223 2002–2003 FATF Report, para. 122.

224 2001–2002 FATF Report, para. 75; 2002–2003 FATF Report, para. 121. Philippines was only withdrawn from the NCCT list in 2005 (2004–2005 FATF Report, para. 35).

225 2001–2002 FATF Report, para. 75; 2002–2003 FATF Report, para. 122; 2005–2006 FATF Report, para. 46.

226 The application of countermeasures was considered and recommended (as of 31 October 2002) unless the Nigerian Government seriously engages in adopting the measures deemed to be necessary to address the ML deficiencies identified by the FATF (2001–2002 FATF Report, para. 76). Nigeria was de-listed in 2006 and monitored at least for one year (2005–2006 FATF Report, para. 46; 2006–2007 FATF Report, para. 44).

227 2004–2005 FATF Report, para. 36; 2005–2006 FATF Report, para. 46; 2006–2007 FATF Report para. 44; 2007–2008 FATF Report, para. 51.

followed the same path; Myanmar was the last jurisdiction to be de-listed in 2006.[228]

Damage to reputation is a peremptory concern for all jurisdictions, as the Hong Kong authorities emphasised in their 2015 debate on Recommendation 32:

> Past experience suggested that major deficiencies in fulfilling FATF's recommendations would result in a more intensive follow-up process and enhanced scrutiny by FATF and would have a negative impact on Hong Kong's reputation as an international financial centre.[229]

The same concern was raised in the Brazilian Senate when debating the adoption of Law 13,810/2019 and compliance with Recommendation 6:

> Brazil is the only one of the 35 members' countries of the FATF that, according to the organisation, has not yet adopted anti-terrorism measures. We run the risk of being blacklisted by the FATF if this project is not approved. We will be together with North Korea, Iran, and Sudan (...) [The Anastasia report] explained that Brazil runs the risk of "very serious consequences" if the proposal is not approved. The country could end up being suspended from the FATF and classified as 'high risk' or 'non-cooperative'. Some of the consequence could be the end of operations of foreign banks here or the imposition of heavy sanctions against other nations that trade with us. Finally, we will be subject to serious losses, such as the increase in country risk and the cost of financial internal and external debts. The fiscal impact can be quite expressive – said the senator, while defending his report.[230]

228 Ibid.

229 Consultation Paper on the 'Establishment of a Reporting System on the Physical Cross-Boundary Transportation of Large Quantities of Currency and Bearer Negotiable Instruments' (July 2015), Security Bureau, 5–6. On the impact of FATF's ME in the development of Hong Kong's policies and legal framework, amongst others, Young, 'Hong Kong Braces Itself for its Third FATF Evaluation' (2008) 29 *The Company Lawyer*.

230 Senate News Agency (20/02/2019) (free translation) at: https://www12.senado.leg.br/noticias/materias/2019/02/20/bloqueio-imediato-de-bens-de-terroristas-e-aprovado-em-comissoes-e-segue-ao-plenario. For a comparative approach and influence of FATF's Standards in the AML/CFT framework of Brazil and Argentina, while addressing legitimacy concerns and the NCCT list, Maíra Rocha Machado, 'Transnational Legal Processes addressing Money Laundering in Brazil and Argentina' in G. Shaffer (ed), *Transnational Legal Ordering and State Change* (Cambridge University Press 2012).

In the 2017–2018 FATF Report, the FATF highlights the advantages of the blacklisting process:

> The FATF's process helps protect the integrity of the international financial system by issuing a public warning about the risks emanating from the identified jurisdictions. These public warnings also put pressure on the identified jurisdictions to address their deficiencies in order to maintain their position in the global economy. Public identification, and the prospect of public identification, encourages countries to swiftly make significant improvements.[231]

However, blacklisting also entails serious economic repercussions in the designated jurisdictions. The 2021 IMF Paper on the 'Impact of Gray-Listing on Capital Flows: An Analysis Using Machine Learning' reveals that jurisdictions that are listed on the 'Grey List' have "significant negative effects" on capital inflows estimated at 7.6% of their GDP, with foreign direct investment and portfolio flow also affected.[232]

> How much gray-listing affects a country's capital flows is of interests to policy makers, investors, and the Fund. It tells the policy makes about the economic costs of gray-listing and may encourage them to make appropriate investments to address gaps in their countries' AML/CFT regimes.[233]

In this respect, Paul Weiss explains that although "not have any direct legal prohibitions or legal effects on the ability of individuals and entities to engage in transactions", enhanced due diligence deemed from blacklisting may affect business activities as business agents and IFIs may prefer to take a cautious approach, like reducing business activities or imposing stringent requirements, thus making business transactions with a "Grey List jurisdiction more burdensome".[234]

231 At: 53; 30 Years FATF Report, 65–66.

232 Working Paper (Mizuho Kida and Simon Paetzold), 5, 20 and 23.

233 Ibid, 22.

234 'FATF 'Gray Lists' Turkey, Citing Concerns with Turkey's Banking and Real Estate Sectors and Potential Terrorism Financing' (10/11/2021) Economic Sanctions & Anti Money Laundering, at: https://www.paulweiss.com/practices/litigation/economic-sanctions-aml/publications/fatf-gray-lists-turkey-citing-concerns-with-turkey-s-banking-and-real-estate-sectors-and-potential-terrorism-financing?id=41695.

5.2.3.1 *The Case of Indonesia*

Indonesia is a good case-study of success considering that it has been on the NCCT list,[235] on the 'Grey List',[236] and was a candidate to the FATF from 2018 until 2023, being the most recent member.[237]

This jurisdiction was withdrawn from the FATF's ongoing monitoring mechanism in June 2015, resulting from significant efforts from the Indonesian authorities to address the identified deficiencies of its AML/CFT regime pursuant to its MER of July 2008.[238] Indonesia is an APG member since August 1999, and held the APG Co-chair from 2006 to 2008.[239]

In November 2017, Indonesia started its third round of ME, culminating with the adoption of the MER in July 2018, where its reform efforts were recognised:

> Following the last APG mutual evaluation in 2008, Indonesia's AML/CFT regime has undergone significant reform across all areas of the FATF standards. Key reforms include: (i) enacting new ML and TF offences and changes to the designation of LEAs to investigate ML; (ii) introducing targeted financial sanctions (TFS) for terrorism and proliferation financing (although major/fundamental improvements are needed); and (iii) introducing comprehensive preventive measure obligations for FIs and DNFBPs and changes to supervisory arrangements.[240]

At the FATF-MENAFATF Joint Plenary meeting in Paris 2018, Indonesia acquires FATF observer status aspiring full membership. At the time, the Indonesian

235 2006–2007 FATF Report, para. 45.

236 At: https://www.fatf-gafi.org/media/fatf/documents/statements/Public-Statement-24-October-2014.pdf. More information at: https://www.fatf-gafi.org/en/countries/detail/Indonesia.html.

237 At: https://www.fatf-gafi.org/en/publications/Fatfgeneral/outcomes-fatf-plenary-october-2023.html.

238 At: 197–205, at: https://www.fatf-gafi.org/publications/high-risk-and-other-monitored-jurisdictions/documents/fatf-compliance-june-2015.html. Adam Fenton and David Price address the Indonesian AML/CFT legislative efforts to comply with the standards, particularly the Eradication and Prevention of Terrorism Financing Act, in March 2013. The authors point out that being "blacklisted created a powerful incentive to act" and tackle the gaps, whilst "some argued that the new law was only enacted as a response to Indonesia's inclusion in FATF's list", 'Forbidden Funds – Indonesia's New Legislation for Countering the Financing of Terrorism' (2014) 11(3) *Indonesian Journal of International Law*, 392.

239 At: https://apgml.org/.

240 APG MER of Indonesia (September) 2018, para. 6.

Government acknowledged that the APG exercise had been a valuable step in the three-year membership process.[241]

Indonesia undertook a ME assessment as a candidate jurisdiction for membership, and its MER was adopted at the FATF Plenary meeting in February 2023. The efforts of the Indonesian Government to establish a sound AML/CFTCPF regime were commended, however there were still some "shortcomings in their legal framework for targeted financial sanctions on proliferation financing".[242]

On 27 October 2023, Indonesia reported some progress and made an undertaking to an action plan addressing the "key technical and effectiveness issues identified during the evaluation".[243] On this basis, the FATF granted membership status to Indonesia, making it the 40th member.

5.2.3.2 *The Case of Turkey*

In a different position, Turkey, a FATF member, is currently and, once again, on the 'Grey List' following its MER (December) 2019, as noted. Serious shortcomings were identified, including "gaps in banking, real estate, gold and precious stones dealers' supervision," absence of a comprehensive legal framework to comply with the UN targeted financial sanctions related to FT and PF, and absence of transparency and BO requirements for legal persons and legal

241 See the declaration of the Central Bank of Indonesia, 'International Appreciation of Compliance and Effectiveness of Anti-Money Laundering and Terrorism Financing in Indonesia' (30/07/2018), Bank of Indonesia website, at: https://www.bi.go.id/en/iru/highlight-news/Pages/International-Appreciation-of-Compliance-and-Effectiveness-of-Anti-Money-Laundering-and-Terrorist-Financing-in-Indonesia.aspx/. Also, 'Indonesia Obtains FATF Observer Status' (05/07/2018) *Jakarta Post*, at: https://www.thejakartapost.com/news/2018/07/05/indonesia-obtains-fatf-observer-status.html.

242 Eg. Indonesia was rated 'PC' in relation to Recommendations 6, 7, 8 and 25 (Executive Summary Report, 12). More at: https://www.fatf-gafi.org/en/countries/detail/Indonesia.html.

243 At: https://www.fatf-gafi.org/en/publications/Fatfgeneral/outcomes-fatf-plenary-october-2023.html.

244 Action plan: (i) dedicating more resources to the supervision of AML/CFT compliance by high-risk sectors and increasing on-site inspections; (ii) applying "dissuasive sanctions" for breaches of AML/CFT, including unregistered money transfers; (iii) enhancing use of financial intelligence to support money laundering investigations; (iv) undertaking more complex money laundering investigations and prosecutions; (v) fixing responsibilities and measurable performance objectives for anti-terror finance authorities; (vi) conducting more financial investigations in terrorism cases; (vii) concerning targeted financial sanctions under the UN's anti-terror resolutions, and pursuing actions against UN-designated groups; and, (viii) implementing a risk-based approach to supervision of

arrangements.[244] Although some progress has been achieved, Turkey remains in 'enhanced follow-up'.[245]

Turkish authorities have shown their discontent for being placed on the 'Grey List' in a statement to the *media* by the Ministry of Treasury and Finance in October 2021:

> Despite our work on compatibility, placing our country on the Grey List is an undeserved outcome (…) in the coming period, necessary measures will continue to be taken in co-operation with FATF and all relevant institutions, to ensure that our country is removed from this list, which it does not deserve, as soon as possible.[246]

The consequences of being on the 'Grey List' are well-highlighted in the *media*: "a grey-listing downgrade strains countries' ties to foreign banks and investors that follow FATF rankings, suggesting the move could further weigh on Turkey's lira, which touched a record low earlier on Thursday".[247]

There is however some expectation in relation to next the FATF's Plenary meeting in June 2024, considering the FATF's statement in February:

> At its February 2024 Plenary, the FATF made the initial determination that Türkiye has substantially completed its action plan and warrants an on-site assessment to verify the implementation of the AML/CFT reforms has begun and is being sustained, that the, and that the necessary political commitment remains in place to sustain implementation in the future.[248]

Expectations are even higher, following an alleged FATF on-site visit to Turkey in May to Turkey to evaluate the AML/CFT/CPF reforms undertaken by the

non-profit organisations to prevent their abuse for terrorist financing. at: https://www.fatf-gafi.org/publications/high-risk-and-other-monitored-jurisdictions/documents/increased-monitoring-october-2022.html.

245 At:https://www.fatf-gafi.org/en/publications/High-risk-and-other-monitored-jurisdictions/Increased-monitoring-february-2024.html.

246 'Finance Watchdog 'Grey Lists' Turkey in Threat to Investment' (21/10/2021) *Reuters*, at: https://www.reuters.com/business/finance-watchdog-grey-lists-turkey-threat-investment-2021-10-21/ or 'Explained: Why Has the Global Terror Finance Watchdog Put Turkey Under the Lens?' (22/10/2021) *The Indian Express*, at: https://indianexpress.com/article/explained/financial-action-task-force-turkey-7584633/.

247 Ibid, *Reuters*.

248 At:https://www.fatf-gafi.org/en/publications/High-risk-and-other-monitored-jurisdictions/Increased-monitoring-february-2024.html.

Turkish Government as mentioned in the *media*,[249] and statements by the Turkish Government that all measures under the action plan are in place.[250]

5.2.3.3 *The Case of Iran*

As referred in Chapter 2, Section 7.2. above, Iran has been blacklisted for the past two decades.[251] In 2016, the Iranian Government made a firm political commitment to rectify its AML/CFT deficiencies, in which a target-oriented action plan (2016–2018) was drawn by the FATF with a comprehensive set of measures outlined in the 2015 Joint Comprehensive Plan of Action (JCPOA). At the time, Iran already had adopted a new AML Code (2008) and bylaw (2010), and set up an AML/CFT Ministerial Co-ordination Council and a FIU (2010).[252]

Positive steps were attained with the JCPOA, including the: adoption of a CFT law, introduction of a cash declaration system, reinforcement of CDD measures and the role of the Central Bank of Iran, as regulator of all financial and credit institutions. As a result, Iran was withdrawn from the 'Black List' during that period.[253] As Steven Terner comments:

---

249 'Finance Watchdog Visited Turkey Ahead of 'Grey List' Decision, Sources Say', Jonathan Spicer and Ebru Tuncay (07/05/2024) *Reuters*, at: https://www.reuters.com/world/middle-east/finance-watchdog-visited-turkey-ahead-grey-list-decision-sources-say-2024-05-07/.

250 According to Anadolou Agency: "Turkish Treasury and Finance Minister, Mehmet Simsek, said Friday that the process to remove Türkiye from the FATF Grey List has reached its final stage. He stressed that the task force decided that Türkiye had completed all the items of an action plan meant to further strengthen AFL and CFT systems." In 'Türkiye 'Substantially' Completed Action Plan to Be Removed from Financial Action Task Force's 'Grey List': Watchdog – Türkiye Makes Key Reforms Ensuring Sanctions for Money Laundering, Financing Terrorism to Improving Asset Recovery System Says FATF', Gökhan Ergöçün (24/02/2024) *Anadolou Agency*, at: https://www.aa.com.tr/en/economy/turkiye-substantially-completed-action-plan-to-be-removed-from-financial-action-task-force-s-grey-list-watchdog/3146367#.

251 2008–2009 FATF Report, 17; 2009–2010 FATF Report, 28–29; 2011–2012 FATF Report, 30; 2016–2017 FATF Report, 39–40.

252 'Iran: IMF Evaluates Iran's Legislative and Institutional Efforts to Combat Money Laundering and Terrorism Financing' (13/04/2018) Library of Congress, at: https://www.loc.gov/item/global-legal-monitor/2018-04-13/iran-imf-evaluates-irans-legislative-and-institutional-efforts-to-combat-money-laundering-and-terrorism-financing/.

253 2015–2016 FATF Report, 40; 2017–2018 FATF Report, 56; 2019–2020 FATF Report, 39. For an analytical study of the AML/CFT Iranian legislation and measures taken against the AML/CFT international instruments, including the Forty Recommendations, amongst others, Mansour Rahmdel, 'FATF and Money Laundering in Iran' (2018) 21(3) *Journal of Money Laundering Control*. Also, European Institute for Export Compliance webpage on Iran, at: https://www.eifec.org/iran-fatf-gafi-aml.

> The signing of the JCPOA in 2016 was a significant step toward Rouhani's goals of economic recovery and global reintegration. Not only did it begin the process of lifting international sanctions related to Iran's nuclear weapons program, but it also came with the temporary removal of Iran from the FATF's blacklist, pending its willingness to achieve compliance with the FATF's anti-money laundering and anti-terrorism financing protocols.[254]

However, the absence of progress, particularly the failure to ratify the Palermo Convention and Convention for the Suppression of the Financing of Terrorism in accordance with the FATF Standards proved decisive,[255] leading to the reinstatement of countermeasures in 2019,[256] with Iran remaining on FATF's 'Black List' ever since.[257]

Additionally, another major factor was the non-approval of two bills consistent with the Forty Recommendations to improve the existing AML and CFT laws.[258] In March 2021, the *media* reports that President Rouhani, in a televised speech, advocated the adoption of the bills to "complete Iran's action plan", claiming:

> All countries have adopted [FATF standards]. Right and left. West and East. If it's something bad, then why has everybody gone for it? (...) Rouhani also said that while the adoption of the two bills may not solve all the country's problems, but officials who opposed them should

254 'Does Iran Want to Be Removed from the FATF Blacklist?' (01/04/2021) Gulf State Analytics, at: https://gulfstateanalytics.com/does-iran-want-to-be-removed-from-the-fatf-blacklist/; ibid. See, 'Global Watchdog Places Iran on Terrorism Financing Blacklist' (21/02/2020) *Reuters*, at: https://www.reuters.com/article/us-iran-fatf-idUSKBN20F1Z6.

255 2018–2019 FATF Report, 56; 2019–2020 FATF Report, 39. Iran is a party to the 1988 Vienna Convention however it has not yet ratified the other two Conventions. At: https://treaties.un.org/pages/ViewDetails.aspx?src=IND&mtdsg_no=XVIII-11&chapter=18&clang=_en and https://treaties.un.org/pages/ViewDetails.aspx?src=TREATY&mtdsg_no=XVIII-12&chapter=18&clang=_en.

256 The 2019–2020 FATF Report states: "In October 2019, the FATF exhorted members to increased supervisory examination for branches and subsidiaries of financial institutions based in Iran; introduce enhanced reporting mechanisms or systematic reporting of financial transactions; and increased external audit requirements for financial groups with respect to any of their branches and subsidiaries located in Iran", 39.

257 At:https://www.fatf-gafi.org/en/publications/High-risk-and-other-monitored-jurisdictions/Call-for-action-february-2024.html.

258 2019–2020 FATF Report, 39.

> consider how they would explain to the people how not ratifying them will hurt the country.[259]

The fact is that the Iranian political elite was/is divided as regards Iran's allegiance to FATF. Former President Rouhani viewed the co-operation with the FATF as a solution to lift international sanctions against Iran (to improve foreign trade and promote economic recovery). Others, differently, "argue that passing legislation to join the FATF could hamper Iran's support for its allies, including Lebanon's Hezbollah".[260] Former President Raeesi, a conservative, went farther by accusing the FATF of being a 'puppet' of the USA and EU, defending closer ties with the East, and criticising the previous administration's pledges to the FATF.[261]

Iran's isolation from the global financial system is often mentioned. Brian O'Toole sceptically comments: "In practice, this [re-imposition of counter-measures] means significant due diligence on or even total cut-off of the target's banks, greatly hampering the jurisdiction's ability to conduct cross-border financial transactions".[262] Similarly, former Government officials recently commented to the *media* that one of the consequences of Iran "being black-listed by the FATF stymied efforts to import Covid vaccines, including those distributed through the WHO Covax program".[263]

---

259 'Iran's FATF Debate Heats Up as Nuclear Deal Remains in Limbo' (03/03/2021) *Aljazeera*, at: https://www.aljazeera.com/news/2021/3/3/irans-fatf-debate-heats-up-as-nuclear-deal-remains-in-limbo. Terner commented that "when Hassan Rouhani was elected President of the Islamic Republic of Iran in 2013, he was given a mandate (...) to bring Iran's banking policies up to international standards so that Iran could be removed from the Financial Action Task Force's (FATF) blacklist of 'Non-Compliant Countries or Territories' (NCCTs)", (n 254).

260 *Reuters* (n 249).

261 'Iran's President Raisi Expresses Skepticism on FATF Accession' (22/09/2021) *Old Iran International*, at: https://old.iranintl.com/en/world/iran%E2%80%99s-president-raisi-expresses-skepticism-fatf-accession.

262 'FATF Blacklists Iran, But Does It Matter?' (24/02/2020) Atlantic Council, at: www.atlanticcouncil.org/blogs/iransource/fatf-blacklists-iran-but-does-it-matter/. The impact of Iran's being in the 'Black List' (Recommendation 19) has profound consequences in the financial and economic systems, already facing huge economic pressure from USA financial sanctions plus the difficulty in engaging in economic relations with the rest of world, including Russia and China as foreign banks.

263 (n 261).

5.2.3.4 *The Case of* DPRK

The other jurisdiction on the 'Black List' is North Korea, as mentioned (Chapter 2, Sections 7.2. and 9 above). Although being listed for more than 20 years, North Korea has taken some valuable steps in the direction of the common global effort to counter ML/FT.

North Korea has acceded the 1988 Vienna Convention on 2007, ratified the Convention for the Suppression of the Financing of Terrorism in 2013, acceded the Palermo Convention in 2016,[264] and has been an observer jurisdiction of the APG since 2014.[265]

Furthermore, it has adopted in April 2016 a new AML/CFT law in line accordance with the FATF standards by establishing, *inter alia*, a national coordinating committee, enhanced CDD and record keeping measures, STRs, a FIU, AML/CFT supervisory and regulatory provisions, legal assistance, and enhancing international co-operation.[266]

Dae Un Hong, when addressing the DPRK's AML/CFT policy efforts, comments on the DPRK's aspirations of becoming an APG member or even a FATF member, when stating:

> It appears the objective of this law is to enhance the government's control over the growing – both formal and informal – financial sector, thereby increasing government revenue and establishing a basis for North Korea's demand for easing the ongoing international financial sanctions, elevating its status to a full member of the APG, and eventually becoming a member of the FATF.[267]

Bradley Babson also mentions this objective:

> North Korea aspires to be a member of the Asia-Pacific Group (...) [W]hile North Koreans are making efforts to learn international business

264 At: https://www.northkoreaintheworld.org/multilateral/international-treaties.

265 2012–2013 APG Report, 22; 2013–2014 APG Report, 19.

266 'North Korea: Anti-Money Laundering and Anti-Terrorism Financing Law Adopted', (19/05/2016) Library of Congress, at: https://www.loc.gov/item/global-legal-monitor/2016-05-19/north-korea-anti-money-laundering-and-anti-terrorism-financing-law-adopted/.

267 'North Korean Laws Since 2016: What They Imply of the Country's Future' (25/02/2021) 38 NORTH, at: https://www.38north.org/2021/02/north-korean-laws-since-2016-what-they-imply-for-the-countrys-future/. Also, in the *media:* 'North Korea Adopts Anti-Money Laundering Law' (18/05/2016) *NK NEWS*, at: www.nknews.org/2016/05/north-korea-adopts-anti-money-laundering-law. The possibility of DPRK to be a member of the FATF is highly unrealistic.

> practices, come into compliance with standards for anti-money laundering and terrorist finance established by the Asia-Pacific Group of the Financial Action Task Force, and are becoming more sophisticated in their outreach efforts.[268]

Nonetheless, the impact of being blacklisted is well noted in the *media,* Rhee Yoojin research fellow for the Reunification Business Department at Korea Development Bank in Seoul, commented to *NK News* that: "[t]his has been a bar that prohibits foreign finance organisations' from advancing into North Korea".[269]

As it is self-evident, this process of 'naming and shaming' is a powerful mechanism,[270] a kind of 'wake-up call' for jurisdictions to commit at the highest political level and engage in substantive reforms,[271] lest their economic and financial reputations may be compromised. As stated in the 2015–2016 Report:

> [B]eing labelled as a country with a weak AML/CFT framework can have serious consequences. Additional measures will apply to financial transactions with the country. As a result, international trading partners will face higher costs, or may no longer be able to do business at all. Unless the country takes urgent action to strengthen its AML/CFT measures in order to remove itself from FATF's enhanced scrutiny, it could see a negative impact on its position in the global economy.[272]

The cases discussed in this Section strongly suggest that the prospect or 'threat' of being publicly exposed and inserted in either one of the lists[273] places enormous pressure on jurisdictions, which endeavour all their efforts to comply with the FATF Recommendations and build a robust and effective AML/CFT/

---

268 'The North Korean Economic System: Challenges and Issues' (2016) *International Journal of Korean Studies,* 169–170, at: https://www.ncnk.org/resources/publications/BradBabson_NKEconomicSystem_ICKSSpringSummer2016.pdf.

269 *NK NEWS* (n 267).

270 2015–2016 FATF Report, 38.

271 30 Years FATF Report, 66.

272 2015–2016 FATF Report, 38.

273 The 25 Years FATF Report states: "Trading partners will be facing higher costs due to additional measures imposed on high-risk countries, or, as financial institutions seek to minimise their risks, they may find they can no longer do business with them at all. All this can have serious consequences for the economy of countries that the FATF identifies as having strategic AML/CFT weaknesses", 19.

CPF regime.[274] It should be added that the lists of the FATF are reproduced on the websites of regional bodies[275] and FIU jurisdictions.[276]

Both mechanisms – the ME process and blacklisting – reflect FATF's far-reaching policy and decision-making powers under its role as a *guardian* and *arbiter* of the international financial system, namely, to self-empower with the authority to call at world-level the adoption of countermeasures (sanctioning power), including to non-FATF members, either belonging to an FSRB or not.

These cases also reveal the behaviour of members, FSRBS and FRSBS jurisdictions, revealing in particular a tacit acceptance of the FATF's powers without challenge, which suggests an implicit assumption of the FATF's position as a full-fledged organisation. Furthermore, only a select few formal IOS have the capacity to call for countermeasures on a worldwide scale.

In a concise paragraph, Ghoshray succeeds in explaining the widespread impact of FATF's work:

> Without treaty obligations and legal specificity, the FATF creates enforceability via an interconnected set of Recommendations covering an array of proscribed behavior. The social isolation and reputational ignominy that results from being blacklisted incentivises jurisdictions to conform to the Recommendations and guidelines. Thus, in achieving compliance success in shaping the policies and laws of many countries within an interconnected framework, the FATF requires a succinct, cohesive institutional structure. Manifested within the FATF standards is a developed internal ordering framework, which allows its soft law norms to exert pressure for global conformity through reputational and social pathways.[277]

In keeping with the preceding thoughts, Doron Goldbarsh correctly observes "it seems that adoption [of AML/CFT measures] is a question of 'when' rather than 'if' as there is no room for choice".[278] FATF's leadership and authoritative capacity to persuade jurisdictions all over the world to implement its policies,

274 2006–2007 FATF Report, para. 45; 2007–2008 FATF Report, para. 52–53.

275 Eg. CFATF public statements, at: https://www.cfatf-gafic.org/home/public-statements. The APG publishes FATF public statements on its website, at: https://apgml.org/about-us/page.aspx?p=6ee636fb-ae8c-4269-83e1-d8bc40320f92.

276 Eg. Australia FIU, at: https://www.austrac.gov.au/fatf-updates-global-mltf-risk-4; Macao (China) FIU, at: https://www.gif.gov.mo/en/standard/highriskjurisdict.html; Malta FIU, at: https://fiaumalta.org/news/fatf-public-statements-23-february-2024/.

277 (n 2) 541.

278 (n 128) 129.

standards and procedures (MER, FUR, ICRG) are so sound that Governments feel driven to comply for fear of reputational damage.[279]

As regards the fourth element, it is contended that the FATF operates on the international plane, under international law, in a distinctive manner, and that it is distinctively recognised as a separate legal person by its members, associate members, and FSRBs' jurisdictions.

6 External Recognition by Other Subjects of International Law

The other crucial element to consider when qualifying an organisation as an international legal person is the inter-relation with other subjects of international law. In Wessel's autonomy test, it is described as the *existence of external behaviour of other subjects towards the legal person,* while in Klabbers' it is an additional element identified as 'external recognition'.

The external relations dimension necessitates a behaviour analysis of how international actors perceive FATF. Is the FATF distinguished on the international plane and by its international actors as an autonomous and independent organisation? Is it eligible to the same international standing as other IOs?

6.1 *The FATF's Legal Status and External Participation*

The global recognition of FATF as *the* leading organisation setting AML/CFT/CPF universal standards is undeniable (eg. Resolutions of the UNSC explicitly echo this status),[280] notwithstanding the ambiguity around its legal status.

This ambiguity regarding its legal nature is also visible when referred by other IOs or international institutions. Some Resolutions of the UNSC suggest that the FATF is an IO by mentioning the organisation side-by-side with other recognised IOs, as if on equal footing. For instance, Annex I of Resolution 2253 (2015) establishes:

> To consult with the member States and other relevant organisations, including the International Air Transport Association (IATA), the International Civil Aviation Organisation (ICAO), the World Customs

279 Ibid.

280 Eg. UNSCR 2610 (2021), Preamble, para. 33 in which it recognises and endorses the "essential role" of the "in setting global standards for preventing and combatting money laundering, terrorist financing, and proliferation financing and its Global Network of FATF-style regional bodies".

> Organisation (WCO), INTERPOL, the Financial Action Task Force (FATF).[281]

Similarly, Annex I of Resolution 2368 (2017) refers:

> To consult with member States, relevant representatives of the private sector, including financial institutions and relevant non-financial businesses and professions, and international and regional organisations, including FATF and its regional bodies.[282]

In other Resolutions, references to FATF are undefined, such as paragraph 27 of the Preamble of Resolution 2617 (2021), which states: "[*a*]*cknowledging* the important work on countering the financing of terrorism of United Nations entities and other multilateral bodies and forums, *reiterating* the essential role of the Financial Action Task Force (FATF)".

The same pattern of referencing the FATF can also be seen in the CoE. For example, the Explanatory Report to the 2005 Convention on Laundering, Search, Seizure and Confiscation of the Proceeds from Crime and on the Financing of Terrorism (2005 Warsaw Convention)[283] refers to the FATF together with the EU and UN: "some of these changes have already been or are currently being included in standards set by other international *fora* (EU, UN, FATF)".[284]

Statements made by the EU are even more ambiguous. The EU either categorises FATF as "the leading international body devoted to the fight against money laundering", as is the case in paragraph 7 of the Preamble of 2nd AML Directive 2001/97/EC or in paragraph 5 of the Preamble of 3rd AML Directive 2005/60/EC or makes references to the organisation side-by-side with other IOs, as is the case of the Proposal for a Directive of the EU Parliament and of the Council amending EU Directive 2015/849 on the Prevention of the Use of the Financial system for Money Laundering or Terrorist Financing that refers "relevant reports issued by Union and international organisations such as the European Banking Authority (EBA), the European Central Bank (ECB), Europol, the Bank for International Settlements (BIS), and the FATF"[285] and

281 Sub-para.(u). Also, sub-para.(u) of Annex I of UNSCR 2368 (2017) and of UNSCR 2610 (2021).

282 Sub-para.(w).

283 Warsaw, 15/05/2005 (CETS 198).

284 Para. 21, at: https://rm.coe.int/16800d3813Ibid.

285 EU Commission Paper, Strasbourg, 05/07/2016 COM (2016) 450 FINAL, 2016/0208 (COD), 9.

the case of paragraph 3 of the Preamble of EU Directive 2018/1673 stating: "[the EU] should continue to take particular account of the Financial Action Task Force (FATF) Recommendations and instruments of other international organisations and bodies active in the fight against money laundering and terrorist financing".

This practice of placing the FATF with other major IOs may lead us to infer an implicit recognition of the FATF as an IO. In a different vein, both the IMF and the Basel Committee identify the FATF as 'an international body' in charge of developing and promoting international standards to counter ML/FT/PF.[286]

In statements from several jurisdictions, references are made to the FATF as an IO or mentioned in an equal standing with other IOs (eg. Australia,[287] Saudi Arabia[288] or USA[289]), while others refer to the FATF as an international body (eg. Canada,[290] Japan[291] or Singapore[292]).

6.2 *FATF's Institutional Participation*

The institutional participation of FATF in other IOs or international institutions, or bodies outside the Global Network is unclear and quite vague due to the lack of public information regarding FATF's observer status.

The Global Forum on Transparency and Exchange of Information for Tax Purposes (Global Forum) is one of the exceptions by expressly referring that the FATF became an observer in 2017.[293] The CTED is another example by referrig to FATF as a partner in its list of IOs together, *inter alia* with the IMF, WB, OAS, WCO and IMO.[294]

---

286 At: https://www.imf.org/external/np/leg/amlcft/eng/aml4.htm and https://www.mas.gov.sg/-/media/MAS/Regulations-and-Financial-Stability/BCBS-Guidelines-for-AML CFT-June-2017.pdf, 1, footnote 2.

287 See Australia Senate Committee Reports, Legal and Constitutional Legislation Committee, Provisions of the Anti-Terrorism Bill (No. 2) 2005, November 2005, 'Chapter 7 – Anti-Money Laundering and Terrorism Financing', para. 7.3.

288 At: https://www.sama.gov.sa/en-us/news/pages/news08022015.aspx.

289 At: https://www.federalregister.gov/documents/2021/04/05/2021-06922/beneficial-ownership-information-reporting-requirem.

290 (n 176) 14.

291 At: https://www.japantimes.co.jp/news/2014/11/19/national/crime-legal/diet-enacts-law-freeze-terrorist-assets-japan.

292 At: https://www.mlaw.gov.sg/news/parliamentary-speeches/second-reading-speech-by-senior-minister-of-state-for-law--indra5.

293 Global Forum on Transparency and Exchange of Information for Tax Purposes, Multilateral Co-operation Changing the World (10 Years Global Forum Report), 9.

294 At: https://www.un.org/securitycouncil/ctc/content/partnerships (last visited 15/05/2024).

Nonetheless, FATF's observership rules are official and publicly known, and reciprocity is a pre-condition to grant FATF's observer status, so it is reasonable to infer that FATF enjoys observer status in IOs, such as the OAS, OSCE, OCDE, IMF, WB or WCO.[295]

As noted, the growing recognition of FATF's role and level of participation in international affairs is echoed in its agenda, leading to some fundamental institutional changes, like the creation of the positions of Vice-President and Deputy Executive Secretariat and the two-year office term for FATF President and Vice-President.[296]

The three FATF's representatives (President and the Vice-president and the Executive Secretary) attend meetings and conferences with relevant international stakeholders, including with the private sector, such as the Wolfsberg Group or the International Banking Federation,[297] and provide statements and speeches.[298]

According to the 30 Years FATF Report, since 2017, the FATF President has had a seat at the highest-level meetings of organisations like the UN, IMF, WB, and the G-20 Finance Ministers and Central Bank Governors.[299]

6.3 *FATF's External Impact in Other IOs and International Institutions*

The normative and regulatory work developed by the FATF has had a substantial impact on other IOs and international institutions or bodies in the field of countering ML/FT/PF. Noteworthy, the use of the Forty Recommendations as a source of law for other international legal instruments.

6.3.1 The Council of Europe

The 2005 Warsaw Convention is a good illustration. Based on the existing international standards, particularly, the Forty Recommendations and the SR on FT (as revised in 2003), this Convention updates and complements the 1990 Convention on Laundering, Search, Seizure and Confiscation of the Proceeds from Crime.[300] The 2005 Warsaw Convention Explanatory Report states that:

295 The HR Special Rapporteur mentions that the FATF as observer status at the IMF, WB, OECD, UN (eg. UNIDC, Sanctions Committees), A/74/335, para. 31.

296 FATF Report to the G-20 Leaders' Osaka Summit 2019, para. 7.

297 2004–2005 FATF Report, para. 31.

298 Partnership and co-operation with the private sector and civil society is of key importance for the success of FATF's mission, as noted in Chapter 2, Section 9.

299 30 Years FATF Report, 78; 2020–2021 FATF Report, 26; 2022–2023 FATF Report, 8.

300 Strasbourg, 08/11/1990 (CETS 141). See the 2005 Warsaw Convention Explanatory Report, para. 10, 15 or 24. At: https://rm.coe.int/16800d3813. The EU Commission, MEMO/05/331, on the 'Nouvelle Convention du Conseil de l' Europe relative au Blanchiment, au

> As regards the prevention of money laundering and the financing of terrorism, the drafters of this Convention considered it necessary to ensure conformity of the provisions included in this instrument with those adopted by other international bodies. In that respect, they wished explicitly, in paragraph 1, to refer to the revised Recommendations of the FATF, which are integrated in the Council of Europe *acquis* through MONEYVAL.[301]
>
> In addition, some of these changes have already been or are currently being included in standards set by other international *fora* (EU, UN, FATF), which the new Convention cannot ignore. Rather, the text of the new Convention must be brought into line with these new developments to ensure mutual consistency with these standards and to make possible harmonised domestic responses in an appropriate legal format.[302]

Expectedly, numerous provisions are 'extracted' or 'drawn' up from the FATF Recommendations. This is the case of Article 3(2) on confiscation measures which sets a list of categories of offences in the Appendix "identical to the one contained in the glossary to the revised FATF Recommendations",[303] or Article 9 on the laundering offence that takes into account FATF Recommendation 1 by providing that "each country should at a minimum include a range of offences within each of the designated categories of offences"[304] or that "procedure against money laundering may be started even if the predicate offence has been committed abroad".[305]

Article 13(1) on measures to prevent money laundering makes a specific reference to FATF:

> Each Party shall adopt such legislative and other measures as may be necessary to institute a comprehensive domestic regulatory and supervisory

Dépistage, à la Saisie et à la Confiscation des Produits du Crime et au Financement du Terrorisme' (No. 198), 21/09/2005 states: "The new Convention takes into account the other international instruments in this area, in particular the recommendations of the FATF", 2.

301 Explanatory Report, ibid. para. 117.

302 Ibid, para. 21. Also, para. 15: "the Committee shall draw up an additional protocol to Convention ETS No. 141, in order to update and complement it as necessary".

303 Ibid, para. 68. It is mentioned that the "categories of offences contained in the Appendix of the Convention reproduce textually the glossary appended to the FATF Recommendations", para. 99.

304 Ibid.

305 Ibid, para. 107 and the report in relation to the FIU provisions and functions.

> or monitoring regime to prevent money laundering and shall take due account of applicable international standards, including in particular the recommendations adopted by the Financial Action Task Force on Money Laundering (FATF).[306]

Part of the *corpus* of the provision is based on FATF's Recommendations like paragraphs 2 and 3 as regards CDD measures or BO,[307] or the meaning of "legal and natural persons which engage in activities which are particularly likely to be used for money laundering purposes"[308] or the expression "subject to safeguards" resulting from professional secrecy or legal professional privilege.[309]

Article 48 of the Convention that sets a monitoring mechanism also makes a specific reference to FATF clarifying that it will not cover areas which are already covered by other "existing monitoring systems (such as MONEYVAL or FATF)" to avoid overlapping but it "will at the same time take advantage of them", in particular their MER, public summaries and other reports.[310]

Article 54 together with Article 13 establishes a "simplified amendment procedure" to update the Appendix that contains "a list of categories of offences to which reference is made to in Articles 3.2, 9.4 and 17.5, and which is textually taken from the Glossary to the FATF Recommendations", and follows the evolution of international law and standards.[311]

6.3.2 The European Union

The Forty Recommendations are also a source of inspiration or even a legislative driving-force within the EU legislative framework. Concepts, terminology and language from the Recommendations, INotes and benchmarks from the methodology may be found in several EU legal instruments. This circumstance has been a gradual trend throughout the years where an effort to adopt a common and uniform language is envisioned within the EU.[312]

---

306 Ibid, para. 117.

307 Ibid, para 118 (eg. KYC and CDD, identification of the ultimate BO, mandatory STR, record keeping, training and internal audit, AML monitoring, detection of cash couriers).

308 FATF Recommendations 5 and 12. Ibid, para.119.

309 FATF Recommendation 16. Ibid, para. 120.

310 Ibid, para. 297–298.

311 Ibid, para. 309–310. This Appendix was already amended pursuant to Ministers' Decision adopted on 22/10/2014, at: https://rm.coe.int/1680482daf. List of precedent crimes (same as FATF's list), at: https://rm.coe.int/CoERMPublicCommonSearchServices/DisplayDCTMContent?documentId=0900001680482daf.

312 Preamble, para. 7 of EU Regulation 2015/847 on Information Accompanying Transfers of Funds: "In the Union's revised strategy on terrorist financing of 17 July 2008 (the 'Revised strategy'), it was pointed out that efforts must be maintained to prevent terrorist

The EU accounts five Directives on the Prevention of the Use of the Financial System for the Purpose of Money Laundering and Terrorist Financing together with other related legislation.[313] The Directive 91/308/EEC was the first Directive targeting money laundering related to drugs offences and imposing obligations on the financial sector. Although making a minor reference in the Preamble part to FATF's Recommendations, the Directive's *ratio* and the influence of the 1990 Forty Recommendation are patent all over the text. In paragraph 12 of the Preamble, it is stated:

> Whereas any measures adopted by the Community in this field should be consistent with other action undertaken in other international fora; whereas in this respect any Community action should take particular account of the recommendations adopted by the Financial Action Task Force on money laundering, set up in July 1989 by the Paris summit of the seven most developed countries.

The 2nd AML Directive 2001/97/EC amends Directive 91/308/EEC by extending its scope in terms of offences and covering a wider range of professions and activities in accordance with the 1996 Forty Recommendations.[314] This intention is clearly expressed in the Preamble part of the Directive (and mirrored in the amendments):

> There has been a trend in recent years towards a much wider definition of money laundering based on a broader range of predicate or underlying offences, as reflected for example in the 1996 revision of the 40

financing and to control the use by suspected terrorists of their own financial resources. It is recognised that FATF is constantly seeking to improve its Recommendations and is working towards a common understanding of how they should be implemented".

313 Eg. EU Directive 2019/1153 Laying Down Rules Facilitating the Use of Financial and Other Information for the Prevention, Detection, Investigation or Prosecution of Certain Criminal Offences or Commission Directive 2006/70/EC as regards the definition of PEPS and technical criteria for SCDD, and exemption grounds, although not making specific reference to FATF standards, it is possible to identify FATF's standards, language and benchmarks.

314 Eg. Extends the CDD obligations and STR to DFNBPS, including to the legal profession (FATF's typologies on ML techniques are referred), to *bureaux de change*, money transmitters, and investment firms' activities. Preamble, para. 8: "A wider range of predicate offences facilitates suspicious transaction reporting and international cooperation in this area. Therefore, the Directive should be brought up to date in this respect". Also, 2001–202 FATF Report, para. 60.

> Recommendations of the Financial Action Task Force (FATF), the leading international body devoted to the fight against money laundering.[315]

The 3rd AML Directive 2005/60/EC is even more straightforward as regards its source of inspiration. Paragraph 5 of the Preamble clearly explains that:

> The measures adopted by the Community in this field should therefore be consistent with other action undertaken in other international fora. The Community action should continue to take particular account of the Recommendations of the Financial Action Task Force (...) Since the FATF Recommendations were substantially revised and expanded in 2003, this Directive should be in line with that new international standard.

This Directive aligns with the 2003 Forty Recommendations and Nine SRS, which incorporate the fight against FT. It was later replaced by the 4th AML EU Directive 2015/849, where substantial changes pursuant to the 2012 FATF Recommendations were introduced.[316] According to paragraph 4 of the Preamble:

> The measures adopted by the Union in that field should therefore be compatible with, and at least as stringent as, other actions undertaken in international fora. Union action should continue to take particular account of the FATF Recommendations (...) the relevant Union legal acts should, where appropriate, be aligned with the International Standards on Combating Money Laundering and the Financing of Terrorism and Proliferation adopted by the FATF in February 2012 (the 'revised FATF Recommendations').[317]

315 Preamble, para. 7. Also, Preamble, para. 3 of EU Directive 2015/849: "In June 2003, the Financial Action Task Force (FATF) revised its Recommendations to cover terrorist financing and provided more detailed requirements in relation to customer identification and verification, the situations where a higher risk of money laundering or terrorist financing may justify enhanced measures and also the situations where a reduced risk may justify less rigorous controls. Those changes were reflected in Directive 2005/60/EC of the European Parliament and of the Council and in Commission Directive 2006/70/EC".

316 Eg. Introduction of tax crimes (Articles 3 and 57), requirements related to PEPS (Articles 3, 20–23), sharing of information (Article 51) or RBA (Articles 4, 18 or 30).

317 4th AML EU Directive 2015/849.

The above Directive was amended by the 5th AML EU Directive 2018/843 following the developments and improvements of FATF's Recommendations. Indeed, it reinforces transparency requirements by providing wider access to information on BO of legal persons, trusts and similar legal arrangements,[318] and establishing central registries or central data systems, by requiring CDD and control measures to providers engaged in exchange services between virtual currencies and fiat currencies and custodian wallet providers.[319] It also widens the powers of the FIUs and access to information.[320]

In the context of strengthening the AML/CFT framework of the EU and the influence of FATF's Recommendations, EU Regulation 1889/2005 on Controls of Cash Entering or Leaving the Community should be underlined, by adopting norms consistent with SR IX (Cash couriers) requiring jurisdictions "to take measures to detect physical cash movements, including a declaration system or other disclosure obligation".[321] This Regulation was replaced by EU Regulation 2018/1672 on Controls of Cash Entering or Leaving the Union that also endeavours to comply with FATF standards and in particular with Recommendation 32.[322]

Similarly, EC Regulation 1781/2006 on Information on the Payer Accompanying Transfers of Funds aiming at implementing SR VII on wire transfers and respective INote.[323] This Regulation was repealed by EU Regulation 2015/847 on Information Accompanying Transfers of Funds, which ensures a higher degree of transparency in the transfer of funds, *inter alia*, by carrying out a RBA, reinforcing information on the payer and the payee, facilitating tracking down of fund transfers on cross-border transactions.[324] The Regulation aims at implementing FATF Recommendation 16 on 'Wire Transfers' and the revised INote.[325]

318 Preamble, para. 4 and 28, and Article 30(4) or Article 32(a).

319 Preamble, para. 8 and 9, and Articles 2(1), 3 or 47(1).

320 Preamble, para. 16–18, and Articles 30(6) or 32(9).

321 Preamble, para 4. The language adopted in the Regulation reflects the language of FATF's Recommendations. See, Preamble, para. 5 of EU Regulation 2015/847.

322 Preamble, para. 6: "The Union is represented in the FATF by the Commission and has committed itself to the effective implementation of the FATF's recommendations". Also, para. 8 and 38.

323 Preamble, para. 2: "[EU] should ensure that Special Recommendation VII on wire transfers (SR VII) of the Financial Action Task Force established by the Paris G-7 Summit of 1989 is transposed uniformly throughout the European Union". Also, para. 3, 5 and 17.

324 Preamble, para. 2, 3, 4, 7 and 23.

325 Preamble, para. 5: "The implementation and enforcement of this Regulation, including FATF Recommendation 16, represent relevant and effective means of preventing and combating money-laundering and terrorist financing". Similarly, EU Directive 2015/849, Preamble, para. 4: "The measures adopted by the Union in that field should therefore be

6.3.3 The UNSC and Other International Institutions

The role of the Forty Recommendations as a source of inspiration for the Resolutions of the UNSC has been addressed in Section 4 above, and the co-operation work with its bodies is discussed in Chapter 2, Section 9 above.

The recognition of the FATF as global standard-setter and of the functions performed by the Global Network preventing and countering FT and PF;[326] the endorsement of the "comprehensive international standards set forth in the FATF" together with the Palermo Convention and the Convention for the Suppression of the Financing of Terrorism;[327] the acknowledgement of the value of the FATF and FSRBS' MERS for the "purposes of designing targeted technical assistance and capacity-building efforts" to assist jurisdictions in need to fully fulfil their international obligations to prevent and counter FT/PF;[328] and the role of the FATF as an expert consultation partner for the bodies of the UNSC[329] are sound pointers of FATF's extensive influence and credibility within the UNSC's anti-terrorism framework, as well as sound pointers of FATF's legitimacy and credibility conferred by the UNSC.

The incorporation of FATF's Recommendations and other documents into the framework of other international institutions or bodies can also be demonstrated, for instance in the operative modules of the IMF[330] and WB,[331] or in the AML/CFT Guidelines[332] and in the Revised Core

---

compatible with, and at least as stringent as, other actions undertaken in international for a (…) [The EU] should continue to take particular account of the FATF Recommendations (…) [EU] legal acts should, where appropriate, be aligned with the International Standards on Combating Money Laundering and the Financing of Terrorism and Proliferation adopted by the FATF in February 2012". The need to adjust and co-ordinate EU's action/measures in accordance with FATF's efforts to implement global AML/CFT policies is highly emphasised.

326 UNSCR 2610 (2021), Preamble, para. 33.

327 UNSCR 2482 (2019), op.para. 3.

328 UNSCR 2462 (2019), op.para. 33 and 35.

329 UNSCR 2610 (2021), op.para. 102.

330 At: http://www.imf.org/external/pp/longres.aspx?id=4684 or https://www.imf.org/en/Publications/Policy-Papers/Issues/2016/12/31/Guidance-Note-for-Staff-on-Undertaking-Targeted-Risk-Based-Reports-on-the-Observance-of-PP4684. See specific guidance on targeted or risk-based ROSCS, 2000–2001 FATF Report, para. 36; 2001–2002 FATF Report, para. 53; 2002–2003 FATF Report, para. 38.

331 2000–2001 FATF Report, para 36; 2001–2002 FATF Report, para 53; 2002–2003 FATF Report, para. 98.

332 The Guidelines on 'Sound Management of the Risks related to Money Laundering and Financing of Terrorism' to the Banking Sector have been revised in July 2020 to include guidance on cooperation and information exchange between prudential and AML/CFT supervisors. Reference is made to FATF standards and benchmarks all over the document.

Principles[333] of the Basel Committee. As affirmed in the Basel Guidelines:

> In March 2013, the FATF also issued Financial Inclusion Guidance, which has also been considered by the Committee in drafting these guidelines. The Committee's intention in issuing this paper is to support national implementation of the FATF standards by exploring complementary areas and leveraging the expertise of both organisations. These guidelines embody both the FATF standards and the Basel Core Principles for banks operating across borders and fits into the overall framework of banking supervision. Therefore, these guidelines are intended to be consistent with and to supplement the goals and objectives of the FATF standards, and in no way should they be interpreted as modifying the FATF standards, either by strengthening or weakening them.[334]

Another example is the Global Forum that introduces Recommendations of the FATF related to BO and respective INotes (eg. Recommendations 10 (CDD), 22 (DNFBPS:CDD), 24 and 25) into its international tax standards as parts of the requirements. As referred in the 10 Year Report of the Global Forum:

> The incorporation into the Global Forum's standard of the requirement to ensure the availability of beneficial ownership information for all legal entities and arrangements has important synergies with the work of the FATF, which makes recommendations on measures geared to anti-money laundering and combatting the financing of terrorism. The FATF definition has been adopted in both the EOIR and AEOI standards.[335]

In the version of June 2017, the Basel Committee endorses the national implementation of the FATF standards "by exploring complementary areas and leveraging the expertise of both organisations." and some "cross-references to FATF standards" are included in the document to assist banks in complying with national requirements based on the implementation of those standards, respectively para. 3 and 4. At: https://www.mas.gov.sg/-/media/MAS/Regulations-and-Financial-Stability/BCBS-Guidelines-for-AMLCFT-June-2017.pdf. These ideas are reiterated in the 2020 revision.

333 Revised 'Core Principles for Effective Banking Supervision' (September 2012), banks should be required to "have adequate policies and processes, including strict customer due diligence (CDD) rules to promote high ethical and professional standards in the banking sector and prevent the bank from being used, intentionally or unintentionally, for criminal activities", and ensure sound banking supervision and reporting of suspicious transactions. An RBA is also recommended, and guidance is provided. Language and specific reference are also made to FATF (eg. Principle 29 on the Abuse of Financial Services).

334 Para 3.

335 At: 17. It also mentions that "[i]n 2015, in response to the call of the G-20 Leaders who invited the Global Forum to draw on the work of the Financial Action Task Force (FATF)

Likewise, the FATF has been a model and a source of inspiration at institutional, policy and *modus operandi* levels for other IOs, institutions or regimes; this topic is addressed in Chapter 5 below.

In conclusion, evidence suggests that the FATF generally meets the external recognition criterion, being perceived as an IO on the international plane.

7 The Relevance of the Will of the Members

Paragraph 48 of the 2019 Mandate, under Section IV, entitled 'Legal Effect of the Mandate; Accountability', expressly states that: "This Mandate is not intended to create any legal rights or obligations".

From this wording, it may be interpreted either that members do not intend to confer any rights or obligations to the organisation (ie. it is not an international legal person and, consequently, deprived of legal personality) or that FATF's actions are not aimed at imposing rights or obligations upon its members, or both.

This book questions whether the intention (will) of the members is determinative of FATF's legal personhood, despite its informal nature (Section 3 above). It is argued that the evolutionary character and *modus operandi* of the organisation, including its external dimension, on the international plane, carry more weight when ascertaining the legal standing of FATF.

The fact is that the FATF has progressively evolved – mandate, institutional framework and functions – and incorporated a number of features that are commonly attributed to formal IOs, including the exercise of public authority functions.

Doctrinal works and the ICJ Opinion in *Reparation of Injuries* have addressed the theme of the constitutive source of the acquisition of legal personality of IOs. As described in Chapter 3, the subjective or will of the founders' theory is not the prevailing and, if applied, the FATF would never be qualified as an IO.[336]

Scholars, such as Seyersted, argue that an IO's "international legal personality flows" from the simple fact that it exists in the legal system, based on

with respect to beneficial ownership, the Global Forum agreed to enhance its EOIR standard by including a new requirement on the availability of beneficial ownership information. This measure helped to further limit the risk of letterbox companies being misused to conceal financial flows", 8–9.

336 This theory has been associated with the legalist approach theory or the realism school of thought. It is not compatible with the current features of the international legal system.

objective criteria, rather than from the members' intention, and that it is international law itself that bestows rights and obligations to the organisation.[337]

Along these lines, Odello, citing Brownlie in relation to the absence of some features in the GATT, but still considered (by the latter) as vested with legal personality, concludes that "international subjects are to be defined by the international legal system, on the basis of criteria that do not necessarily depend on the will of the States that create each institution".[338]

Klabbers underlines that "it is not up to the drafters to decide on legal personality: that is rather something to be decided by the legal system concerned".[339] By the same token, Jones asserts that "the concept of personality indicates that it ought logically to derive through operation of the rules of the relevant legal system, rather than being bestowed by particular actors".[340]

The subjective theory was also rejected in the ICJ Opinion in *Reparation of Injuries*. The Court emphasised that the intention of the members must be analysed from an objective perspective, ie. if members created an organisation to perform certain functions (*factual existence*) and if granted *specific objective* characteristics (capacities) to the organisation to properly operate and exercise its functions (functionalist test) at international level, then the existence and operation of such an organisation can only be explained if entrusted with legal personality.[341]

In other words, in the dynamics of the international system, members' (subjective) intention to create (or not) an organisation with rights and obligations

337 (n 7) 51.

338 (n 9) 360–361.

339 'Institutional Ambivalence by Design: Soft Organizations in International Law' (2001) 70(3) *Nordic Journal of International Law*, 415. Jones states that references to the intention of the founding States "do not suggest that such intention is constitutive of personality", 'Legal Personality and the Responsibility of International Organisations' (Dissertation for LLB (Hons), University of Otago, October 2013), at: https://www.otago.ac.nz/law/research/journals/otago065260.pdf, 18.

340 Ibid, 37.

341 ICJ Reports 1949, 178–179. If the ICJ adopted the subjective personality theory, the Court would not be able to have recognised the UN's ability to claim damages because there must be an express norm in the UN Charter attributing legal personality to the organisation. The absence of such a norm means that the members did not intend to grant legal personality to the UN. According to this theory, the EU would not have legal personality between its constitution in 1992 (Maastricht Treaty) and 2007 (Treaty of Lisbon), due to the absence of a specific norm that confers legal personality to the organisation. As Amerasinghe elucidated, "[i]t is not some subjective intention of the minds of the founders but an objective that was to be found in the circumstances of creation and constitution of the UN", 'International Legal Personality Revisited' (1995), republished in F. Johns (ed), *International Legal Personality* (Routledge 2010), 243–246.

under international law becomes somehow secondary or even irrelevant, considering the *objective intention of the members* (the creation of the IO) and the *empirical existence* of the organisation. The fact that it operates and possesses a considerable number of characteristics recognised by the international legal system as attributable to an IO is another central element to bear in mind.[342] Therefore, the intention of the members in granting certain functions and capacities for the organisation to fulfil its mission must be understood from an objective and pragmatic point of view.

While affirming that the FATF has no legal standing on the international plane, members have developed an organisation with authoritative decision-making that sets international standards and operational procedures across jurisdictions in a vertical structure of integrated networks.

In this respect, Klabbers, when addressing both the OSCE and FATF's legal nature, concludes that:

> [W]hile the FATF is a strange creature set up by the G-7 and located within and administered by the OECD, it too functions much like a regular organisation (...) the FATF seems fairly formalised: it has a Secretariat, it meets at regular intervals, there are procedures to provide for the presidency and vice-presidency, et cetera.[343]

Aligning with the idea that the FATF may be an IO, Borlini and Montanaro write:

> [T]he FATF bears many of the 'typical' characteristics of international organisations. First, it has its own recourses and a permanent structure in order to ensure effective and continuous activity. Second, it monitors the implementation of its Recommendations in member's domestic legal systems. Third, its officials enjoy the same immunities and privileges of OECD's officials. In light of these above, it is possible to argue that at least

342 As Jones refers the "highest source of authority" lies in the international realm (n 339) 25.

343 At the time the FATF was a temporary organisation, as Klabbers commented: "The most curious aspect of its existence is perhaps that is lifespan is not unlimited: it operates on mandates that are valid for a number of years. This may be seen as a sign of deformalisation (if no longer deemed desirable, it can easily be disbanded), but that only strengthens the general point that all institutional structures will combine elements of the formal and informal", 'Formal Intergovernmental Organizations' in J.K. Cogan, I. Hurd and I. Johnstone (eds), *Oxford Handbook of International Organizations* (Oxford University Press 2016), 137.

> some of the rules of international law applicable to international organisations (eg. rules of immunity) could be applied to FATF.[344]

Nonetheless, the fact is that in the 2019 Mandate, Ministers had the opportunity to clarify FATF's legal position on the international plane, including a change of its current name and format, but decided "to work together in the form of a task force"[345] and confirmed that there is no intention of legally bind its members.[346]

Yet, as Akande explains, it is not the format or the name that determines the nature of an organisation; what is materially relevant is its *acquis institutionel*:

> In considering, whether or not a body or institutional structure qualifies as an international organisation, one must consider the substance of the structure established by States rather than whether it is formally designated as an international organisation. The key is whether the above criteria are fulfilled rather the designation of the organisation.[347]

In dispute is the fact that the FATF and its members have been giving conflicting and ambivalent signals that challenge or even refute the quoted paragraph 48, such as:

- In the 30 Years FAFT Report, the FAFT states that it is an IO;[348]
- In the 2019 Ministerial Declaration, Ministers expressly affirm that the FATF will hold its members and jurisdictions from the Global Network accountable in event of failing to implement the FATF Standards;[349]
- In the HLPOs it is mentioned that the FATF is a standard-setter, guardian and arbiter of the international financial system;[350]
- In its 2018–2019 Report, FATF states that: "countries need to transpose the new binding requirements into their national legal, regulatory and operational framework";[351]

344 (n 185) 1024–1026.

345 2019 Mandate, para. 5. Also, 2012–2020 Mandate (para. 5); 2008–2012 Mandate (para. 8); 2004–2008 Mandate (para. 16).

346 Ibid. para. 48. It should be noted that this declaration only appears in the 2019 and 2012–2020 Mandates (para. 48). The 2008–2012 Mandate only mentions accountability (para. 26).

347 (n 11) 254–255.

348 At: 83–84.

349 Para. 4 and 14.

350 At: 13.

351 At: 22. The FATF refers in its 2019–2020 Report that it "finalised binding international standards for virtual assets and virtual asset service providers (VASPs)", 13.

- The FATF proclaims that its role is to give practical effect to the relevant UN Conventions and Security Council Resolutions;[352]
- The FATF calls on a regular basis its members and non-FATF members (global network) to apply enhance due diligence or countermeasures based on 'Grey' and 'Black' Lists.

This ambiguity is also reinforced by other factors. In this regard, a few key moments should be highlighted:

- The 2003/2004 formal partnership with the IMF/WB;
- Resolution 1617 (2005) of the UNSC endorsing for the first time FATF's Recommendations and the work of the FATF;
- The 2012 Revised Recommendations setting a new universal paradigm to counter ML/FT and PF;
- The HLPOs that formally institutionalised the relationship between the FATF and its FSRBs;
- The formal setting of the Global Network;
- The transformation of the FATF into a permanent organisation;
- Resolution 2462 (2019) of the UNSC endowing the FATF, its standards and FSRBs with a new level of legitimisation; and
- The suspension of a member for violating core principles of the organisation.

Considering the above and after 30 Years of FATF's existence, it is fair to question: what kind of organisation members have built in terms of international institutional law? Can the FATF be described as an organisation that results from a plain coalition of wills, a shared expectation? Can its constitutional body be considered a 'gentlemen's agreement' or a joint collective act of mere political nature?[353] Can its decisions and actions be classified, as Golia Jr and Peters define, simple "collective decisions with public relevance at global level"?[354] When the FATF demands that both members and non-members to take collective actions, such as adopting countermeasures, are these requests just political declarations of a shared expectation? Is the behaviour of jurisdictions drifted by pure voluntary commitment or, differently, does it bear a sense of legal obligation? Ultimately, what is the genuine intention of the members when drafting paragraph 48 of the 2019 Mandate, and what is the meaning and scope of that paragraph today, when compared to the behaviour of the organisation, members and non-members, whether from a political, legal or practical perspective?

352 30 Years FATF Report, 40.

353 Aust, *Modern Treaty Law and Practice* (3rd edn, Cambridge University Press 2013), 28.

354 (n 115) 47.

These doubts have been to some extent addressed by the ICJ Opinion in *Reparation of Injuries* in relation to the UN:

> The Charter has not been content to make the Organisation created by it merely a centre 'for harmonising the actions of nations in the attainment of common ends' (Article 1, para. 4). It has equipped that centre with organs, and has given it special tasks (...) It could not carry out the intentions of its founders if it was devoid of international personality. It must be acknowledged that its Members, by entrusting certain functions to it, with the attendant duties and responsibilities, have clothed it with the competence required to enable those functions to be effectively discharged.[355]

Now and then, it is difficult to draw a line between moral, political and legal obligations, especially when facing a gradual institutional evolution of an organisation where the level of commitment rises *in tandem* with compliance requirements and supervision mechanisms.

The expansion of FATF's powers may be understood as a manifestation of Guzman's 'Frankenstein' syndrome, where the organisation acts beyond the powers conferred by its members and against the interests established by the members, 'the creature' turning against its creator.[356] However, this does not seem to be the case with the FATF.

Members have intentionally conferred and developed policy and lawmaking powers, monitoring and sanctioning powers, and public functions, as well as funded FATF activities from national budgets, exercised ministerial oversight, and provided clear and undeniable political and institutional support.

Furthermore, the FATF has been bestowed with two capabilities: the ME process and blacklisting, which can be understood as a transference of powers from members to the organisation. Although intrusive into their domestic affairs and with an impact, even interference, on their national policies, members have accepted the FATF's monitoring and enforcement processes, which include assessment ratings, recommendations, action plans and red flag statements.

It is therefore believed that there is sufficient material evidence that FATF members, non-FATF members, other IOs and international actors have adopted a consistent and systematic behaviour towards FATF's Recommendations,

355 ICJ Reports 1949, 178–179.

356 'International Organizations and the Frankenstein Problem' (2013) 24(4) *European Journal of International Law*, 999–1000.

action plans and calls for countermeasures as if dealing with a full-fledged IO. In practice, this objective behaviour contradicts whatever the implication contained in paragraph 48.

8 Summary

The FATF is an international legal person that bears rights and duties under international law. Based on the five essential elements to assert the legal personhood of the FATF, it is considered that the FATF meets them all and that it may be qualified as an IO:

i) Membership: it has been proven that its members are States, regional IOs and other entities (jurisdiction) with recognised status under international law;
ii) Created under international law: it has been proven that it is created by acts of international law, such as Declarations, and other international collective acts of a constitutive nature;
iii) To have an organ with a distinct will: it has been proven that it has a separate and independent institutional setting, which assures the distinct and autonomous will of the organisation *vis-à-vis* its members. It is a permanent organisation with an autonomous institutional framework with organs that have decision-making capacity and act on behalf of the organisation, including a Secretariat with administrative apparatus and independent financial resources (financial autonomy) and headquarters arrangements. It exercises its functions and powers pursuant to the interests of the organisation and in a distinct manner from its members;
iv) To operate on the international plane according to international law: it has been proven that it is entrusted with a number of legal capacities, developed either explicitly or implicitly, expressing an autonomous will and independent standing from its members on the international plane. Its capacities are broad and far-reaching (AML/CFT/CPF global standard-setter, keeper, and arbiter). The impact of FATF's Recommendations, ME process and backlisting across the world is undeniable, including the possible emergence of customary international law through a body of practice and the general acquiescence of members and non-members;

v) External recognition by other subjects of international law: it has been proven that FATF interacts with other international stakeholders on the international plane, and that its role has been endorsed and legitimised by relevant IOs and other international bodies; the Resolutions of the UNSC under Chapter VII of the UN Charter also favour an implicit (if not explicit) perception that the FATF is a full-fledged IO.

CHAPTER 5

Relevance and Challenges

In this Chapter, it is discussed how the study of the FATF may be of relevance for public international law, in particular to international institutional law, if the FATF is considered a new *species* of IOs. The implications FATF faces as an international legal person and the challenges it encounters in carrying out its public functions are also addressed.[1]

1 Why Does the FATF Case Matter? Why Is It Relevant to International Institutional Law and Public International Law?

In the preceding Chapter, the legal personhood of the FATF is tested based on the criteria outlined in Chapter 3 as essential for classifying an organisation whenever such organisation does not possess the traditional and irrefutable criteria of being treaty-based, created by States, and having an organ of its own with a distinct will (*volunté distincte*).[2]

The case-study of the FATF is framed in previous legal theoretical work, international legal sources, and in the dynamics of the international legal system, which is itself the main driving force (source) of the evolutionary character of the FATF.

A coherent, structured and comprehensive reasoning of five interconnected elements is applied to determine whether the FATF is an IO. The research also provides a myriad of factors and indicators in different spheres, addressing the

1 A. von Bogdandy and M. Goldman define the 'exercise of international public authority' as "any kind of governance activity by international institutions, be it administrative or intergovernmental" that interferes in the lives of individuals, private associations, enterprises, States, or other public institutions. 'Authority' is described as the legal capacity to determine others and to reduce their freedom, ie. to unilaterally shape their legal or factual situation, either through binding or non-binding instruments. 'The Exercise of International Public Authority through National Policy Assessment' (2008) 5 *International Organizations Law Review*, 259, 261–264.

2 As Di Stasi argues "[i]t is indisputable that the theoretical models of IOs, based on their formal attributes rather than on the way in which they function, find it hard to take into consideration the increased differentiation in types of IOs together with the growing complexity of institutional regimes", 'About Soft International Organizations: An Open Question' in R. Virzo and I. Inagravallo (eds), *Evolutions in the Law of International Organizations* (Brill/Nijhoff 2015), 48.

 DOI:10.1163/9789004715134_006

five elements and establishing the cornerstone criterion: the *volunté distincte* (autonomy) of the FATF.

The FATF may be a sound example of how the original nature of an organisation may evolve into a full-fledged IO, beyond the initial intention of members and its informal framework, due to the gradual evolution of its mandate, institutional framework, and functions, including global governance, along with a body of practice within the organisation and a body of practice between itself and other international actors in the international domain.

How might the findings of this case-study be relevant in public international law and, in particular, international institutional law?

They are relevant in the sense that the FATF may be an example of a new *species* of IOs, of organisations that bring together all the objective elements necessary to be considered subjects of international law, ie. with international legal personality and capacity, especially when entrusted with public functions (*vel non*).

These organisations, like treaty-based IOs, are also a creation resulting from the dynamics and changing needs of the international community; however their position in the international legal system remains ambiguous, in a kind of legal *vacuum* if not scrutinised. As Angela Di Stasi comments, there is a wide spectrum of institutional designs "characterising the constellation of soft IOs" that "in some cases makes their inclusion in the category of hard or soft IOs uncertain".[3]

A clear-cut understanding of the legal status of the FATF on the international plane, by determining the criteria that confer and characterise such standing (and how they are articulated), may enable us to identify other organisations that share analogous features and provide some clarity and legal certainty as to the international legal system's architecture of the twenty-first century.

Another step in the right direction is to recognise that there is no categorical or authoritative definition of what is an IO and that the traditional and common elements that characterise an IO, ie. understood as the requisites for an organisation to be considered an international legal person, have often been contested as in the case of IPU, OSCE or EU, as mentioned in Chapter 3 above. It is therefore necessary to devise a pragmatic and contemporary conceptual approach that does not ignore the objective reality of today's international institutions

As Klein and Sands comment:

3 Ibid, 18.

> [T]he threat of international terrorism, weapons of mass destruction, the war in Iraq, global warning and trade disputes amongst other developments have underscored the limits on the role and functions of international organisations (…) We will have to make do with what we have, adapted to deal with new realities. Evolution, not revolution.[4]

Considering the diversified nature and design patterns of IOs, as well as the potential emergence of new forms or models, it may be argued that we are beholding the birth of a new generation that *stretches the definition of IOs*, as mentioned by Ayelet Berman and Wessel.[5]

This empirical analysis and conceptual approach contributes to the ongoing debate on the main elements that qualify an IO, stressing the risk of categorisation, overlooking or neglecting relevant objective and empirical elements offered by the international legal system, such as *how* the institutional framework of the organisation has evolved, *what* are the real and effective powers of that organisation, *how* the organisation operates in practice on the international plane, *how* the organisation is perceived by other international actors, and *whether* its members and peers have tacitly or expressly recognised its status as an IO.

This fact-finding and considerations are all the more significant when the FATF is most likely inspiring and shaping other organisations. In this context, the FATF can be understood as a contemporary or *avant-garde* IO model, and if it serves as an exemplary model for a new generation of IOs, it is important to examine any shortcomings and suggestions for improvement.

We may be witnessing a new global trend in international institutional law where the founding of IOs and their constitutional instruments are less formal and more dynamic in nature. Where organisations have a higher degree of flexibility and adopt pragmatic approaches to international community concerns, but are still part of the international legal system, bound by principles of international law and no less accountable.[6] This reality should not be neglected,

4 '(Re)Writing on the Law of International Organizations: Options and Challenges' (2008) 5 *International Organizations Law Review*, 222.

5 'The International Legal Form and Status of Informal International Lawmaking Bodies: Consequences for Accountability', in J. Pauwelyn, R. Wessel and J. Wouters (eds), *Informal International Lawmaking* (Oxford University Press 2012).

6 As Shams comments: "while the Financial Action Task Force operated globally as a supranational organ with substantial sanctioning powers that stems from the dominance of its members in global financial market, it continued to operate internally on a basis of strict commitment to unanimity. This dual nature of FATF is becoming a typical example of the emerging structures of global governance. Innovations in international law are essential

requiring an in-depth analysis and an unequivocal understanding of their legal status.

1.1 *The FATF as an Institutional Model*

1.1.1 The Asia-Pacific Group on Money Laundering

Of all existing FSRBS, the APG is the only regional body that has faithfully reproduced the FATF's original institutional model. One probable reason may be the fact that the APG is one of the oldest "and more established FSRBS", as commented by the FATF President at the APG Annual Meeting in July 2011.[7]

According to the APG 2019 Terms of Reference (as amended), the nature and purpose of the regional group is as follows:

> The APG is an autonomous, pro-active inter-governmental organisation contributing to the reduction of serious crime in the Asia/Pacific Region and is established by agreement among its members. It does not derive from an international treaty and it is not part of any international organisation.[8]

In the refereed document, the technical nature and non-political inter-governmental organisation character are highlighted.[9] Its website states vaguely that the APG "was officially established as an autonomous regional anti-money laundering body".[10]

The APG was established in 1997, 'importing' the FATF's original model and design:

i) An informal organisation created through a political declaration of States (founding members)[11] and a constitutional body formed of diverse legal instruments;

---

to fill gaps in governance that are created by new realities. These innovations, however, should continue to be subject to scrutiny and responsive criticism", 'Club Multilateralism and Global Supranationalism: The Case of FATF' in J.B. Attanasio and J.J. Norton (eds), *Multilateralism v Unilateralism: Policy Choices in a Global Society* (British Institute of International and Comparative Law and SMU Dedman School of Law 2005), 482.

7 At: 11.

8 Section 3.1, last amended in July 2023 (last visited 15/05/2024).

9 Section 1.

10 Before it was stated the "APG is a regional multilateral organisation whose strategic mission is to counter ML/FT and PF in the Asia-Pacific Region" without defining 'regional multilateral organisation'. At: http://www.apgml.org/about-us/page.aspx?p=32a60063-49e9-4954-ac79-d306ddff5cac (last visited 15/05/2024).

11 Australia, Bangladesh, China, Hong Kong (China), Japan, New Zealand, Philippines Singapore, Sri Lanka, Chinese Taipei, Thailand, USA, Vanuatu.

ii) A fixed life-spam (5 and 8 years, successively renewed);
iii) A Plenary, a Governance Committee (previous Steering Group), and a Secretariat;
iv) Decision-making by consensus;
v) Periodic Ministerial-level meetings (high-level political body);
vi) Hosting arrangement with Australia;[12]
vii) Financing by established quotas from members and donations.

Since its inception, the APG Terms of Reference (Mandate) has been successively renewed in concordant with FATF's mandate and lifespan. The 2003–2004 APG Report portrays this situation when it refers to the letter from APG Co-Chairs to the relevant Ministers and Central Bank Governors to seek their agreement to extend APG's mandate until December 2012, namely to "mirror the FATF, whose mandate was recently extended until December 2012".[13]

Also in line with the previous, the APG 2011 Terms of Reference in which members agreed to: "Extend its mandate for a further eight years from 31 December 2012 to 31 December 2020 to coincide with the Financial Action Task Force's (FATF's) term".[14]

At the APG Annual Plenary meeting in August 2019, members decided to extend APG's mandate until 31 December 2028,[15] while acknowledging the change in FATF's status from a temporary to a permanent body (to become effective in 2020). The APG Co-chairs noted that not only the APG would oversee the functioning of the new format, but they also 'left the door open' for a similar review at the APG:

> One notable achievement at the 2019 annual meeting was the unanimous agreement among all members to extend the APG mandate beyond 2020 to December 2028 with an agreement to monitor the effect of the FATF's recent decision to move from a time-limited standard eight-year mandate term to unlimited mandate. Should the membership feel it necessary to re-visit our renewed mandate for this purpose, the membership may decide to do so.[16]

12 The APG's peculiarity of a co-chair presidency derives from the arrangement with the Australian Government who hosts the APG Secretariat Headquarters in Sydney and "provides administrative, IT, legal, finance, human resources and other essential services". See Section 5.2. of Terms of Reference.

13 2003–2004 APG Report, 15.

14 Section 2.7.

15 2018–2019 APG Report, 7; Section 2.11. of Terms of Reference.

16 Ibid, 4.

1.1.2 The Global Forum on Transparency and Exchange of Information for Tax Purposes

The Global Forum, which, like the FATF, is the organisation responsible for implementing and monitoring the application of high universal standards on global transparency and exchange of information, fostering global co-operation between tax authorities, and ensuring the security of the financial system and economies is another example of where the institutional and operational characteristics of the FATF can be fully observed.[17]

The Global Forum was established in 2000 with a limited partnership aiming at combating tax havens, including blacklisting jurisdictions that have stringent bank secrecy regimes.[18] In 2009, it was subject to a restructure under the umbrella of the OECD[19] and a call from the G-20 due to the 2007/2008 financial crisis and a number of financial scandals involving tax evasion, tax havens and offshore financial centres.[20] At the G-20 London Summit in 2009, G-20 Leaders agreed:

> [T]o take action against non-cooperative jurisdictions, including tax havens. We stand ready to deploy sanctions to protect our public finances and financial systems. The era of banking secrecy is over. We note that the OECD has today published a list of countries assessed by the Global Forum against the international standard for exchange of tax information.[21]

Following the Summit, the Global Forum reviewed its mandate by strengthening the standards on transparency and exchange of information for tax purposes and ensuring that they are swiftly and universally applied. Inspired by the FATF, it established a Secretariat and a thorough peer review and

17 At: *ww.oecd.org/tax/transparency/*. This organisation deals with tax evasion, tax havens, offshore financial centres, information exchange agreements, money laundering and tax co-operation. Membership expanded from 89 to 171 members, including all OECD and G-20 countries, all IFCs and a number of developing countries. At: http://www.oecd.org/tax/transparency/who-we-are/members (last visited 15/05/2024).

18 From 2000–2009, it comprised OECD countries and IFCs that committed to implement the international standard on tax transparency and exchange of information on request.

19 Council Decision C(2009)122/FINAL, 25/07/2009.

20 10 Years Global Forum Report, 7. Tax havens were divided in a 'blacklist' of countries not committed to the standard and a 'Grey List' of countries not yet substantially implemented the standard. See plans for the G-20 Pittsburgh Summit in 2009, at: http://www.g20.utoronto.ca/g20plans/g20leaders090818.pdf. Also, 'OECD Names and Shames Tax Havens' (03/04/2009) *BBC*, at: http://news.bbc.co.uk/2/hi/business/7980848.stm.

21 Para. 15.

monitoring mechanism "to all jurisdictions that share its values". This mandate was approved at the Global Forum Plenary meeting held in Mexico in 2019.[22]

Parallel to the FATF, the Global Forum is composed of a Plenary, Steering Group, Secretariat and WGs (a Peer Review Group for the Exchange of Information on Request, a Peer Review Group for the Automatic Exchange of Information and a Crypto-Asset Reporting Framework Group).

Equivalent to the FATF Secretariat, the Global Forum Secretariat is designated as "self-standing", although based in the OECD's Centre for Tax Policy and Administration. Its tasks and resources were also gradually broadened in line with the membership expansion. Presently, the Secretariat integrates more than 50 persons with differentiated backgrounds from finance, tax administration, legal and advisory firms and academia, representing approximately 40 nationalities.[23]

The Global Forum is the decision-making body that sets the priorities and work plans of the organisation, where each member has equal standing and decisions are made by consensus.

Analogous to FATF's original institutional design, the mandate of this organisation is successively renewed. The initial three-year term expired on 31 December 2012,[24] with a three-year term renewal until 31 December 2015,[25] and after, with a five-year period renewal until 31 December 2020 to complete the peer review process.[26] One of the outcomes of the Global Forum Plenary Meeting, on 17–19 November 2021, was the members' decision to expand the mandate for three more years, from 1 January 2023 to 31 December 2025.[27]

Comparable to the FATF, the Global Forum is entrusted with a major responsibility of ensuring worldwide compliance with the international standards through peer reviews and monitoring mechanisms, targeting members

22 A mechanisms of exchange information that may also allow "developing countries to benefit from the new more co-operative tax environment". Summary of Outcomes of the Meeting of the Global Forum on Transparency and Exchange of Information for Tax Purposes (01-02/09/2009).

23 At: https://www.oecd.org/tax/transparency/who-we-are/secretariat/ (last visited 15/05/2024).

24 Council Decision C(2009)122/FINAL.

25 Council Decision C(2012)148, 15/11/2012.

26 Council Decision C(2015)127, 29-30/10/2015.

27 At: https://www.oecd.org/tax/transparency/documents/2021-global-forum-Plenary-meeting-statement-of-outcomes.pdf. Also, the OECD (2023) 'Handbook for Peer Reviews on Transparency and Exchange of Information on Request: Second Round', Global Forum on Transparency and Exchange of Information for Tax Purposes, 6.

and non-members,[28] issuing ratings ('NC', 'PC', 'LC' and 'C') and recommendations,[29] and publishing its reports.[30] Technical assistance programmes and training to guarantee that the standards are implemented are also offered.[31]

Jurisdictions are assessed against the international standard on tax transparency and the international standard on exchange of information for tax purposes: i) Exchange of Information on Request (EOIR), where a tax authority can request information in the context of a tax investigation,[32] and ii) Automatic Exchange of Information (AEOI), where a pre-defined set of information on financial accounts held by non-residents is automatically exchanged.[33]

Like the FATF, the publication of the assessments and ratings bears a reputational impact and serious economic costs, as mentioned in the Global Forum webpage:

---

28 Teams of legal, operational and cybersecurity experts conducted peer reviews based on agreed Terms of Reference and methodology (assessment criteria) with the support of the Secretariat. Assessments rely on jurisdictions' input, exchange of information and on-site visits. A report with recommendations is drafted, discussed, and later submitted to the Global Forum for adoption. At: https://www.oecd-ilibrary.org/taxation/global-forum-on-transparency-and-exchange-of-information-for-tax-purposes-peer-reviews_2219469x.The OECD Handbook is very clear when it states that it "is intended to assist the assessment teams and assessed jurisdictions participating in the Global Forum's peer reviews and nonmember reviews, under the second round of reviews on transparency and exchange of information on request", ibid, 5.

29 At: https://www.oecd.org/tax/transparency/documents/exchange-of-information-on-request-ratings.htm. The last OECD information for blacklisting non-compliant jurisdictions dates back from 2009. There is reference to a publication of a 'Black List' of 35 tax havens in 2000. At: https://en.wikipedia.org/wiki/Global_Forum_on_Transparency_and_Exchange_of_Information_for_Tax_Purposes (acceded on 15/05/2024). Joel Slemrod and John D. Wilson, 'Tax Competition with Parasitic Tax Havens' (2009) 93 (11–12) *Journal of Public Economics*, 1261–1262.

30 10 Years Global Forum Report. See: https://www.oecd.org/tax/transparency/country-monitoring/.

31 The peer review process intends to be a fair process and aims at ensuring that the "standards are properly implemented and on the basis of a level playing field". Global Forum webpage – 'Monitoring the Implementation of the Standards', at: https://www.oecd.org/tax/transparency/what-we-do/.

32 The first peer review of the EOIR was conducted in 2010 focusing on technical compliance, *ie.* assessing the legal framework in place, the second peer review was executed in 2016, and include the legal framework in place as well as the implementation of the standard in practice (effectiveness).

33 The AEOI also followed the same practice (after 2017/2018). The last review also focused on whether jurisdictions are ensuring that financial institutions are reporting complete and accurate information to exchange.

> When combined with the publication of the results of the reviews, including the ratings, there is a reputational impact encouraging any recommendations to be addressed. Furthermore, the proper implementation of the standards provides international investors with comfort that the jurisdictions in which they are investing have a sound regulatory framework to ensure tax compliance, with some development banks making their investments conditional on positive outcomes from the Global Forum's peer review processes.[34]

1.1.3 FATF Cyber-Style Security Body Proposal

Another inspiration of the FATF model is the theoretical proposal of having a global cyber security organisation similar to FATF. A 'FATF Cyber-Style Security Body' that would be responsible for setting standards and guidance to combat cyber security risks and to ensure good governance practices.[35]

Kevin Newmeyer, proponent of this hypothesis, favours the characteristics of the FATF, emphasising its advantages as a model. The author points to the following as valuable aspects: the limited and selective membership of the FATF; "the development of subordinate regional organisations" (FSRBS);[36] the compliance mechanism;[37] the 'name and shame' policy (blacklisting);[38] the G-7 and G-20 endorsement and a general political commitment to FATF Standards;[39] and technical assistance, including donors. As Newmeyer explains:

> A new body, modelled on the successful Financial Action Task Force with a mandate to improve international cybersecurity, offers an alternative to the current chaos. The body should be chartered by the G-20 and include representation from the private sector and pertinent international bodies. The key to success will be the political will of the membership (...)

34 Global Forum webpage – 'Issuing Compliance Ratings', at: https://www.oecd.org/tax/transparency/what-we-do/; 10 Years Global Forum Report. The main distinction between the FATF and the Global Forum is that the latter comprises 171 jurisdictions with equal status, and non-compliance is associated to OECD Conventions.

35 The author claims that "cybersecurity demands a global response". 'The FATF as a Model for Internet Governance' (2011), 4. At: https://ieeexplore.ieee.org/document/5978781.

36 Ibid, 3.

37 "The FATF establishes the policies and recommendations which are then passed on to the FSRBS", ibid, 2.

38 The "threat of blacklisting, it is effective in bringing pressure to bear on recalcitrant nations", ibid, 1.

39 Ibid, 4.

> Finally, the body must be able to recommend to its member States the corrective and punitive measures necessary to improve cyber domain security for all users.[40]

1.2 *The FATF as a Model at Operational Level*

The FATF evaluation process and blacklisting can also serve as a model. The ME process has been a model for the OECD WG on the application of the OECD Anti-Bribery Convention[41] and the Global Forum (as mentioned above), while the NRA and the blacklisting mechanism developed by the FATF, for instance, have modelled the EU framework.

The implementation and enforcement of the OECD Anti-Bribery Convention is conducted by a peer-review monitoring mechanism similar to that of the FATF. The process is conducted in four stages: i) legal framework (technical compliance); ii) practice (effectiveness); iii) enforcement and cross-cutting issues and non-implementation; and iv) enforcement and cross-cutting issues tailored to specific country needs and failure to implement Recommendations (enhanced measures).[42]

The monitoring system is well explained in the webpage of the OECD Anti-Bribery Convention:

> Following the adoption of the evaluation report, the OECD Working Group on Bribery monitors the evaluated country's efforts to implement the Working Group's recommendations. In the event that the country has failed to take action to effectively implement these recommend actions, the OECD Working Group on Bribery can employ additional measures to address an evaluated country's inadequate implementation or continued failure to implement the OECD Anti-Bribery Convention.[43]

The Global Forum also introduced a monitoring system inspired by FATF ME process to oversee the implementation of international standards on tax transparency and exchange of information, which consists of peer review, methodology, benchmarks, assessment, and technical assistance, as mentioned.[44]

---

40 Ibid.

41 At: www.oecd.org/daf/anti-bribery/countrymonitoringoftheoecdanti-briberyconvent ion.htm.

42 Ibid.

43 Ibid.

44 The 10 Years Global Forum Report states: "The implementation of the international standards on transparency and exchange of information has been swift and global. Only few jurisdictions have fallen short in meeting the commitments made to the Global Forum.

In terms of the EU, the EU has drawn heavily from FATF Recommendation 1 (NRA and RBA) when developing its own 'Supranational Risk Assessment Report'. A necessary tool for the Commission to assess the ML/FT risks in the EU, especially to identify, analyse, and address risks "affecting the internal market and relating to cross-border activities".[45]

The first Supranational Risk Assessment Report was published in June 2017.[46] The goal of mapping the risks and the means to mitigate them is well-highlighted in the last Supranational Risk Assessment Report, published in October 2022. In the Report, the European Commission states:

> The 2022 Commission SNRA is made up of two documents: this report and a detailed Staff Working Document, which read together provide a comprehensive mapping of risks on all relevant areas, as well as the necessary recommendations to counter them (...) As with the previous reports, this third edition analyses the present ML/TF risks and proposes comprehensive action to address them. It also assesses the degree to which the Commission's recommendations for mitigating measures in the 2019 Report have been implemented and evaluates the remaining risks.[47]

Also based on FATF's experience and its backlisting mechanism, the EU decided to identify "third-country jurisdictions which have strategic deficiencies in their national AML/CFT regimes", thereby creating its own 'Black List'.[48] Such power is delegated to the Commission,[49] which compiles the EU list based on member States' assessments and "information from international organisations and standard-setters in the field of AML/CFT, such as FATF public statements, mutual evaluations or detailed assessment reports or published follow-up reports".[50]

They are provided with support to advance their regulatory environment and practices", 37. See OECD (2023) Handbook for Peer Reviews (n 27).

45 Articles 6–8 of EU Directive 2015/849, as amended by EU Directive 2018/843.

46 COM(2017) 340 final, 26/06/2017. The second Report was adopted by COM(2019) 370 final, 24/07/2019.

47 COM(2022) 554 final, 27/10/2022, 2.

48 Preamble, para. 28. See Articles 9, 13, 16, 18, 19, 64 of EU Directive 2015/849 as amended by EU Directive 2018/843.

49 Article 290 of the Treaty on the Functioning of the EU and Articles 9 and 64 of EU Directive 2015/849 as amended by EU Directive 2018/843.

50 Preamble, para. 13 of EU Directive 2018/843. Also, Article 16 and Annex II of the same Directive where it is stated that the Commission should consider "third countries which, on the basis of credible sources such as mutual evaluations, detailed assessment reports

The first EU List of High-Risk Third Countries was issued in July 2016, identifying 11 countries (Commission Delegated Regulation (EU) 1675/2016), and has been regularly amended, in July 2018 (Commission Delegated Regulation (EU) 2018/1467, adding jurisdictions), in May 2020 (Commission Delegated Regulation (EU) 2020/855, adding 12 jurisdictions and deleting six), in January 2022 (Commission Delegated Regulation (EU) 2022/229, listing 23 jurisdictions and de-listing five), and in December 2023 (Commission Delegated Regulation (EU) 2024/163, listing 25 jurisdictions and de-listing two).[51]

The EU Commission has identified 132 high-risk jurisdictions under EU Directive 2015/849 to be assessed until 2025,[52] which means that business relationships and transactions with these jurisdictions will be subject to additional checks and control measures under enhanced customer due diligence.[53]

This understanding that the ME process can serve as a model for other organisations, is self-perceived by the FATF in its 2010–2011 FATF Report, when it states:

> The FATF not only promotes the endorsement of the Forty Recommendations but also measures how effectively they have been implemented. Through its Mutual Evaluation process, the FATF has been very successful at ensuring that the standards are well applied by its jurisdictions and has been a model for many other organisations.[54]

1.3 *The FATF Regime as a Model for Other Regimes of Global Concern*

The FATF's overall regime can also be seem as an *optimum* model for other topics of global concern requiring co-ordinated multilateral action.

---

or published follow-up reports, have requirements to combat money laundering and terrorist financing consistent with the revised FATF Recommendations and effectively implement those requirements".

51 Also: https://finance.ec.europa.eu/financial-crime/anti-money-laundering-and-countering-financing-terrorism-international-level_en#strategic-deficiencies.

52 List of Countries in the Scope of the EU Assessment on High Risk Third Countries under Directive (EU) 2015/849 and List of Priority of 1 Countries, at: https://finance.ec.europa.eu/document/download/eb46278d-00eb-4791-9ffe-c1c9b5bb1ea2_en?filename=list_of_scoping-priority-hrtc_aml-cft-14112018.pdf. Also, EU Commission webpage - 'AML and CFT at International Level', at: https://finance.ec.europa.eu/financial-crime/anti-money-laundering-and-countering-financing-terrorism-international-level_en#:~:text=at%20international%20level-,Anti%2Dmoney%20laundering%20and%20countering%20the%20financing%20of%20terrorism%20at,countering%20the%20financing%20of%20terrorism (last visited 15/05/2024).

53 Preamble, para. 12 and Articles 18, 18a of EU Directive 2018/843.

54 2010–2011 FATF Report, 5.

Jakobi regards the FATF as a model for co-operation on security governance since the FATF has managed to create a 'transnational security space' in the field of AML/CFT via its unique framework and doings.[55]

The author enumerates five elements that can build a transnational security space: i) comprehensive security concept; ii) multi-purpose rationalisation; iii) public-private co-operation; iv) multi-model governance; and v) private and public sectors obligations. The author concludes that the FATF reunites them all.

Indeed, it is possible to find examples of FATF's actions that correspond to each of the above elements: i) the Forty Recommendations; ii) the methodology, monitoring system, blacklisting and the Global network); iii) co-operation between supervisors and regulators; iv) layers of 'binding' and non-binding instruments, HLPOs, as well as the hierarchy between the FATF and FRSBs; and v) relationship between FIUs and FIs.

According to Jakobi:

> The FATF [is] a special case in global governance, and its success is hard to replicate, this 'special status' is not fixed. The FATF's particularity is the creation of multiple networks and, with these, transnational security spaces that did not exist before (...) It can be a model for future security governance in other fields than just representing a single case.[56]

Bravo also believes that the FATF's AML regime can be, after a comparative analysis of the international efforts to combat both money laundering and human trafficking, a useful model for combating trafficking in human beings more effectively. This assessment covered institutions, international instruments, and adopted measures, including blacklisting.[57]

The author underlines not only FATF's international standards, but also the impressive compliance rates, which are linked to the evaluation mechanism (methodology) and reputation ('name and shame' policy) that are in place

55 'Governing Illicit Finance in Transnational Security Spaces: The FATF and Anti-Money Laundering' (2018) 69 *Crime, Law and Social Change*, 173. For the author, the FATF may be a global governance model because of its procedures, standards, and the setting to a network that ensures compliance, including in the private sector.

56 Ibid, 187.

57 'Follow the Money? Does the International Fight Against Money Laundering Provide a Model for International Anti-Trafficking Efforts?' (2008) 6(1) *University of St. Thomas Law Journal*, 141. The author compares the effectiveness of FATF's blacklisting and the USA Annual Report on Human Trafficking, concluding that FATF's is more successful in terms of compliance rates.

as decisive factors. Although questioning the genuine international political determination and strength of jurisdictions to effectively fight human trafficking, Bravo summarises the following:

> Although no definitive answer is yet possible regarding the relative effectiveness and success of the two regimes, it does appear that the FATF's anti-money laundering mission and campaign is more effective. Some of these mechanisms and methodologies have been identified in this article, and there is little doubt that, if there is political will, some aspects of the anti-money laundering model could be adopted and adapted to the international fight against human trafficking.[58]

Another interesting example is FATF's Recommendations and compliance system being proposed as a model for new standards, such as to fight corruption in the context of money laundering.

In face of the lack of progress as regards the negotiations of the Additional Protocol to the Merida Convention (APUNCAC) aiming at implementing "international requirements to report beneficial ownership of funds involved in certain financial transactions", Stuart Yeh suggests resorting to FATF as a solution to overcome such an impasse. The author proposes the adoption of 19 Specific Recommendations.[59]

The difficulty in reaching a consensus over the text of the Protocol and the inherent hurdle to have a binding international legal instrument (national ratification procedures), as well as to implement it, where countries choose the implementation method in accordance with their constitutional frameworks, could be overcome using FATF's influential role and operational methods. As elucidated by Yeh:

> In principle, if the members of FATF are in agreement, FATF could simply adopt the model recommendations (...) Implementation of the recommendations via FATF would avoid the lengthy, time-consuming process of drafting an international convention, resolving disputes about detailed language, and reconciling the discordant views of diverse UN member States. It would avoid the need to build the level of consensus needed for signature and ratification in each member State. Instead, FATF could

58 Ibid, 202–203.

59 'New Financial Action Task Force Recommendations to Fight Corruption and Money Laundering' (2022), at: www.mdpi.com/2075-471X/11/1/8.

> simply agree to promulgate a new set of recommendations that are not, in principle, controversial.[60]

The *rationale*, the standards' features (concise, clear, consensus-based, objective), the broad range of application of the Recommendations, and the *modus operandi* (monitoring and blacklisting) of the FATF are underscored by Yeh as an alternative and reliable solution/model to implement universal standards to counter corruption.[61]

> The FATF shapes the regulations written in response to the FATF recommendations, thereby shaping the capacity of domestic authorities to pursue criminals dealing in illegal drugs, human trafficking, and other crimes. The intergovernmental body sets international standards that aim to prevent these illegal activities and the harm they cause to society. As a policy making body, the FATF works to generate the necessary political will to bring about national legislative and regulatory reforms in these areas.[62]

Aside from the preceding examples, it may also be affirmed that the influence of FATF's regime is quite broad. Indeed, it is possible to identify excerpts of FATF's Recommendations, definitions, and benchmarks in the UNODC Model Laws on Anti-Money Laundering . The UNODC has developed two model laws, one for common law legal systems and another for civil law legal systems, to assist them in "drafting AML legislation in order to be in full compliance with the applicable UN Conventions and the FATF Recommendations".[63] Furthermore, the influence of the FATF is noticeable at the level of jurisdictions in their national laws[64] and

60 Ibid,18.

61 As the author explains: "While FATF recommendations are not legally binding in the way that an international convention is binding, over 200 countries and jurisdictions have committed to the implementation of FATF recommendations (…) [FATF recommendations] are, therefore, extremely influential in shaping the international AML regulatory regime", Ibid, 2.

62 Ibid, 13.

63 At: https://www.unodc.org/unodc/en/legal-tools/model-treaties-and-laws.html.

64 Eg. The Anti-Money Laundering and Counter Financing of Terrorism Amendment Act 2017 of New Zealand, incorporates language from FATF's Standards and benchmarks, at: https://www.legislation.govt.nz/act/public/2017/0035/latest/DLM7161207.html#DLM7161200. Law No. 14/2022/QH15; Anti-Money Laundering Law of 15/11/2022 of Vietnam also absorbs FATF's wording into its domestic law. At: https://thuvienphapluat.vn/van-ban/EN/Tien-te-Ngan-hang/Law-14-2022-QH15-Anti-Money-Laundering/547270/tieng-anh.aspx. Forsman evaluates the 30 years Swedish AML/CFT legal system and the influence of FATF

regulations.[65]

The UN, the CoE, and the EU have also enacted international legal instruments or adopted legislation and regulations based on FATF Standards. As mentioned in Chapter 4, Section 6, these instruments intentionally 'transplant' some of the FATF's standards and benchmarks.

The above illustrates and symbolises FATF's recognition of *public auctoritas*, as well as how profound and embedded the Forty Recommendations are at international level. It also shows their cascading effect on other institutions and jurisdictions' legal frameworks.[66] This drift also contributes to the argument that FATF's Recommendations may have evolved into customary international law through general practice and *opinio iuris*.

2 Implications and Challenges as a Subject of International Law with Public Authority

2.1 *The FATF as a Subject of International Law and Public Authority*

In public international law, the FATF, as a subject of international law, enjoys active and passive international legal personality, bearing rights and obligations under international law. However, there is no explicit norm in international law asserting what rights or duties IOs have, as noted by Schermers and Blokker:

> The fact that an international organisation is an international person does not mean that it is in the same position as a State in the context of international relations. To be an international person means only *to be*

into Sweden's' law, indirectly through EU law either directly through its regular assessments. '30 Years of Combating Money Laundering in Sweden and Internationally – Does the System Function as Intended?' (2020) 1 *Sveriges Risbank Economic Review*, 33, 43–46.

65 Eg. Instruction No. 1/2019 on AML/CFT Preventive Measures, Gaming Inspection and Coordination Bureau, Macao (China), at: https://dicj.gov.mo/web/files/anticrime/DICJ_Instruction_01_2019_ractification_en.pdf; 2021 Regulations on AML/CFT Operations Matters Conducted by Attorneys, Chinese Taipei Ministry of Justice, at: https://law.moj.gov.tw/ENG/LawClass/LawAll.aspx?pcode=I0030049; 2022 Regulation and Supervision of Trust Business, supervisory policy manual, Hong Kong Monetary Authority, at: https://www.hkma.gov.hk/media/eng/doc/key-functions/banking-stability/supervisory-policy-manual/TB-1.pdf.

66 Forsman, although recognising the uncertainty surrounding the legal nature of FATF Recommendations – are they binding or not (?), claims that they are not legally binding, but "are binding in practice" because the consequences can be very serious for non-compliant jurisdictions, (n 64) 28–29.

> *capable* of bearing rights and duties. No answer is given to the question of what rights and duties individual organisations have.[67]

Like any other IO, FATF's legal capacities derive from its basic documents (legal instruments that form its constitutional body), treaties or agreements by which it is bound, customary international law, general international law, soft law and body of practice.[68]

These capacities, as mentioned in Chapter 3, vary from organisation to organisation and are broadly developed either explicitly or implicitly according to the organisation's needs to achieve its purposes and adequately perform its functions.[69] As properly observed by Sands and Klein:

> The precise scope of those rights and duties will vary according to what may reasonable be seen as necessary, in view of the purposes and functions of the organisation in question, to enable the latter to fulfil its tasks. Therefore, the *test is a functional* one; reference to the functions and powers of the organisation exercised on the international planc and not to the abstract notion of personality, will along give guidance on what powers may properly be implied.[70]

FATF's specific legal capacities, such as policy and lawmaking, monitoring, sanctioning, and public functions authority, have been established in the rules of the organisation. According to Article 2(b) of DARIO, the 'rules of the organisation' include *inter alia* the "constituent instruments, decisions, resolutions and other acts of the international organisation adopted in accordance with those instruments, and established practice of the organisation".[71]

67 *International Institutional Law* (5th rev edn, Martinus Nijhoff Publishers 2011), 993.

68 Amerasinghe, *Principles of the Institutional Law of International Organizations* (2nd rev ed, Cambridge University Press 2005) 17–21.

69 ICJ Opinion 1949, 180. Also, para. 7 of General Commentary to DARIO and para. 15 of the Commentary to Article 2 of DARIO. IOs are established to perform a specific task and their functions and powers differ due their diversity and purposes.

70 *Bowett's Law of International Institutions* (6th ed, Sweet & Maxwell 2009) 477.

71 Also, Article 2(j) of 1986 Vienna Convention on the Law of Treaties between States and IOs or between IOs. See para. 16–19 of the Commentaries to Article 2 of DARIO: "The definition seeks to strike a balance between the rules enshrined in the constituent instruments and formally accepted by the members of the organisation, on the one hand, and the need for the organisation to develop as an institution, on the other hand". It includes acts either "regarded as binding or not, insofar as they give functions to organs or agents in accordance with the constituent instruments of the organisation."

The general legal capacities recognised by general international law and customary international law to IOs, in particular: to have the capacity to contract, to acquire and dispose of immovable and movable property, to institute legal proceedings, to have property and assets, to enjoy jurisdiction immunity, to enjoy the inviolability of the premises and archives, to enjoy the inviolability of the communications, to be exempted of taxes and custom duties, to conclude treaties, to be entitled to privileges and immunities, including its personnel, to bring international claims both to member and non-member States for direct injuries into the organisation and to claim for reparation (compensation) should equally be inferred.[72]

As regards *ius tractum*, the 1986 Vienna Convention on the Law of Treaties between States and International Organisations or between International Organisations notes that IOs' "possess the capacity to conclude treaties, which are necessary for the exercise of their functions and the fulfilment of their purposes".[73]

Typically, such treaty-making capacity is not explicit in the founding instruments of the IOs,[74] they are implied (interpretation and implied powers doctrine) from these instruments as a requirement for the organisation to properly perform its functions.[75]

In this regard, I agree with Akande's reasoning that a minimum treaty capacity to conclude certain types of agreements should be presumed for all IOs, namely headquarter agreements, privileges and immunities agreements

72 See, the 1946 Convention on the Privileges and Immunities of the UN, 1947 Convention on the Privileges and Immunities of the Specialised Agencies, 1986 Vienna Convention on the Law of Treaties between States and IOs or between IOs. Amerasinghe rightly mentions that "there is a strong presumption in the absence of contrary indication that such powers are enjoyed by international organisation *qua* international persons, because they are necessary for the discharge of their functions and the fulfilment of their purposes", (n 68) 102.

73 Preamble, para. 12.

74 Brownlie also concurs and asserts that such 'treaty-making power' "may be established by interpretation of the instrument as whole and resort to the doctrine of implied powers", *Principles of Public International Law* (6th ed, Oxford University Press 2003), 684.

75 As Amerasinghe explains "privileges and immunities are not necessarily expressly mentioned in the constituent instrument", (n 68) 102. Treaty-making capacity is inferred even if not provided in the founding treaty and, as long as, it does not contradict the founding treaty and the rules of the organisation. See Preamble, para. 13–14 of the 1986 Vienna Convention on the Law of Treaties between States and IOs or between IOs.

with the host State, and agreements for settling claims by and against the organisation.[76]

As regards *ius legationis*, it is consensual that IOs require a "certain minimum of freedom and legal security for their assets, headquarters, and of the establishments, for their personnel and representatives"[77] to safeguard the autonomy of the organisation and the total independence of its agents when discharging their duties. Immunities and privileges vary from IO to IO.

The above *ratio* is well reflected in the 1946 Convention on the Privileges and Immunities of the UN, in the 1947 Convention on the Privileges and Immunities of the Specialised Agencies or in the 1975 Vienna Convention on the Representation of States in their Relations with International Organisations of a Universal Character. Article 105 of the UN Charter also stipulates that:

> [The UN] shall enjoy in the territory of each of its Members such privileges and immunities as are necessary for the fulfilment of its purposes and that representatives of the Members of the United Nations and officials of the Organisation shall similarly enjoy such privileges and immunities as are necessary for the independent exercise of their functions in connection with the Organisation.

Regarding FATF's *ius tractum* and *ius legationis*, there is a substantial lack of publicly available information.[78] This includes details about FATF's headquarters arrangements and whether the organisation and its personnel enjoy any

76 'International Organizations' in M. Evans (ed), *International Law* (3rd ed, Oxford University Press, 2011), 258. Bronwlie comments that "IOs are commonly given immunity on a functional basis from municipal law", (n 74) 703.

77 Brownlie states that "by analogy, with the privileges and immunities accorded to diplomats, the requisite of privileges and immunities in the respect of territorial jurisdictions of host States are recognise in the customary law. However, there is yet no general agreement on the precise content of the customary law concerning the immunities of international organisations. The minimum principle appears to be that officials of international organisations are immune from legal process in respect of all acts performed in their official capacity". Ibid, 685.

78 Tilahun mentions that the FATF "signed a memorandum of understanding for the establishment of an International Training and Research Institute (TREIN) in Busan". 'The Re-organization of the FATF as an International Legal Person and the Promises and Limits to Accountability' in A. Arcuri and F.C. Kund (eds) *Technocracy and Multi-level Governance: What Role for Accountability?* (Routledge 2021), On-line version, 9, at: https://papers.ssrn.com/sol3/papers.cfm?abstract_id=4127120. This fact could be a positive sign of FATF's *ius tractum* capacities.

sort of privileges and immunities because they are under the auspices of the OECD, despite not being part of the OECD.[79]

FATF's actions are limited to its functions, powers and aims in accordance with the rules of the organisation (principle of speciality and doctrine of attributed powers), meaning that it must act accordingly and cannot stray from the aims of the IO (*ultra-vires* and implied doctrines).

The FATF, as any IO, is bound by the rules and underlying general principles of international law (Chapter 3). Principles such as free consent, good faith, *pacta sunt servanda,* equality, reciprocity, and the ones embodied in the UN Charter like the principles of the equal rights and self-determination of peoples, of the sovereign equality and independence of all States, of non-interference in the domestic affairs of States, of the prohibition of the threat or use of force and of universal respect for, and observance of, human rights and fundamental freedoms, environment protection should be observed by the FATF.[80]

The principles of mutual co-operation, dialogue, and respect for territorial integrity were recently invoked as core principles of the organisation in the FATF Public Statement of March 2022 in the exceptional context of the Russian Federation invasion of Ukraine. These general principles of international law have been reiterated in subsequent FATF statements on the same

79 Borlini and Montanaro, 'The Evolution of the EU Law against Criminal Finance: The 'Hardening' of FATF Standards within the EU' (2017) 48(4) *Georgetown Journal of International Law*, 18. Of public knowledge, what is known is that the OECD procedures for hiring FATF staff are applied (at: www.fatf-gafi.org/en/the-fatf/job-opportunities.html), as well as the OECD contribution scale for member fees (2019 Mandate, para. 47).

80 Eg. Preamble, para. 4, 7, 15 of the 1986 Vienna Convention on the Law of Treaties between States and IOs or between IOs. See General Principles of Law (Consolidated text – A/CN.4/L.971, 21/07/2022) and ILC work on general principles of law, at: https://legal.un.org/ilc/guide/1_15.shtml. Amongst others, Megan Donaldson and Surabhi Ranganathan, 'Accountability' in J. Klabbers (ed), *The Cambridge Comparison to International Organizations Law* (Cambridge University Press 2022) 53; Nowrot, 'Global Governance and International Law' (2004) Institute für Wirtschaftsrecht, 18–19, at: https://doczz.net/doc/6078592/global-governance-and-international-law. The author alerts to the need of abiding a set of common principles and obligations "since a failure to bring major actors under the international rule of law imposes unnecessary risks on the inherently frail international legal system", 18–19. Daniel Bradlow outlines some of such principles which may derive from general or customary international law, such as: principles of sovereignty, non-discrimination (treatment of legal and natural persons), environmental responsibility and good faith. 'A Framework for Assessing Global Economic Governance' (2013) 36 *International & Comparative Law Review*, 984–985, 987–988.

subject and politically upheld by FATF Ministers in both the 2022 and 2024 Ministerial Declarations.[81]

Being a subject of international law also means that the FATF may be accountable in case of an internationally wrongful act (omission or action), including breach of international law, and liable for damages reparation.[82] As astutely observed by Jean d'Aspremont: having a *volunté distincte* implies having a *responsibilité distincte*.[83]

In this respect, the principles and rules set forth in DARIO are a valuable legal resource to ascertain international responsibility.[84] The general principle in international law is that "international responsibility is the inherent consequence of international legal personality", hence IOs are responsible for their wrongful actions in the international arena and, exceptionally, their members.[85]

---

81 See Chapter 2, Section 4.2. and Chapter 4, Section 4 above.

82 Article 34 of DARIO indicates that reparation may be in the form of: restitution, compensation and satisfaction.

83 'Abuse of the Legal Personality of International Organizations and the Responsibility of Member States' (2017) 4 *International Organizations Law Review*, 93. Jones explains the personality-responsibility correlation: "The concept of personality distinguishes between the actors included in a legal system and those which are not, and for that reason is commonly taken to mean the capacity to bear rights and owe obligations enforceable under that legal system. An essential feature of holding rights is the ability to bring claims against legal persons infringing those rights and the necessary corollary is that claims must be able to be brought against anybody with personality that breaches an obligation. As such, international responsibility follows directly from international legal personality", 'Legal Personality and the Responsibility of International Organizations' (Dissertation for LLB (Hons), University of Otago, October 2013), 6–7.

84 Amongst others, Amerasinghe (n 68) 384–386; Kristina Daugirdas 'Reputation and the Responsibility of International Organizations' (2015) 25(4) *European Journal of International Law*, 992; Blokker, 'Member State Responsibility for Wrongdoings of International Organizations: Beacon of Hope or Delusion?' in A.S. Barros, C. Ryngaert and J. Routers (eds), *International Organizations and Member State Responsibility: Critical Perspectives* (Brill/Nijhoff 2016), 38 and 47; Leube, 'Can the EU Be Held Accountable for Financing Development Projects that Violate Human Rights' (2017) 48 *Georgetown Journal of International Law*, 1253–1256; Donaldson and Ranganathan criticise the narrow scope of the DARIO where "responsibility only arose where there had been non-compliance with an international obligation (by definition, most likely in relations between IOs and States rather than between IOs and third parties), and because the ILC's work did not purport to say anything about the primary rules which might give rise to these obligations", (80) 59–60.

85 Amongst others, Amerasinghe (n 68) 384–386; d'Aspremont (n 83) 93–96. Blokker clearly mentions that "responsibility of the organisation is the rule, and the member State responsibility the exception", (ibid) 39. International responsibility is a general principle

The non-recognition of FATF's legal personality would imply that the organisation is not internationally accountable, and that responsibility would fall upon FATF's members.[86] As correctly recalled by Barros, "when States created International Organisations they do not leave their international obligations behind".[87]

From another perspective, States may take advantage of an organisation's informal character to avoid, as Alan Boyle emphasises, their "domestic treaty ratification process" and "perhaps to escape democratic accountability for the policy to which they have agreed".[88] However, while benefiting from being cleared from their constitutional constraints and political accountability mechanisms,[89] it is also true that States are relieving the international

of law and of customary international law, see DARIO and ILC 2001 Draft Articles on Responsibility of States for Internationally Wrongful Acts with Commentaries.

86 In this respect, Amerasignhe comments: "Such rights, obligations and powers would be vested collectively in all the creating States, which may not have been the intention behind the creation of the organisation", 'International Institutional Law – a Point of View' (2008) 5 *International Organizations Law Review*, 147; same author (n 68) 69. Jones contends that "organisations that lack of personality under international law are not liable under international law, which means that the responsibility will devolve upon the member States to which the wrongful act is attributable.", (n 83) 7. Also, Golia Jr and Peters, 'The Concept of International Organization' in J. Klabbers (ed), *The Cambridge Companion to International Organizations Law* (Cambridge University Press 2022), 47. Within this context, Bouwhuis suggests using "the domestic legal analogy regarding the personality and responsibility of legal persons and incorporated legal persons without personality (…) even though without legal personality, incorporated legal persons are liable for their actions and, ultimately, its members", 'The International Law Commission's Definition of International Organizations' (2012) 9 *International Organizations Law Review*, 455.

87 'Member States and the International Legal (Dis)order: Accounting for the Notion of Responsible Governance', in A.S. Barros, C. Ryngaert and J. Routers (eds), *International Organizations and Member State Responsibility: Critical Perspectives* (Brill/Nijhoff 2016), 50. According to Brownlie, "[g]eneral international law provides criteria according to which an organisation may be held to be unlawful in conception and objects, and, apart from this, particular acts in the law may be void if they are contrary to a principle of *ius cogens*.", (n 74) 701.

88 'Soft Law in International Lawmaking' in M. Evans (ed), *International Law* (3rd ed, Oxford University Press 2011), 125. Dinah Shelton also claims the use of non-binding instruments not to circumvent domestic constituencies, but as an *alternative pressure mechanism to dissenting States or free riders* to solve a global problem over the objections of States or of non-compliant States, *Commitment and Compliance: The Role of Non-Binding Norms in the International Legal System* (Introduction) (2000), at: http://papers.ssrn.com/sol3/papers.cfm?abstract_id=2234113. In a different and critical perspective, amongst others, d'Aspremont (n 83) 1032, 1088–1089.

89 Abbot and Snidal argue that "*soft legalisation* provides a rational adaptation to uncertainty", by permitting States "to capture the 'easy gains' when there is lack of knowledge, differences or uncertainties as regards the outcome of the bargain. It provides

responsibility of the organisation from any breach of international law and placing themselves in a position of being held accountable for such a breach.

On the other hand, the possibility of 'zero' international responsibility is also unacceptable, as rightly pointed out by Kristina Daugirdas:

> If the IOs were not responsible, then their member States would be responsible in their stead, and this outcome contradicts the separate legal personality of the IO (…) The alternative – that nobody would be responsible – is widely considered intolerable.[90]

DARIO provides clarity on situations where IOs and their members may breach international obligations and the consequences of such breaches.[91] However, there are no norms as regards third party dispute settlement mechanisms or other complaint mechanisms (eg. for human rights violations) or norms establishing which institutions should oversee the wrongdoings of IOs, resulting in IOs building themselves their own watchdog mechanisms.[92] There is also the

---

a framework in which States can adapt their arrangement as circumstances change and can pursue 'harder gains' through further negotiation. Soft law avoids the sovereignty costs associated with centralised adjudication or other strong delegation and is less costly than repeated renegotiation in light of new information". 'Hard and Soft Law in International Governance' (2001) 54(3) *International Organization*, 444. Also, Christiane Ahlborn, 'To Share or Not to Share? The Allocation of Responsibility between International Organizations and their Member States' (2013) Amsterdam Law School Research Paper No. 2013–73, https://papers.ssrn.com/sol3/papers.cfm?abstract_id=2361075. Petman outlines the risks of "deformalisation of international law, substituting traditional legal instruments like treaties with informal decisions and recommendations, and international organisations with expert bodies and other informal organs that may be less accountable than traditional organisations. This development could potentially further undermine the already tenuous democratic control with international decision-making and the rule of law in international affairs", 'Deformalization of International Organizations Law' in J. Klabbers and A. Wallendahl (eds), *Research Handbook on the Law of International Organizations* (Edward Elgar 2011/2014), 433–434.

90 (n 84) 994–995.

91 Several Articles of DARIO provide situations in which members may be internationally liable, including Article 58 (Aid or Assistance by a State in the Commission of an Internationally Wrongful Act by an IO), Article 59 (Direction and Control Exercised by a State over the Commission of an Internationally Wrongful Act by an IO), Article 60 (Coercion of an IO by a State), Article 61 (Circumvention of International Obligations of a State member of an IO), Article 62 (Responsibility of a State member of an IO for an Internationally Wrongful Act of that Organisation) and Article 63 (Effect of this Part). The DARIO explains that there may be situations with a plurality of subjects to be accountable for and that States are not entirely free to disregard their international obligations.

92 von Bogdandy and Mateya Steinbrück Platise comment on DARIO's gap for not providing remedies for individuals against HR violations pertained by IOs. Domestic courts, as well

fact that there has been a lack of practice in using DARIO over the last decade to shed some light on these issues.[93]

The notion that members bear exclusive responsibility for FATF's actions, including breaches of international law, in virtue of its informal nature, is highly questionable and quite unsatisfactory.[94] The FATF has reached a high and mature stage of institutional development, assuming public *auctoritas* functions with the general acquiescence of its members and other IOs. It has an individual standing in international relations, and such a standing should include responsibility and accountability mechanisms.

The question of international responsibility assumes higher relevance when it relates to the active and preeminent role that some IOs play in the contemporary scenario in terms of global governance when they are entrusted with

as mechanisms, such as the WB Inspection Panel, are mentioned as alternatives. 'ARIO and Human Rights Protection: Leaving the Individual in the Cold' (2012) 9(1) *International Organizations Law Review*, 73–75. Blokker also mentions this gap in DARIO: the absence of institutions to determine whether the IO committed wrongful acts or of a compulsory external system for review of IOs acts. The author mentions that IOs' monitoring is exercised by general international law and directly and indirectly by IO's members, (n 84) 38. Amongst others, d'Aspremont criticises the fact that DARIO "is limited do the creation of IOs and not the decision-making process of International Organisations", (n 83) 102–103.

93 Boon, 'New Directions in Responsibility: Assessing the International Law Commission's Draft Articles on the Responsibility of International Organisations' (2011) *Yale Journal of International Law*, Seton Hall Public Law Research Paper No. 2011-01, 8–9; Wouters and Jed Odermatt, 'Are All International Organizations Created Equal?' (2012) 9(1) *International Organizations Law Review*, 9; d'Aspremont, 'The Articles on the Responsibility of International Organizations: Magnifying the Fissures in the Law of International Responsibility' (2012) 9 *International Organizations Law Review*; Daugirdas (n 84) 992; Leube (n 84) 1253–254; Boon and Frederic Megret, 'New Approaches to the Accountability of International Organisztions' (2019) 16 *International Organizations Law Review*. Also, para. 5 to General Commentary of DARIO.

94 Borlini and Montanaro comment: "Furthermore, the peculiar characteristics of the FATF make it more difficult to determine whether it can qualify as an international organisation. Determining the nature of the FATF is not a mere theoretical exercise. In fact, should it qualify as a full-fledged international organisation, it would probably be, at least to some extent, subject to the rules of international law applicable to international organisations", (n 79) 17. Ebikake also mentions that "while the role of the FATF remains unclear in international law. This is important for the purpose of responsibility, as the law on State responsibility clearly states when a State is responsible, in the event of a breach, and the consequence in international law", 'Money Laundering: An Assessment of Soft Law as a Technique for Repressive and Preventive Anti-Money Laundering Control' (DPhil Thesis, Liverpool John Moores University, 17/05/2021), 33, at: https://researchonline.ljmu.ac.uk/id/eprint/16216/1/THE%20THESIS.pdf.

public authority, affecting States and individuals, such is the case of the UN/UNSC, NATO, EU, or the IMF.[95]

As Klabbers accurately comments: "there is an increasing need to think of ways and means to exercise control, both political and judicial over the exercise of public authority".[96] In a forthright manner, Kristen Boon summarises the call for higher accountability standards:

> Demands for accountability are partly a function of international organisations expanding authority and power; the call for accountability has been strongest where international organisations exercise governance functions or affect individual rights.[97]

---

95 Amongst others, Mirko Sossai, 'UNSC Res.1373 (2001) and International Lawmaking: A Transformation in the Nature of the Legal Obligations for the Fight against Terrorism?' (Agora on Terrorism and International Law, Inaugural Conference of the European Society of International Law, Florence 2004), at: https://scholar.google.com/citations?view_op=view_citation&hl=en&user=oocVk_kAAAAJ&citation_for_view=oocVk_kAAAAJ:GnPB-g6toBAC; Alvarez, *International Organizations as Law-Makers* (Oxford University Press 2005), 10–11; Erika de Wet, 'The Security Council as Law-Maker, the Adoption of (Quasi)-Judicial Decisions', in R. Woldrum and V. Röben (ed), *Developments of International Law in Treaty-Making* (Springer 2005); Björn Elberling, 'The Ultra Vires Character of Legislative Action by the Security Council' (2005) 2(2) *International Organizations Law Review*; Andrea Bianchi, 'Assessing the Effectiveness of the UN Security Council's Anti-Terrorism Measures: the Quest for Legitimacy and Cohesion' (2006) 17(5) *European Journal of International Law*; Wessel, 'The Rule of Law and the Security Council: The New Procedures for the Legal Protection of Individuals in the Fight against Terrorism' (2008) University of Amsterdam, First draft prepared for the CONNEX/*Ius Commune* Workshop 'Accountability and the Rule of Law at International Level', at: https://research.utwente.nl/en/publications/the-rule-of-law-and-the-security-council-the-new-procedures-for-t; Boon (n 93) 4; Antonios Tzanakopoulos, *Disobeying the Security Council – Countermeasures against Wrongful Sanctions* (Oxford University Press 2011); Christiane Ahlborn, 'The Rules of International Organizations and the Law of International Responsibility' (2011) Amsterdam Law School Research Paper No. 2011-04, at: http://papers.ssrn.com/sol3/papers.cfm?abstract_id=1825182; Enzo Cannizzaro and Paolo Palchetti, 'Ultra-Vires Acts of International Organizations' in J. Klabbers and A. Wallendahl (eds) *Research Handbook on the Law of International Organizations* (Edward Elgar Publishing 2011); Wessel and Dekker, 'Identities of States in International Organizations' (2015) 12(2) *International Organizations Law Review*, 24; Wessel and Blockmans, 'The Legal Status and Influence of Decisions of International Organisations and Other Bodies in the European Union' in P. Eeckhout and M. Lopez-Escudero (eds), *The European Union's External Action in Times of Crisis* (Hart Publishing 2016), 226 *et seq*; Boon and Megret (n 93) 6.

96 'The Paradox of International Institutional Law' (2008) 5 *International Organizations Law Review* 19, 22–23.

97 (n 93) 4.

Some IOs have developed and expanded their original powers, as set out in their constituent instrument, to an extent that was not foreseen or possible to predict by their founders.[98] Factual circumstances and practice were decisive in this expansion, however, this phenomenon also contributes to a growing concern in terms of accountability and international responsibility in case of misuse or abuse, especially when affecting individual rights.[99]

In this respect, for example the cases of the involvement of UN peacekeeper agents in trafficking in persons during the UN Peacekeeping Operations in Bosnia (1995–2002),[100] which was acknowledged by the UN after conducting investigations, or the failure to investigate alleged cases of torture and due process of law violations by NATO officers of the Stabilisation Force in Bosnia and Herzegovina (SFOR),[101] or the outbreak of cholera in Haiti (2010) believed to be caused by Nepal UN peacekeepers, or the case of NATO's intervention in Libya under Resolution 1973 (2011) of the UNSC, when pilots mistakenly bombed civilian targets and caused extensive damage.[102]

98 Eg. the UN peacekeeping operations were not stipulated in the UN Charter, or the IMF and WB involvement in post-conflict situation. In this respect, Boon, 'Open for Business': International Financial Institutions, Post-Conflict Economic Reform, and the Rule of Law' (2007), at: http://nyujilp.org/wp-content/uploads/2013/02/39.3-Boon.pdf. On the legislative power of the UNSC, amongst others, Alvarez (n 95) 182–217; Bianchi (n 95) 1357; Tzanakopoulos (n 95).

99 Amongst others, Mielle Bulterman, 'Implementation of Financial UN Sanctions: Jurisdictional Problems related to Genuine Global Governance' in P. Slot and M. Bulterman (eds), *Globalisation and Jurisdiction* (Kluwer Law International 2004); Wessel (n 95). Wouters and Philip De Man note that IOs "decisions and actions may violate the individual rights of citizens, which is further ground for arguments criticising these organisations for not upholding democratic principles", 'International Organizations as Law-Makers' (2009) Leuven Centre for Global Governance Working Paper No. 21, 20, at: https://ghum.kuleuven.be/ggs/publications/working_papers/new_series/wp21-30/wp21.pdf.

100 UNSCR 1035 (1995) and UNSCR 1423 (2002). Amongst others, 'The Apparent Lack of Accountability of International Peace-Keeping Forces in Kosovo and Bosnia-Herzegovina', Report of the Amnesty International (Amnesty International, April 2004).

101 The SFOR was established under Resolution 1088 (1996) of the UNSC. Gisela Hirschmann offers a number of cases while emphasising the role of third parties as 'supervisors' of IOs', especially when related to HR violation. In this regard, entities as the OSCE, CoE, OHCR, IOM, NGOs (eg. HR Watch, Ombudsman, civil society play an important role. 'Guarding the Guards: Pluralist Accountability for Human Rights Violations by International Organisations' (2019) 45(1) *Review of International Studies* 45(1).

102 Amongst others, Boon (n 93), 1–4; Hirschmann, ibid. Boon and Megret also provide several examples: UN Peacekeeping Operations, NATO, WB, UNSC, (n 93). Klabbers also offers examples of misuse or wrongdoing of certain IOs in the field of HR and others, and the lack of control and international accountability. For instance, the WB is regularly condemned for failing to pay attention to the effects of its policies on HR or the WTO

Additional examples include the IMF being criticised for violating economic, social, and cultural rights of individuals residing in States that borrow from the organisation[103] or the establishment of an independent complaint mechanism by the WB for local communities that claimed that have been adversely affected by WB-funded projects.[104]

INTERPOL also had to reform its notification system and introduce oversight mechanisms and remedies after allegations of violation of basic human rights in virtue of individuals wrongly named in INTERPOL Red Notices, as well as data protection concerns.[105]

There is also criticism concerning the financial sanctions imposed by the UNSC in its Resolutions to counter terrorism under Chapter VII of the UN Charter. These criticisms pertain to the listing of individuals, the freezing of assets, the reporting procedure, the lack of human rights safeguards, and the compatibility of the international obligations with other international human rights instruments (refer to the ECJ Kadi case),[106] which originated the setting

---

of sacrificing environmental considerations, labour standards and principles of human rights. 'Contending Approaches to International Organizations: Between Functionalism and Constitutionalism' in J. Klabbers and A. Wallendahl (eds), *Research Handbook on the Law of International Organizations* (Edward Elgar 2011/2014).

103 Amongst others, Alvarez (n 95) 632–633; Schermers and Blooker (n 67) 1077–1078; Daugirdas (n 84) 991–993.

104 At: https://www.worldbank.org/en/programs/accountability/brief/overview. Amongst others, Klabbers (n 102) 3 and 16; Blokker (n 84) 43–44. Donaldson and Ranganathan provide a brief overview of the WB accountability reforms (n 80).

105 A new statute of the Commission for the Control of INTERPOL's Files was adopted in March 2017, strengthening its ability to provide an effective remedy for individuals unduly designated in the Red Notices. Amongst others, Alex Tinsley, 'Echoes of Kadi: Reforms to Internal Remedies at INTERPOL' (20/01/2017), *European Journal of International Law* (blog), at: https://www.ejiltalk.org/echoes-of-kadi-reforms-to-internal-remedies-at-interpol/. Also, Report of the CoE 'Abusive Use of INTERPOL System: The Need for More Stringent Legal Safeguards' (Doc. 14277, 29/03/2017) Committee on Legal Affairs and Human Rights, CoE Parliamentary Assembly; EU Study 'Misuse of INTERPOL's Red Notices and Impact on Human Rights – Recent Developments', (PE 603.472, January 2019), Policy Department for External Relations Directorate General for External Policies of the Union; Report of the CoE 'Assessing INTERPOL Reform and Extradition Proceedings: Building Trust by Fighting Abuse' (Doc. 14997, 15/10/2019), Committee on Legal Affairs and Human Rights, CoE Parliamentary Assembly.

106 In this context, the ECJ Kadi's judgment should be underpin. The ECJ confirmed that "the obligations imposed by an international agreement cannot have the effect of prejudicing the constitutional principles of the EC Treaty, which include the principle that all Community acts must respect fundamental rights [due process of law and the right to be heard], that respect constituting a condition of their lawfulness which it is for the Court to review in the framework of the complete system of legal remedies established by the Treaty". ECJ, Joined Cases C-402/05 and C-415/05 *Kadi and Al Barakaat,* para. 285.

of basic humanitarian expenses, the implementation of procedural safeguards, and the creation of the Ombudsperson.[107]

There should be an understanding that the exercise of public powers brings up questions of an international law *ethos*. It should be argued that IOs, particularly organisations exercising this public authority power (*acta ius imperii*) and that can potentially affect the rights of individuals when carrying out their mission, must be bound by a set of general international norms and principles.[108]

This topic has been the subject of vast literature, where contending theoretical approaches between constitutionalism and functionalism are studied (eg. Klabbers).[109] Some scholars advocate that there is an emerging international constitutional law (eg. Erika de Wet),[110] others claim the development

---

Patricia Schneider, strongly criticises the UNSC sanctions process (blacklisting procedure since Resolution 1237 (1999)), referring ECJ's judgments, the ECHR and the creation of the Ombudsperson as forms of reacting and protecting the rights of individuals, 'Sanctioned Until Proven Innocent – Reviewing the UN and EU Smart Sanctions Regime for Blacklisted Terror Suspects' in M. Brzoska (ed), *European Peace and Security Policy: Transitional Risks of Violence* (NOMOS Bloomsbury 2014). Also, Barros as regards Kadi case and the creation of the Ombudsperson of the Sanctions Committee, (n 87) 70–71.

107 Eg. UNSCR 1452 (2002), op.para. 1(a) introduces basic expenses as an exception to assets freezing; UNSCR 1730 (2006), op.para. 1 establishes a focal point to receive de-listing requests; UNSCR 1904 (2009), op.para. 19–21 establish the Ombudsperson; UNSCR 2161 (2014), op.para. 63(b) allows claims of individuals for de-listing (through the focal point) of false or mistaken identity; UNSCR 2368 (2017), op.para. 81(b) introduces the concept of extraordinary expenses. More at: https://www.un.org/securitycouncil/ombudsperson.

108 Akande makes an accurate remark on this matter: "It is a reflection of the significant role that international organisations play in international affairs and in the exercise of public power that attention is now being paid to the question of what limits of their powers are and the principles relating to when and how these organisations may be held accountable or responsible for the exercise of such powers", (n 76) 253. Amongst others, von Bogdandy, 'Globalization and Europe: How to Square Democracy, Globalization and International Law' (2004) 15(5) *European Journal of International Law*; Wouters and De Man (n 99) 20, Julia Arato, 'Treaty Interpretation and Constitutional Transformation: Informal Change in International Organizations' (2013) 38(2) *Yale Journal of International Law*.

109 The author addresses functionalism and constitutionalism as modes of controlling IOs activities. After the analysis of pros and cons, it addresses alternative control mechanism beyond a rule-based approach, a body of rules of global administrative law or transnational administrative law (due process, proportionality, balancing of interest) associated to an ethical-based behaviour, (n 102).

110 'The International Constitutional Order' (2006) 55(1) *International Comparative Law Quarterly*, 51–76; same author 'The Emerging International Constitutional Order: The Implications of Hierarchy in International Law for the Coherence and Legitimacy of International Decision-Making' (2007) 10(2) *PER/PELJ*. Also, Arato (n 108) 299. Barros that states the "need to discipline the exercise of public power through constitution-like principles", (n 87) 67. Christoph Möllers sets a body of constitutional standards for global

and application of global administrative law principles founded on domestic administrative law (eg. Nico Kirsch).[111]

A gradual need to uphold principles and norms of global administrative law or an *imperative corpus of fundamental principles* binding and limiting IOs actions (constitutionalism approach) is generally acknowledged.[112] Therefore, regardless of the theoretical debate, there is an undisputable consensus among scholars that certain fundamental principles and norms whether of constitutional or administrative law nature, such as the rule of law, legitimacy, due process, proportionality, accountability, participation and transparency, often referred to as principles of good governance, should guide and bind IOs.[113]

---

administration: i) rule of law and judicial review; ii) democratic standards, iii) HR; iv) substitute standards (accountability); v) rule-making; vi) administrative adjudication; vii) independent authorities; and viii) hybrid organisations. 'Constitutional Foundations of Global Administration' in S. Cassesse (ed), *Research Handbook on Global Administrative Law* (Edward Elgar Publishing 2016).

111 'The Pluralism of Global Administrative Law' (2006) 17(1) *European Journal of International Law*. Amongst others, Jared Wessel, 'Financial Action Task Force: A Study in Balancing the Sovereignty with Equality in Global Administrative Law' (2006/2007) 13(1) *Widener Law Review*, 169; Klabbers, 'Checks and Balances in the Law of International Organizations' (2007) 13 *Ius Gentium*; ne Dubois and Nowlan, 'Global Administrative Law and the Legitimacy of Sanctions Regimes in International Law'(2010) 36 *Yale Journal of International Law*; Bradlow (n 80) 984–985; Klabbers, 'The EJIL Foreword: The Transformation of International Organizations Law' (2015) 26(1) *European Journal of International Law*, 76; Barros (n 87) 62–63. Harlow analysis the concept of administrative global law and a set of values and principles like rule of law, due process, legality, impartiality, proportionality transparency, accountability (developed from domestic administrative law and trade relations), and the promotion of good governance values, including HR values and the need to control (check and balances). 'Global Administrative Law: The Quest for Principles and Values' (2006) 17(1) *European Journal of International Law*. Dan Sarooshi comments that "domestic public law and administrative law principles are of a general application to international organisations that exercise conferred powers of governance, since there is an inextricable line between domestic public law and the activist of the government", 'Role of Domestic Public Law Analogies in the Law of International Organizations' (2008) 5 *International Organizations Law Review*, 237.

112 Wouters and De Man commented these principles represent and guarantee certain democratic values and would serve to close the democratic gap, (n 99) 20. Golia Jr and Peters also outlined that "every exercise of 'public' power (or 'authority') is legitimate only if and to the extent that it is constituted, constrained and guided by (constitutional and/or administrative) law. Such approaches also provide material standards – ranging from checks and balances in the organisations over the protection of human rights and transparency and participation/inclusion in decision-making up to some form of independent review – for institutional design and reform", (n 86) 32.

113 On general principles of good governance, amongst others Bradlow (n 80) 984–988. As regards soft organisations, Pauwelyn, Wessel and Wouters mention that *informal international lawmaking* can be improved with a threshold of principles – called 'procedural

Whenever the exercise of public functions affects the lives of individuals, especially the enjoyment of rights and freedoms, there is a *due diligence standard* that should be applied by States, as creators and members of IOs, to safeguard the protection of individuals, given that individuals are the "ultimate beneficiaries of the international community"[114] or ultimate "stakeholders".[115]

There are several oversight mechanisms that IOs may be subject to and be liable for their decisions and actions, including participatory decision-making processes, complaint or auditing mechanisms, Ombudsman or inspection panels, internal proceedings, and dispute settlement or judicial review. All of them are embodied in Gisela Hirschmann's concept of *pluralist accountability*. A multi-layer and non-exclusive mechanism of accountability involving international, regional, national courts, NGOs, experts commissions where the reputation of IOs is a 'pull factor' for compliance.[116]

---

meta-norms' – to achieve the necessary institutional balance (checks and balances) and to legitimise informal IOs' authority. According to the authors, procedural meta-norms reinforce: i) authority, procedure and substance by extending consultation beyond service providers, ii) source and authority of the norm-creating body by increasing transparency, openness and neutrality in the norms' procedural elaboration and by increasing substantive quality and consistency, and overall acceptance (consensus) of the norm. However, it may be questioned if procedural meta-norms suffice to overcome the lack of substantive meta-norms or general principles of international law, such as the rule of law, legitimacy, accountability, proportionality. 'When Structures Become Shackles: Stagnation and Dynamics in International Lawmaking' (2014) 25(3) *European Journal of International Law*, 733–763.

114 Barros (n 87) 62–63.

115 Barros recalls "States own omission in due diligence of HR obligations" in relation to International Organisations, claiming that both subjects are equally responsible, ibid, 70–71. Daugirdas develops the idea of member States' obligation to exercise due diligence in order to supervise IOs to which they are members, especially when the acts of these IOs may harm individual's rights, breach international obligations or to prevent abuses. The author criticises DARIO for framing these obligations to narrowly, 'Member States' Due Diligence Obligations to Supervise International Organizations' (2020) *Law & Economic Papers*, University of Michigan Law School, 13–16, at: https://papers.ssrn.com/sol3/papers.cfm?abstract_id=3539181. Golia Jr and Peters understand "autonomy not exclusively in the relationship between the organisation and its members, but also in relation to individuals and third parties who may be affected by an organisation's actions and omissions." Therefore, the need to "look beyond the membership is the fact that all organisational behaviour produces military, environmental, economic or financial externalities for humans, often independent from the latter's citizenship in a member State. Humans may therefore be the 'stakeholders' of organisations, beyond the member States, seen as the 'shareholders'", (n 86) 41.

116 Hirschmann develops the concept of 'pluralist accountability' in the global governance context for HR violations by IOs. Policies and actions of IOs are increasingly affecting individuals' fundamental rights and freedoms, and therefore must be accountable.

In line with previous scholars, I consider that there is a cross-fertilisation of ethical and legal values and principles of the international legal system that extend beyond the constituent instruments that should guide and frame IO's *modus operandi*, especially when they perform public functions (global governance matters).[117]

Furthermore, the FATF is part of this exclusive circle of world-leading organisations endowed with public authority, which makes the aforementioned concerns and comments valid to the FATF.

The Forty Recommendations, along with their normative dimension and subsequent actions, such as the ME, ICRG, and blacklisting, have a transversal and cross-sector impact. These actions affect a diversity of stakeholders, including States, individuals and legal persons, and cover a wide range of subject matters (eg. legal, financial, law enforcement, regional co-operation), and they involve both the public and private sectors, as mentioned.

The FATF not only establishes *universal standards* (policy and lawmaking), acting as a global standard-setter, but also ensures their application through solid compliance and supervisory mechanisms, acting as a global keeper, and is able to call for countermeasures (blacklisting), including non-members, acting as a global arbiter.

In order to perform its functions, the FATF assembles a spectrum of three distinct capacities within a single organisation. This is outstanding, and one wonders how many IOs around the world combine these three capacities/ functions.

Pluralist accountability is exercised through a variety of actors (eg. Parliaments, HR Committees, Ombudsperson, NGOs) in different spheres and stages (eg. standard-setting, monitoring, information, sanctioning, reviews), (n 101). On the role of civil society in the sphere of global governance and means available, amongst others, Jan Aart Scholte, 'Global Governance, Accountability and Civil Society' in J.A. Scholte (ed), *Building Global Democracy? Civil Society and Accountable Global Governance* (Cambridge 2011).

117 Amongst others, Sarooshi highlights the intersection between the legal rules governing the exercise of public powers of governance (domestic and international levels), (n 111) 237. Marco Macchia develops a set of legal principles that should frame the global environment, such as the principle of legality, legal certainty and jurisdification of procedural norms, prohibition of arbitrariness, principle of equality and the duty to give reasons, transparency and disclosure of information, principle of effective judicial review, by providing examples (eg. UN, WTO, UNHCR). 'The Rule of Law and Transparency in the Global Space', in S. Cassesse (ed), *Research Handbook on Global Administrative Law* (Edward Elgar Publishing 2016).

2.2 FATF's *Exercise of Public Functions, Gaps and Improvement*

Bearing in mind the above, it is important to ascertain whether FATF, in the hypothesis of being a new *species* of IOs, has any shortcomings or aspects that deserve amelioration, especially considering the conferred powers of global governance and the principles of good governance.

In this respect, there are inherent shortfalls, such as its 'club-member' character and unbalanced relationship with the FRSBs jurisdictions, as well as general shortfalls that may fall in any IO exercising public functions, such as: accountability, sovereignty and transparency concerns, and unintended consequences.[118]

2.2.1 The 'Club-Member' Character

One crucial aspect to ponder is FATF's controversial 'club-member' character, which has been subject to strong criticism by experts, academics, and practitioners when addressing rule-making neutrality and hegemonic governance.[119]

---

118 About IOs accountability, theoretical approaches, and modes, having the WB has an example, and directions for the future, see Donaldson and Ranganathan (n 80). Amongst others, Blokker, 'Comparing Apples and Oranges? Reinventing the Wheel?' (2008) 5(1) *International Organizations Law Review*, 208; Klabbers, 'Controlling International Organizations: A Virtue Ethics Approach' (2011) 8(2) *International Organizations Law Review*; Golia Jr and Peters (n 86).

119 Stessens states that "the FATF is perceived as a rich man's club", 'The FATF 'Black List' of Non-Cooperative Countries or Territories' (2001) 14 *Leiden Journal of International Law*, 208. Broome describes the FATF "[a]kin to a private club", *Anti-Money Laundering – International Practice and Policies* (Sweet and Maxwell Asia 2005), 561. Hülsse names it a "club organisation" and comments that "legitimation and effectiveness have become central concerns of the FATF". 'Even Clubs Can't Do Without Legitimacy: Why the Anti-Money Laundering Blacklist Was Suspended' (2008) 2(4) *Regulation & Governance*, 466 and 472. Beekarry refers to "a very exclusive club with no convention-based status and limited membership to a selected few". 'The International Anti-Money Laundering and Combating the Financing of Terrorism Regulatory Strategy: A Critical Analysis of Compliance Determinants in International Law' (2011) 31(1) *Northwestern Journal of International Law & Business*, 190. Rodiles characterises the FATF as a "selective club" nature of "like-minded actors". 'The Design of UN Sanctions through the Interplay with Informal Arrangements' in L. van den Herik (ed), *Research Handbook on UN Sanctions and International Law* (Edward Elgar Publishing 2017), 181. Romaniuk and Keatinge highlighted that "scholars draw attention to FATF's unique structure, designed as is to maximise the influence of powerful States (…) For Dan Drezner, FATF is an exemplar case of 'club inter-governmental organisations' wherein 'great powers were able to cajole, coerce, and enforce a global anti-money laundering standard into existence". 'Protecting Charities from Terrorists … and Counterterrorists: FATF and the Global Effort to Prevent Terrorist Financing through the Non-Profit Sector' (2018) 69(2) *Crime, Law and Social Change*, 279. Tilahun, calls it a "a club-like institution dominated by a select group of like-minded states", (n 78) 1.

The FATF integrates 40 members, including the world's wealthiest or most economically developed jurisdictions and emerging economies,[120] who are the decision-makers within a Global Network of 206 jurisdictions, as stated in Chapter 2 above.

This 'dominance' has been criticised. In the 2023 RUSI Roundtable about 'The Future of the Financial Action Task Force – Improving the Least Bad Option?', it was mentioned that: "Global South voices are frequently sidelined or ignored as 'access to the microphone'" is determined and argued that AML/CFT/CPF priorities, blacklisting and action plans are decided by the "Global North countries".[121]

The legitimacy challenges posed by the FATF involve various aspects – political, legal, institutional, and practical. All were debated at the RUSI Roundtable, and in particular its "club-like nature", which is a critical aspect and an obstacle to legitimate and transparent governance. One of the conclusions was that:

> [A]ddressing the closed and club-like nature of the mutual evaluation process was high on the list of priorities for the roundtable participants – both those that observe the process from the outside as well as those that have experienced the process and its implications. (…) But beyond continuing to enact measures that enhance transparency, the gravest task for the FATF will be to rectify inequalities between Global South countries and the Global North.[122]

The low level of representativeness and participation of FRSBs members (166) in FATF decision-making raises therefore major concerns about legitimacy,

120 As noted, G-20 members are also members of the FATF. As the HR Special Rapporteur commented: "The Task Force is at the centre of a very complex ecosystem comprising entities from most major international and regional organisations whose mandate and activities intersect with that of the Task Force", A/74/335, para. 31. As Ghoshray comments that "[i]n the absence of either an IMF or WTO type of umbrella to effectuate majority participation, the FATF seems to gravitate towards a minority imposition of a global agenda paradigm. This exposes the majority of jurisdictions to hegemonic subservience, which is not conducive to developing compliance convergence". 'Compliance Convergence in FATF Rulemaking: The Conflict Between Agency Capture and Soft Law' (2014/2015) 59(3) *New York Law School Law Review*, 532–533.

121 The 2023 RUSI Roundtable (November) was divided in two sub-topics: 'FATF's Processes and Mechanics' and 'FATF's Engagement with the Outside World" with no conclusive suggestion, (2024 RUSI Conference Report) at: https://www.rusi.org/explore-our-research/publications/conference-reports/future-financial-action-task-force-improving-least-bad-option.

122 Ibid, 5–6.

fairness, and transparency. These concerns are well articulated by the HR Special Rapporteur:

> [T]hat de facto, universally enforced rules are effectively imposed by a rather small core group of States representing the globe's most advanced economies. Given the weight of financial and economic power underpinning the (technically) legally non-binding set of standards, following the direction set by the Financial Action Task Force is not merely optional for States with lower levels of financial and economic development. Such circumstances inevitably raise concerns related to State sovereignty and the legitimacy of regulatory processes.[123]

Nonetheless, several steps have been adopted to enhance legitimacy and transparency, including new members, associate membership status, joint activities, technical assistance, the Global Network, and most notably the HLPOs and the Universal Procedures. The latter documents provide a clear institutional relationship framework (formal basis) between the FATF and FSRBs and their jurisdictions, increasing transparency and legitimacy by strengthening and formalising their level of participation and representativeness in decision-making processes.[124]

Even so, and although considerable steps have been taken to engage FSRBs jurisdictions in FATF's decision-making processes and affairs, the decision-making power remains in the FATF (*octopus head*), meaning that, in the end, the final decision will be based on the values, interests, and resources of the wealthy nations, as noted.[125] The regional bodies merely express their views

123 A/74/335, para. 45; about FATF's and its role in countering terrorism and FT, including legitimacy and transparency and HR concerns, para. 28–46.

124 In 2008, Hülsse and Kerwer address some of the concerns regarding the legitimacy of the FATF, arguing that expertise as well as acceptance of new members and broader participation of jurisdictions in the rule-making process contributed significantly to the organisations' legitimacy. The authors mention that both 'technocratic participation' (experts from governments and private sector) and 'democratic participation' (States' participation, including non-members) can be found in FATF's decision making processes, thus strengthening *input and output-legitimacy* of the Forty Recommendations. Nevertheless, the authors stress the need to improve non-FATF members' participation. 'How International Organizations Rule the World: The Case of the Financial Action Task Force' (2011) 2(1) *Journal of International Organisations Studies*, 53–59.

125 Jared Wessel in a very critical comments that "networks such as the FATF regulate globalisation, a phenomenon that challenges the very notion of State sovereignty by de-emphasising State power (…) the FATF is incapable of respecting the traditional notion of sovereignty and deliberative equality while at the same time attempting to set the civil liberty/security trade-off within and between jurisdictions via the traditional

as associate members, but there is no assurance that the 'Big-40' will consider them. There is no voting right, veto or other mechanism in place to ensure that their views are considered.

This lack of participation (democracy deficit) of non-FATF members and transparency clouds FATF's legitimacy, rule of law and accountability, as correctly underpinned by Gathii:

> Notably, while the participation of non-member States would give voice to constituencies that are not currently represented in the decision-making of international institutions, it is also crucial to promote additional mechanisms that would give such poor States control over decisions and policies of international institutions that affect them – such as those of the FATF. It is only by rejecting the inevitability of FATF-type driven lawmaking that there can be redefinition of the choices made in centres of power that are insensitive to the concerns of those without a voice within them.[126]

This situation and the differing positions are also evidenced at the 2023 RUSI Roundtable about the FATF:

> These power imbalances are mirrored in, and largely sustained through, the existing relationship between the FATF and its global network of FSRBs. Any reforms successful at minimising the FATF's legitimacy deficit must therefore address how the FATF is often seen by the majority of the world: the rich world setting agendas and establishing processes for the developing world to implement, and in which it has minimal input.[127]

command-and control model of regulation", (n 111) 185. Addressing this matter as regards 'soft' organisations, Berman and Wessel, 'The International Legal Status of Informal International Lawmaking Bodies: Consequences for Accountability', in J. Pauwelyn, R. Wessel and J. Wouters (eds), *Informal International Lawmaking* (Oxford University Press 2012).

126 'Financial Action Task Force and Global Administrative Law' (2010) *Journal of the Professional Lawyer, Forthcoming*, Albany Law School Research Paper Series No. 10, 8. As Tilahun comments "the FATF exercises a lawmaking power over virtually the entire global society without having formal delegation of authority by most States or without meaningfully ensuring their participation in its decision-making", (n 78) 5.

127 (n 121) 4.

2.2.2 Unbalanced Relationship with the FSRBs Jurisdictions and Risk of Detachment

In addition to the previously mentioned, there is also a major reality gap between the FATF members and the other members belonging to the FSRBs that overshadows the implementation of the FATF Standards.[128] Most of these jurisdictions are economically dependent and/or low-capacity jurisdictions; they are not at the same playing field level as FATF's members.

Therefore, it is not surprising that jurisdictions outside the membership of the FATF exhibit more deficiencies or difficulties in complying with the FATF Standards, whereas, in contrast, FATF members demonstrate high compliance levels.[129]

According to the 2022 FATF Status Report, "FATF Member countries account for about 85% of global GDP and 59% of the global population".[130] This Report visibly displays the existent discrepancies between members of the FATF and the FSRBs:

- FATF members have a good perception of the ML/FT risks and of the RBA achieving 80% substantial or high effectiveness ratings, FSRBs members only 19% achieve a substantial or high effectiveness ratings;[131]
- On BO and transparency requirements only about half (52%) of the 120 assessed jurisdictions have adequate laws and regulatory structures in place, and only 9% have effectively implementing these laws;[132] only 1% of FSRBs are effectively prosecuting and convicting ML, and none are pursuing ML risk investigations (data from Immediate Outcome 7);[133]
- 82% of FSRBs members show ratings of either low or moderate in relation to Immediate Outcome 11 (prevention and suppression of PF).[134]

Although, recognising that jurisdictions "have diverse legal, administrative and operational frameworks and different financial systems, and so cannot all take identical measures to counter these [AML/CFT] threats",[135] the fact is

128 See the jurisdictions nominated in the 'Grey List'. Also, FATF Consolidated Table of Assessment Ratings of May 2024.

129 2018–2019 FATF Report, 46; 2022 FATF Status Report; 2021 IMF Paper on the 'Impact of Gray-Listing on Capital Flows: An Analysis Using Machine Learning' (Working Paper Kida and Paetzold); 2022 WB Report on 'National Assessments of Money Laundering Risks: Learning from Eight Advanced Countries' (Joras Ferwerda and Peter Reuter).

130 At: 9.

131 At: 5.

132 At: 6.

133 At: 39.

134 At: 46.

135 2017–2018 FATF Report, 37.

that all 206 jurisdictions are asked to implement and comply with the FATF's Standards and are subject to the same ME process and monitoring mechanisms, regardless of not sharing equal capacities and resources as the 'Big-40' and having other emerging priorities.

Indeed, small and low-capacity jurisdictions are subject to enormous efforts at the most different levels: political and legal (law reforms), financial (budget allocation), human (equipped staff), including a mindset change among all players (government, private sector, and individuals).[136] Technical assistance and training, though necessary, are often insufficient to resolve the root causes of the problems when they are structural rather than conjectural.

There are also inconsistencies and a lack of awareness of the realities and contexts of countries and regions. Jason Sharman provides, as an illustration, the case of the diversion of funds from "African and Caribbean countries from anti-AIDS programmes to meet the FATF Standards".[137] And Tayo Oke also refers to them when addressing Western modules and initiatives (assistance, programmes, and proposals) related to AML and PEPs in Africa:

> African leaders themselves have shown little enthusiasm for the raft of legislation being encouraged (and in many cases enacted) as useful tools in prosecuting cases of money laundering involving PEPS. It is further contented that the reason for this antipathy lies in the fact that although these legislations have been construed in universal principles, they have *ipso-facto*, been construed outside the socio–legal context of the African PEP.[138]

136 FATF's lawmaking activity it implies to track all its preparatory works and studies as regards the updating of the standards, as well as its guidance papers as regards their correct implementation, it almost involves full time officials specifically assigned to follow exclusively FATF's matters.

137 'The Bark is the Bite: International Organizations and Blacklisting' (2009) 16(4) *Review of International Political Economy*, 8. Also, the 2023 RUSI Roundtable about the FATF: "At the same time, for many countries in the Global South, it is challenging to justify putting sufficient resources into the fight against money laundering. This is not seen as among the most pressing of their various national challenges, such as providing security and the rule of law or addressing the impacts of climate change and the fallout of the Covid-19 pandemic. This may explain, in part, why so many countries in Africa, for example, appear to be regularly placed on and off the Grey List. It is a reflection of competing political, economic and social priorities that they face", (n 121) 4.

138 'Extra-Territorial Money Laundering Legislation: Criminal Sanction, Deterrence, and the African PEP' (2013) 39(4) *Commonwealth Law Bulletin*, 631. The author highlights the particular socio-political and legal context of African countries and its political elite which make it problematic to implement measures to counter ML, corruption and bribery. There is a governance pattern in Africa where PEPs dominate significant elements of the

There is a *de facto* unequal relationship between the FATF members, those who set the rules, standards and procedures, and the non-FATF members.[139] This uneven circumstance is acknowledged by the FATF Executive Secretariat at a 2019 RUSI meeting about the FATF Strategic Review, when addressing FATF's Strategic Review and the 5th Round of ME, the representative of the FATF poses an insightful question: "Should evaluations continue to treat all countries identically, regardless of risk and of the capacity of countries to implement the FATF Standards?"[140]

This sort of detachment from other jurisdictions' socio-economic realities, combined with the imposition of high levels of compliance, not only builds a *fragmented* Global Network, in which FATF standards are implemented at *two velocities*, but also creates a sense of frustration, scepticism, and reluctance towards the organisation by non-FATF jurisdictions.[141]

---

judiciary, legislative and executive branches. There is this "endemic nature" of political corruption in Africa that results from its cultural and social background (the political elites governed by a maze of tribal/ethnic groups) and not from being "third world countries or under-developed"; a mindset often implicit in Western countries, reason why part of the technical assistance related to PEPs by Western countries is inadequate to Africa reality. Also, Bianchi referring to Samoa, as representative of the Pacific Island, expressing the concerns and limited resources of the Islands to comply with their reporting obligations and with the 'pressing priorities' of the FATF, (n 95) 897.

139 Sharman highlights the costs of compliance with AML/CFT measures in the developing countries, referring to African and Caribbean countries. The implementation of measures in these countries by the private sector, such as CDD/KYC, STRs, policy changes, information campaigns, and the establishment of the FIU, FATF's templates and guidance in the public sector for these countries imply a substantial financial and human resources burden (n 137). Turner also comments on the unbalanced burden place upon developing countries, including the costs posed in their private and public actors to implement the 'recommended' AML/CFT policies. 'The Financial Action Task Force: International Regulatory Convergence through Soft Law' (2014) 59 *New York Law School Law Review*, 557. Antoniette Verhage addresses the uneven level playing field countering AML/CFT in the world, having as reference African countries; although using the AML/CFT "same building blocks and building institutions", there is a *differential* in resources (even in EU countries), generating different levels of compliance. 'Global Governance + Global Compliance? The Uneven Playing Field in Anti-Money Laundering' in J. van Erp, W. Huisman and G. Walle (eds), *The Routledge Handbook of White-Collar and Corporate Crime in Europe* (Routledge 2015).

140 FATF's Executive Secretariat Speech (18/11/2019), at: http://www.fatf-gafi.org/publications/fatfgeneral/documents/rusi-fatf-strategic-review.html. See Executive Summary, 2022 FATF Status Report.

141 Beekarry comments that "countries are reluctant to comply with such norms which they consider developed without their consent but inconsistent with the realities of their economic and financial systems and rules. States in Africa and part of Asia have all along argued that the norms do not match their financial environment", (n 119) 191. Oke states

Another factor to consider is the overall burden and pressure that small or low-income economies face with the implementation of the standards and the ME process, including the application of the methodology alongside the ICRG process and potential blacklisting and its action plans.

The complexity of this process, which implies implementing an action plan and specific timelines, as well as the burden that falls on the jurisdictions under monitoring mechanism is highlighted, for instance, by the South African authorities:

> South African authorities submitted a Post Observation Period Report to the FATF Joint Group on 28 November 2022. The FATF Joint Group responded to South African authorities with preliminary analysis/comments on 16 December 2022. South African authorities responded to the preliminary analysis/ comments by the Joint Group on 3 January 2023, in line with the timelines in our follow-up process. The revised and updated Post Observation Period Report responds to the preliminary analysis/ comments by the Joint Group. (…) The Joint Group will report to the FATF's International Co-operation Review Group (ICRG) on the progress that South Africa has made in addressing the deficiencies that were identified (…) before the ICRG makes a final recommendation to the FATF Plenary ahead of its meeting of 22–24 February 2023.[142]

Firstly, the constant amendment of the Recommendations, INotes and ME methodology affects national sectors at different levels, requiring permanent follow-up and update, sometimes undermining a possible upgrade for delisting remaining on the 'Grey List', if that is the case.

Secondly, the lack of understanding and flexibility by some assessors of the jurisdiction's particularities or difficulties, including domestic background, capacities and resources, and regional context that may affect the assessment or the implementation of the action plan.

---

that "[m]oney laundering may be universally recognised and growing problem, but combating it successfully requires further understanding of regional peculiarities, even if these sometimes appear unpalatable to world leaders.", (n 138) 645. Ghoshray refers the asymmetries of the negotiating power and the economic gap between developed countries and low-capacity jurisdictions undermining convergence, (n 120) 534–535.

142 'Enactment of Key Money-Laundering and Combating Terrorism Financing Laws' (06/06/2023) Media Statement, Department of National Treasury of South Africa, at: https://www.fsca.co.za/Regulatory%20Frameworks/Pages/AMLCFT.aspx.

Thirdly, FATF/ICRG's action plans and respective timeframes are often too demanding and stringent, calling into question their proportionality, adequacy and even fairness, reason why 'Grey List' jurisdictions are seldom delisted after a year,[143] despite FATF claims that this is not a "punitive process".[144]

2.2.3 Accountability, Sovereignty, Transparency

Like other IOs with a global governance mandate, there are also accountability, sovereignty and transparency concerns and room for improvement. As remarked by Ruth Grant and Robert Keoane note that "those who govern are held accountable to the governed". Though it is impossible to be subject to the same "models of State control", there are instruments in the context of global governance to legitimise and control the exercise of public functions by IOs (*pluralistic* or *multi-layered* accountability).[145]

The role of FATF as a global standard-setter, guardian and arbiter to counter ML/FT/PF is undisputable. However, the exercise of public functions implies higher responsibilities and scrutiny, including being governed by principles of good governance and oversight mechanisms, given that its decisions and actions have ramifications at the global, regional, and national scales and affect the sphere of persons.

No institution is free from scrutiny, particularly when carries heavy leadership tasks with global outreach, such as ensuring the stability and integrity of the international financial market.

The institutional design of the FATF (non-treaty-based) together with its lawmaking (universal recommendations),[146] monitoring, and sanctioning

143 Most action plans require amending or adopting new legislation, putting high pressure on Governments and Parliaments, especially when national parliaments have their own agenda and procedures (eg. public consultation), being almost impossible, even in democratic societies, to approve a new bill in one year.

144 2020–2021 FATF Report, 56.

145 'Accountability and Abuses of Power in World Politics' (2004) Global Administrative Law Series, IILJ Working Paper 2004/7, 2. The authors identify seven types of accountability mechanisms and consider their applicability to States, NGOs, multilateral organisations, multinational corporations, and transgovernmental networks. Hierarchical accountability, supervisory accountability, fiscal accountability, legal accountability, market accountability, peer accountability and public reputational accountability, 16–18. At: http://iilj.org/wp-content/uploads/2016/08/Grant-etal-Accountability-and-Abuses-of-Power-in-World-Politics-2004-2.pdf. Maria Bergstrom also proposes a multi-layered accountability system due to the diversity of actors (public and private) entrusted with 'enforcement' powers in the implementation of the AML standards. 'From Global Rules and Standards to Enforceable National Provisions: The Case of Anti-Money Laundering Regulation and Implementation' (2013) 58 *Scandinavian Studies in Law*.

146 A/74/335, para. 29, 39, 46.

powers (ME and blacklisting) transcend conventional IOs design-setting, traditional international lawmaking, and traditional behaviour of States, reflecting a diverse format of multilateral negotiation and co-operation. In a critical comment, the HR Special Rapporteur states:

> That evolving process has significant effects on the legitimacy of the traditional consensus required to create international law and the intrusions into State sovereignty that follow the shift from hard to soft law proliferation in counterterrorism regulation. The Special Rapporteur is of the view that the interests of a sizeable number of (non-dominant) States are being neglected in the emerging regulatory practice of forum-shopping. There are grave dangers that informal and selective institutions drive lawmaking in ways that oust the admittedly challenging, political contestation that characterises multilateral diplomatic negotiations.[147]

There is a lack of parliamentary oversight. National parliaments, both from FATF members and non-members, are in general excluded from FATF lawmaking processes and decision-making. There is no direct or even indirect parliamentary participation, national scrutiny, or oversight mechanisms for FATF policies. This fact raises concerns about legitimacy, accountability, and transparency, particularly in democratic societies.[148]

147 A/74/335, para. 27.

148 A/74/335, para. 20: "[FATF Recommendations] formulated in processes that are non-transparent and not accessible to all States, in order to present as regular conduct and practices that which would previously have been considered a challenge to State sovereignty". Also, A/74/335, para. 18; HRC/40/52, 01/03/2019, para. 31. The need to improve parliamentary scrutiny was also addressed, amongst others, UK House of Lords, European Union Committee – Nineteenth Report-Money Laundering and the Financing of Terrorism (2008–09), (2009 House of Lords Report), para. 30 and 32. Drezner calls attention to the disruption of democratic sovereignty with this new form of multilateral co-operation led by the USA and EU, and the use of these "coercive methods". 'On the Balance between International Law and Democratic Sovereignty' (2011) 2(2) *Chicago Journal of International Law*, 336. 2015 Study on 'Countering Terrorism or Constraining Civil Society? The Impact of FATF Recommendations on NPOs in Central and Eastern Europe and Central Asia', Statewatch and Human Security Collective (2015 Statewatch and Human Security Collective Study), also observes that "[y]et despite its global policy-making role, there is no intergovernmental convention underpinning or regulating the activities of the FATF", 4. About the need for accountability mechanisms and institutional transparency, amongst others, Tilahun (n 78). In the 2023 RUSI Roundtable about the FATF, it was reported that "[s]ome participants felt that signing a political declaration under those circumstances, with threat of further sanction in the form of being blacklisted, was a form of 'blackmail'.", (n 121) 2.

Goldbarsht addresses this issue when commenting on how the Australian parliament was confronted with a *fait d'accompli* as regards FATF's membership and the absence of formal *checks and balances* in the legislative process related to FATF Recommendations. This situation challenges the *grundnorm* of the separation of powers between the legislative and the executive.[149] In a pertinent remark, Goldbarsht mentions:

> The causal relationship between both FATF MERS and Australian legislation in the field of CFT support the argument that two legislative forums exist, the Australian parliament constitutes the formal legislative forum; while in meeting out the Recommendations, the FATF – an organisation which Australia joined following a decision of the executive branch which was neither made nor accepted *a fortiori* by the Parliament – constitutes the legislative forum in a practical sense.[150]

Sovereignty and reputation costs[151] are not just related to the lack of parliamentary supervision or low representation of developing countries in standards' decision-making, they are also reflected in the monitoring and sanctioning of regulatory processes imposing short, medium, and long-term policies and measures that interfere in the sovereign domain of jurisdictions. These influence national political agendas, defining Government's priorities, and confining internal policies with socio-economic costs for States and their respective population.[152]

---

149 'Who's the Legislator Anyway: How the FATF's Global Norms Reshape Australian Counter Terrorist Financing Laws' (2017) 45(1) *Federal Law Review*, 127–130, 149. Also, A/74/335, para. 29.

150 Ibid, 150.

151 As commented by the FATF Executive Secretariat (2019): "However, the motivation is generally to avoid a bad report, and the consequences of that, including potential naming and shaming by FATF in the grey or blacklist, as this increases the costs of doing business in those countries and deters foreign direct investment, as well as affecting their international reputation". At: http://www.fatf-gafi.org/publications/fatfgeneral/documents/rusi-fatf-strategic-review.html.

152 Amongst others, Drezner (n 148) 336; Ghoshary (n 120) 533–535, A/74/335, para. 32 and 41. Hanafi Amrani strongly criticises the clash between FATF's standards and State's sovereign power to develop and implement their own policies. The author claims that this is a violation of treaties and general principles of law, like the principle of non-interference, sovereign equality and territorial integrity. The author contends that FATF's "recommendations come down to coercion". 'Anti-Money Laundering as International Standards and the Issue of State Sovereignty' (2015) 12(2) *Indonesian Journal of International Law*, 171. Alvarez mentions that the "new and sophisticated forms of lawmaking and compliance mechanisms that are being imposed on members outside the traditional paradigm of

The 2017 IMF Paper on 'Loss of Correspondent Banking Relationships (CBRs) in the Caribbean: Trends, Impact, and Policy Options'[153] indicates for instance that blacklisting of Belize was the "main causal factor" for the loss of offshore relationships, and that the strategic deficiencies found in the AML/CFT framework of the Bahamas, in the CFATF MER (November) 2007 was one of the factors for CBRs withdrawal.[154] The 2021 IMF Paper on the 'Impact of Gray-Listing on Capital Flows: An Analysis Using Machine Learning' reveals a decrease of capital inflows and foreign direct investment in jurisdictions that were on the 'Grey List'.[155]

A 2023 Study by Louis de Koker, John Howell and Nicholas Morr was conducted to understand the correlation between FATF's blacklisting and corresponding economic impact in the designated jurisdictions. The study covers 177 jurisdictions, gathers data from 2000 to 2020 from the blacklisted jurisdictions, and assesses various variables.[156] The authors observed that:

> A major finding is that net official development assistance (ODA), International Bank for Reconstruction and Development (IBRD) loans, and International Development Association (IDA) credits seem to reduce during greylisting periods and this reduction endures after the country becomes de-listed. This is of significant concern as such reduction

lawmaking (agreements)" are *shrinking the domain reservé of States.* 'International Organizations and the Rule of Law: Challenges Ahead', forthcoming in The International Legal Order: Essays Commemorating the 10th Anniversary of the Xiamen Academy of International Law 2016, 600 *et seq.*

153 Working Paper (Trevor Alleyne, Jacques Bouhga-Hagbe, Thomas Dowling, Dmitriy Kovtun, Alla Myrvoda, Joel Okwuokei and Jarkko Turunen).

154 Ibid, respectively 36 and 33.

155 At: 5 and 18–19. Ryder mentions the skepticism of some as regard the RBA falling on different activity sectors, in which, for instance, FIs act "as frontline financial policemen". 'The Financial Services Authority and Money Laundering, a Game of Cat and Mouse' (2008) 67(3) *Cambridge Law Journal*, 641–642. Asim Jusic makes a cost/benefit compliance analyses of Kuwait's AML/CFT framework (2013–2015). The author concludes that compliance costs for the private sector, particularly FIs, like a KYC system, RBA, STRs, are higher and outweigh the benefits. "The experience of many countries suggests the application of FATF standards frequently results in strong negative economic and social effects, ie. harm to smaller businesses and financially most vulnerable populations through the rising of costs of services of FIUS and DFNBPs, eventually hindering, rather than promoting, overall economic development". 'Kuwait's Administrative Risk-Based Model for the Prevention of Money Laundering: Costs and Benefits of Compliance with the Financial Action Task Force (FATF) Standards' (2017) 31 *Arab Law Quarterly*, 132–133.

156 'Economic Consequences of Greylisting by the Financial Action Task Force' (2023) 11 *Risks.*

may impact disproportionately on developing economies and their populations.[157]

Although FATF's backlisting main objective is to encourage designated jurisdictions to improve and undertake necessary reforms in their AML/CFT/CPF regimes, it seems that it may also have a counterproductive effect of being able to 'isolate' the jurisdiction by reducing external financial assistance during the ICRG process and even afterwards. This has a significant economic impact especial for low-income jurisdictions that depend on foreign economic assistance. According to the authors, "[t]hese findings are of concern from a development policy perspective" for blacklisted jurisdictions.[158]

It is clear that the FATF actions have a far-reaching impact, shaping domestic systems with political, legal, and practical consequences. Furthermore, jurisdictions/Governments are held accountable at international, regional, and national levels in case of non-compliance, but who holds FATF accountable?[159] Highly critical, Shams comments:

> The FATF is an unaccountable institution. The sanctions applied by the FATF can be serious for the survival of a small economy. Any country that sustains damage by an FATF action will not have any venue for redress.[160]

Shams is partially correct; the fact is that FATF's existing accountability mechanisms (internal and external)[161] do not differ substantially from formal IOs. On the other hand, it is possible to assert that the FATF has broader and more open participation mechanisms than most IOs. The FATF is subject to public scrutiny through public consultation processes (eg. amending Recommendations

157 Ibid, 2. There was positive improvement in the banking sector, but also a negative one with regards to the decreased in net foreign assets and the increase in debt in the earlier listing phases. GDP growth rates are also impacted. The study reveals that "negative indicators are less visible in the dataset in Period IV (2016)", 23.

158 Ibid, 2.

159 2022 Ministerial Declaration, para. 10: "The FATF holds jurisdictions from the Global Network accountable for the lack or deficient implementation of the Recommendations". Also, 2024 Ministerial Declaration, para. 2.

160 (n 6) 482.

161 See Chapter 2. Internal accountability is performed by the members (eg. reports, budget statements, public consultation papers, and open stocktakes) and Ministers (internal political control); external oversight is performed by the UNSC, G-7 and G-20. Beekarry mentions partnership with the IMF and WB as a factor for "additional oversight for legitimacy and accountability of FATF's actions", (n 119) 194.

or Guidance Papers)[162] and promotes regular consultative forums with the private sector and NPOs/civil society.

Notwithstanding the above, there is always room for improvement, particularly given the fact that there is little information about whether the ICRG makes a previous assessment of the resources or institutional capacity of jurisdictions before drafting action-plans, or whether there is room for negotiation, or what happens if there is no agreement with the designated jurisdiction.[163] Is there a peer review panel or an appeal mechanism for jurisdictions to contest FATF's (ICRG) action plans or blacklisting?[164] How do you challenge the FATF's 'technical decisions' that bear national political, social, and economic costs?[165]

162 Eg. The public consultation in relation to Recommendations 24 and 25, respectively at: https://www.fatf-gafi.org/en/publications/Fatfrecommendations/R24-public-consultation-oct-2022.html and https://www.fatf-gafi.org/en/publications/Fatfrecommendations/R25 public-consultation-oct22.html.

163 Usually ICRG's action plans call for reforms at legal, regulatory and/or operational levels.

164 In a critical remark, Keatinge notes: "the FATF needs to recognise that it should be more transparent and be able to provide greater assurance of independence and oversight particularly to those that are subject to its decisions and recommendations. If – as it repeatedly states – it is a purely technical body, the FATF and its activities should be overseen by an independent governance board; its evaluations should be independently reviewed, not subject to the evidently politicised horse-trading that occurs currently", 'The Financial Action Task Force Should Embrace the Opportunity to Reform', (2019) RUSI Financial Crime and Security Studies Centre, at: https://rusi.org/explore-our-research/publications/commentary/financial-action-task-force-should-embrace-opportunity-reform. Also, Tilahun, who proposes a formal mechanism at the FATF Secretariat to receive complains from external stakeholders, (n 78) 11.

165 During the Covid-19 pandemic, some jurisdictions on the 'Grey List' saw their re-assessment suspended (upgrading and de-listing) regardless of their domestic efforts to be de-listed with obvious socio-economic costs. What happens for jurisdictions that stay in this sort of limbo or stand-by, is there any review or redress? Consider the case of Bahamas, which took significant steps to respond to the CFATF and FATF action plan after being blacklisted and the subsequent consequences of the delay of the FATF/ICRG on-site meeting. In the CFATF Plenary in November 2018, Bahamas received an upgrade on 13 ratings, reaching compliance levels with FATF Recommendations as "top FATF member States". While such progress was recognised by the FATF in February 2020, travel restrictions because of pandemic prevented the visit of the FATF scheduled for April, and Bahamas remained on the 'Grey List'. In May 2020, Bahamas was 'threatened' "that it would be placed on the European Union's 'AML Blacklist' as a result of the country's listing on the FATF Grey-List". See, Office of The Attorney General, Press Release (24/09/2020): 'Bahamas Makes Significant Strides in Fight against Financial Crime: Update on the Bahamas' National Identified Risk Framework', at: https://www.bahamasembdc.org/bahamas-makes-significant-strides-in-fight-against-financial-crime-update-on-the-bahamas-national-identified-risk-framework/.

Criticisms of inconsistencies, duality of criteria, and lack of transparency also undermine FATF's aims and actions, as well as affect its legitimacy and credibility in terms of global governance.[166] In a striking remark in relation to FATF's role as the global AML/CFT/CPF 'watchdog', Broome mentions:

> If [FATF] is going to be lawmaker, policemen, prosecutor and judge, it needs to do so against a set of very well considered public criteria. Transparency is important and yet the processes have been remarkable lacking in transparency.[167]

Indeed, there is a *certain degree of opacity* in some bodies and proceedings of the FATF that seem to be embodied in a 'secrecy veil'.[168] The non-existence

---

166 Broome (n 119) and Hülsse (n 119) refer inconsistencies of the NCCT process, the later, mentioning that the FATF did not apply the "same rigour to its own members" like Turkey and Greece, questioning why Cambodia was on the NCCT list and not Vietnam, and claiming that the NCCT list "was never comprehensive", being for many countries "unreasonable and unfair", respectively, 565–566 and 465. Sharman also mentions double standards practice in relation to Seychelles, Antigua & Barbuda and Cook Islands designation, questioning the evidence and the effectiveness of the exercise, (n 137). In the same line of thought, Arba Metz-Dworkin criticises the withdrawal of Argentina from the blacklist in 2014 "without proof that Argentina's new laws and mechanisms were functioning to properly deter illegal activity". The author claims that Argentina should have remained blacklisted. 'A Call for Sanctions: Argentina's Black-Market Currency Whitening and Violations of International Anti-Money Laundering Conventions and Protocols' (2016) 48 *George Washington International Law Review*, 468. Couvée also refers this situation by exemplifying that the USA could have triggered the ICRG review in 2016, 'Exclusive: FATF Spared Large Economies from Pressure Over AML Gaps' (06/01/2023) *ACAMS*, at: https://www.moneylaundering.com/news/exclusive-fatf-spared-large-economies-from-pressure-over-aml-gaps/.

The 2023 RUSI Roundtable also states "that also been noted that the vast majority of the countries on the Grey List are Global South countries and there have been claims that the FATF has previously rejected changes to its thresholds which would have made it more likely that major economies, such as the UK or the US, would be grey-listed", (n 121) 4.

167 Ibid, 568.

168 About FATF's secretive nature and proceedings, 2009 House of Lords Report (n 148), para. 31: "FATF decision-making and policy-making structures were insufficiently transparent to warrant their own uncritical acceptance"; A/HRC/40/52, 01/03/2019, para. 30. Hayes refers that although FATF is "accountable to the Ministers of its membership", "the absence of publicly agreed rules on, for example, decision-making, openness and transparency, access to information, budgetary scrutiny, parliamentary control or oversight mechanisms, the organisation can only claim to be democratically accountable in the narrowest sense", 'Counter-Terrorism, 'Policy Laundering' and the FATF: Legalizing Surveillance, Regulating Civil Society', (2012) Transnational Institute and Statewatch Report (2012 Hayes Report), 17–18.

of a clear and publicly known body of rules regarding decision-making, like how consensus is reached, or its institutions, such as the rules governing the Steering Committee, who are its members, who are the members of the ICRG, how are ICRG's action plans designed and approved, what are the ICRG's procedures[169] or the host arrangement with the OECD, raises concerns about the rule of law and operational transparency.[170]

In contrast, the OECD provides a good example of institutional transparency. All relevant rules of the organisation are available, namely the Document on the Government Structure, Rules of Procedure, Financial Regulations, Staff Regulations, Rules and Instructions, Code of Conduct.[171]

Nevertheless, there are some positive signs that indicate progress within the FATF in terms of rule of law and principles of good governance. For the first time, in the 2024 Ministerial Declaration, under the topic of 'Promoting Robust and Inclusive Governance', FATF Ministers affirm that the organisation must carry out its mission based on the values of "integrity, accountability, and transparency".[172]

This is a milestone statement, given that neither the FATF's mandate nor the HLPOs explicitly mention these principles. It likely considers some critical views on the subject, thereby enhancing the FATF's credibility. It also makes a difference by addressing "equality and diversity" and women empowerment within the framework of the FATF. This statement bears particular significance because it is now part of FATF's *acquis* and overseen by the Ministers.

However, there is still room for improvement. A depiction is the method of publication of some core documents. In May 2024, the FATF publishes the 'Methodology for Assessing Technical Compliance with the FATF Recommendations and Effectiveness of AML/CFT/CPF Systems' and the 'Procedures for the FATF AML/CFT/CPF Mutual Evaluations, Follow-Up and

169 Amongst others, Hayes observations as regards the absence of "adequate democratic control of the FATF and public accountability" and "a Secretariat that is unwilling to even disclose the nationality of the seven governments which sit on the FATF's Steering Board", ibid, 34, 37. At the 2009 House of Lords Report, the author of the report refers that it requested information about the composition and functioning of the Steering Group but the request was refused, (n 148) para. 31.

170 Despite criticism, positive steps were undertaken including the: publication of budget statements, creation of the website, dissemination of the MERs, e-news, forum, and, again, the approval of the HLPOs that establishes a set of rules to enhance transparency and accountability.

171 At: https://www.oecd.org/legal/internal-rules.htm.

172 Para. 21.

ICRG', both "approved" in the FATF Plenary meeting in March 2022.[173] The 2022–2023 FATF Report also mentions that:

> The Methodology, which was approved by the FATF in March 2022, but is not yet in effect, will be the foundation for all assessments conducted in the 5th round of mutual evaluations. The Procedures, also approved in March 2022, describe the steps for assessment and follow-up processes.[174]

The documents were made available on the FATF's website "for information sharing only" for two years, stating respectively that: "The Methodology in this document is not yet in effect" and "The procedures in this document are not yet in effect".

Both documents came into effect in May 2024 and are publicly available. However, the front page of the Methodology displays that it was "adopted in February 2022" and the cover "Last updated April 2024",[175] while the front page of the Procedures indicates that it was "adopted in March 2022" and the cover "Last updated May 2024".

The publication of the 2023 Universal Procedures, referenced in the outcomes of the FATF Plenary meeting in October 2023, is even more striking; the document was never made publicly available. This document's front-page states that it was "adopted in October 2023" and "Updated in May 2024".

This method of publication raises questions about FATF's procedural transparency: (i) How can the new methodology mention that the approval date is February 2022, when it took place during the FATF Plenary meeting in March 2022? (ii) How to reference a document dated from 2022 or 2023 when it was only finalised and entered into effect in May 2024? (iii) What were the reasons for keeping the 2023 Universal Procedures publicly unavailable? (iv) Were these documents subject to a confirmation process by its members? If so, why not in the upcoming FATF Plenary meeting in June 2024? If not, were they 'ratified' or confirmed by an out-of-session process? (v) What was the role of

173 "As a result of this Strategic Review, the FATF finalised and approved the *FATF Methodology* to assess countries' actions to combat money laundering and the financing of terrorism and proliferation, and the *FATF Procedures* for the fifth round of mutual evaluations. The FATF will now prepare these documents for publication on the FATF website". At: https://www.fatf-gafi.org/en/publications/Fatfgeneral/Outcomes-fatf-plenary-march-2022.html.

174 At: 36.

175 The on-line first version was completed in February 2022, later revised in February 2024 to take into consideration the recent amendments to the Forty Recommendations and INotes. This method of publishing and dating the documents is misleading because it can mislead users to think that these documents were already in force in 2022.

the FSRBs in the revision process of the "Universal Procedures"? Was there any consultation process?[176]

2.2.4 Unintended Consequences

In February 2021, the FATF formally acknowledged the unintended consequences resulting from the misinterpretation or incorrect implementation of its standards. This phenomenon became more perceptible with the adoption of the 2012 Recommendations that reinforced the standards and introduced the *RBA* as a new foundation paradigm,[177] and with the 2013 Methodology that introduces *effectiveness* as a separate assessment tool.[178]

Jurisdictions facing new and more demanding standards and assessment requirements, together with a certain degree of unpreparedness are two ground factors that may have contributed, to some extent, to the inadequate application of the Recommendations.[179] Furthermore, the fear of reputational damage in the event of backlisting may have potentially paved the way to overzealous application of the Recommendations.[180]

176 2023 Universal Procedures: "Before updating the Universal Procedures, the FATF should consider the impact of any changes on the FSRBs. Where any evaluation procedure of an assessment body continues to be inconsistent with the Universal Procedures, the FATF Secretariat would provide a paper to allow for a discussion by FATF's Evaluation and Compliance Group (ECG)", 5.

177 Jurisdictions are requested to identify, understand and assess their national-level vulnerabilities (risks) within their AML/CFT regimes. See 2022 WB Report on 'National Assessments of Money Laundering Risks: Learning from Eight Advanced Countries' when it states that a "meaningful risk-based approach requires a good understanding of how risks are distributed", 29.

178 See Chapter 2.

179 Koker comments on the lack of understanding by some financial operators, DFNBPS, and even from regulators/supervisors of the meaning of RBA. There is also possible misplayed guidance, as well as to proper notion of the meaning of "proportional and adequate measures to mitigate the risk". 'Financial Action Task Force Standards and Financial Inclusion: What Should Be Done – and What Should Not Be Done – to Improve the Alignment between Integrity and Inclusion Policy Objectives' (23/08/2020) *La Trobe Law Tech*, 15–16. Also, 2015 Report on 'Unintended Consequences of Anti-Money Laundering Policies for Poor Countries', *Center for Global Development*, CGD Working Group Report (2015 CGD Report), 5.

180 The same is valid for FATF's (ICRG) action plans. Michael Pisa mentions that "critics contend that supervisors and financial institutions in some developing countries, wary of crossing a regulatory redline, have erred on the side of caution by implementing laws and company policies that are more stringent than those required by the FATF. The result, they argue, is a culture of rigid, non-risk-based 'overcompliance' that makes it more difficult to provide financial services to the poor", 2019 Paper 'Does the Financial Action Task Force (FATF) Help or Hinder Financial Inclusion? A Study of FATF Mutual Evaluation Reports', *Center for Global Development*, CGD Policy Paper 143 (2019 Pisa Report), 3.

A project to understand the existence, causes and extent of the negative impact of some of the FATF Recommendations was conducted in collaboration with different stakeholders, resulting in the 'High-Level Synopsis Stocktake of the Unintended Consequences of the FATF Standards' (2021 FATF Synopsis Stocktake),[181] where four areas were identified: de-risking, financial exclusion, undue targeting of NPOs and the curtailment of human rights (with a focus on due process and procedural rights).[182]

2.2.4.1 *De-risking*

According to FATF's definition de-risking is: "the phenomenon of financial institutions terminating or restricting business relationships with clients or categories of clients to avoid, rather than manage, risk in line with the FATF's risk-based approach".[183] FIs are asked to adopt a RBA on the basis of materiality and risk with their clients (CDD/KYC) and implement adequate preventive measures to identify and mitigate ML/TF/PF risks.

However, FIs have adopted a conservative approach of not providing certain financial services to high-risk activities, market segments, or clients in order to mitigate the risk and avoid heavy fines, monitoring and prosecution and/or reputational damage in case of non-compliance with the AML/CFT/CPF standards and the RBA. Measures may include denying or terminating certain financial services to NPOs, firms, MVTS, retail customers or corresponding banking from countries profiled as high-risk or 'considered vulnerable'.[184]

In reality, a conservative approach is less costly, less time-consuming, safer and easier than a case-by-case RBA analysis. This situation and its impact have been acknowledged in the 2015 CGD Report on 'Unintended Consequences of Anti-Money Laundering Policies for Poor Countries' of the Center for Global Development, as regards banks in Australia, UK and USA that ceased to provide

181 At: https://www.fatf-gafi.org/media/fatf/documents/Unintended-Consequences.pdf.

182 Financial exclusion and inadequate application of Recommendation 8 have been identified and object of FATF's Typologies, Best Practices, Guidance Papers, and targeted in FATF's Standards, including prompting amendments to Recommendations and/or INotes, and 2013 Methodology.

183 At: https://www.fatf-gafi.org/en/publications/Fatfgeneral/Rba-and-de-risking.html.

184 2017 IMF Paper on Loss of CBRs in the Caribbean: Trends, Impact, and Policy Options demonstrates that "compliance costs associated with the due diligence required to meet these standards, combined with low expected profits and the large fines and reputational damage for violations, are primary reasons given for withdrawing CBRs", 16. On this subject, also, the Opinion of the European Banking Authority (EBA) on De-Risking which analyses the factors and consequences of de-risking (EBA/Op./2022/01, 05/01/2022), at: https://www.eba.europa.eu › *Publications* › *Opinions*.

services to small money transfer operators (MTOs) in certain regions, affecting jurisdictions where these operations and services are an important source of revenue and a way for migrant workers to send money home.[185]

Jurisdictions are requested to conduct an NRA (Governments), a sectorial RBA (regulators/supervisors) and an operational RBA (FIs and DFNBPs), a three-tiered RBA assessment involving all stakeholders, namely public and private sectors. However, this is a complex and costly task. For low-income and lower middle-income economies, transversal requisites, such as financial and human resources, that are required to conduct an RBA on a case-by-case basis can be discouraging or even detrimental, leading to choose a 'safe' approach.[186]

2.2.4.2 *Financial Exclusion*

Financial exclusion is the denial of financial services. The FATF has been paying attention to this phenomenon aiming at bringing more individuals into the formal financial system where transactions can be more easily monitored. This strategy reduces the ML/FT/PF risks and attempts to change the practice of relying in systems like hawala, unlicensed MVTS or cash couriers.[187]

The 2017 WB Global Findex Database on 'Measuring Financial Inclusion and the Fintech Revolution', covering 140 economies, concluded that in high-income economies 94% of adults have an account while in developing economies only 63% do. It is stated:

185 At: viii, 15 *et seq*. On the economic and social impact of FATF's standards, their implementation, the application of the RBA and consequences in the NPO sector in poor countries, see the 2015 Statewatch and Human Security Collective Study (n 148) or EBA Opinion on De-risking, ibid.

186 About the consequences of de-risking such as financial exclusion and the use of less transparent channels amongst others, Koker (n 179); EBA Opinion on De-risking, ibid, para. 8 and 10. Also, A/HRC/50/23, paras. 42–45, A/70/371, para.s. 42–44; A/HRC/40/52, para. 51 and 62.

187 The FATF recognised that financial integrity and financial inclusion as complementary and mutually beneficiary in the FATF Guidance on 'Anti-Money Laundering and Terrorist Financing Measures and Financial Inclusion' (2013 and 2017). In 2012, Ministers stated that financial exclusion is a "real risk" factor to the implementation of FATF's Recommendations, especially to jurisdictions "with capacity constraints", para. 6. In 2019, Ministers reiterated that the FATF "will continue to promote financial inclusion and encourage proportionate and effective implementation of the FATF standards by countries in line with the risk-based approach", para.13.

> Many poor people around the world lack the financial services that can serve these functions, such as bank accounts and digital payments. Instead, they rely on cash – which can be unsafe and hard to manage.[188]

The 2021 WB Global Index Database on 'Financial Inclusion, Digital Payments, and Resilience in the Age of Covid-19', accounting 123 economies, indicates some improvement; from 2017 to 2021, the average rate of account ownership in developing economies increased 8%, from 63% to 71% of adults.[189]

In order to increase financial inclusion, the RBA concedes some flexibility to FIs, namely, the use of *simplified customer due diligence* (SDD) measures like exemptions and simplifications procedures for clients that present a low risk profile, reducing time, proceedings, costs and encouraging the use of the formal financial channel.

However, regardless of global efforts, practice has shown that some jurisdictions apply stricter measures, such as residential address verification or other identification requirements,[190] instead of applying risk-based SDD measures, consisting of a proportionality test and an RBA on a case-by-case basis. This scenario is more common in low-income jurisdictions that prefer to apply a safer approach, especially if they are under the ME or ICRG processes.[191] As noted by Michel Pisa:

> [D]eveloping countries continue to implement laws that are not risk based and impose more stringent account opening requirements for low-income and low risk persons or products than those required by

188 At: 1 (Asli Demirgüç-Kunt, Leora Klapper, Dorothe Singer, Saniya Ansar and Jake Hess). One of the findings indicates that the use financial technology, including the use of mobile phones and the internet to execute financial transactions are two examples on how digital technology can promote financial inclusion and reduce costs, 2.

189 Executive Summary (Demirgüç-Kunt, Klapper, Singer, Ansar), 2. On the challenges, benefits to financial inclusion but also on the risks of using new technologies if not well-regulated and governed (digital identification); Douglas Arner, Dirk Zetzsche, Ross Buckley and Janos Barberis, 'The Identity Challenge in Finance: From Analogue Identity to Digitized Identification to Digital KYC Utilities' (2019) 20(4) *European Business Organization Law Review*.

190 Pisa comments that according to the 2017 WB Survey on 'Global Financial Inclusion and Consumer Protection' of 124 jurisdictions: 75% required proof of address to open an account; 69% required proof of nationality or legal status; 44% required proof of income; and 35% (n 180) 12. Amongst others, Mathew Ferreira, Albert Van der Linden and Barry Cooper, 'Proof of Address Must Fall' (2018), at: https://cenfri.org/articles/proof-of-address-must-fal.

191 Koker (n 179) 6, 13–15.

the global standards, due to uncertainty over how to implement the RBA and fear of being publicly identified for shortcomings in their AML/CFT framework.[192]

2.2.4.3 *Undue Restrictions for Non-profit Organisations*

Reports and studies from the NPO community[193] and experts[194] have indicated and proven undue restrictions in the NPO sector/civil society by misinterpretation, misuse, excessive or even unjustified measures under the pretext of countering terrorism or CFT, including implementing and complying with FATF Recommendation 8, seriously undermining the legitimate activities of NPOs.[195]

---

192 (n 180) 12.

193 Eg. Reports or studies from the Global NPO Coalition, at: https://fatfplatform.org or from the Charity & Security Network, at: https://charityandsecurity.org/search-page/. Also, 2012 Hayes Report (n 168); 2015 Statewatch and Human Security Collective Study (n 148); 2015 CGD Report (n 179); 2017 Report on 'Challenges Facing Civil Society Organisations Working on Human Rights in the EU', European Union Agency for Fundamental Rights; 2019 Report on 'FATF's Recommendation 8 on Non-profit Organisations: A New Tool to Unfairly and Dangerously Shrink Civil Society Space', Working Group on Torture & Terrorism (OMCT-SOS-Torture Network Members) (2019 OMCT-SOS Report).

194 Amongst others, HR Special Rapporteurs to the UN General Assembly or to the HRC. Eg. A/70/371, 18/09/2015 examines the negative impact of counterterrorism legislation and other measures on civil society, para. 7–8, 17–30 or 42; A/HRC/23/39, 24/04/2013, para. 26; A/HRC/40/52; A/HRC/50/23, 10/05/2022; A/HRC/50/49, 12/05/2022. Also, 2010 WB Report on 'Non-Profit Organisations and the Combatting of Terrorism Financing: A Proportionate Response' (Emile van der Does de Willebois and others), Working Paper No. 208 (2010 De Willebois Report); 2016 Global Survey of the Implementation by member States of Security Council Resolution 1373 (2001) (S/2016/49) compiled by the CTED (2016 Global Survey); the 2020 Joint Report (S/2020/493) of the CTED and the Analytical Support and Sanctions Monitoring Team pursuant to Resolutions 1526 (2004) and 2253 (2015) concerning Islamic State in Iraq and the Levant (ISIL) (Da'esh), Al-Qaeda and the Taliban and Associated Individuals and Entities on Actions taken by Member States to Disrupt Terrorist Financing, prepared pursuant to Paragraph 37 of Security Council Resolution 2462 (2019) (2020 CTED Joint Report). This last report is based on 112 replies to questionnaires by member States, concluding that 54% of responding States never identified cases of terrorism financing through the NPO, and most reporting States never dealt with a case of misuse of an NPO for terrorism-financing purposes, para. 78–79.

195 A/70/371, para. 7–8, 10. 2009 Report on 'Tackling the Financing of Terrorism' from the UN Counter-Terrorism Implementation Task Force states that: "It is important to be realistic about the actual use of this sector for terrorism financing. As a percentage of the total NPO financial flows, TF-related funds are very small", UN Counter-Terrorism Implementation Task Force (CTITF WG), 16–17. Also, Romaniuk and Keatinge provide a background on the evolution of Recommendation 8 (ex-SR VIII) raising doubts and pointing the lack of evidence, stating that "within a few short years, NPO found themselves subject to

Although recognising the essential role of NPOs in society,[196] the original text of Recommendation 8 and its INote (2012 Recommendations) refer that indistinctly all NPOs were "particularly vulnerable" to FT, asking countries to "ensure that they cannot be misused", leading to incorrect assumptions and interpretations.[197]

A 2015 Study on 'Countering Terrorism or Constraining Civil Society? The Impact of Financial Action Task Force Recommendations on Non-Profit Organisations in Central and Eastern Europe and Central Asia' from the Statewatch and Human Security Collective concludes that the "FATF R8 compliance mechanism (i) is an important vehicle for the imposition of NPO regulations worldwide, and (ii) can override parliamentary scrutiny of draft legislation that has a critical impact on freedom of association and expression".[198]

Some jurisdictions have actually introduced unbalanced or disproportionate measures, including overregulation of the standard or non-differentiation of high and low risk NPOs for ME or ICRG assessment purposes[199] or have intentionally adopted measures that hinder HR and humanitarian work.[200]

---

international soft law that reflected an empirically unfounded global consensus concerning their relative vulnerability", (n 119) 276.

196 See original para. 1 of INote of Recommendation 8 (2012) and para. 2 of INote of Recommendation 8 as amended in 2016.

197 It is important to recall the historical background of Recommendation 8 which replicates former SR VIII, adopted in 2001 after 9/11 events. See, A/74/335, para. 34 or, amongst others, Romaniuk and Keatinge (n 119) 267–268.

198 At: 53.

199 Eg. Obligation to register or de-registration, burdensome, complex or excessively bureaucratic procedures and documentation for registration; restriction or denial of financial services; intrusive supervision, such as excessive audit, monitor (eg. assembly notes or lists of members and personnel); or dissuasive sanctions, such as accounts freezing, fines, decertification or de-licensing. Also, A/70/371, para. 17–30; 42, HRC/40/52, para. 31 or 42; A/HRC/50/23, para. 37–39 provide concrete examples. Amongst others, Lia van Broekhoven and Sangeeta Goswami, 'Can Stakeholder Dialogues Help Solve Financial Access Restrictions Faced by Non-profit Organisations That Stem from Countering Terrorism Financing Standards and International Sanctions?' (2021) 163 *International Review of the Red Cross*. The authors make an overview of different type of financial restrictions to NPO and stakeholders dialogue, progress achieved and room for improvement.

200 As stated in the 2019 OMCT-SOS Report: "[I]n the name of counterterrorism and security, they [NGOs and human rights defenders] are arrested, arbitrary detained, prosecuted, sentenced to heavy prison terms, attacked, threatened and harassed, for documenting human rights violations and calling on their governments to fulfil their legal obligation to respect the fundamental rights of all citizens. These patterns have been particularly pronounced in countries that have a poor human rights record and repressive practices but have also occurred in countries that pride themselves on upholding fundamental values of democracy and human rights", 1. Also, A/HRC/40/52, para. 31 and 42; A/64/226, 04/08/

This negative bearing on NPOs derives not only from Governments but also from other sectors of society. A 2017 Report on 'Financial Access for US NonProfits' from the Charity & Security Network provides relevant data as to the effect of Recommendation 8, including de-risking and stringent regulatory measures by the private and public sectors, enlightening that this "impact is global and not limited to conflict zones or fragile and failing States", but also impacting in democratic States.[201]

Many NPOs had to re-consider their humanitarian assistance operations in vulnerable areas to terrorism, including financial support for their staff on the ground, due to the costs in finding practical solutions to provide a minimum of adequate and safe assistance; and these costs were not only monetary, time was also of essence to promptly delivery humanitarian assistance.[202]

As a result, and under pressure, the FATF adopted several measures, including providing guidance to assist in the adequate implementation of Recommendation 8 (2013 and 2015),[203] engaging in constructive

2009, para. 114 and 118; A/HRC/20/27, 21/05/2012, para. 65 and 75; A/70/371, para. 30; A/HRC/50/23, para. 18–32 on access to foreign funding.

201 Executive Summary (Sue Eckert, with Kay Guinane and Andrea Hall). The study includes a universe of 8,665 NPOs with operations abroad (eg. education, development/poverty reduction, humanitarian relief, public health, medical services, HR/democracy building and peace operations/peace building), two thirds experienced banking problems, with the most common reasons being: delays of wire transfers, which can last up to several months (37%), unusual documentation requests (26%), increased fees (33%), account closures (6%) and refusal to open accounts (10%). Fifteen percent of the NPOs have these types of constraints on a regular basis, and 45% are involved in humanitarian relief work. Also, 2015 CGD Report (n 179); A/HRC/40/52, para. 62; A/HRC/50/23, para. 42–45. In 2019, the Dutch Gender Platform Women and Human Security Collective reported the impact of CFT measures on 20 Dutch NGOs working on women's human rights and gender equality and concluded that 85% experienced increased demands in terms of compliance (ie. banks, donors, MTS), 70% faced onerous information requests and delays in transfers and 45% faced denials of transfers. 'Shadow Report on UNSCR 2242 – Protecting Us by Tying Our Hands – Impact of Measures to Couter Terrorism Financing on Dutch NGO's Working on Women's Human Rights and Gender Equality', 21-30.

202 Amongst others, Global NPO Coalition on FATF Reply to EBA, ibid, 2; Executive Summary of the 2017 Report on 'Financial Access for US NonProfits' states that 42% of American NPOs reported that sometimes were forced to carry cash. 2015 CGD Report mentions that the "HSBC closed the bank account of several NPOs including the Cordoba Foundation, a think tank that receives money from the UK government for work to prevent terrorism" and that NPOs working in conflict zones had to resort to less regulated and transparent alternative channels, (n 179) 38.

203 Eg. 2013 and 2015 Best Practices on Combatting the Abuse of NPOs; 2014 Guidelines on Combatting the Abuse of NPOS; 2019 Guidance on Terrorist Financing Risk Assessment. Also, A/HRC/43/46, 21/02/2020, para. 11; A/70/371, para. 23 and 27.

dialogue with the NPO sector (Chapter 2, Section 9.2. above),[204] and amending Recommendation 8 and its INote to clarify which type of NPOs should be subject to supervision and to an RBA (June 2016). The principle of proportionality was incorporated into the standard, and a specific reference added: CFT measures should be "implemented in a manner which respects countries' obligations under the Charter of the United Nations and international human rights law."[205]

Regardless of efforts to mitigate the adverse impact of relevant laws and policies related to the incorrect implementation of Recommendation 8, they were/are not sufficient to override the practice, as different sources continue to report misapplication and abuses.[206]

In November 2021, the Global NPO Coalition reported to the FATF President that the Israeli Government validated the designation of six Palestinian NGOs on HR and humanitarian aid as terrorists to conform with international standards by citing FATF Recommendation 8 and its INote.[207] As a reaction, the Global NPO Coalition expressed great concern with the potential politicisation of FATF's Standards, process and impact on international human rights, humanitarian, and refugee law.

In March 2022, in a virtual side event of the 49th Session of the UN Human Rights Council, Karen Janjua (Community World Service Asia) referred that following the 2018 ME of Pakistan, the National Counter Terrorism Authority adopted new legislation with vague terminology under FATF Guidance, leading to supervisory 'harassment' and abusive investigations, with 65,000–110,000 Pakistani NPOs registrations being revoked. These legislative changes aimed to remove Pakistan from FATF's 'Grey List'.[208]

204 A/74/335, para. 42. See: www.fatfplatform.org.

205 Para. 2.

206 A/74/335, para. 34–35; A/HRC/20/23, para. 33–39; 2019 OMCT-SOS Report (n 193); Koker (n 179) 11. Amongst others, Georgios Pavlidis, 'The Dark Side of Anti-Money Laundering: Mitigating the Unintended Consequences of FATF Standards' (2023) 2 *Journal of Economic Criminology*.

207 At: https://fatfplatform.org/news/global-coalition-letter-to-fatf-on-israeli-designation-of-6-npos-using/ *or* https://fatfplatform.org/assets/Global-Coalition-Response-re-Israel-UN-Letter-Citing-FATF.pdf.

208 'The Financial Action Task Force (FATF) and the Case of Pakistan', *Respect, Protect and Fulfil: Guaranteeing Access to Resources as a State Responsibility*, at: https://charityandsecurity.org/news/un-human-rights-councils-49th-session-side-event-on-restrictions-on-access-to-resources-debilitating-impact-on-civil-society/. Hayes mentions the cases of FATF evaluators endorsing or encouraging restrictive NPO regulations on Burma/Myanmar, Cambodia, Colombia, Egypt, India, Indonesia, Paraguay, Russia, Saudi Arabia, Sierra Leone, Tunisia and Uzbekistan, 2012 Hayes Report (n 168) 10. In the 2015 Statewatch and Human Security Collective Study, it is stated that: "Hungary and India provide the

As a corollary of huge political and public pressure, given extensive evidence from many stakeholders, especially the fact that the Recommendation interferes with matters of high relevance, such as human rights and humanitarian relief,[209] in October 2023, the FATF agreed to amend Recommendation 8 and its INote to address these concerns, explaining that not all NPO sector is affected and that jurisdictions need to assess FT risks without "disrupting or discouraging legitimate NPO activities".[210]

2.2.4.4 *Curtailment of Human Rights with a Focus on Due Process and Procedural Rights*

The potential misuse of FATF's Standards in the context of human rights is also refereed in the 2021 FATF Synopsis Stocktake, namely due process and procedural rights (eg. due process, right to be heard, right to legal representation, right to fair trial, right to appeal and legal remedies) in relation to Recommendation 5 on the 'Criminalisation of Terrorist Financing Offence' and Recommendation 6 on 'Targeted Financial Sanctions related to Terrorism and Terrorist Financing' (application of UNSC Resolutions under Chapter VII of the UN Charter).[211]

---

most clear-cut examples in this report of States unduly restricting the legitimate activities of civil society organisations; in both cases laws that were passed at least partly to satisfy FATF requirements were used to justify and enact repressive legislation.", (n 148), 53–54. The case studies from the 2019 OMCT-SOS Report also reveal a common link: the need jurisdictions to show progress after the MER's recommendations, ICRG action plan, and/or fear of being blacklisted. The report indicates that several amendments were undertaken under the guidance or supervision of the FATF which are highly questionable as regards HR protection. See, Thailand's case, the Government had to withdraw the NPO bill because of claims that it restricted severely HR, such as freedom of expression and association, and established discriminatory restrictions against organisations that receive foreign funds, (n 193). The International Commission of Jurists has underscored "the imprecise and overbroad language of the draft law, which would allow for abusive and arbitrary application by the Thai authorities on 'Not-for-Profit Organisations'". 'Thailand: Repressive Draft Law on the Operation of Not-for-Profit Organisations Must Be Revised or Scrapped' (31/03/2021) International Commission of Jurist, at: https://www.icj.org/thailand-repressive-draft-law-on-the-operation-of-not-for-profit-organizations-must-be-revised-or-scrapped/.

209 Expert reports, such as the HRC, CTED/CTC, IMF, WB and NPOs.

210 At: https://www.fatf-gafi.org/en/publications/Fatfgeneral/outcomes-fatf-plenary-october-2023.html.

211 At: 5–6. In relation to the lack of due process and human rights and the fight against terrorism, amongst others, Gacinto della Cananea, 'Return to the Due Process of Law: The European Union and the Fight against Terrorism' (2007) 32 *European Law Review*; Jared Genser and Kate Barth, 'When Due Process Concerns Become Dangerous: The Security

The FATF recognises that the use of excessive broad meaning of terrorism and FT definitions may lead to investigations and prosecutions other than terrorists or those supporting terrorism, including human rights activists, and to the application of wrongful preventive measures, namely restrictions on the freedom of expression, association or manifestation.[212]

By way of illustration, FATF's President's reply to the HR Rapporteur in relation to Serbia in 2020:

> We share your concerns regarding the allegations that Serbia misused its Law on the Prevention of Money Laundering and the Financing of Terrorism with the aim to restrict or coerce civil society actors for their work and criticism of the Government. The FATF takes such allegations seriously and considers actions such as the ones subject to these allegations antithetical to our Standards, particularly the risk-based approach set out in Recommendation 8 in relation to NPOs.[213]

The FATF also acknowledges that the use of certain ML/FT investigative techniques, or for assets' freezing purposes may involve: i) arbitrary or unlawful interference with privacy or risk of racial, political or religious profiling; ii) covert surveillance on the freedom of expression, peaceful assembly and association; and iii) gathering and sharing of personal information, such as social security, tax records, transaction records and travel records.[214]

Aside from the ones referred above, there are also reports that some jurisdictions have implemented asset freezing regimes pursuant to UNSCR 1373 (2001) without adequate procedural human rights safeguards, *inter alia*: insufficient information on the grounds for listing, absence of an independent or impartial

Council's 1267 Regime and the Need for Reform' (2010) 33(1) *Boston College International and Comparative Law Review*; Rodiles (119).

212 2016 Global Survey discloses that "a number of shortcomings" in domestic counter-terrorism legislation, excessive restrictions, and lack of law enforcement oversight, para. 397, 399 and 437. This is reiterated by the HR Special Rapporteur, when underpins that these overly broad terrorism and FT definitions "can lead to relevant laws targeting conduct protected under international human rights law or, at least, that which is not terrorist in nature and thereby to the misapplication of law and of resources.", A/74/335, para. 39. Also A/HRC/50/49, para. 16–17 and 20–21.

213 At: https://spcommreports.ohchr.org/TMResultsBase/DownLoadFile?gId=35813.

214 2016 Global Survey, para. 398, 402 and 413; 2020 CTED Joint Report, para. 73–74; Koker (n 179) 10–12.

authority to review the decision, unclear de-listing and unfreezing procedures, delays in de-listing or arbitrary assets freezing.[215]

Furthermore, assets freezing encompasses other human rights, such as social and economic rights like basic living expenses, family expenses and right to property, which can be equally affected by overzealous restrictions on managing funds or by the absence or delays in exemptions.[216]

While the implementation of these Recommendations is directly associated with the application of UNSC Resolutions under Chapter VII of the UN Charter, there are a number of FATF Standards, criteria and benchmarks, including CDD, KYC, information sharing, new investigative techniques that deal with the right to privacy, data protection and non-discrimination, which are also fundamental rights.[217] Akin to the NPO sector, the exercise of human rights has been hampered or at risk by domestic legislation of some jurisdictions under the pretext of countering terrorism and FT, and pertaining to comply with the FATF Standards.[218]

According to the HR Special Rapporteur, the responsibility for balancing both international obligations relating to human rights, humanitarian law

---

215 In many jurisdictions, such procedures are either absent or unknown and insufficiently used in practice. See 2016 Global Survey, para. 416; 2020 CTED Joint Report, para. 30. Furthermore, a potential conflict of values and interests may rise in other spheres. For example, the 2015 Statewatch and Human Security Collective Study questions the balance between MONEYVAL's mandate to implement CFT requirements and CoE's obligations under Articles 1 (obligation to respect HR), 10 (freedom of expression) and 11 (freedom of assembly and association) of the ECHR (n 148) 10, 54–55. Borlini and Montanaro also address the tension between the "incorporation of FATF soft law standards" into EU's legal framework, especially the compatibility with EU constitutional fundamental rights and freedoms, providing as examples, the ECJ ruling *Jyske Bank Gibraltar* (Case C-212/11) related to the freedom to provide services under Article 56 TFEU and the ECJ ruling *Ordre des Barreaux* (Case C-305/05) related to the right to a fair trial under Article 6 of the ECHR. Both cases where analysed in light of the existing EU/domestic AML/CFT legislation, as well as the right to privacy, data protection and the principle of proportionality, (n 79) 1040, 1060–1061.

216 Eg. Basic living expenses. Amongst others, Bulterman, 'Implementation of Financial UN Sanctions: Jurisdictional Problems related to Genuine Global Governance' in P. Slot and M. Bulterman (eds.), *Globalization and Jurisdiction* (Kluwer Law International 2004), 262–266; Bianchi (n 95) 907–908.

217 A/74/335, para. 44; A/HRC/40/52, para. 31. Amongst others, Mirja Ciesiolka, 'Protecting the Right to Privacy while Combating Terrorism Finance' (05/08/2019) University of Zurich, at: https://www.ohchr.org/sites/default/files/Documents/Issues/Terrorism/SR/Submissions/Mirja_Ciesiolka_GA74CT.pdf.

218 Amongst others, Colin Tyre QC, 'Anti-Money Laundering Legislation: Implementation of the FATF Forty Recommendations in the European Union' (2010) 69 *Journal of the Professional Lawyer*.

and refugee law and the fight against terrorism and FT rests not only on all FATF and FSRBS members,[219] but also with the FATF,[220] especially when its Recommendations have been endorsed by the UNSC, therefore requiring higher standards of commitment and responsibility of the UN core values.[221] The Special Rapporteur also notes that there is a human rights standard gap in FATF's framework and that FATF should introduce "comprehensive human rights benchmarking" into its standards.[222]

3 Summary

The FATF is a recognised organisation with global governance responsibilities with more than 30 years of existence that recently celebrated the tenth anniversary of the 2012 Forty Recommendations. These recommendations have been continuously updated to face new threats and needs of the international community.[223]

The FATF may take the opportunity to carry out a self-assessment of its strengths and weaknesses, as well as to analyse the effectiveness of its global enforcement mechanism and the impact of its actions outside the financial sector,[224] given the complexity of the impact at domestic national level and

219 A/74/335, para. 38.

220 A/74/335, para. 44.

221 A/74/335, para. 33, 44, 46; A/70/371, para. 9–11; A/HRC/50/23, para. 67. It is also a fact that after the 9/11, even the UNSC adopt a number of Resolutions to counter terrorism under Chapter VII of the UN Charter with scarce human rights' reference.

222 A/74/335, para. 46 and 55 (also, para. 27, 36–38, 43–44, 66); A/HRC/50/23, para. 36 and 67. Amongst others, Ciesiolka (n 217) 6–7. Young rightly mentions that ME assessors should not endorse AML/CFT national measures "that are in obvious breach of fundamental principles of domestic law or international human rights law". 'Policing and Prosecution of Money Laundering' in V. Mitsilegas, S. Hufnagel and A. Moiseienko (eds), *Research Handbook on Transnational Crime* (Edward Elgar Publishing 2019),140.

223 Keatinge comments that the FATF has "missed a golden opportunity [2019 Mandate] to reflect on its own shortcomings and effectiveness" instead of exclusively looking at the "shortcomings of others via its evaluation process" (n 164).

224 Keatinge critically observes that the FATF "has no basis on which to determine whether its actions (...) are genuinely effective in achieving a reduction in financial crime; it is merely assumed that the implementation of its standards have the desired result", ibid. Gelemerova mentions "it is indeed a panopticon built on quicksand (...) one may wonder what is more threatening: the age-old laundering phenomenon or the control hunger of the authorities, learning so little of their own panopticon", *The Anti-Money Laundering System in the Context of Globalization: A Panopticon Built on Quicksand?* (Wolf Legal Publishers 2011), 258. Amongst others, Nance, 'The Regime that FATF Built: An Introduction to the Financial Action Task Force' (2018) 69 *Crime Law and Social Change,*

the sensitive nature of certain subjects addressed by the FATF, such as human rights.

As regards the inherent shortfalls of the FATF, the organisation might consider improving its institutional design, including format and procedures,[225] as well as making an explicit reference to its core principles in the Mandate and the HLPOs and adding a human rights standard to them. A more equitable participation or representation *ratio* of the FSRBs jurisdictions in decision-making could be ensured to increase its legitimacy and transparency.

Through FATF statements and Ministerial Declarations, these core principles, values, and principles of good governance have been progressively incorporated into FATF *aquis*, marking constructive steps in this direction. Yet, it would be beneficial to adopt a single instrument that includes such *acquis* in a coherent, systematic, and comprehensive manner.

There is also this complex and uneasy situation in which the FATF is at the vertex of the hierarchical structure with decision-making capacity and public functions (global standard-setter, keeper, and arbiter), but with a less formal institutional design when compared to the formal institutional design of most of its regional bodies (Chapter 2, Section 8 above).

The FATF could establish a more formal institutional background by adopting a formal instrument, not necessarily treaty-based, such as a MoU like the ESAAMLG and MENAFATF, and by establishing publicly known rules of procedure for its internal bodies.

The ME and ICRG processes should be more open and inclusive, incorporating a holistic approach with proportionate, flexible, and realistic solutions by taking into consideration the factual capacity of jurisdictions and their national and regional contexts in order to implement FATF's Standards and action plans.

Regarding the FATF's general shortcomings, the organisation might consider establishing a comprehensive *checks and balances* system and improving

---

123; Gallant, 'Promise and Perils: The Making of Global Money Laundering, Terrorist Finance Norms' (2010) 13(3) *Journal of Money Laundering Control*, 180; Michael Brzoska, 'A Good Thing Gone Too Far? External Assessments and Counterterrorist Finance-Related Measures in the European Union' in M. Brzoska (ed), *European Peace and Security Policy: Transitional Risks of Violence* (NOMOS Bloomsbury 2014). Barbara Vettori also comments on the little scientific knowledge about the effectiveness and efficiency of the AML countermeasures and the questions there reason why they are not assessed. 'Evaluating Anti-Money Laundering Policies: Where Are We?' in B. Unger and D. van der Linde (eds), *Research Handbook on Money Laundering* (Edward Elgar Publishing 2013).

225 According to Tilahun the FATF is a soft organisation, (n 78). See remarks on Chapter 2, footnote 91.

its internal and external oversight mechanisms. This could involve the introduction of a peer review panel, an appeals process, or a complaint mechanism, which would promote broader public accountability.[226]

In relation to the unintended consequences of FATF Standards, the FATF Plenary decided to analyse how it could refine its work and mitigate them.[227] The FATF has already addressed concerns related to Recommendation 8, but de-risking and financial exclusion continue to be problematic.

Paradoxically, the 2021 FATF Synopsis Stocktake also demonstrates that, while attempting to ensure the safety and integrity of the financial market, the incorrect implementation of the international AML/CFT standards by the different stakeholders (eg. Government, regulators, FIs) either by overregulation, over supervision, oversanctioning or even by adopting a conservative RBA, etc, has the perverse effect of encouraging the use of non-formal, non-regulated, or less regulated financial channels, thus reducing transactions' transparency and increasing the risk of ML/FT/PF.

The FATF backlisting process has also another unintended consequence that requires improvement. While the FATF backlisting process, as previously mentioned, is not a 'punitive' measure, it can have a double-edged impact; it not only highlights the global AML/CFT/CPF deficiencies of the designated jurisdictions, but it also has the potential to economically isolate them. The case of jurisdictions under the 'Grey List' that may be losing or seeing reduced foreign development aid and funds during the ICRG process, or even after being delisted, questions the *rationale* of the monitoring and sanctioning process.[228]

It should be emphasised that the issues of legitimacy, rule of law,[229] transparency, and accountability gaps are common challenges for all IOs exerting

226 2012 Hayes Report (n 168) 37–38. Keatinge comments that while the "FATF itself commits to enhancing the transparency of the financial system, but not of itself. There is sadly little 'new' in the FATF's new mandate beyond the agreement that it should be open-ended, arguably a retrograde step, reducing accountability.", (n 164). The author argues that by transforming FATF's into a permanent body the accountability mechanisms have been reduced (before there was a scrutiny every 8 years). I do not share the same point of view because there is now a bi-annual meeting at the highest level.

227 At: https://www.fatf-gafi.org/en/publications/Fatfgeneral/Plenary-march-2022.html.

228 As Koker, Howell and Morr mention: "[p]unitive economic consequences, especially in relation to development aid and funding, would seem to run counter to the spirit and objective of the Period IV listings. (…) FATF listing processes that trigger negative economic consequences for countries that are committed to resolving deficiencies and are swiftly acting in terms of an agreed action plan to do so, should be subjected to close policy scrutiny by all FATF stakeholders", (n 156) 23.

229 On the rule of law as a paradigm, amongst others, Blokker (n 118); Klabbers (n 118); same author (n 111). Alvarez mentions the work carried out by the UN, including UNSC Resolutions referencing, the Rule of Law Coordination and Resource Group and the

public authority, nonetheless the FATF should reflect on them to validate its role on the international plane in a manner that is consistent with the principles of good governance.

Enhancements such as these would increase the FATF's legitimacy and credibility while providing strong evidence that the organisation is firmly committed to ethical governance values and high scrutiny standards, particularly when claiming for the integrity and transparency of the global financial sector. Additionally, they would demonstrate that the FATF is living up to the political legitimacy that is being bestowed upon it by other relevant IOs, such as the UN/UNSC, IMF, or WB, as well as States.

An open and constructive debate about the mandate, powers and actions of the FATF, including transparent regulation and oversight mechanisms, as well as the inclusion of core principles, values and an international human rights standard in its constitutional instruments should be envisioned.

affirmation of the rule of law as a general principle of the UN. The rule of law should be understood and exported to other IOs as a principle and associated with "good governance", for this goal the contribution of the Resolution of the General Assembly on the rule of law at the national and international levels (A/RES/64/116, 15/01/2010) should be underscored (para. 4 of the Preamble), (n 152) 46–47.

CHAPTER 6

Conclusion

The FATF is an unconventional IO that illustrates the dynamics of the international legal system. The same dynamics that gave rise to the emergence of IOs in the nineteenth century to address collective challenges is changing the configuration of traditional IOs and international lawmaking in the twenty-first century towards new patterns and realities in global governance.

This study on the FATF is pertinent because it clarifies the legal status of this organisation endowed with the heavy responsibility of safeguarding the integrity and security of the international financial system by countering money laundering, financing of terrorism and the financing of the proliferation of weapons of mass destruction in the international legal system.

The institutional metamorphosis of the FATF is a sound example on how the original nature of an organisation can evolve into a full-fledged IO, regardless of the initial intention of the members and the informal nature of the body. The gradual evolution of the FATF's mandate, institutional setting, and *modus operandi* on the international plane has changed its *modus constituendi*. In its evolution, the interaction between the different international actors, including members, non-members, UN/UNSC, EU, IMF, WB, G-20, in the international domain plays a crucial role in the manifestation of a general practice and acquiescence of the FATF's legal status.

A coherent, structured, and comprehensive five-elements *rationale* is conceptualised and applied to ascertain the legal personhood of an organisation when lacking the traditional and consensual elements of being treaty-based, created by States, and 'having an organ of its own' with a distinct will (*volunté disctincte*). This approach provides a rational basis to establish whether the organisation has a separate and autonomous will from its members.

On the basis of this conceptual approach, it has been demonstrated that the FATF meets all the essential criteria and qualifies as an IO:

1. Membership: it has been proven that its members are States, regional IOs and other entities (jurisdictions) with recognised legal status under international law;
2. Created under international law: it has been proven that it is created and developed by acts of international law, such as Declarations and other international collective acts of a constitutive nature that build and mould its constitutional framework and fulfil a parallel function to that of treaties or statutes of a formal IO;

 | DOI:10.1163/9789004715134_007

3. To have an organ with a distinct will: it has been proven that it has a separate and independent institutional setting (*acquis institutionel*), which assures the distinct and autonomous will of the organisation *vis-à-vis* its members. It is a permanent organisation with an autonomous institutional framework with organs that have decision-making capacity and act on behalf of the organisation, including a Secretariat with administrative apparatus, independent financial resources (financial autonomy), and headquarters arrangements;
4. To operate on the international plane according to international law: it has been proven that it is entrusted with a number of legal capacities, developed either explicitly or implicitly, expressing an autonomous will and independent standing from its members on the international plane. Its capacities are broad and far-reaching. The FATF self-perceives as the global standard-setter, keeper and arbiter for AML/CFT/CPF, assembling altogether a spectrum of capacities typically associated to formal IOs. The organisation has the authority to backlist and call for countermeasures to members and non-members, an authority granted to a selected few formal IOs. The impact of FATF's Recommendations, ME process and backlisting across the world is undeniable, including the possible emergence of customary international law through a body of practice and the general acquiescence of members and non-members;
5. External recognition by other subjects of international law: it has been proven that FATF interacts with other international stakeholders on the international plane, and that its role has been endorsed and legitimised by relevant IOs and other international bodies; the Resolutions of the UNSC under Chapter VII of the UN Charter also favour an implicit (if not explicit) perception that the FATF is a full-fledged IO.

The empirical analysis and contemporary conceptual approach contribute to the ongoing debate in public international law and international institutional law on the key elements that characterise an IO in international institutional law. This study stresses the risk of categorisation, overlooking or neglecting relevant objective and empirical elements offered by the international legal system, such as: (a) *how* the institutional framework of the organisation has evolved, *what* are the real and effective powers of that organisation; (b) *how* the organisation operates in practice on the international plane; (c) *how* the organisation is perceived by other international actors; and (d) *whether* its members and peers tacitly or expressly recognise its status as an IO.

The FATF is an *institutional legal fact*, created by and under the rules of general international law and customary international law and, consequently, with international legal personality, bearing rights and obligations under international law. It is endowed with public functions as a global standard-setter, keeper, and arbiter and is therefore bound to general principles and rules of international law and capable of being held internationally accountable.

The findings of this study are significant at a time when the FATF is inspiring and shaping other organisations, most likely being considered a contemporary or *avant-garde* IO model. Further studies should be conducted to assess its shortcomings and identify areas for improvement, especially within the framework of good governance and oversight mechanisms, as its decisions and actions have ramifications on a global and national scale, as well as on natural and legal persons.

The mandate and powers of the FATF are complex, broad, and multidisciplinary, comprising policy and lawmaking powers, monitoring and sanctioning powers that extend to non-members. The FATF has built a network of nine regional bodies that interconnects 206 jurisdictions across the world. An ingeniously designed system involving co-ordination, common interpretation and application of the Recommendations, common compliance, and articulated supervisory mechanisms. The concept of an *octopus-effect network* provides a faithful image of the internal and external *modus operandi* of the FATF's creative framework.

FATF's case-study paves the way for a more accurate analysis of other organisations with analogous characteristics that act on the international plane and hold public authority functions, but whose evolving legal nature remains unsettled, thus operating in a kind of institutional and accountability *vacuum* that overshadows clarity and legal certainty in the architecture of the international legal system of the twenty-first century.

The international legal system is not hermetic. A new generation of IOs is emerging, less formal and more dynamic in nature, with pragmatic approaches to international community concerns, which challenge the traditional axioms relating to the core criteria that qualify an IO, but which are nevertheless part of the international legal system, bound by the principles of international law and no less accountable.

It is hoped that this study will provide a deeper understanding of the FATF and its effective place in the international legal system, identifying possible trends and even the emergence of novel models of IOs that escape the institutional-building paradigm as subjects of public international law.

Bibliography

Books

An Anatomy of the World Trade Organization – The Anatomy Series of International Institutions in K. Adamantopoulos (ed) (Kluwer Law International 1997).

Alexander, K., *Economic Sanctions – Law and Public Policy* (Palgrave Macmillan 2009).

Alvarez, J., *International Organizations as Law-Makers* (Oxford University Press 2005).

Amerasinghe, C.F., *Principles of the Institutional Law of International Organizations* (2nd rev edn, Cambridge University Press 2005).

Armstrong, D., L. Lloyd and J. Redmond, *International Organization in World Politics* (3rd edn, Palgrave Macmillan 2004).

Aust, A., *Modern Treaty Law and Practice* (3rd edn, Cambridge University Press 2013).

Barkin, S.J., *International Organisations – Theories and Institutions* (2nd edn, Palgrave Macmillan 2013).

Broome, J., *Anti-Money Laundering – International Practice and Policies* (Sweet and Maxwell Asia 2005).

Brownlie, I., *Principles of Public International Law* (6th edn, Oxford University Press 2003).

Dai, X., *International Institutions and National Policies* (Cambridge University Press 2007).

Dinh, N.Q., P. Daillier, and A. Pellet, *Droit International Public* (3rd edn, L.G.D.J 1987).

Dinh, N.Q., P. Daillier, and A. Pellet, *Direito Internacional Público* (4th edn, Fundação Calouste Gulbenkian 1999).

Domingo, R., *The New Global Law* (Cambridge University Press 2011).

Evans, M. (ed), *International Law* (3rd edn, Oxford University Press 2011).

Gelemerova, L., *The Anti-Money Laundering System in the Context of Globalisation: A Panopticon Built on Quicksand?* (Wolf Legal Publishers 2011).

Informal International Lawmaking, J. Pauwelyn, R. Wessel and J. Wouters (eds) (Oxford University Press 2012).

Klabbers, J., *An Introduction to International Institutional Law* (2nd edn, Cambridge University Press 2009).

Rittberger, V., B. Zangl, and A. Kruck, *International Organization* (2nd edn, Palgrave Macmillan 2012).

Sands, P., and P. Klein, *Bowett's Law of International Institutions* (6th edn, Sweet & Maxwell 2009).

Schermers, H., and N. Blokker, *International Institutional Law* (5th rev edn, Martinus Nijhoff Publishers 2011).

Seyersted, F., *Objective International Personality of Intergovernmental Organizations – Do Their Capacities Really Depend Upon Their Constitutions* (Krohns Bogtrykkeri (ed), København, Copenhagen 1963).

Seyersted, F., *Common Law of International Organizations* (Martinus Nijhoff 2008).

Slaughter, A.M., *A New World Order* (Princeton University Press 2004).

Tzanakopoulos, A., *Disobeying the Security Council – Countermeasures against Wrongful Sanctions* (Oxford University Press 2011).

Book Chapters

Akande, D., 'International Organizations' in M. Evans (ed), *International Law* (3rd edn, Oxford University Press 2011).

Alvarez, J., 'International Organizations: Then and Now' (2006), republished in E. Kwakwa (ed), *Globalization and International Organizations* (Ashgate Publishing Limited 2011).

Amerasinghe, C.F., 'International Legal Personality Revisited' (1995), republished in F. Johns (ed), *International Legal Personality* (Routledge 2010).

Amerasinghe, C.F., 'The Law of International Organizations: A Subject Which Needs Exploration and Analysis' (2004), republished in E. Kwakwa (ed), *Globalization and International Organizations* (Ashgate Publishing 2011).

Aufricht, H., 'Personality in International Law' (1943) republished in F. Johns (ed), *International Legal Personality* (Routledge 2010).

Barros, A.S., 'Member States and the International Legal (Dis)order: Accounting for the Notion of Responsible Governance' in A.S. Barros, C. Ryngaert and J. Routers (eds), *International Organizations and Member State Responsibility: Critical Perspectives* (Brill/Nijhoff 2016).

Bederman, D., 'The Souls of International Organizations: Legal Personality and the Lighthouse at Cape Spartel' (1995/1996), republished in F. Johns (ed), *International Legal Personality* (Routledge 2010).

Bengoetxea, J., 'The EU as (More Than) an International Organization' in J. Klabbers and A. Wallendahl (eds), *Research Handbook on the Law of International Organizations* (Edward Elgar Publishing 2011).

Berman, A., and R. Wessel, 'The International Legal Form and Status of Informal International Lawmaking Bodies: Consequences for Accountability' in J. Pauwelyn, R. Wessel and J. Wouters (eds), *Informal International Lawmaking* (Oxford University Press 2012).

Berman, A., S. Duquet, J. Pauwelyn, R. Wessel, and J. Wouters, 'Introduction and Key Issues Surrounding Informal International Lawmaking' in A. Berman, S. Duquet, J.

Pauwelyn, R. Wessel and J. Wouters (eds), *Informal International Lawmaking: Case Studies* (Torkel Opsahl Academic EPublisher The Hague 2012).

Blokker, N., 'Preparing Articles on Responsibility of International Organizations: Does the International Law Commission Take International Organizations Seriously? A Mid-Term Review' in J. Klabbers and A. Wallendahl (eds), *Research Handbook on the Law of International Organizations* (Edward Elgar Publishing 2011).

Blokker, N., 'Member State Responsibility for Wrongdoings of International Organizations: Beacon of Hope or Delusion?' in A.S. Barros, C. Ryngaert and J. Routers (eds), *International Organizations and Member State Responsibility: Critical Perspectives* (Brill/Nijhoff 2016).

Blokker, N., and R. Wessel, 'Revisiting Questions of Organisationhood, Legal Personality and Membership in the OSCE: The Interplay between Law, Politics and Practice' (final draft to be published in M.S. Platise, C. Moser and A. Peters (eds), *Revisiting the Legal Status of the OSCE* (Cambridge University Press 2018)).

Boyle, A., 'Soft Law in International Lawmaking' in M. Evans (ed), *International Law*, (3rd edn, Oxford University Press 2011).

Brunnée, J., 'Reweaving the Fabric of International Law? Patterns of Consent in Environmental Framework Agreements' in R. Wolfrum and V. Röben (eds), *Developments of International Law in Treaty-Making* (Springer 2005).

Brzoska, M., 'A Good Thing Gone Too Far? External Assessments and Counterterrorist Finance-Related Measures in the European Union' in M. Brzoska (ed), *European Peace and Security Policy: Transitional Risks of Violence* (NOMOS Bloomsbury 2014).

Bulterman, M., 'Implementation of Financial UN Sanctions: Jurisdictional Problems Related to Genuine Global Governance' in P. Slot and M. Bulterman (eds), *Globalisation and Jurisdiction* (Kluwer Law International 2004).

Cannizzaro, E., and P. Palchetti, 'Ultra-Vires Acts of International Organizations' in J. Klabbers and A. Wallendahl (eds), *Research Handbook on the Law of International Organizations* (Edward Elgar Publishing 2011).

Chiti, E., and R. Wessel, 'The Emergence of International Agencies in the Global Administrative Space: Autonomous Actors or State Servants?' in R. Collins and N. White (eds), *International Organizations and the Idea of Autonomy: Institutional Independence in the International Legal Order* (Routledge 2011).

Crawford, J., and S. Olleson, 'The Nature and Forms of International Responsibility' in M. Evans (ed), *International Law* (3rd edn, Oxford University Press 2011).

d'Aspremont, J., 'The Multifaceted Concept of the Autonomy of International Organizations and International Legal Discourse' in R. Collins and N. White (eds), *International Organizations and the Idea of Autonomy: Institutional Independence in the International Legal Order* (Routledge 2011).

Damais, A., 'The Financial Action Task Force' in W.H. Muller, C.H. Kalin and J.G. Goldsworth (eds), *Anti-Money Laundering: International Law and Practice* (John Wiley & Sons 2007).

Davison, R., 'Soft Law 'Regimes and European Organizations' Fight against Terrorism and Money Laundering' in L. Holmes (ed), *Terrorism, Organised Crime and Corruption – Networks and Linkages* (Edward Elgar Publishing 2007).

De Wet, E., 'The Security Council as Law-Maker, the Adoption of (Quasi)-Judicial Decisions' in R. Wolfrum and V. Röben (eds), *Developments of International Law in Treaty-Making* (Springer 2005).

Di Stasi, A., 'About Soft International Organizations: An Open Question' in R. Virzo and I. Ingravallo (eds), *Evolutions in the Law of International Organizations* (Brill/Nijhoff 2015).

Donaldson, M. and S. Ranganathan, 'Accountability' in J. Klabbers (ed), *The Cambridge Companion to International Organizations Law* (Cambridge University Press 2022).

Donnelly, S., 'Informal International Lawmaking: Global Financial Market Regulation' in A. Berman, S. Duquet, J. Pauwelyn, R. Wessel and J. Wouters (eds), *Informal International Lawmaking: Case Studies* (Torkel Opsahl Academic EPublisher, The Hague 2012).

Eden, P., 'International Measures to Prevent and Supress the Financing of Terrorism' in P. Eden and T. O'Donnell (eds), *September 11, 2001: A Turning Point in International and Domestic Law?* (Transnational Publishers, Ardsley 2005).

Gazzini, T., 'The Personality of International Organizations' in J. Klabbers and A. Wallendahl (eds), *Research Handbook on the Law of International Organizations* (Edward Elgar Publishing 2011).

Golia Jr, A., and A. Peters, 'The Concept of International Organization' in J. Klabbers (ed), *The Cambridge Companion to International Organizations Law* (Cambridge University Press 2022).

Jenks, W., 'The Legal Personality of International Organizations' (1945), republished in F. Johns (ed), *International Legal Personality* (Routledge 2010).

Klabbers, J., 'Contending Approaches to International Organizations: Between Functionalism and Constitutionalism' in J. Klabbers and A. Wallendahl (eds), *Research Handbook on the Law of International Organizations* (Edward Elgar Publishing 2011).

Klabbers, J., 'Formal Intergovernmental Organizations' in J.K. Cogan, I. Hurd and I. Johnstone (eds), *Oxford Handbook of International Organizations* (Oxford University Press 2016).

Lauterpacht, H., 'The Subjects of International Law' (1970), republished in A. Bianchi (ed), *Non-State Actors and International Law* (Routledge 2009).

Lavenex, S., 'Globalization and the Vertical Challenge to Democracy' in H. Kriesi, S. Lavenex, F. Esser, J. Matthes, M. Bühlmann and D. Bochsler (eds), *Democracy in the Age of Globalization and Mediatization* (Palgrave Macmillan 2013).

Macchia, M., 'The Rule of Law and Transparency in the Global Space' in S. Cassesse (ed), *Research Handbook on Global Administrative Law* (Edward Elgar Publishing 2016).

Machado, M.R., 'Transnational Legal Processes Addressing Money Laundering in Brazil and Argentina' in G. Shaffer (ed), *Transnational Legal Ordering and State Change* (Cambridge University Press 2012).

Matveev, A., 'The OSCE Identity Crisis' in IFSH (ed), *OSCE Yearbook 1999* (Baden-Baden 2000).

Möllers, C., 'Constitutional Foundations of Global Administration' in S. Cassesse (ed), *Research Handbook on Global Administrative Law* (Edward Elgar Publishing 2016).

Muldoon, J.P., 'New Types of Organizations and the Global Governance in the Twenty-First Century: The Case of ICANN' in J.E. Oestreich (ed), *International Organizations as Self-directed Actors – A Framework Analysis* (Routledge 2012).

Nance, M., 'Naming and Shaming in Financial Regulation: Explaining Variation in the Financial Action Task Force on Money Laundering' in H.R. Friman (ed), *The Politics of Leverage in International Relations – Name, Shame and Sanction* (Palgrave Macmillan 2015).

Nijman, J, 'Paul Ricoeur and International Law: Beyond 'the End of the Subject' – Towards a Reconceptualization of International Legal Personality' (2007), republished in F. Johns (ed), *International Legal Personality* (Routledge 2010).

Nowrot, K., 'Reconceptualising International Legal Personality of Influential Non-state Actors: Towards a Rebuttable Presumption of Normative Responsibilities' (2006), republished in F. Johns (ed), *International Legal Personality* (Routledge 2010).

Petman, J., 'Deformalization of International Organizations Law' in J. Klabbers and A. Wallendahl (eds), *Research Handbook on the Law of International Organizations* (Edward Elgar Publishing 2011).

Png, C.A, 'International Legal Sources III – FATF Recommendations' in W. Blair, R. Brent and T. Grant (eds), *Banks and Financial Crime – The International Law of Tainted Money* (2nd edn, Oxford University Press 2017).

Rodiles, A., 'The Design of UN Sanctions through the Interplay with Informal Arrangements' in L. van den Herik (ed), *Research Handbook on UN Sanctions and International Law* (Edward Elgar Publishing 2017).

Schneider, P., 'Sanctioned Until Proven Innocent – in Reviewing the UN and EU Smart Sanctions Regime for Blacklisted Terror Suspects' in M. Brzoska (ed), *European Peace and Security Policy: Transitional Risks of Violence* (NOMOS Bloomsbury 2014).

Scholte, J.A., 'Global Governance, Accountability and Civil Society' in J.A. Scholte (ed), *Building Global Democracy? Civil Society and Accountable Global Governance* (Cambridge 2011).

Shams, H., 'Club Multilateralism and Global Supranationalism: The Case of FATF' in J.B. Attanasio and J.J. Norton (eds), *Multilateralism v Unilateralism: Policy Choices in a Global Society* (British Institute of International and Comparative Law and SMU Dedman School of Law 2004).

Shawn, D., 'Informal International Lawmaking: Global Financial Market Regulation' in A. Berman, S. Duquet, J. Pauwelyn, R. Wessel and J. Wouters (eds), *Informal International Lawmaking: Case Studies* (Torkel Opsahl Academic EPublisher, The Hague 2012).

Shelton, D., 'International Law and 'Relative Normativity' in M. Evans (ed), *International Law* (3rd edn, Oxford University Press 2011).

Simonet, L. and H.G. Lüber, 'The OSCE and its Legal Status: Revisiting the Myth of Sisyphus' (OSCE Yearbook 2016).

Sollier, J., 'The United Nations Security Council – and the Efforts to Combat Money Laundering and the Financing of Terrorism', in W.H. Muller, C.H. Kalin and J.G. Goldsworth (eds), *Anti-Money Laundering: International Law and Practice* (John Wiley & Sons Ltd 2007).

Tilahun, N., 'The Re-organization of the FATF as an International Legal Person and the Promises and Limits to Accountability' in A. Arcuri and F. Coman Kund (eds) *Technocracy and Multi-level Governance: What Role for Accountability?* (Routledge 2021).

Ulfstein, G., 'Reflections on Institutional Design – Especially Treaty Bodies' in J. Klabbers and A. Wallendahl (eds), *Research Handbook on the Law of International Organizations* (Edward Elgar Publishing 2011).

Van den Broek, M., 'Harmonization of Substantive Norms in Preventive AML Policy' in B. Unger, J. Ferwerda, M. Van den Broek and I. Deleanu (eds), *The Economic and Legal Effectiveness of the European Union's Anti-money Laundering Policy* (Edward Elgar Publishing 2014).

Verhage, A., 'Global Governance + Global Compliance? The Uneven Playing Field in Anti-Money Laundering' in J. van Erp, W. Huisman and G.V. Walle (eds), *The Routledge Handbook of White-Collar and Corporate Crime in Europe* (Routledge 2015).

Vettori, B., 'Evaluating Anti-Money Laundering Policies: Where Are We?' in B. Unger and D. van der Linde (eds), *Research Handbook on Money Laundering* (Edward Elgar Publishing Inc 2013).

Wessel, R., and E. Kica, 'Political Economy and the Decisions of International Organizations: Choosing Governance Arrangements through Informality' in A. Fabbricotti (ed), *Political Economy of International Law* (Edward Elgar Publishing 2016).

Wessel, R., and S. Blockmans, 'The Legal Status and Influence of Decisions of International Organisations and Other Bodies in the European Union' in P.

Eeckhout and M. Lopez-Escudero (eds), *The European Union's External Action in Times of Crisis* (Hart Publishing 2016).

White, N., and A. Abass, 'Countermeasures and Sanctions' in M. Evans (ed), *International Law* (3rd edn, Oxford University Press 2011).

Young, S., 'Policing and Prosecution of Money Laundering' in V. Mitsilegas, S. Hufnagel and A. Moiseienko (eds), *Research Handbook on Transnational Crime* (Edward Elgar Publishing 2019).

Zanghì, C., *Diritto delle Organizzazioni Internazionali* (3rd edn, G. Giappichelli Editore 2013).

Journal Articles and Online Publications

Abbot, K., and D. Snidal, 'Why States Act through Formal International Organizations' (1998) 42(1) *Journal of Conflict Resolution*.

Abbot, K., and D. Snidal, 'Hard and Soft Law in International Governance' (2001) 54(3) *International Organization*.

Adorno, R., 'The Invaluable Role of Soft Law in the Development of Universal Norms in Bioethics' (2007), at: http://www.unesco.de/wissenschaft/bis-2009/invaluable-role-of-soft-law.html?&L=0.

Ahlborn, C., 'The Rules of International Organizations and the Law of International Responsibility' (2011) Amsterdam Law School Research Paper No. 2011-04, at: http://papers.ssrn.com/sol3/papers.cfm?abstract_id=1825182.

Ahlborn, C., 'To Share or Not to Share? The Allocation of Responsibility between International Organizations and their Member States' (2013) Amsterdam Law School Research Paper No. 2013–73, at https://papers.ssrn.com/sol3/papers.cfm?abstract_id=2361075.

Alexander, K., 'The International Anti-Money Laundering Regime: The Role of the Financial Action Task Force' (2001) 4(3) *Journal of Money Laundering Control*.

Alvarez, J., 'International Organizations and the Rule of Law: Challenges Ahead' (2016) forthcoming in The International Legal Order: Essays Commemorating the 10th Anniversary of the Xiamen Academy of International Law.

Amerasinghe, C.F., 'International Institutional Law – A Point of View' (2008) 5 *International Organizations Law Review*.

Amerasinghe, C.F., 'Comments on the ILC's Draft Articles on the Responsibility of International Organizations' (2012) 9 *International Organizations Law Review*.

Amrani, H., 'Anti-Money Laundering as International Standards and the Issue of State Sovereignty' (2015) 12(2) *Indonesian Journal of International Law*.

Arato, J., 'Treaty Interpretation and Constitutional Transformation: Informal Change in International Organizations' (2013) 38(2) *Yale Journal of International Law*.

Arner, D., D. Zetzsche, R. Buckley, and J. Barberis, 'The Identity Challenge in Finance: from Analogue Identity to Digitized Identification to Digital KYC Utilities' (2019) 20(4) *European Business Organization Law Review*.

Arsić-Đapo, J., 'Another Brick in the Wall – Building Up the OSCE as an International Organization One Agreement at a Time' (2017) 14 *International Organizations Law Review*.

Ayers, A., 'The Financial Action Task Force: The War on Terrorism Will Not Be Fought on the Battlefield' (2002) 18(3) *New York Law School Journal of Human Rights*.

Beekarry, N., 'The International Anti-Money Laundering and Combating the Financing of Terrorism Regulatory Strategy: A Critical Analysis of Compliance Determinants in International Law' (2011) 31(1) *Northwestern Journal of International Law & Business*.

Bergstrom, M., 'From Global Rules and Standards to Enforceable National Provisions: The Case of Anti-Money Laundering Regulation and Implementation' (2013) 58 *Scandinavian Studies in Law*.

Bianchi, A., 'Assessing the Effectiveness of the UN Security Council's Anti-terrorism Measures: The Quest for Legitimacy and Cohesion' (2006) 17(5) *European Journal of International Law*.

Blazejewski, K., 'The FATF and its Institutional Partners: Improving the Effectiveness and Accountability of Transgovernamental Networks' (2008) 22(1) *Temple International & Comparative Law Journal*.

Blokker, N., 'Comparing Apples and Oranges? Reinventing the Wheel?' (2008) 5(1) *International Organizations Law Review*.

Blokker, N., and R. Wessel, 'Introduction: First Views at the Articles on the Responsibility of International Organizations' (2012) 9(1) *International Organizations Law Review*.

Boon, K., 'Open for Business': International Financial Institutions, Post-Conflict Economic Reform, and the Rule of Law' (2007), at: http://nyujilp.org/wp-content/uploads/2013/02/39.3-Boon.pdf.

Boon, K., 'New Directions in Responsibility: Assessing the International Law Commission's Draft Articles on the Responsibility of International Organizations' (2011) *Yale Journal of International Law*, Seton Hall Public Law Research Paper No. 2011-01.

Boon, K., and F. Megret, 'New Approaches to the Accountability of International Organizations' (2019) 16 *International Organizations Law Review*.

Borlini, L., 'The Financial Action Task Force: An Introduction' (2015) 2 *Anti-corruption Research Center (U4 BRIEF)*, at: https://papers.ssrn.com/sol3/papers.cfm?abstract_id=3834449.

Borlini, L., 'Soft Law, Soft International Organizations e Regolamentazione 'Tecnica' di Problemi di Sicurezza Pubblica e Integrità Finanziaria' (2017) 2 *Rivista di Diritto Internazionale*.

Borlini, L., and F. Montanaro, 'The Evolution of the EU Law against Criminal Finance: The 'Hardening' of FATF Standards within the EU' (2017) 48(4) *Georgetown Journal of International Law*.

Bouwhuis, S., 'The International Law Commission's Definition of International Organizations' (2012) 9 *International Organizations Law Review*.

Bradley, B., 'The North Korean Economic System: Challenges and Issue' (2016) *International Journal of Korean Studies*, at: https://www.ncnk.org/resources/publications/BradBabson_NKEconomicSystem_ICKSSpringSummer2016.pdf.

Bradlow, D., 'A Framework for Assessing Global Economic Governance' (2013) 36 *International & Comparative Law Review*.

Bravo, K., 'Follow the Money? Does the International Fight against Money Laundering Provide a Model for International Anti-trafficking Efforts' (2008) 6(1) *University of St. Thomas Law Journal*.

Bravo, K., 'Challenges to the Caribbean Economic Sovereignty in a Globalising World' (2011) *Michigan State University College of Law Journal of International Law*.

Brownlie, I. and Goodwin-Gill, G.S, 'Joint Opinion on the International Legal Personality of the Inter-Parliamentary Union' (1999), at: http://www.ipu.org/finance-e/opinion.pdf.

Calcara, G., 'A Transnational Police Network Co-operating Up to the Limits of the Law: Examination of the Origin of INTERPOL' (2020) 11(4) *Transnational Legal Theory*.

Cananea, G., 'Return to the Due Process of Law: the European Union and the Fight against Terrorism' (2007) 32 *European Law Review*.

Churchill, R., and G. Ulfstein, 'Autonomous Institutional Arrangements in Multilateral Environmental Agreements: A Little-Noticed Phenomenon in International Law' (2000) 94(4) *American Journal of International Law*.

Ciesiolka, M., 'Protecting the Right to Privacy while Combating Terrorism Finance' (05/08/2019) University of Zurich, at: https://www.ohchr.org/sites/default/files/Documents/Issues/Terrorism/SR/Submissions/Mirja_Ciesiolka_GA74CT.pdf.

Couvée, K. 'Exclusive: FATF Spared Large Economies from Pressure Over AML Gaps' (06/01/2023) *ACAMS*, at: https://www.moneylaundering.com/news/exclusive-fatf-spared-large-economies-from-pressure-over-aml-gaps/.

d'Aspremont, J., 'Softness in International Law: A Self-Serving Quest for New Legal Materials' (2008) 19(5) *European Journal of International Law*.

d'Aspremont, J., 'The Articles on the Responsibility of International Organizations: Magnifying the Fissures in the Law of International Responsibility' (2012) 9 *International Organizations Law Review*.

d'Aspremont, J., 'Abuse of the Legal Personality of International Organizations and the Responsibility of Member States' (2017) 4 *International Organizations Law Review*.

Daugirdas, K., 'Reputation and the Responsibility of International Organizations' (2014) 25(4) *European Journal of International Law*.

Daugirdas, K., 'Member States' Due Diligence Obligations to Supervise International Organizations' (2020) Law & Economics Papers, University of Michigan Law School, at: https://papers.ssrn.com/sol3/papers.cfm?abstract_id=3539181.

de Oliveira, S., 'The Governance of the Financial Action Task Force: An Analysis of Power and Influence Throughout the Years' (2018) 69 *Crime, Law and Social Change*.

de Schoutheete, P., and S. Andoura, 'The Legal Personality of the European Union' (2007) LX(1) *Studia Diplomatica*.

De Wet, E., 'The International Constitutional Order' (2006) 55(1) *International and Comparative Law Quarterly*.

De Wet, E., 'The Emerging International Constitutional Order: The Implications of Hierarchy in International Law for the Coherence and Legitimacy of International Decision-Making' (2007) 10(2) *Potchefstroom Electronic Law Journal/Potchefstroomse Elektroniese Regsblad*.

Delston, R., and S. Walls, 'Reaching Beyond Banks: How to Target-Based Money Laundering and Terrorist Financing Outside the Financial Sector' (2009) 41(1) *Case Western Reserve Journal of International Law*.

Doyle, T., 'Cleaning Up Anti-Money Laundering Strategies: Current FATF Tactics Needlessly Violate International Law (Financial Action Task Force)' (2002) 24(2) *Houston Journal of International Law*.

Drezner, D., 'On the Balance between International Law and Democratic Sovereignty' (2001) 2(2) *Chicago Journal of International Law*.

Dubois, P.H., and A. Nowlan, 'Global Administrative Law and the Legitimacy of Sanctions Regimes in International Law' (2010) 36 *The Yale Journal of International Law*.

Ebikake, E., 'Money Laundering: An Assessment of Soft Law as a Technique for Repressive and Preventive Anti-Money Laundering Control' (DPhil Thesis, Liverpool John Moores University, 17/05/2021), at: https://researchonline.ljmu.ac.uk/id/eprint/16216/1/THE%20THESIS.pdf.

Elberling, B., 'The Ultra Vires Character of Legislative Action by the Security Council' (2005) 2(2) *International Organizations Law Review*.

Ellis, J., 'Shades of Grey: Soft Law and the Validity of Public International Law' (2012) 25(2) *Leiden Journal of International Law*.

Ezewudo, C., 'The Money Laundering and Terrorist Financing: An Insight into the Money Laundering (Prohibition) Act of 2004, Laws of Nigeria' (Dissertation LLM 2011-2012, Institute of Advanced Legal Studies, School of Advanced Study, University of London 03/09/2012), at: http://sas-space.sas.ac.uk/4736/1/Chibueze_Ezewudo_LLM_ICGFREL_dissertation.pdf.

Fenton, A., and D. Price, 'Forbidden Funds – Indonesia's New Legislation for Countering the Financing of Terrorism' (2014) 11(3) *Indonesian Journal of International Law*.

Ferreira, M., A. Van der Linden and B. Cooper, 'Proof of Address Must Fall' (2018), at: https://cenfri.org/articles/proof-of-address-must-fal.

Forsman, M., '30 Years of Combating Money Laundering in Sweden and Internationally – Does the System Function as Intended?' (2020) 1 *Sveriges Risbank Economic Review*.

Gaja, G., 'Articles on the Responsibility of International Organizations' (July 2014) *United Nations Audiovisual Library of International Law*, at: http://legal.un.org/avl/ha/ario/ario.html.

Gallant, M., 'Tax and Terrorism: A New Partnership?' (2007) 14(4) *Journal of Financial Crime*.

Gallant, M., 'Promise and Perils: The Making of Global Money Laundering, Terrorist Finance Norms' (2010) 13(3) *Journal of Money Laundering Control*.

Gallant, M., 'Money Laundering Consequences – Recovering Wealth, Piercing Secrecy, Disrupting Tax Havens and Distorting International Law' (2014) 17(3) *Journal of Money Laundering Control*.

Gathii, J.T., 'Financial Action Task Force and Global Administrative Law' (2010) *Journal of the Professional Lawyer, Forthcoming*, Albany Law School Research Paper Series No. 10.

Genser, J., and K. Barth, 'When Due Process Concerns Become Dangerous: the Security Council's 1267 Regime and the Need for Reform' (2010) 33(1) *Boston College International and Comparative Law Review*.

Ghoshray, S., 'Compliance Convergence in FATF Rulemaking: The Conflict between Agency Capture and Soft Law' (2014/2015) 59(3) *New York Law School Law Review*.

Goldbarsht, D., 'Who's the Legislator Anyway: How the FATF's Global Norms Reshape Australian Counter Terrorist Financing Laws' (2017) 45(1) *Federal Law Review*.

Grant, R., and R. Keohane, 'Accountability and Abuses of Power in World Politics' (2004) Global Administrative Law Series, IILJ Working Paper 2004/7, at: http://iilj.org/wp-content/uploads/2016/08/Grant-etal-Accountability-and-Abuses-of-Power-in-World-Politics-2004-2.pdf.

Gulati, R., P. Phanish, and M. Tushman, 'Meta-Organization Design: Rethinking Design in Inter-Organizational and Community Contexts' (2012) 33(6) *Strategic Management Journal*.

Guzman, A., 'International Organizations and the Frankenstein Problem' (2013) 24(4) *European Journal of International Law*.

Habibi, H., and S. Zanershan, 'The Role & Position of FATF in International Law System' (2021) 20(45) (Abstract), *Journal of Legal Research*.

Harlow, C., 'Global Administrative Law: The Quest for Principles and Values' (2006) 17(1) *European Journal of International Law*.

Harlow, C., 'Composite Decision-Making and Accountability Networks: Some Deductions from a Saga' (2012) Jean Monnet Working Paper 04/12, at: http://jeanmonnetprogram.org/paper/composite-decision-making-and-accountability-networks-some-deductions-from-a-saga/.

Hillgenber, H., 'A Fresh Look at Soft Law' (1999) 10(3) *European Journal of International Law*.

Hirschmann, G., 'Guarding the Guards: Pluralist Accountability for Human Rights Violations by International Organisations' (2019) 45(1) *Review of International Studies*.

Höbek, T., 'Legal Attributes of International Organizations in the Absence of a Constituent Legal Document. The Case of the OSCE' (2011) University of Vienna, at: https://backend.univie.ac.at/fileadmin/user_upload/s_rechtswissenschaft/Doktoratsstudium_PhD/Expose1/Europarecht/Legal_Attributes_of_International_Organizations_in_the_absence_of_a_constituent_legal_document.pdf.

Hülsse, R., 'Even Clubs Can't Do Without Legitimacy: Why the Anti-Money Laundering Blacklist Was Suspended' (2008) 2(4) *Regulation & Governance*.

Hülsse, R., and D. Kerwer, 'How International Organizations Rule the World: The Case of the Financial Action Task Force' (2011) 2(1) *Journal of International Organisations Studies*.

Jackson, J., 'The Financial Action Task Force: An Overview' (2017) Congressional Research Service Report, at: https://sgp.fas.org/crs/misc/RS21904.pdf.

Jakobi, A., 'Governing Illicit Finance in Transnational Security Spaces: the FATF and Anti-Money Laundering' (2018) 69 *Crime, Law and Social Change*.

Jayasuriya, K., 'Globalization, Law, and the Transformation of Sovereignty: The Emergence of Global Regulatory Governance' (1999) 6(2) *Indiana Journal of Global Legal Studies*.

Jones, G., 'Legal Personality and the Responsibility of International Organisations' (Dissertation for LLB (Hons), University of Otago, October 2013), at: https://www.otago.ac.nz/law/research/journals/otago065260.pdf;.

Jusic, A., 'Kuwait's Administrative Risk-Based Model for the Prevention of Money Laundering: Costs and Benefits of Compliance with the Financial Action Task Force (FATF) Standards' (2017) 31 *Arab Law Quarterly*.

Keatinge, T., 'The Financial Action Task Force Should Embrace the Opportunity to Reform' (2019) *RUSI Financial Crime and Security Studies Centre*, at: https://rusi.org/explore-our-research/publications/commentary/financial-action-task-force-should-embrace-opportunity-reform.

Khagram, S., 'Possible Future Architectures of Global Governance: a Transnational Perspective/Prospective' (2006) 12(1) *Global Governance*.

Klabbers, J., 'The Redundancy of Soft Law' (1996) 65 *Nordic Journal of International Law*.

Klabbers, J., 'Institutional Ambivalence by Design: Soft Organizations in International Law' (2001) 70(3) *Nordic Journal of International Law*.

Klabbers, J., '(I Can't Get No) Recognition: Subjects Doctrine and the Emergence of Non-state Actors' – Essays in International Law for Martii Koskenniemi 2003 *Nordic Cosmopolitanism*,.

Klabbers, J., 'The Concept of Legal Personality' (2005) 11 *IUS GENTIUM*.

Klabbers, J., 'Two Concepts of International Organization' (2005) 2(2) *International Organizations Law Review*.

Klabbers, J., 'Checks and Balances in the Law of International Organizations' (2007) 13 *IUS GENTIUM*.

Klabbers, J., 'The Paradox of International Institutional Law' (2008) 5(1) *International Organizations Law Review*.

Klabbers, J., 'Controlling International Organizations: A Virtue Ethics Approach' (2011) 8(2) *International Organizations Law Review*.

Klabbers, J., 'The EJIL Foreword: The Transformation of International Organizations Law' (2015) 26(1) *European Journal of International law*.

Klein, P., and P. Sands, '(Re)Writing a Handbook on the Law of International Organizations: Options and Challenges' (2008) 5 *International Organizations Law Review*.

Knobel, A., and M. Meinzer, 'Don't Forget the Trust: Amendments Needed in FATF's Recommendations and in EU's AML Directive', Tax Justice Network, Drilling Down to the Real Owners – Part 2 (28/06/2016). at: https://www.taxjustice.net/wp-content/uploads/2016/06/TJN2016_BO-EUAMLD-FATF-Part2-Trusts.pdf.

Koker, L., 'Financial Action Task Force Standards and the Financial Inclusion: What Should Be Done – and What Should Not Be Done – to Improve the Alignment between Integrity and Inclusion Policy Objectives' (23 August 2020) *La Trobe Law Tech*.

Koker, L., J. Howell and N. Morr, 'Economic Consequences of Greylisting by the Financial Action Task Force' (2023) 11 *Risks*.

Koppell, J., 'Global Governance Organizations: Legitimacy and Authority in Conflict' (2008) 18(2) *Journal of Public Administration Research and Theory*.

Krisch, N., 'The Pluralism of Global Administrative Law' (2006) 17(1) *European Journal of International Law*.

Leube, K., 'Can the EU Be Held Accountable for Financing Development Projects that Violate Human Rights' (2017) 48 *Georgetown Journal of International Law*.

Livermore, M., 'Authority and Legitimacy in Global Governance: Deliberation, Institutional Differentiation and the Codex Alimentarius' (2006) 81 *New York University Law Review*.

Marceau, G., 'IGOs in Crisis? Or New Opportunities to Demonstrate Responsibility?' (2011) 8(1) *International Organizations Law Review*.

McRae, D., 'General Agreement on Tariffs and Trade' (United Nations Audiovisual Library of International Law, 22/09/2021 – This Introductory Note was written in June 2021), at: https://legal.un.org/avl/pdf/ha/gatt/gatt_e.pdf.

Metz-Dworkin, A., 'A Call for Sanctions: Argentina's Black-Market Currency Whitening and Violations of International Anti-Money Laundering Conventions and Protocols' (2016) 48 *George Washington International Law Review*.

Morgan, J., 'Dirty Names, Dangerous Money: Alleged Unilateralism in U.S. Policy on Money Laundering' (2003) 21(3) *Berkeley Journal of International Law*.

Nance, M., 'Re-thinking FATF: An Experimentalist Interpretation of the Financial Action Task Force' (2018) 69 *Crime, Law and Socials Change*.

Nance, M., 'The Regime that FATF Built: An Introduction to the Financial Action Task Force' (2018) 69 *Crime Law and Social Change*.

Newmeyer, K., 'The FATF as a Model for Internet Governance' (2011), at: https://ieeexplore.iee.org/stamp/stamp.jsp?tp=&arnumber=5978781.

Nowrot, K. 'Global Governance and International Law' (2004) *Institute für Wirtschaftsrecht*, at: https://opendata.uni-halle.de/bitstream/1981185920/76421/1/BeitraegeTWR_33.pdf.

O'Toole, B., 'FATF Blacklists Iran, But Does It Matter?' (24/02/2020) *Atlantic Council*, at: www.atlanticcouncil.org/blogs/iransource/fatf-blacklists-iran-but-does-it-matter/.

Odello, M., 'The Developing Legal Status of the Organisation for Security and Co-operation in Europe' (2006) XXII *Anuario Espanol de Derecho Internacional*.

Oke, T., 'Extra-Territorial Money Laundering Legislation: Criminal Sanction, Deterrence, and the African PEP' (2013) 39(4) *Commonwealth Law Bulletin*.

Pascu, G., and C.T. Luminosu, 'The Legal Personality of the European Union – between the Maastricht Treaty and the Draft Treaty establishing a Constitution for Europe – Reality and Perspectives' (2006) 6(3) *Romanian Journal of European Affairs*.

Pauwelyn, J., 'Informal International Lawmaking: Framing the Concept and Research Questions – Mapping the Action and Testing Concepts of Accountability and Effectiveness' (Project Framing Paper, February 2011), at: https://www.researchgate.net/publication/228147656_Informal_International_Lawmaking_Framing_the_Concept_and_Research_Questions.

Pauwelyn, J., R. Wessel and J. Wouters, 'When Structures Become Shackles: Stagnation and Dynamics in International Lawmaking' (2014) 25(3) *European Journal of International Law*.

Pavlidis, G., 'The Dark Side of Anti-Money Laundering: Mitigating the Unintended Consequences of FATF Standards' (2023) 2 *Journal of Economic Criminology*.

Pingel, I., 'Privileges and Immunities of the Organization for Security and Co-operation in Europe (OSCE)' (2018) *Max Planck Institute for Comparative Public Law and International Law*, MPIL Research Paper Series No. 2018–37.

Purdă, N., 'Aspects on the International Legal Personality of International Organizations' (2012) 2, *Challenges of the Knowledge Society*.

Rahmdel, M., 'FATF and Money Laundering in Iran' (2018) 21(3) *Journal of Money Laundering Control*.

Raustiala, K., 'The Architecture of International Co-operation: Transgovernamental Networks and the Future of International Law' (2002) 43(1) *Virginia Journal of International Law Association*.

Romaniuk, P., and T. Keatinge, 'Protecting Charities from Terrorists ... and Counterterrorists: FATF and the Global Effort to Prevent Terrorist Financing through the Non-profit Sector' (2018) 69(2) *Crime, Law and Social Change*.

Rosas, A., 'The European Court of Justice and Public International Law' (Speech at the CoE Committee of Legal Advisers on Public International Law on 23/03/2018), at: https://rm.coe.int/statement-delivered-by-judge-allan-rosas-at-the-55th-cahdi-meeting-55t/16807b3b04.

Runjic, L., 'The Legal Nature and Status of Interpol in the Context of Contemporary International Law' (22nd International Scientific Conference on Economic and Social Developments – Legal Challenges of Modern World, Split 2017), at: https://papers.ssrn.com/sol3/papers.cfm?abstract_id=3166171.

Ryder, N., 'The Financial Services Authority and Money Laundering, a Game of Cat and Mouse' (2008) 67(3) *Cambridge Law Journal*.

Samara, C., 'International Responsibility of International Organizations (The Draft Articles of the International Law Commission)' (2017), at: https://papers.ssrn.com/sol3/papers.cfm?abstract_id=3480061.

Samridha, N., 'Money Laundering: Current Issues and Challenges' (15/11/2010) *Legal Services India* (*blog*), at: https://www.legalservicesindia.com/article/436/Money-Laundering.html#google_vignette.

Sarooshi, D., 'The Role of Domestic Public Law Analogies in the Law of International Organizations' (2008) 5 *International Organizations Law Review*.

Schulte-Kulkmann, N., 'The Architecture of Anti-Money Laundering Regulation in the People's Republic of China – Shortfalls and Requirements for Reform' (2006) 14(4) *European Journal of Crime, Criminal Law and Criminal Justice*.

Sellers, M.N.S., 'International Legal Personality' (2005) 11 *IUS GENTIUM*.

Sharman, J., 'The Global Anti-Money Laundering Regime and Developing Countries: Damned If They Do, Damned If They Don't?' (International Studies Association Annual Conference, San Diego, 22–25 March 2006).

Sharman, J., 'The Bark is the Bite: International Organizations and Blacklisting' (2009) 16(4) *Review of International Political Economy*.

Shelton, D., 'Commitment and Compliance: The Role of Non-binding Norms in the International Legal System (Introduction)' (2000), at: http://papers.ssrn.com/sol3/papers.cfm?abstract_id=2234113.

Shinfield, J. and M. Bellofiore, 'Canada: Revised FATF Recommendations: What Effect Will They Have in Canada?' (2012), at: http://www.mondaq.com/canada/x/168544/Financial+Services/Revised+FATF+Recommendations+What+Effect+Will+They+Have+In+Canada Tax Crimes.

Slaughter, A.M., 'Liberal International Relations Theory and International Economic Law' (1995) 10(2) *American University International Law Review*.

Slemrod, J., and J. D. Wilson, 'Tax Competition with Parasitic Tax Havens' (2009) 93 (11–12) *Journal of Public Economics*.

Smellie, A., 'The Work of the Caribbean Regional Division of the Financial Action Task Force' (1993) 19(2) *Commonwealth Law Bulletin*.

Sossai, M., 'UNSC Res.1373 (2001) and International Lawmaking: A Transformation in the Nature of the Legal Obligations for the Fight against Terrorism?' (Agora on Terrorism and International Law, Inaugural Conference of the European Society of International Law, Florence 2004), at: https://scholar.google.com/citations?view_op=view_citation&hl=en&user=0ocVk_kAAAAJ&citation_for_view=0ocVk_kAAAAJ:GnPB-g6toBAC.

Stessens, G., 'The FATF 'Black List' of Non-cooperative Countries or Territories' (2001) 14 *Leiden Journal of International Law*.

Tinsley, A., 'Echoes of Kadi: Reforms to Internal Remedies at INTERPOL' (20/01/2017) *European Journal of International Law* (blog), at: https://www.ejiltalk.org/echoes-of-kadi-reforms-to-internal-remedies-at-interpol/.

Turner, N.W., 'The Financial Action Task Force: International Regulatory Convergence through Soft Law' (2014) 59 *New York Law School Law Review*.

Tyre, C., 'Anti-Money Laundering Legislation: Implementation of the FATF Forty Recommendations in the European Union' (2010) 69 *Journal of the Professional Lawyer*.

Unger, B., and J. Ferwerda, 'Regulating Money Laundering and Tax Havens: The Role of Blacklisting' (2008) Utrecht School of Economics, Tjalling C. Koopmans Research Institute, Discussion Paper Series 08–12.

Vabulas, F., and D. Snidal, 'Informal Intergovernmental Organizations (IIGOs)' (International Political EcoNo.my Society Conference, University of Wisconsin 2011), at: http://ncgg.princeton.Edu/IPES/2011/papers/S330_rm3.pdf.

van Broekhoven, L., and S. Goswami, 'Can Stakeholder Dialogues Help Solve Financial Access Restrictions Faced by Non-profit Organizations That Stem from Countering Terrorism Financing Standards and International Sanctions?' (2021) 103 *International Review of the Red Cross*.

von Bogdandy, A., 'Globalization and Europe: How to Square Democracy, Globalization and International Law' (2004) 15(5) *European Journal of International Law*.

von Bogdandy, A., and M. Goldmann, 'The Exercise of International Public Authority through National Policy Assessment' (2008) 5 *International Organizations Law Review*.

von Bogdandy, A., and M.S. Platise, 'ARIO and Human Rights Protection: Leaving the Individual in the Cold' (2012) 9(1) *International Organizations Law Review*.

Weiss, P., 'FATF 'Gray Lists' Turkey, Citing Concerns with Turkey's Banking and Real Estate Sectors and Potential Terrorism Financing' (2021), at: https://www.paulweiss.com/practices/litigation/economic-sanctions-aml/publications/fatf-gray-lists-turkey-citing-concerns-with-turkey-s-banking-and-real-estate-sectors-and-potential-terrorism-financing?id=41695.

Wessel, J., 'Financial Action Task Force: A Study in Balancing the Sovereignty with Equality in Global Administrative Law' (2006/2007) 13(1) *Widener Law Review*.

Wessel, R., 'Revisiting the International Legal Status of the EU' (2000) 5 *European Foreign Affairs Review*.

Wessel, R., 'The Rule of Law and the Security Council: The New Procedures for the Legal Protection of Individuals in the Fight against Terrorism' (2008) (First draft prepared for the CONNEX/Ius Commune Workshop Accountability and the Rule of Law at International Level, University of Amsterdam), at: https://research.utwente.nl/en/publications/the-rule-of-law-and-the-security-council-the-new-procedures-for-t.

Wessel, R., 'Towards World Legislation? The Exercise of Public Authority by International Institutions' (2010) (Conference World Legislation: Perspectives from International Law, Legal Theory and Political Philosophy (First draft)), at: https://ramseswessel.eu/Publications/Conference-papers/.

Wessel, R., 'Informal International Lawmaking as a New Form of World Legislation?' (2011) 8 *International Organizations Law Review*.

Wessel, R., and I. Dekker, 'Identities of States in International Organizations' (2015) 12(2) *International Organizations Law Review*.

Whitaker, E., 'Compliance among Weak States: Africa and the Counter-Terrorism Regime' (2010) 36 *Review of International Studies*.

Wouters, J., and P. De Man, 'International Organizations as Law-Makers' (2009) Leuven Centre for Global Governance Working Paper No. 21, at *SSRN:* https://ssrn.com/abstract=1767888 *or* http://dx.doi.org/10.2139/ssrn.1767888.

Wouters, J., and J. Odermatt, 'Are All International Organizations Created Equal?' (2012) 9(1) *International Organizations Law Review*.

Yeh, S., 'New Financial Action Task Force Recommendations to Fight Corruption and Money Laundering' (2022), at: www.mdpi.com/2075-471X/11/1/8.

Young, S., 'Hong Kong Braces Itself for its Third FATF Evaluation' (2008) 29 *The Company Lawyer*.

Index